T0092852

# 2D Game Development
# with Unity

# 2D Game Development
# with Unity

Franz Lanzinger

CRC Press
Taylor & Francis Group
Boca Raton London New York

CRC Press is an imprint of the
Taylor & Francis Group, an **informa** business

First edition published 2021
by CRC Press
6000 Broken Sound Parkway NW, Suite 300, Boca Raton, FL 33487-2742

and by CRC Press
2 Park Square, Milton Park, Abingdon, Oxon, OX14 4RN

© 2021 Franz Lanzinger

CRC Press is an imprint of Taylor & Francis Group, LLC

Reasonable efforts have been made to publish reliable data and information, but the author and publisher cannot assume responsibility for the validity of all materials or the consequences of their use. The authors and publishers have attempted to trace the copyright holders of all material reproduced in this publication and apologize to copyright holders if permission to publish in this form has not been obtained. If any copyright material has not been acknowledged please write and let us know so we may rectify in any future reprint.

Except as permitted under U.S. Copyright Law, no part of this book may be reprinted, reproduced, transmitted, or utilized in any form by any electronic, mechanical, or other means, now known or hereafter invented, including photocopying, microfilming, and recording, or in any information storage or retrieval system, without written permission from the publishers.

For permission to photocopy or use material electronically from this work, access www.copyright.com or contact the Copyright Clearance Center, Inc. (CCC), 222 Rosewood Drive, Danvers, MA 01923, 978-750-8400. For works that are not available on CCC please contact mpkbookspermissions@tandf.co.uk

*Trademark notice*: Product or corporate names may be trademarks or registered trademarks and are used only for identification and explanation without intent to infringe.

ISBN: 978-0-367-34911-0 (hbk)
ISBN: 978-0-367-34907-3 (pbk)
ISBN: 978-0-429-32866-4 (ebk)

Typeset in Minion
by codeMantra

# Contents

# Acknowledgments

A BIG THANK YOU TO THE MANY PEOPLE AND ORGANIZATIONS who made this book possible.

First and foremost, thank you Atari Coin-Op! That's where I got my start in the game industry at the ripe old age of 26 in 1982. Unfortunately, Atari Coin-Op no longer exists, but the unparalleled influence of that small group of pioneers continues to this day.

A HUGE thank you to the thousands of people who built and continue to build Unity, Blender, GIMP, Audacity, and MuseScore. This book relies heavily upon their contribution and generosity for making this valuable software available at no cost to the developer.

Thank you to the millions of players who love games and play them maybe just a little too much. Without you, none of this would exist, not the games, the game companies, nor the thousands of jobs and careers in game development.

Thank you to Rick Adams of CRC Press, who has been a real joy to work with.

If I forgot to thank you, please insert your name here. You know who you are.

Finally, thank you Susan for your love and support throughout the years.

# Author

**Franz Lanzinger** is an independent game developer, author, and pianist. He is the owner of Lanzinger Studio located in Sunnyvale, California. His game development career spans almost forty years starting with the coin-op classic *Crystal Castles* at Atari in 1982 and continuing with *Ms. Pac-man* and *Toobin'* for the NES, published by Tengen in 1990.

Mr. Lanzinger has been an indie game developer since 1991. He worked on SNES' *Rampart*, *Championship Pool*, and *NCAA Final Four Basketball*, as well as *Gubble* for the PC, Mac, and Playstation. He is currently working on a remake of *Gubble* for PC, Mac and consoles, using Unity and Blender. In his spare time, he teaches piano and works as an accompanist for the Valley Chorale and the Serendipity Choir. Go to franzlanzinger.com for the latest news about Mr. Lanzinger.

# Introduction and Overview

IN THIS BOOK, YOU'LL LEARN TO DEVELOP 2D GAMES USING UNITY. *2D Game Development with Unity* combines a practical, hands-on, step-by-step approach with explanations of the theory behind it all. This book covers the major aspects of 2D game development with Unity. In addition to Unity, you'll use Blender and GIMP for graphics creation, Audacity for sound effects, MuseScore for music, and SourceTree for version control. All of this software is free to use, and much of it is open source. If you carefully work through this book, you'll learn a great deal. You'll be ready to make your own original games, whether as a solo developer, as a contributor to a small team, or as an employee at a large game company.

This book is divided into two parts. Part I explores the tools and theory behind 2D game development. You'll make a few small games, and a larger one, to get started. Then, in Part II, you'll build a 2D game with many of the features typically found in commercial games.

You'll experience the joys and occasional frustrations of game development: The awesome feeling of making your character move for the first time, and the pain of thinking it's going to work, only that it doesn't, and you have no clue as to why. It's all part of the process, and there's nothing quite like it.

In the first two chapters, you'll start with a thorough review of the foundations: math and coding. You should already know some algebra, geometry, and trigonometry. A background in calculus and more advanced university level math is not needed for this book, but it can be very helpful for advanced game development. You should have at least some coding experience, preferably in some dialect of C. If you're brand new to coding, you can still follow along with this book, but you would benefit from learning more about coding ahead of time before diving into this book.

In subsequent chapters, you'll explore the creation of art, music, and sound for games. And, of course, you'll learn how to use Unity to put all that art, music, and sound together to make games.

Part II is devoted to making a single, larger 2D game. You'll learn about coding in C#, using Unity, creating characters, controlling the characters, GUI creation, debugging, testing, and much more.

You are strongly encouraged to follow along and build the games as you're reading this book. That is the best way for you to learn. Actually, it's the only way! All code and game assets are available for download at franzlanzinger.com, so you don't really need to type in the code or draw anything, but you'll learn much more if you build everything "from

scratch" along with this book. You'll also have the opportunity to branch out and do things a bit differently from this book. That's the main advantage of doing game development yourself. You then have total control over your game. Soon you'll know enough to make that next awesome, original hit game.

Game development can be a daunting, exciting, and highly rewarding endeavor. There's a lot to learn, and some aspects may seem difficult at first. Don't let that stop you! It's incredibly fun and satisfying, so go and make some games!

# I

## The Basics of Game Development

# First Steps

I**N THIS CHAPTER**, you'll take your first steps as a game developer. You'll install Visual Studio and Unity. You'll explore C# and some basic mathematical concepts. Best of all, you'll make your first game, a simple game in Visual Studio. Your goal is to learn how to use these game development tools. There's no better way than to dive right in and make something with them.

This book was written to let you follow along with a series of steps. By doing this, you will experience firsthand what it's like to be a game developer. There are hundreds of numbered steps in this book, requiring you to pay very close attention and to do them in order, one by one. Many of the step descriptions are followed by additional explanations, descriptions, or screen shots.

You'll need to have access to a PC or Mac to follow along with the steps in this book. Your system needs to meet the development system requirements for Unity. In January 2020, the Unity company released the 2019.3 version of Unity. That is the version used for this book. Here is a summary of the system requirements for that version of Unity:

- OS: Windows 7 and Windows 10, 64-bit versions only; macOS 10.12.6+.

- CPU: X64 architecture with SSE2 instruction set support.

- Graphics API: DX10, DX11, and DX12-capable GPUs. Mac Metal capable.

Look at *unity.com* for details. While not strictly necessary, it's highly recommended that you have at least 1920×1080 resolution for your screen. A multiple monitor setup with a fairly recent graphics card is a good idea in order to enjoy Unity even more. If you don't have multiple monitors, the use of Virtual Desktops in Windows, or Mission Control on your Mac, is a worthwhile alternative.

If your system meets the requirements listed above, it will also meet the requirements for the other software used in this book. And yes, you'll need fairly fast internet access, the faster the better. Some of your downloads will be large and time consuming, but once your software is installed, you'll be able to work on your game without internet access.

If you're like most game developers, you'll have access to several systems, old and new, laptops and desktops. Your older laptops may not be compatible with Unity, but they can likely be used for doing Visual Studio projects and for the creation of graphics, sound, and music. They may be good enough for testing your games. Testing on older systems is an important facet of game development if you intend to distribute your game for play on PCs or Macs.

This book focuses on the development of games for PCs and Macs. Unity got its name from its ability to create games once and deploy them to many targets such as desktops, consoles, and mobile devices. All games in this book will run on PCs and Macs, and most of them can be modified to run on consoles and/or mobile devices with some effort. The process of taking a game from an existing platform to another one is called *porting*. Porting is easy in Unity when compared to writing your own game engine and getting it to work on all of your target platforms. Each platform has a long list of specific requirements, especially if your goal is to produce a commercial release. The number of supported platforms for Unity stands at 25 as of 2020. You'll need to do your own research on the current details of porting to, and developing for your intended target platforms.

It's easier to learn the basics of C# inside of Visual Studio rather than Unity. You'll want to have Visual Studio installed anyhow when using Unity, so in the next section you'll install Visual Studio.

## VISUAL STUDIO

Visual Studio is Microsoft's suite of development tools. It supports a plethora of languages, among them C#. In this section, you'll install the free version of Visual Studio. The Visual Studio 2019 community edition can be downloaded at *visualstudio.microsoft. com*. Go ahead and install this. Under Workloads select "Universal Windows Platform development." On a Mac, follow the specific instructions for Mac installation. This is a somewhat large install, so be sure you have enough disk space and time to download and install.

To test out whether the install worked, the first step is always to write a "Hello World!" program. This is a minimal program that only displays the text "Hello World!".

<Step 1> Run Visual Studio 2019 Community Edition.

<Step 2> Sign in or create a Microsoft Account, if necessary. This is only needed the first time you run Visual Studio.

<Step 3> Click on "Create a new project" in the Get started panel, as shown in Figure 1.1. On a Mac, this interface looks different, but you'll also see a way to create a new project.

<Step 4> Click on "Language" and select C#.

<Step 5> Click on C# Console App (.NET Framework) or (.NET Core). Compare your screen with Figure 1.2.

Get started

Clone or check out code

Get code from an online repository like GitHub or Azure DevOps

Open a project or solution

Open a local Visual Studio project or .sln file

Open a local folder

Navigate and edit code within any folder

Create a new project

FIGURE 1.1   The Get started panel in Visual Studio 2019.

Create a new project

Recent project templates

Console App (.NET Framework)  C#

Blank Solution

Search for project templates

Language ▾                Platform ▾                Project type ▾

Filtering by: C#                                   Clear filter

WPF App (.NET Framework)
Windows Presentation Foundation client application
    C#    Windows    Desktop

Class Library (.NET Standard)
A project for creating a class library that targets .NET Standard.
    C#    Android    iOS    Linux    macOS    Windows
    Library

Console App (.NET Framework)
A project for creating a command-line application
    C#    Windows    Console

Windows Forms App (.NET Framework)
A project for creating an application with a Windows Forms (WinForms) user interface
    C#    Windows    Desktop

Back        Next

FIGURE 1.2   Creating a new project in Visual Studio 2019.

**<Step 6>** Click on Next.

**<Step 7>** Enter Project Name "Hello World".

On a Mac, use the project name "HelloWorld". On a Mac, project names may not contain spaces, nor can you have an exclamation mark.

**<Step 8>** Optional: Enter a project location.

This would be a good time to set up a folder for all the projects for this book. It's up to you to name and create that if you wish.

**<Step 9>** Click Create.

**<Step 10>** Add this line of code inside the Main function:

```
Console.WriteLine("Hello World!");
```

Your screen should now look similar to Figure 1.3.

On a Mac, you won't have to type in the Console.WriteLine line of code, as it's there already. Also, there's only a single "using" line.

**<Step 11>** Control-F5 to compile and run it.

This step automatically saves your work, compiles it, and runs it. When running the console app, a popup window appears and prints "Hello World!" in the window followed by "Press any key to continue . . .". And before you go hunting for the "Any" key on your keyboard, just press the spacebar. There is no

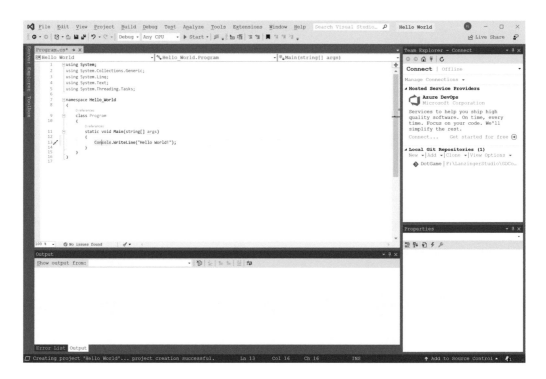

FIGURE 1.3 Hello World program in Visual Studio.

"Any" key on your keyboard. Search for "any key video" online for some very funny videos about this dilemma.

**\<Step 12\>** Exit.

You're now ready to use Visual Studio 2019. In the next few sections, you'll learn the basics of C# and make a simple game using Visual Studio.

## WHAT IS C#

C# (pronounced C Sharp) is the programming language used in this book and by Unity. C# is one of the many descendants of the granddaddy of them all, C. As of 2019, C# is one of the top programming languages in terms of both job demand and popularity. As a side benefit to reading this book, you'll learn the basics of C#, and programming in general.

To get started with game development, it is helpful to first learn your programming language well enough to do the job. C# is a large language, but only a relatively small subset of C# is necessary to make games in Unity.

Basic computations often look identical in C and C#. For example, the following code runs and produces the same result in both languages:

```
int i;
int x = 0;
for (i=0; i<10; i++)
{
  x = x + i;
}
// the value of x is 45 at the end of this computation.
```

Before learning more about C#, you'll start by examining different kinds of numbers and how they are represented on computers.

## NUMBERS

Numbers are the fundamental entities for Computer Game Development. Graphics, sound, and game logic are all represented by numbers in a computer game. In this section, you'll review some of the different types of numbers in mathematics and then look at how they are represented on your computer and in C#.

Here are some common types of numbers in mathematics: natural numbers, integers, rational numbers, real numbers, and complex numbers. Let's examine each of them.

*Natural numbers* are used for counting things. They start at one, so zero isn't considered a natural number. Mathematicians view numbers as unlimited. There is no such thing as a largest natural number. The set of natural numbers is infinite.

*Integers* introduce the concept of *negative number*. They are used for counting things that could possibly be zero or negative, such as a bank balance, for example.

*Rational numbers* are numbers of the form a/b with a and b integers, where b must be non-zero. Examples are 1/3, 12/35, –1/1000, 34/–1. *Decimal numbers* such as 10.43 are a special category of rational numbers because they can always be written as a rational number, for example 10.43 = 1043/100.

*Real numbers* are numbers with a possibly infinite number of decimal digits, such as pi = 3.1415926… or the square root of 2 = 1.4142… Real numbers are important for advanced mathematics, but because of their infinite nature, they cannot be directly represented on computers. Some real numbers are called *irrational* as they cannot be represented as a rational number, for example the aforementioned square root of 2.

*Complex numbers* are numbers of the form a + bi, where a and b are real numbers and i is the square root of –1. Complex numbers are rarely used in game development, but are commonly used in advanced mathematics.

It is important to distinguish between numbers in mathematics and numbers in computer programs. In mathematics, there is no upper limit for the size of numbers, but on a computer, the fixed amount of available memory requires a limit on the size of numbers. The next section shows the implications of this in C#.

## INTS, FLOATS, AND DOUBLES

In this section, you'll explore three types of numbers in C#. Here's an example:

```
int i = 17;
float x = 17.0f;
double y = 17.0;
```

What we have here is the number 17 represented in three different ways. The first is as an int, the second as a float, and the third as a double. You would call all of these "seventeen," but on your computer, they are represented in three very different ways. The int version is a 32-bit integer, stored in four consecutive bytes as 0x00000011. That x stands for hexadecimal. The float version also uses up 32 bits, but it's a different bit pattern: 0x41880000. The double version uses 64 bits stored in eight consecutive bytes as follows: 0x4031000000000000. You don't need to understand the details of how this works, just that floats and doubles are stored in this way. Game developers tend to use 32-bit integers and floats, mainly because they are adequate for most games as well as faster and more space-efficient than the alternatives.

Notice the letter f at the end of the float 17. That is the way you tell C# that the number is a float rather than a double. When coding in Unity, this distinction becomes important as you will see later on in this book.

It's time to experiment with these numbers by writing some code using ints, floats, and doubles.

**<Step 1>** In Visual Studio, create a new C# console project and call it NumberTest.

**<Step 2>** Insert the following code into Main:

```
int i = 17;
float x = 17.0f;
double y = 17.0;
Console.WriteLine("i={0},x={1},y={2}", i, x, y);
```

If you're on a Mac, you can leave the Hello World! line at the beginning.

**<Step 3a>** For Mac users only: Visual Studio – Preferences – Key Bindings – Scheme. Select Visual Studio (Windows). Click on OK.

This will make your keyboard shortcuts the same as for Windows. For example, to save a file is <Ctrl> S rather than <command> S. In this way, the keyboard shortcuts mentioned in this book work both on Windows and on Macs. You may use the Mac Key Bindings instead if you prefer those, but then you won't match the book's instructions in a few places. Be aware that this setting applies to Visual Studio only, so on other applications such as Unity or Audacity you'll be using <command> instead of <Ctrl>.

**<Step 3b>** Run NumberTest using <Ctrl>-F5. The output from this should be

```
i=17,x=17,y=17
Press any key to continue . . .
```

This really simple exercise shows how to declare variables, assign values to them, and then to access those values in a `Console.WriteLine` statement. All three variables show 17 as their value. Next, you're going to do some computations with those numbers.

**<Step 4>** Insert the following code at the end of Main after the existing `Console.WriteLine` statement:

```
i = i + 1;
x = x * 2;
y = y / 3.0;
Console.WriteLine("i={0},x={1},y={2}", i, x, y);
```

**<Step 5>** Again, run the code using <Ctrl>-F5. The output from this should be

```
i=17,x=17,y=17
i=18,x=34,y=5.66666666666667
Press any key to continue . . .
```

The variable `i` is one larger, `x` got doubled, and `y` divided by 3. `y` isn't really 17/3 but rather a close approximation. Because `y` is declared as a `double`, it has about 15 significant digits.

**<Step 6>** Change the declaration of `y` to `float` and run the program again.

You probably got two errors when you did that. That's because you also need to add an `f` at the end of the 17.0 in the declaration, and the 3.0 in the division. You are also seeing the location of the errors underlined in red. To see the error messages, on a Mac, click on the red error message on top. On a PC, look at the Error List in the panel at the bottom. You may need to expand the Error list panel by dragging the boundary up.

Visual Studio can be helpful for avoiding C# coding errors. It won't catch all coding errors right away, but if you see a red squiggly underline in the code editor, chances are high that you goofed. It's useful to know that hovering the mouse over a squiggly red line will pop up a short explanation.

**\<Step 7\>** Fix the errors by adding f's after the constants and try again.

The value of y is now 5.666667. The number of printed digits for y is now 7 instead of 15 because you have only 32 bits instead of 64 bits available to store the number. You'll now move on and test out some additional ways to do computations in C#.

**\<Step 8\>** Add the following code to Main:

```
double z;
i = 17 % 12;    // remainder function
x = (float)i + 3.0f;    // casting an integer to a float
z = Math.Sqrt(2.0);    // square root of 2
y = 1.0f / (float)Math.Sin(Math.PI * 0.25); // sqrt(2)
Console.WriteLine("i={0},x={1},y={2},z={3}", i, x, y, z);
```

Then run it and compare your results with this:

```
i=5,x=8,y=1.414214,z=1.4142135623731
```

Try to understand what's going on here. The variable i is computed as the remainder of dividing 17 by 12, thus 5. The expression (float)i converts the integer i to a float. This is called *casting*. The variable z, a double, is used to store the result of the built-in Math.Sqrt function. The Math functions use doubles, so if your code primarily uses floats, you'll often need to cast the results of Math functions to floats as indicated in the computation for y. That strange expression to compute y also results in the square root of 2. Oh, and the letters after the double slashes are comments and are ignored by C#.

**\<Step 9\>** Save your project.

You have just experienced one of the basic principles of good programming practice. Writing small bits of test code to try out features of a programming language is the best way to learn to use these features. You can freely experiment and even try to break things. When you're comfortable with your test code and fully understand it, you'll be ready to use what you learned in your actual project.

You're now ready to tackle the next topic, random numbers.

## RANDOM NUMBERS

In this section, you'll learn about random numbers in game design. Random numbers have been used in computer games since the very beginning. They are essential for any game with random elements such as shuffling a virtual deck of cards, slot machines, dice, and procedurally generated data. They are also great for fooling your players into thinking that you created sophisticated AI, when in fact your creatures just got lucky and acted smart.

The first thing to realize is this: Random numbers on computers aren't really random. They are generated using a deterministic algorithm which generates a sequence of numbers that appear to be random. The numbers appear random because these sequences pass certain statistical tests, but under the hood, they aren't random at all. It is possible to build

hardware that generates truly random numbers, but this is actually a bad thing for software development. You want to be able to recreate your "random" number sequence for testing purposes.

This brings us to the concept of a *seed*. Computer generated pseudo-random number sequences start with a seed, which is just another word for the first number in the random sequence. The random number algorithm computes each number in the sequence using only the previous number as input. If you want to recreate the same sequence, you simply start with the same seed. If you want a different random sequence compared to the last time you executed the program, you start with a different seed. Commonly used techniques to make these random numbers seem more random are to base the seed on the system clock or to increment the seed from game to game. Feel free to search the internet for additional discussions about randomness and random number generators.

In the following project, you will explore how to create and use random numbers in your C# based games.

**<Step 1>** In Visual Studio, create a new C# console project with the name "RandomTest".

**<Step 2>** Enter the following code to Main and run it multiple times:

```
Random rnd = new System.Random();
int randomnumber = rnd.Next(1,10);
Console.WriteLine("randomnumber = {0}", randomnnumber);
```

It's highly likely that you will see different numbers on subsequent program executions.

This code needs some explanation. The first line creates a new random number generator and you called it "rnd". The rnd.Next call returns a random number between 1 and 10. The result will be greater than or equal to 1, but strictly less than 10.

**<Step 3>** Go and insert a seed number into the System.Random() call like this:

```
Random rnd = new System.Random(42516);
```

Now, when you run the code, you'll get the same output every time because the seed is the same.

In the next step, you'll generate random doubles.

**<Step 4>** Remove the seed, then insert the following code:

```
double randomdouble = rnd.NextDouble();
Console.WriteLine("randomdouble = {0}", randomdouble);
```

You should see random doubles greater than or equal to 0.0 and less than 1.0.

## NUMBER GAME

This is a book about game development, so it's about time for you to make your first game. This is a simple number guessing game. There's not much to the design, but don't let that fool you. It's not going to be all that easy.

The core of the design is this: The game asks the player to guess an integer between 1 and 10 inclusive. The "inclusive" means that 1 and 10 are valid guesses. If the player guesses correctly, he wins. If not, the game gives a hint about the number. If the player guesses too low, the game prints "higher," or else "lower." Then, the player gets to try again.

This game is simple enough that you won't need to use Unity. A small Visual Studio Console app written in C# is perfectly adequate.

**<Step 1>**  Create a Visual Studio console app named "NumberGuess".

**<Step 2>**  Add code which prints a message that asks the player to guess a number, then exits. Run your code.

Here comes the most important lesson in this book. Are you ready? If you learn nothing else, learn this: Write your code one small piece at a time, and immediately test each piece before you go on to create the next one. This isn't a game at all yet, just a console app that prints some text and exits. It's basically Hello World with different text. The book doesn't tell you right away how to code this. Here's your chance to show that you remember how to do this. Or, if you don't remember how to output text in C#, you can look it up from a previous code listing in this book. Your code should look similar to this:

```
static void Main(string[] args)
{
    Console.WriteLine("Guess the number from 1 to 10: ");
}
```

Next, you'll generate the number that the player needs to guess.

**<Step 3>**  Put in code that generates a random integer from 1 to 10. Do this before asking for the guess.

Here is the code for this step:

```
static void Main(string[] args)
{
    Random rnd = new Random();
    int number = rnd.Next(1, 10);
    Console.WriteLine("Guess the number from 1 to 10: ");
}
```

Well, this code runs, but it appears to execute the same way as the previous version. To help test it you'll temporarily put in a WriteLine statement so you can see the value of number.

**<Step 4>**  Insert the following statement immediately after the `rnd.Next` statement:

```
Console.WriteLine("number = {0}",number);
```

You can now run the code and check that the number being generated is indeed between 1 and 10. There is one problem though. How do you know that all the possible numbers 1, 2, 3, …, 8, 9, 10 are being generated with equal frequency? Here is some code that checks this:

```
for (int i = 1; i <= 10; i++)
{
    int counter = 0;
    for (int j = 1; j < 1000; j++)
    {
        number = rnd.Next(1, 10);
        if (number == i) counter++;
    }
    Console.WriteLine("Frequency of {0} is {1} out of 1000",
                      i, counter);
}
```

When you run this code, you'll see a problem. The frequency for the numbers from 1 to 9 is about 100, but 10 has a frequency of 0. The problem lies with the `rnd.Next(1,10)` statement. It generates random numbers between 1 and 10, but not 10 itself. To fix this, you need to change the 10 to an 11. Now when you run the code everything looks good and you may remove the test code. Because you hate to throw this code away, you do the following. Instead of deleting it, comment it out by surrounding it with /* and */.

You're finally ready to move on and do the next step.

**<Step 5>** Insert the following code:

```
int guess;
bool valid;
valid = Int32.TryParse(Console.ReadLine(), out guess);
if (valid) if (guess == number)
{
    Console.WriteLine("You Win");
    return;
};
Console.WriteLine("You Lose");
```

This code lets the player enter one string, and if it matches the random number the player wins, otherwise he loses. Then the game exits. This code introduces several new C# concepts.

The variable `valid` is declared to be `bool`. A `bool` (pronounced Boolean after George Boole) has just two possible values, `true` or `false`. The next line reads a string from the console, converts it to a 32-bit integer, and stores the result in the variable guess. If the players enter an invalid input the `TryParse` call fails and returns false. Otherwise the code compares the guess with the number and if they are equal the player wins.

As you can see, it took quite a bit of code to deal with something as simple as getting an integer from the player and testing it, but that's the nature of programming. In coding, things are often quite a bit more difficult that you might at first expect. This is why it's so very difficult to predict the time it'll take to program something, even if it's very simple.

To make matters worse, the game isn't even done yet. There's still the matter of looping back to the beginning to give the player additional chances at guessing the number. You also need to add code to explain to the player what went wrong when the input isn't a valid number.

**<Step 6>** Replace the code after the declaration of `valid` with this:

```
while (true)
{
    valid = Int32.TryParse(Console.ReadLine(), out guess);
    if (valid) if (guess == number)
       { Console.WriteLine("You Win"); return; };
    if (!valid)
    {
        Console.WriteLine("Invalid input, try again");
        continue;
    }
    if (guess<number)
        Console.WriteLine("too low, please try again");
    else
        Console.WriteLine("too high, please try again");
}
```

Congratulations! You reached your first major milestone, the first playable version of your first game! You're almost finished with the game, and it's playable. It's not really fun, but that doesn't matter right now. Your goal was to learn how to create a simple, playable game.

The next step will fix the most glaring problem: the code tells you what the number is that you're trying to guess, but that surely makes the game way too easy.

**<Step 7>** Remove the output of `number`. Then play the game and try to win.

Now you're getting somewhere. It's no longer totally obvious how to win. Rather than continue the development of this game, it's time to wrap things up by putting in a quick title.

**<Step 8>** Add the following line at the beginning of Main:

```
Console.WriteLine("Number Guess");
```

You're going to shelve this game now. It's just a small exercise on your way to making games in Unity.

**<Step 9>** Save and exit Visual Studio.

## IMPORTANT: NOTES FOR MAC USERS

If you are following along with this book on a Mac, here are some important notes. Macs can be wonderful development machines, so by all means, continue to use your Mac if that is your preferred computer. You can skip this section if you're only using Windows.

All of the software tools used in this book are available both for Windows 10 and for Mac OS. There can be slight differences between Mac and Windows versions, but for the most part they are close to the same. The devil lies in the details. The keyboard shortcuts are different sometimes, and the screenshots do not match exactly, or in some rare instances not at all.

From here on in, this book will usually assume that you're using Windows. You can still follow along on your Mac, but you will need to adjust the keyboard shortcuts, and you'll

have to live with the slightly different screen shots. Occasionally, the Menu structures are different, but the same set of choices is always available. It helps to use the same software version numbers as the corresponding Windows version number recommended in the book. Also, be sure to go to www.franzlanzinger.com for the latest compatibility notes and additional help for Mac users.

## INSTALLING UNITY

In this section, you'll install Unity and take it for a quick spin. Go to *www.unity.com* and install the Personal, Plus, or Pro edition of version 2019.3.0f6. You'll need to check the financial eligibility conditions to see which version you are eligible to use. This book is compatible with all three editions. This book was produced and tested with the Personal Edition, version 2019.3.0f6. Check the author website www.franzlanzinger.com for the latest compatibility information if you are interested in following along with this book using a different version of Unity.

This book was originally developed on Windows. The screen captures were done on the author's 4K monitor running Windows 10. On a Mac, your screen might look a little different from the corresponding Windows screen captures. Also, make sure to read or reread the previous section for Mac users. Note that the author tested on a 2015 iMac using Unity Version 2018.2.8f1, which is similar but not exactly the same as Windows Unity 2019.3.0f6. See the author website for more details about this.

Unity is a real-time development platform for making games and similar applications for a wide variety of targets. With Unity, you can develop for PCs, Macs, game consoles, VR, and mobile devices. The name "Unity" implies that you can develop your game once and then deploy it to many platforms. It is without a doubt the world's most popular game engine with half of all released games developed using Unity, according to a rough estimate by Unity's CEO in 2018. Only a few very large game development studios take the plunge and write their own game engines for their games.

Now that you've installed Unity your logical next goal will be to create a "Hello World" project. This will be quite a bit different from the Hello World project for Visual Studio. No coding will be necessary. You'll simply add a GUI object with the text "Hello World." Follow the next few steps to do this:

<Step 1> Run the Unity Version that you just installed, click on New. Use the name HelloUnity. Choose the 2D Template, select Location, Create Project. Wait about a minute or two.

<Step 2> GameObject – UI – Text. Set Pos X and Pos Y to 0 in Inspector Panel.

<Step 3> Play the game by clicking on the Play arrow, middle top of the window.
You should see a blue screen with "New Text" in the middle. This "game" is just a static screen.

<Step 4> Stop playing the game by clicking the Play arrow again, and then change the text from "New Text" to "Hello World!" in Inspector panel.

**\<Step 5\>** Play and then stop.

**\<Step 6\>** File – Save. File – Exit. (On a Mac it's Unity – Quit.)

Special instructions for Mac users may not be there in the remainder of the book. Please read the previous section for Mac users if you haven't done so already.

In the next chapter, you'll learn more about how to code in the Unity environment using C#.

# Programming C# in Unity

THIS CHAPTER COVERS the basics of programming C# in Unity. In each section, you'll create a small Unity project. Those projects explore some C# programming features as well as how to use them in Unity. This book focuses on those portions of C# necessary for coding games in Unity. C# as a whole is a much larger language. You'll be just fine learning a smaller subset and sticking with it as you work through the rest of this book. In the more distant future, when you become more experienced as a game developer, you may wish to learn more advanced C# techniques.

## THE DEFAULT C# SCRIPT IN UNITY

<Step 1> Create a 2D project in Unity and use "DataTypes" as the name.

You can use the Unity Hub to do this. In the hub you select which version of Unity you'll be using. It is recommended that you use 2019.3.0f6 so that you're using the same version as the one used during the creation of this book. Using a more recent version will probably work, but there may be minor differences. Creating a new Unity project may take some time, possibly a minute or two depending on your system.

<Step 2> Edit – Preferences… – External Tools – External Script Editor. (Unity – Preferences on Mac.)

This step may be unnecessary for you. If necessary, select Visual Studio 2019 (Community). As mentioned earlier, this book assumes that you're using Visual Studio as your code editor.

<Step 3> Layout – Revert Factory Settings…

This dropdown menu is at the top right corner of the Unity Editor window. Your screen should look like Figure 2.1.

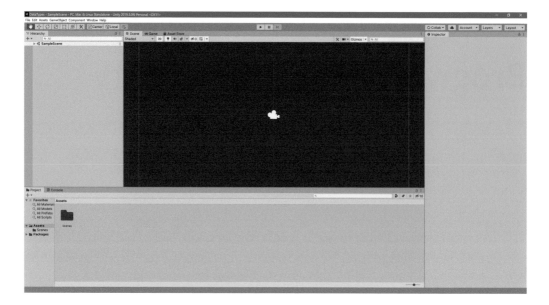

FIGURE 2.1    Unity Screen Default Layout.

**\<Step 4a\>**  In the Project panel, click on the+icon below the Project tab. Then click on C# Script. Type DataTypesTest and \<Enter\> (\<Return\> on Mac) to name it.

**\<Step 4b\>**  Expand the SampleScene in the Hierarchy by clicking on the small triangle to the left of the bold text.

**\<Step 4c\>**  Drag the newly created script from the Assets panel on top of the Main Camera in the Hierarchy panel.

**\<Step 5a\>**  Left-click on DataTypesTest in the Assets panel to select it.
    Your screen should look like Figure 2.2.
    In the Inspector panel on the right, in the Assembly Information section, you see the current contents of the script. Your next step allows you to edit this script in Visual Studio.

**\<Step 5b\>**  Double-click on DataTypesTest in the Assets panel.
    You should see Visual Studio 2019 open as a separate window. If you're doing this for the first time, this might take a minute or so. If you have a multi-monitor setup, this would be a good time to move the Visual Studio window to another monitor. In Windows, the Visual Studio window should look similar to Figure 2.3.
    The Mac display is somewhat different, but it works similarly.

For the rest of this book, code won't be displayed as a graphic figure, but as text:

```
using System.Collections;
using System.Collections.Generic;
using UnityEngine;
```

FIGURE 2.2    Creating a script in Unity.

FIGURE 2.3    Visual Studio showing the DataTypesTest script.

```
public class DataTypesTest : MonoBehaviour
{
    // Start is called before the first frame update
    void Start()
    {

    }

    // Update is called once per frame
    void Update()
    {

    }
}
```

The colors of the text may or may not match your screen. Using different colors for different types of code entities is called Color-Coding. Color-coding the C# code in Visual Studio is a useful automatic feature to help programmers make sense of it all and to help prevent bugs. Before you move on, you'll examine this script line by line.

At the beginning are three lines that start with using. These lines are examples of *using directives*. These directives give you access to objects in System.Collections, System.Collections.Generic, and UnityEngine. You can safely ignore these directives for now, but you do need to have them at the top of all of your Unity C# files.

Before you continue your exploration of this file, you need to review your knowledge of animations and frames. Unity is designed to create animations on the various supported target devices. Animations are a sequence of *frames*. Each frame is a graphic image designed to be displayed quickly and in sequence. Movies usually run at 24 frames per second, television broadcasts typically at 25 or 30 frames per second. Video game frame rates vary. They look good at 60 frames per second, though 30 or a bit less is considered acceptable depending on the type of game. Unity renders frames at a target framerate. The default target framerate depends on the device. You can control this in code if you wish.

It's time to return to examining the default file. After the three "using" directives, you see the class definition DataTypesTest with two methods: Start and Update. The Unity engine renders some number of frames each second. The Start method is called some time before the first frame is rendered. The Update method is automatically called once per frame. These methods contain no statements, so they don't do anything yet. They are there to speed up your editing later on when you insert code into them. If you know you'll never need them, it's safe to delete them.

A note about the terminology for *methods* vs. *functions*: In this book, the words "method" and "function" are used interchangeably. The word "function" sometimes designates a method that returns a value. For example, in mathematics, the square root function takes a nonnegative number as input and returns the square root of that number. The official term in C# is "method" but it's OK to call methods "functions" whether they return a value or not. When a method doesn't return a value, it is declared with the keyword void.

## NUMERIC DATA TYPES

In this section, you'll explore some of the numeric data types in C#. Examples of numeric data types are bytes, 32-bit integers, and floating point numbers. A good overview of *all* of

the data types for C# can be found at *docs.microsoft.com*. The C# section of that website is a valuable reference resource straight from the company that created C#. That documentation is intended for experienced software engineers, so you may want to stay away if you're a beginner.

You'll start by looking at the eight integer data types: `sbyte`, `short`, `int`, `long`, and their unsigned cousins: `byte`, `ushort`, `uint`, and `ulong`. The code in the following steps tests these data types. You will use the Console window to look at the output of your code. You open it by selecting Window – General – Console in the Unity window.

**<Step 6>** In the Visual Studio window, insert the following code in `Start`, <Ctrl> S to save, open the Console window if necessary, and click play.

```
int i = 17;
Debug.Log($"i={i}");
i = 2+2;
Debug.Log($"i={i}");
```

In the Console window you should see the following output:

```
i=17
i=4
```

You might see additional text in the Console window, including a time stamp, for example, or additional information about each line.

**<Step 7>** Stop playing the game by clicking on the play arrow again.

It can sometimes be difficult to know whether or not a game is playing. When in doubt, look at the play arrow at the top of the Unity window. The play arrow has a dark background when the game is playing, and a light gray background when it's not.

The Unity Console window may start out as a detached window or as a panel next to the Project panel. In the following steps, you'll try out some of the features of the Console window (or panel).

**<Step 8>** Clear the Console window by clicking on the "Clear" tab of the Console window.

**<Step 9>** Deselect Clear on Play in the Console window if necessary.

**<Step 10>** Run and stop the game several times.

You should get additional output in the Console every time you run the game.

**<Step 11>** Select Clear on Play and then repeat Step 10.

This time the console clears every time you run the game, and then the Start method outputs the same text. The result is that the console appears to do nothing.

**<Step 12>** Insert the following lines:

```
string Timenow = System.DateTime.Now.ToString();
Debug.Log(Timenow);
```

When you run the game multiple times, you'll see the output change slightly where it displays the seconds in the Timenow string.

You're ready to get back to exploring numeric data types.

**<Step 13>** Replace the `Start` method with the code below, and then test it.

```
void Start()
{
    sbyte b_int;
    short s_int;
    int i_int;
    long l_int;

    b_int = 17;
    s_int = 17;
    i_int = 17;
    l_int = 17;

    Debug.Log($"b_int={b_int}");
    Debug.Log($"s_int={s_int}");
    Debug.Log($"i_int={i_int}");
    Debug.Log($"l_int={l_int}");
}
```

There's not much to this code yet. Your next goal is to break it in various ways. This is the best way to experience how your development environment deals with errors. You'll also gain a better understanding of these data types along the way, which is, after all, your real goal.

**<Step 14>** Replace the first 17 with 1000.

You'll immediately get an error in Visual Studio: `Constant value '1000' cannot be converted to a 'byte'`. That's because the range of valid numbers for unsigned bytes is 0 to 255. Below is a table which shows the valid number ranges for the eight integral types in C#:

| Data Type | Bytes | Lower Limit | Upper Limit |
|---|---|---|---|
| Byte | 1 | 0 | 255 |
| Sbyte | 1 | −128 | 127 |
| Ushort | 2 | 0 | 65,535 |
| Short | 2 | −32,768 | 32,767 |
| Uint | 4 | 0 | 4,293,967,295 |
| Int | 4 | −2,127,483,648 | 2,147,483,647 |
| Ulong | 8 | 0 | 18,446,744,073,709,551,615 |
| Long | 8 | −9,223,372,036,854,775,808 | 9,223,372,036,854,775,807 |

It's helpful to understand this table. This will allow you to make an informed decision when selecting which of the integral data types to use in your projects.

**<Step 15>** Replace 1000 with 128, then with -128. Test this.

128 is too high for sbyte, -128 is OK. Notice that you get the error directly in the Visual Studio Editor before even running the game. You can test the other data types in a similar manner if you wish.

**<Step 16>** Insert the following lines and test them:

```
i_int = 2000000000;
i_int = i_int * 2;
```

That big number is 2 billion, i.e. 2 followed by nine zeros. You might expect 4000000000 as the result of that computation, but instead you get −294967296, which is clearly very wrong. This is an example of *overflow*. 32 bits are just not quite enough storage to represent 4 billion. The next step shows how to fix this.

**<Step 17>** Replace those last two lines with this:

```
l_int = 2000000000;
l_int = l_int * 2;
```

You now should get the expected result of 4000000000 because the variable l_int is declared as a long. C# does have a feature that enables overflow checking. With that feature enabled, you will get an error when an overflow occurs. This feature is generally not used by programmers because it's a little bit slower, but it can be useful when searching for bugs. Search for "overflow detection C#" in the C# language specification for more details.

As a general rule, using the int data type is a reasonable choice for representing integers. It's unusual to have to count anything that reaches more than 2 billion. The int data type is probably faster than long and it uses half the storage. The short and byte data types are rarely used except when storing large arrays where the storage savings can be significant. The unsigned integral data types are often used when storing bit patterns.

Next, you're now going to look at floating point numbers. C# has two data types for this, float and double. Here is the data type table for floating point numbers in C#:

| Data Type | Number of Bytes | Approximate Range | Precision |
|---|---|---|---|
| Float | 4 | $\pm 1.5 \times 10^{-45}$ to $\pm 3.4 \times 10^{38}$ | 6–9 digits |
| Double | 8 | $\pm 5.0 \times 10^{-324}$ to $\pm 1.7 \times 10^{308}$ | 15–17 digits |

**<Step 18>** Insert the following code into the Start method, and then test it:

```
float x;
double y;

x = 2;
y = 3;

Debug.Log($"x = {x}");
Debug.Log($"y = {y}");
```

There's not much going on here. You're displaying a float and a double.

**<Step 19>** Set x and y to different values as follows, then test.

```
x = 2.1f;
y = 3.1;
```

The x value now needs an f. In C#, when specifying a float like this it's necessary to append the letter f at the end, as you will see in the following step.

**<Step 20>** Remove the f from 2.1f and see what happens.

You immediately get an error in Visual Studio. You're likely going to see this error in the future because it's easy to forget to type that f when entering code. Unity uses floats for most of its built-in data structures, but the default floating point data type in C# is double.

The next steps do some simple computations with integers and floating point numbers. It's good for you to understand this code before going on to writing actual games.

**<Step 21>** Insert and test:

```
// Conversion from int to float
Debug.Log($"i_int={i_int}");
x = i_int;
Debug.Log($"x = {x}");

// Conversion from float to int
x = 3.14159f;
i_int = (int)x;
Debug.Log($"i_int = {i_int}");
```

When converting ints to floats and vice versa, you can just do an assignment statement for int to float, but you need to do a *cast* when converting from float to int. A cast looks like this: (data type) and it will explicitly convert the following expression to the data type within the parentheses. The next step shows more casting in action:

**<Step 22>** Insert and test:

```
x = (float)(3.3 * 5.7);
Debug.Log($"x = {x}");

i_int = (int)(3.3 * 5.7);
Debug.Log($"i_int = {i_int}");

x = (float)3 / (float)(2 + 5);
Debug.Log($"x = {x}");
```

You should get 18.81 for x, 18 for i_int, and then 0.4285714 for x. The first computation takes the double 3.3, multiplies it by the double 5.7, and then converts it to a float. The second computation casts the 18.81 to an int, which has the effect of dropping the fractional part of 18.81. The last computation is simply the floating point version of 3/7.

## MATH OPERATORS

In C#, *operators* are sequences of one or more special characters such as + - * / & =. Operators can be combined with variables and literals to form expressions. In this section, you'll explore the basic math operators in C#: addition, subtraction, multiplication, division, modulus, increment, and decrement. A solid knowledge of these operators is essential when developing in C#.

**<Step 1>** Create a Unity project with the name `Operators`.

**<Step 2>** Create a script with name `OperatorTest` and drag it onto the `Main Camera` just as you did before in the previous project. Then insert the following code into the `Start` method:

```
int i, j, k, answer;
i = 2;
j = 3;
k = 4;
answer = i + j;
Debug.Log($"answer = {answer}");
```

The first thing to notice is that you're getting a warning in Visual Studio. The warning states that the variable k is assigned but never used. This warning can be ignored for now because you intend to use the variable k in the very next step. It's a good habit to watch out for warnings and to fix them quickly. It is considered poor programming practice to ignore warnings for any significant length of time.

Your output from Step 2 should be "answer=5". It doesn't get much easier than that. You are now ready to do some more experimentation with the C# arithmetic operators.

**<Step 3>** Try out the following code:

```
int i, j, k, answer;
i = 2;
j = 3;
k = 4;
answer = i + j + k;
Debug.Log($"answer = {answer}");
answer = i + j*k;
Debug.Log($"answer = {answer}");
answer = (i + j)*k;
Debug.Log($"answer = {answer}");
answer = i + j + k*1000;
Debug.Log($"answer = {answer}");
answer = (i + j + k)*1000;
Debug.Log($"answer = {answer}");
answer = k/3;
Debug.Log($"answer = {answer}");
answer = k%3;
Debug.Log($"answer = {answer}");
answer = (i + j + k)%7;
Debug.Log($"answer = {answer}");
```

You should get the following answers: 9, 14, 20, 4005, 9000, 1, 1, 2. This code tests the four basic arithmetic operators and the modulus operator. Addition, multiplication, and subtraction are straightforward, but division and modulus aren't quite that easy to understand. The result of an integer division is always an integer with any remainder dropped. The remainder can be obtained by using the modulus operator %. The last answer in the above code example is the remainder of dividing 9 by 7, which is 2. The modulus operator is quite common and useful, so learning it right now is worthwhile.

The use of parentheses is critical when coding complicated expressions. If you know the *order of operation* of the C# operators you can sometimes avoid parentheses, for example, in the expression i+j*k. In that expression, the multiplication is done first, then the addition. That's because multiplication has a higher order of operation than addition. A good rule of thumb is to not rely on your memory of the order of operations, but rather to put in the parentheses. This rule is often broken when it comes to multiplication vs. addition because we are all used to that from algebra. Countless bugs are caused by faulty knowledge of operator precedence, so it's best to put in those parentheses when there's any doubt. Unnecessary parentheses can become necessary when you or someone else modifies your code, so avoid relying on the order of operation rules if there's a good chance that the code will be modified later on.

In the next step you'll test out increment and decrement operators.

**<Step 4>** Try out the following code:

```
answer = 10;
answer++;
Debug.Log($"answer = {answer}");
answer--;
Debug.Log($"answer = {answer}");
++answer;
Debug.Log($"answer = {answer}");
--answer;
Debug.Log($"answer = {answer}");
```

The answers should be 11, 10, 11, and 10. This code uses the increment and decrement operators both in *prefix* and *postfix* mode. In prefix mode, the operator appears before the expression that it affects, and in postfix mode, it appears afterward. There is another difference between prefix and postfix: The postfix version returns the expression and then operates. The prefix version operates and then returns the expression. The following step tests this.

**<Step 5>** Try out the following code:

```
answer = 10;
Debug.Log($"answer = {answer++}");
Debug.Log($"answer = {answer}");
answer = 20;
Debug.Log($"answer = {++answer}");
Debug.Log($"answer = {answer}");
```

The answers should be 10, 11, 21, and 21. Notice that in the postfix code the variable answer is printed and then incremented. The second output statement prints the incremented variable. In the prefix code, the variable answer is incremented first, then printed, thus you get 21 right away.

The next step is really easy, and it's only in here for completeness. The increment and decrement operators are examples of *unary* operators. Two additional unary operators are the plus and the minus operator.

<Step 6> Try the following code:

```
answer = 10;
Debug.Log($"answer = {+answer}");
Debug.Log($"answer = {-answer}");
```

You will get 10 and −10 as the answers. The strange thing about the plus operator is that it doesn't do anything. It's included in C# for consistency and completeness. It complements the `minus` operator, which is used quite frequently. Both the plus and minus operators are prefix only.

So far, you've only used the `int` data type for testing out these operators. Amazingly, they also work for all of other numeric types, though there are some subtle differences.

<Step 7> Try this:

```
Debug.Log("Floating Test");
float x, y;
double z;
x = 10.1f;
z = 50.12345123451234512345;
y = x + 10;
y = x + (float)z;
Debug.Log($"x y z = {x} {y} {z}");
```

The output is **x  y  z  =  10.1  60.22345  50.1234512345123**. What is going on here? The assignment for x needs the f at the end of the literal **10.1f**. If you forget the f, you get an error. Oddly enough the similar statement **x  = 10;** does not cause an error because C# can implicitly convert integer literals to floats. That assignment for z has too many digits but C# quietly truncates the extra ones, no error, no warning. This also happens for floats by the way. The first addition statement implicitly converts the 10 to a float and then performs the addition. The second addition statement needs to have a cast for z to convert it to a float. If you remove the cast, there you get an error. The output for y only has seven digits as that is the limit for floats.

The next step tests out compound assignment statements. For a binary operator op, a compound assignment statement looks like this: x op= y, which is the same as x=x op y.

<Step 8> Insert the following code and test it:

```
int i = 2;
i += 7;
Debug.Log($"i = {i}");
```

The value of `i` will be 9. Compound assignment is a very commonly used feature of C#. It makes your code more readable, and in some cases more efficient, so use it!

## BITWISE OPERATORS

In this section, you'll explore the bitwise operators including AND, OR, XOR, Complement, and the Shifts. These operators correspond to very fast hardware instructions on your

device. These operators should be in every game programmer's arsenal. In this section, you will continue to use the Operators project in Unity.

<**Step 1**> Create a script with name BitOperatorTest and drag it onto the Main Camera just as you did in the previous section. Main Camera now has two active scripts.

<**Step 2**> Select the Main Camera object and disable the OperatorTest script in the Inspector. You do this by clicking on the check box next to the name.

<**Step 3**> Use Visual Studio to insert the following code into the Start method of BitOperatorTest.

```
int a, b, c;
a = 32;
b = a >> 3;
c = a << 3;
Debug.Log($"a,b,c = {a} {b} {c}");
```

This code tests out the two shift operators: right shift >> and left shift <<. The right shift operator shifts the bit pattern of the variable a to the right by three positions, which has the effect of dividing it by 8. Left shift moves the bits to the left, effectively multiplying the variable a by 8. The output of this code should be
```
a,b,c = 32,4,256
```
The next step tests out the logical bitwise operators: & | ~ !.

<**Step 4**> Insert the following code:

```
uint d, e, f;

a = 0x04700_8999;
b = 0x0ffff_0000;

c = a & b;   // AND
d = a | b;   // OR
e = a ^ b;   // XOR
f = ~a;      // Complement

Debug.Log($"a = {a:x}");
Debug.Log($"b = {b:x}");
Debug.Log($"c = {c:x}");
Debug.Log($"d = {d:x}");
Debug.Log($"e = {e:x}");
Debug.Log($"f = {f:x}");
```

This code tests the four bitwise operators AND, OR, XOR, and Complement. Your output should look like this:
```
a,b,c = 32 4 256
a = 47008999
b = ffff0000
c = 47000000
d = ffff8999
e = b8ff8999
f = b8ff7666
```

a and b are simply the input numbers. Notice the underscore in the source code where a and b are assigned. The underscore allows you to separate groups of hexadecimal digits for clarity and has no other effect. The output versions of a and b do not have the underscore. Think of b as a mask. This mask operates on a depending on the operator. c is a but with the rightmost 16 bits masked out. d is the same as a with the leftmost 16 bits set to ffff. e is a with the leftmost 16 bits flipped, and f is the complement of a. This kind of bit manipulation is commonly necessary when dealing with hardware interfaces in video games. It is also used when trying to pack and unpack as much information as possible within arrays of data.

## MATH FUNCTIONS

C# in Unity has a large number of mathematical functions built in via several mathematical libraries. This section experiments with the recommended library for floats: Mathf. There is a similar library called Math which uses doubles. This section assumes that you learned high school trigonometry and remember the basics. You can be a successful 2D game developer without knowing trig, so don't be discouraged if this section is difficult for you. On the other hand, learning the very basics of trig will go a long way toward helping your understanding of the geometry and physics of 2D games.

**<Step 1>** Create a new Unity project named MathTest, create a script called MathTest, and assign it to the Main Camera. Then insert the following code into the Start method:

```
float a = 2.0f;
float b = Mathf.Sqrt(a);

Debug.Log($"Squareroot of {a} is {b}");
```

**<Step 2>** Run the code.

You should get the expected answer of 1.414214. Remember that you're using floats here, so you only get seven significant digits in the answer. As an aside, try to take the squareroot of -2.0f. You might expect to get an error, but instead you get NaN, an abbreviation for not a number. You should avoid this situation by explicitly testing that anything you feed into the squareroot function is non-negative.

The following table lists some of the useful functions and constants in Mathf.

| Constant | Description |
|---|---|
| Mathf.PI | Approximation of pi to 7 digits |
| Mathf.Deg2Rad | Degrees to radians conversion |
| **Function** | **Description** |
| Mathf.Sqrt | Square root |
| Mathf.Sin | Returns the sine of input angle in radians |
| Mathf.Cos | Return the cosine of input angle in radians |
| Mathf.Tan | Return the tangent of input angle in radians |

A complete list of available functions in Mathf is available online.

**\<Step 3\>** Compute the sine of 45 degrees. Then check to see if it matches 1/sqrt(2). Do this by inserting this code:

```
float c = Mathf.Sin(Mathf.Deg2Rad*45.0f);
c = 2.0f * c;
Debug.Log($"Squareroot of 2 is {c}");
```

That's right, the sine of 45 degrees multiplied by 2 is the squareroot of 2. You used the built-in conversion factor `Mathf.Deg2Rad` to convert 45 degrees to radians before computing the sine.

Be aware that the functions in Mathf can be somewhat slower that ordinary operations such as addition or multiplication. In the early days of game development, this was a problem, but these days our computers and phones are so fast that you can do thousands of Mathf computations every frame and not notice a slowdown when playing the game.

2D games usually don't need to use these math functions. When they do, it's usually something pretty elementary like computing the circular motions of game objects using sine and cosine. Another example would be the computation of the Euclidean distance between objects. The formula for this uses a single call to Mathf.Sqrt.

Calling the Mathf functions can sometimes be avoided by doing some algebra, thus speeding up your code. A good example of this is circular collision detection. If you wish to detect when an object is within a threshold distance of another object you might be tempted to use the squareroot function to calculate the distance between the objects and then compare that distance with your desired threshold. This squareroot computation can be avoided by simply squaring the threshold and comparing it with the square of the distance between the two objects.

## MORE C# DATA TYPES

There are quite a few non-numeric data types in C#. In this section, you'll explore Booleans, characters, strings, and arrays. These are all used extensively in game development.

**\<Step 1\>** Create a new Unity project named TypeTest, create a script called TypeTest, and assign it to the Main Camera. Then insert the following code into the `Start` method:

```
bool a, b, c, d;

a = true;
b = false;
c = a && b;
d = a || b;

Debug.Log($"a,b,c,d = {a} {b} {c} {d}");
```

This code tries out the Boolean data type, called `bool` in C#. The operator `&&` is the logical and. The result is only true if both a and b are true. Similarly, `||` is the logical or operator. Your output should be "a, b, c, d = True False False True". The logical operators look similar to the bitwise operators from the bitwise operator section. Note that the logical operators use two characters, whereas the bitwise operators only use a single character.

**\<Step 2\>** Insert the following code at the end of `Start`:

```
a = 3 < 4;
b = 3 > 4;
c = (5 == 7) || (15 == 15);
d = !(5 <= 6);

Debug.Log($"a,b,c,d = {a} {b} {c} {d}");
```

This code uses the comparison operators: less than \< greater than \> equals `==` and less than or equal `<=`. That exclamation mark is the negation logical operator. Here is an explanation of how you get the output `True False True False`. 3 is less than 4 so a is true. 3 isn't greater than 4 so b is false. 5 is not equal to 7 but 15 is equal to 15, so c is true. 5 is less than or equal to 6, but the negation of that is false, so d is false. The comparison operators work with all of the numeric data types. Note that equality testing uses two equal signs, whereas assignment statements use only one equal sign. You can get some pretty strange looking code like this, for example:

```
a = b == c;
```

When b is equal to c, this statement assigns `true` to a.

**\<Step 3\>** Add the following to the Start method:

```
char ac, bc, cc;
ac = 'A';
bc = (char)(ac + 1);
cc = (char)(ac + 32);

Debug.Log($"ac,bc,cc = {ac} {bc} {cc}");
```

This code shows how to use the `char` data type. The output should be ac, bc, cc = A B a. Characters in C# are 16-bit Unicode. The computation for bc takes ac converts it to an integer, adds 1, and then converts it back to a character. The result is, unsurprisingly, 'B'. The computation for cc adds 32 to 'A' which happens to get the lower case character 'a'. There are no built-in character operators in C#. There is, however, very good string support.

Strings are sequences of characters, typically stored as an array of characters with a null character at the end. C# has a built-in string data type. You will be trying out strings in the next several steps.

**\<Step 4\>** Add the following code to `Start`:

```
string mystring;
mystring = "Testing ONE TWO THREE";
```

```
Debug.Log(mystring);
Debug.Log(mystring.ToLower());
```

You are using the built-in string method ToLower which converts all characters of the input string to lower case. You can look up the many other supported string methods online as needed. String manipulation is sometimes necessary in game development, but this really depends on the game. If you're writing a text adventure, you'll use strings a lot. If you're writing a space shooter then not so much.

**<Step 5>** Insert and test the following:

```
int[] myarray = new int[5] { 1, 4, 9, 16, 25 };
Debug.Log($"array elements 0 and 1: {myarray[0]} {myarray[1]}");

myarray[0] = 17;
myarray[1] = myarray[2] * myarray[3];
Debug.Log($"array elements 0 and 1: {myarray[0]} {myarray[1]}");
```

This is a simple example of a one-dimensional integer array in C#. The square brackets after the int indicate that you are declaring the variable myarray as an array. The five numbers that are listed inside of the curly brackets are the initial values. The indices of arrays start at 0, so the first element in a five element array is element 0, the last is element 4. When you run this code, you should get 1 and 4 at the first log statement, 17 and 144 for the second.

In the next step you'll declare and use a two-dimensional float array.

**<Step 6>** Insert and test the following:

```
float[,] My2dimArray = new float[3,4];
My2dimArray[0, 0] = 1.0f;
My2dimArray[1, 0] = 2.3f;
My2dimArray[2, 3] = 4.34f;
Debug.Log($"two dim array [1 0]: {My2dimArray[1,0]}");
```

This is really just an exercise to see if you can type this code, get it to work, and understand what it does. You're setting up a small array, putting in some numbers into the array, and displaying one of those numbers.

Arrays are an efficient way to store larger amounts of data in your program. It's important to know that arrays must fit into the available RAM on your device. If you set up an array that doesn't fit, you should get an error. How about you try to do that and see what happens.

**<Step 7>** Declare an array with 100000000000 elements.

You will get an OverflowException error when you run the code. That's because C# imposes a limit of 4 gigabytes on arrays, regardless of how much RAM is installed on your system. If you declare an array that allocates a little less than 4 gigabytes you may be OK, depending on your operating system and the device you're using. Developers tend to avoid such large arrays because of performance issues.

Yes, C# supports n-dimensional arrays where n is any number, but typically n is at most 3 in real-world applications. Arrays can have elements of any other data type, even other arrays. Arrays of arrays are called *jagged arrays* because the arrays may have different numbers of elements. A listing of a jagged numeric array will not necessarily look like a rectangular array of numbers because each row may have a different number of columns. Similar to jagged arrays, in arrays of strings each element uses up a different amount of data if the strings are of different lengths.

This concludes our discussion of some popular C# data types. You may learn about the other data types in the C# documentation, if you wish.

## IF AND SWITCH

This section explores how to control the flow of your code using two kinds of selection statements: if and switch. The easiest is with the "if" statement.

<Step 1> Create a new Unity project named SwitchTest, create a script called SwitchTest, and assign it to the Main Camera. Then insert the following code into the `Start` method:

```
int a, b;
a = 10;
b = 12;
if (a<b)
{
    Debug.Log("a is less than b");
}
else
{
    Debug.Log("a isn't less than b");
}
```

This code tests the if-else statement. You should see "a is less than b" in the Console window. Try changing the value for a to 15 and running it again. That time you'll see "a isn't less than b".

Note that there are curly brackets surrounding the `Debug.Log` statements. They aren't necessary in this case, but they are recommended in order to avoid some nasty bugs that can occur if you don't put in the brackets. The next steps show this in action.

<Step 2> Remove the curly brackets surrounding the Debug.Log statements, and then edit the code to look like this:

```
if (a<b)
    Debug.Log("a is less than b");
else
    Debug.Log("a isn't less than b");
```

When you test this code, it runs exactly the same way. So far so good.

**<Step 3>** Edit the Start method to look like this:

```
void Start()
{
    int a, b;
    a = 10;
    b = 12;
    if (a < b)
        Debug.Log("a is less than b");
    else
        Debug.Log("a isn't less than b");
        Debug.Log("a still isn't less than b");

    Debug.Log("End of Start Method");

}
```

Your intention here is to execute the two successive indented Debug.Log statements when a isn't less than b. But that's not what the code will do. That second Debug.Log statement that says that a still isn't less than b will always execute, even when a is less than b, because the curly brackets are missing.

**<Step 4>** Put the curly brackets back and test the code again.
The code should work as intended.

**<Step 5>** Remove the else clause with the two Debug.Log statements and set a=15;
This demonstrates that the else clause can be omitted if it's not needed.
The next steps test the switch statement.

**<Step 6>** Insert and test the following code before the "End of Start Method" statement.

```
int testvalue = 1;
switch (testvalue)
{
    case 1:
        Debug.Log("testvalue is 1");
        break;
    case 2:
        Debug.Log("testvalue is 2");
        break;
    default:
        Debug.Log("testvalue default");
        break;
}
```

As you might guess, this statement executes the code in the matching switch section depending on the value of testvalue. For example, you would use the switch statement when coding a finite state machine as shown later in this book.

Switch statements are notorious for causing bugs when programmers forget to put in a break statement. This can easily happen in C++ or C, but C# will trigger a compilation error when a break is missing. Try it! You can have multiple *case labels* sharing the same switch section. So, for example, you can have case 2: immediately followed by case 3: If you do that the associated

switch section is executed whenever `testvalue` is 2 or 3. You can find additional information about the C# switch statement at docs.microsoft.com.

## LOOPS

Looping is what gives computers their immense power. A human would take quite a while to add up the first 1000 square integers. Yes, there's a formula for that, but modern computers can do this by simply adding all those numbers in a few milliseconds. The following code shows how.

**<Step 1>** Create a new Unity project named LoopTest, create a script called LoopTest, and assign it to the Main Camera. Then insert and test the following code in the `Start` method:

```
int sum = 0;
for (int i=1; i<1000; i++)
{
    sum += i * i;
}
Debug.Log($"sum = {sum}");
```

You should get the answer of 332833500. You just used the for loop which executes the loop body for as long as the loop counter `i` stays below the limit of 1000. The loop counter is initialized to 0 and is incremented every time through the loop.

By the way, you have a bug. Remember that you wanted to add the first 1000 square integers, but the loop stops before it gets to 1000. To fix this, change the for loop to this:

```
for (int i=1; i<=1000; i++)
```

You can see that now the test for stopping the loop is "less than or equal", which is what you want. The correct answer is 333833500, 1 million larger. There is a mathematical formula for this which allows you to avoid all those computations.

**<Step 2>** Insert the following code:

```
int numsquares = 1000;
sum = numsquares * (numsquares + 1) * (2 * numsquares + 1) / 6;
Debug.Log($"sum from formula = {sum}");
```

When you run this code, you should get two matching sums.

By the way, you got kind of lucky on this one. If you try this same code with 2000 instead of 1000, you'll get two different negative sums. How on earth can this happen? Well, you used 32-bit integers, and you overflowed. Make all the integers longs and the code will work.

In general, a for loop consists of an initializer, a condition, and an iterator, followed by a block of statements that are repeatedly executed. The following step tests some additional examples of for loops.

**\<Step 3\>** Insert and test the following

```
for (int j = 7; j > 3; j--) Debug.Log($"j = {j}");

int k=0;
for (; ; )
{
    Debug.Log($"k = {k}");
    k++;
    if (k > 4) break;
}

int a, b;
for (a = 0, b = 4; a < 3; a++, b--) Debug.Log($"a,b = {a} {b}");
```

The first loop shows that you can decrement, not just increment. It also demonstrates that you can omit the curly brackets for the loop body if the loop body is just a single statement. This saves some typing, but it's not recommended if you plan on maintaining this code in the future. The second loop is an infinite for loop, except that you exit it via the break statement. The third demonstrates complex initializers and iterators. Notice the commas used to separate the multiple initializing statements and iterator statements.

The next step shows how to nest for loops.

**\<Step 4\>** Insert and test the following code.

```
for (int i = 0; i < 2; i++)
    for (int j = 0; j < 2; j++)
    {
        Debug.Log($"i,j = {i} {j}");
    }
```

This is a simple example of how to nest one for loop inside of another. You can, of course nest more loops inside of each other when needed. Notice that this code has curly brackets for the loop body even though they aren't really needed here.

Next you'll explore the two kinds of *while loops* in C#.

**\<Step 5\>** Insert and test:

```
int power = 2;
while(power<100)
{
    Debug.Log($"power = {power}");
    power *= 2;
}
```

Can you guess what this code will do? When you run it, you'll get the powers of 2 up to and including 64. This form of the while statement executes the code inside of the curly brackets repeatedly. The Boolean condition after the while keyword is tested before the code is executed. If it's false, the execution moves to the code after the closing curly bracket.

The do-while statement works similarly.

**\<Step 6\>** Replace the while loop with this:

```
int power = 2;
do
{
    Debug.Log($"power = {power}");
    power *= 2;
} while (power < 100);
```

This code produces the same output. The difference is that the loop condition is tested after the code block, not before. If you change the initialization to power = 200, then the code block of the loop would be executed once and then exit. The while statement in step 5 would skip over the loop code immediately.

## CLASSES AND METHODS

In this section, you'll explore classes and methods in C#. If you've learned another object-oriented language such as C++, this will seem easy. If it's all new to you, don't worry. Game development can be done with just the basics of object-oriented programming. You'll start by building your own class. A class is just a collection of data and methods as shown in this next step.

**\<Step 1\>** Create a new Unity project named ClassTest, create a script called ClassTest, and assign it to the Main Camera. Then replace the script with the following:

```
using System.Collections;
using System.Collections.Generic;
using UnityEngine;

public class ClassTest : MonoBehaviour
{
    // Start is called before the first frame update
    void Start()
    {
        TreeClass pear = new TreeClass("Mypeartree", "pear", 24);
        Debug.Log(pear.convertString());
    }

    // Update is called once per frame
    void Update()
    {

    }
}

public class TreeClass
{
    string name;
    string kind;
    int age;

    public TreeClass(string name, string kind, int age)
    {
        this.name = name;
        this.kind = kind;
        this.age = age;
    }
}
```

```
public string getName() { return name; }
public string getKind() { return kind; }
public int getAge() { return age; }

public string convertString()
{
    return ("This tree has the name " + this.getName()
        + ".\nMy kind and age: " + this.getKind() +
        " " + this.getAge());
}

}
```

Your output in the Console window should be:

```
This tree has the name Mypeartree
My kind and age: pear 24
```

This is about as simple as it gets. You created your own class with the name TreeClass. It has three instance variables: name, kind, and age. There are five methods: TreeClass, getName, getKind, getAge, and convertString. This class doesn't really do anything other than store information about tree objects and allowing access to these objects. The Start method created a single tree using the TreeClass method, and then used convertString to send the string version of the tree to Debug.Log.

When doing simple Unity programming, you won't often need to create your own classes. Instead, you'll use the classes created for you by Unity and add methods when appropriate. As you get more advanced, you'll learn additional object-oriented programming techniques as needed. If you are an advanced programmer, you may wish to read "Object-Oriented Programming (C#)" in docs.microsoft.com. There you'll find a good overview of the object-oriented features supported by C#.

## C# PROGRAMMING STYLE

As in all programming languages, style matters. If you use good style, your code will be more readable and maintainable. This book strives to follow the following commonly used coding style conventions:

- Use four-character indents and tabs saved as spaces.

- One statement per line.

- One declaration per line.

- One blank line between method definitions and property definitions.

- Place comments on separate lines, not at the end of a line of code.

For the naming of variables, we use PascalCase for method names and class names. We use camelCase for variables and parameters. In case you don't know this, PascalCase runs

words together and separates them via capitalization. camelCase does the same thing, but has the first letter in lowercase, making the capital letters look a bit like humps on a camel. Single character variable names should only be used as loop iterators or in sample code.

Good style for braces is to give each brace its own line, and to use braces in conditional statements no matter the number of lines. Occasionally, one-liner pieces of code may break these rules. You can find additional information about C# style and the coding standard used in this book in Appendix V.

# 2D Graphics with GIMP and Unity

Tʜɪs ᴄʜᴀᴘᴛᴇʀ ᴄᴏᴠᴇʀs the creation of some 2D graphics for a very simple 2D game: Bouncing Donuts. You will use the *GNU Image Manipulation Program* (GIMP). You'll draw a donut and a wooden plank in GIMP, import them into Unity, and then create a simple demo featuring your donut bouncing on three planks. In subsequent chapters, you'll turn this demo into a playable game.

## INTRODUCTION TO GIMP

You will use GIMP to make the graphics for this chapter. GIMP is a cross-platform image editor available for Macs, Windows, and Linux. It is open-source software and may be freely used for any purpose, including commercial projects.

If you haven't done so already, please install GIMP. Go to www.gimp.org for instructions. This book uses GIMP 2.10.14, released in October 2019. You may wish to use a more recent version of GIMP, but be aware that the user interface and feature set might be slightly different if you do that.

During the installation, you'll have the chance to customize GIMP. That is unnecessary to follow along with the steps in this book.

You'll start by drawing something resembling a donut.

<Step 1> Open GIMP.
> Before you start using GIMP, you're going to set up the user preferences to match what's used in this book.

<Step 2> Windows – Single Window Mode.
> Do this several times to see what this does. For the purposes of this book, it's better to use Single Window Mode, so please use that.

<Step 3, Windows> Edit – Preferences.

**\<Step 3, Mac\>** Gimp-2.10 – Preferences.

This opens a Preferences dialog. It's quite extensive and worth exploring once you're familiar with the basics of GIMP. For now, you're going to try to match the settings in the book.

**\<Step 4\>** Window Management – Reset Save Window Positions to Default Values.

You're doing this in case you have moved the windows. You can do this in the future if you'd like to have the default window positions again.

**\<Step 5\>** Exit and relaunch GIMP.

This relaunch is necessary to activate the windows position reset.

**\<Step 6, Windows\>** Edit – Preferences – Theme – Light.

**\<Step 6, Mac\>** Gimp-2.10 – Preferences – Theme – Light.

This book uses a light theme because that looks better on paper.

**\<Step 7\>** Icon Theme – Color – OK.

This is the author's personal preference.

**\<Step 8\>** Go back to Preferences, and then use Icon Size from the Theme – Custom Icon Size.

Move the slider and pick a size for the icons that you like. This book was produced using a 4K monitor, so the author used Huge to make the icons large enough.

**\<Step 9\>** Adjust the window size and panels on the left and right of the window, if necessary. Compare with Figure 3.1.

You are now ready to use GIMP. Just to make sure that you're set up the way you want, do the following:

**\<Step 10\>** Exit GIMP and launch it again.

As you can see, the window size and layout is preserved when you exit and launch again.

Your first goal in using GIMP is to draw a cartoonish donut.

**\<Step 11\>** File – New and choose a size of 512 × 512 pixels – OK.

You need to type in the 512 × 512 and make sure that the units are set to px (short for pixels). These dimensions are chosen to be large enough to let you draw a detailed image, if you wish. Choosing powers of 2 for size dimensions allows you to scale the image down to, for example, 128 × 128, and avoid scaling artifacts. Figure 3.2 shows the completed donut. You will try to draw it just like that.

**\<Step 12\>** Layer – Transparency – Add Alpha Channel.

**\<Step 13\>** Colors – Color to Alpha … and use a white color – OK.

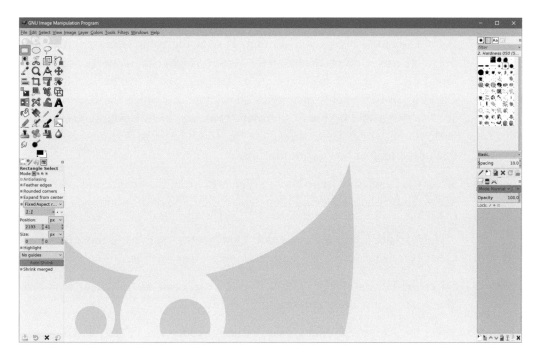

FIGURE 3.1    GIMP setup with Light theme, Color icon theme, and Huge icons on 4K monitor.

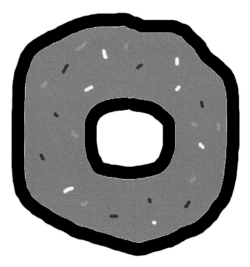

FIGURE 3.2    Donut drawn in GIMP.

The white background color should change to a checkerboard pattern. The checkerboard indicates transparency, also known as alpha. The pixels surrounding the donut and the pixels inside of the donut hole will need to be transparent.

In the following steps, you will be drawing using the Pencil tool and the Paintbrush tool. Before you do that, look at the color selector immediately below the tool icons on the left of the screen. The top left rectangle is the active foreground color; the bottom right rectangle is the active background color. Clicking on those color rectangles allows you to change those colors. There are also two useful keyboard shortcuts. D makes the foreground black and the background white. X exchanges the foreground and background colors. You don't need to hold down shift for those.

<Step 14> Select the Pencil tool (type N) and type X to make the foreground color black. Make the Brush Size 20, and then draw the outline of the donut and the donut hole.

You can use Figure 3.2 as a guide. Don't worry too much if those two circles aren't exactly perfect. A few bumps along the way are fine.

<Step 15> Select the Fill tool (Type <Shift>B) and a tan color as the foreground color. Then click on the donut interior to fill in the donut.

<Step 16> Select the Paintbrush tool (Type P) and make the Brush Size 10. Draw some sprinkles using three different colors: pink, light blue, and white.

You can use <Ctrl> Z (<command> Z on a Mac) to undo your drawings along the way.

Ok, that's enough for now. It's just place-holder graphics. The game industry calls this sort of thing programmer art. If you're a programmer, chances are that your art skills are mediocre, but that doesn't matter. You're trying to make a playable game with art that will likely be replaced by professional graphics later on. And if you're lucky your crudely drawn art will be good enough with a charm all its own. Remember, there's plenty of hit games that shipped with programmer art.

<Step 17> File – Save As to Donut.xcf and File – Export As to Donut.png. Use the png default settings.

Be sure to select your working directory for this book as the directory. The xcf file is the GIMP internal format. Later on, when you load donut.xcf you can continue working on your donut where you left off. The png file is the graphics file that will be used by Unity to display the donut. Unity won't be using the xcf file directly, but you are storing it in the assets folder for easy access.

One more thing: Make sure you capitalized Donut in those filenames. Yes, it matters later on.

<Step 18> Exit GIMP.

In Windows, File – Quit, <Ctrl> Q, or close the window. If you forget to save before quitting, GIMP will remind you to save before letting you quit. On a Mac, GIMP-2.10 – Quit, <command> Q, or close the window.

Next, you're going to set up your Unity game project and import the donut into Unity.

**\<Step 19\>** In Unity, create a new 2D project named BouncingDonuts.

**\<Step 20a\>** Move the donut.xcf and donut.png files into the Assets panel.

There are two ways to do that. You can drag the files directly into the Unity window, or you can copy them into the Assets folder of your Unity project using the operating system interface.

**\<Step 20b\>** Select the Donut in the Assets panel.

There are two donuts in there. Which one should you select? Pick the one that has an icon that looks like a donut. That's the png file. The other one is the GIMP project file. The Unity window should now look like Figure 3.3.

The order of the Assets may be different on your system.

**\<Step 21\>** Drag the Donut into the Hierarchy panel.

Be sure to do this with the.png file, the one with the donut icon.

**\<Step 22\>** Duplicate the Donut Sprite using the Edit Menu.

**\<Step 23\>** Move the duplicated donut to show overlapping donuts as in Figure 3.4.

To do this, select the Move tool (the icon with four arrows), hover the mouse over the red arrow, then drag it after it turns white. That arrow is yellow while you're dragging.

You can now see two donuts overlapping each other. This tests that transparency is working.

FIGURE 3.3　Donut in the Assets panel in Unity.

FIGURE 3.4   Overlapping donuts.

**<Step 24>** Delete the duplicated donut by right-clicking on it in the Hierarchy panel and selecting Delete.

**<Step 25>** Save the BouncingDonuts project and scene and exit Unity.

## BOUNCING DONUTS DESIGN

It's a common misconception that game developers design their games first and then implement them according to those designs. Sometimes, that actually happens, but it's unusual. In the real world, game developers decide on a rough design, start to implement something, then they change the design, implement the changes, and then they do that over and over again until the game is ready for release. Many successful games continue their development after their first release and can stay in development for years or even decades.

For this Bouncing Donut game, all you have right now is a donut and a name. This game is supposed to be an exercise, not meant for release to the public. If you can make it fun and playable that would be a success. You can then reevaluate and decide on how to polish it and release it. Writing a small prototype game first is often the very best way to prepare for the development of a much larger, releasable game.

Bouncing Donuts will be a 2D game with a donut as the main character. There will be other donuts and they'll bounce on the planks and against one another. To keep things as simple as possible you won't scroll the playfield for now. You'll start with your donut at the top left of the playfield and try to bounce the donut into a donut box. As the game evolves, there will be obstacles for the bouncing donut to make the game more challenging. You'll control the donut by manipulating the playfield. You now have enough of a game idea to start development of a simple prototype. You don't have a clear vision for what those other donuts are going to do, so you'll shelve that idea for now.

FIGURE 3.5    Sketch of Bouncing Donuts prototype.

It can definitely help to make a quick sketch of the playfield first. Figure 3.5 shows such a sketch drawn on paper and then captured using a phone.

This is a very rough sketch, the kind you might draw in one minute on a restaurant napkin. It gives you an idea of the scale of some of the objects and will help you get started. The final version will probably look quite a bit different.

## CREATING A WOODEN PLANK IN GIMP

You drew a simple donut sprite in GIMP earlier in this chapter and moved it to Unity. In this section, you'll draw a wooden plank and move it to Unity as well.

<Step 1>  Open GIMP.

Your goal is to make a rectangular plank that looks like it's made of wood. This means you'll need to get a wood texture. There are dozens of ways of obtaining textures. The fastest way to get a texture for a prototype project is to search the internet for textures, pick one, and copy it into GIMP. If you do this, make sure that you record where you got the texture so you can deal with licensing it or replacing it before release. This applies to anything and everything that you grab from the internet.

It may be more satisfying and easier to just make your own texture from scratch. This also ensures that you own the image, which may be important if you plan to do a public release of your game in the future. This is the method you'll use in the next few steps.

<Step 2>  Take a digital photo of a piece of wood and store it in the Assets folder. Call it WoodenPlankPhoto.jpg. Be sure that you're not photographing something proprietary, such as a company logo, or even your neighbor's tree. You could

take a photo of some furniture that you own, or maybe a tree in your own backyard.

Figure 3.6 shows what that photo might look like.

<Step 3> Open the photo in GIMP using File – Open.

<Step 4> If you get a dialog concerning rotation of the image, choose "Keep Original".

<Step 5> Use the Rectangle Select tool (Type R) to grab a rectangular section of wood.
The aspect ratio of the rectangle should be about 6 to 1. In other words, make the rectangle about six times longer than it is wide. You can look at the bottom of the screen to see the pixel dimensions of the rectangle to help you with this.

<Step 6> Edit – Copy.

<Step 7> Edit – Paste as – New Image.

<Step 8> Image – Transform – Rotate 90 degrees clockwise.
This last step is only necessary if your rectangle is vertical. The wooden planks in this game will be horizontal.

<Step 9> Image – Scale Image. Enter Width of 360, Height of 60.

<Step 10> Adjust the zoom level with the + and – keys. It's convenient to use the numpad for this, but typing + and – on your regular keyboard also works.
Your plank should look like Figure 3.7.

<Step 11> File – Export As ... using the filename WoodPlank.jpg, and the Assets folder. You may use the default settings for this export.

<Step 12> File – Save As ... using the filename WoodPlank.xcf, also in the Assets folder.

FIGURE 3.6   Original photo to be used to make a wooden plank texture.

FIGURE 3.7    WoodPlank in GIMP.

> In the next section, you'll make a test animation using the plank and the donut.

**<Step 13>** Exit GIMP.

## THREE PLANKS AND A DONUT IN UNITY

To wrap up this chapter, you'll import the wooden plank into the BouncingDonuts project and make the donut bounce on the wooden plank. You'll then create multiple planks and position them on the screen to match your design sketch.

**<Step 1>** Open the BouncingDonuts project in Unity.

> You should see two new assets, both called WoodPlank, as shown in Figure 3.8.
>
> The asset with the GIMP icon is the GIMP xcf file, which you won't be using in your project. The asset that looks like a wooden plank is the png file that you created using GIMP in the previous section. Double check that the Donut and WoodPlank filenames are capitalized correctly, If not, you can rename them by clicking on the name, waiting, clicking it again, waiting again, and then editing the name with your keyboard. That's not obvious, but that's how Unity does renaming.

**<Step 2>** Drag the WoodPlank asset (the one that looks like a wooden plank) into the Hierarchy panel.

> You should now see the plank in the middle of the Scene.

**<Step 3>** Change the position of the Donut to (0, 3, 0).

FIGURE 3.8    Woodplank assets in Unity.

You do this by selecting the Donut in the Hierarchy or the Scene and editing the X Y and Z properties of the Position in the Transform section in the Inspector panel. While you're at it, you'll scale the donut to be smaller compared to the plank.

**<Step 4>** Change the Scale of the Donut to (0.2, 0.2, 1).

You can safely ignore Z-scales and Z-positions for your 2D sprites in this sprite-based 2D project. They are unused, so yes, it would be better to not have them there at all, but this is how Unity does it.

**<Step 5>** Change the position of the WoodPlank to (0, −3, 0).

This moves the wooden plank lower on the screen.

**<Step 6a>** Click on the Game tab and move the Scale Slider up to 5× and back to 1×.

This shows you a dark blue background. It represents the view the game player will get.

**<Step 6b>** Click on the Scene tab.

You're back in the Scene view where you do the layout of the game as you're developing it.

**<Step 6c>** Hover the mouse over the Scene, and then move the scroll wheel and the mouse to make the Scene view match Figure 3.9.

That icon in the middle represents the Camera. It goes together with the Camera Gizmo, which is that thin white outline.

**<Step 6d>** Click on Gizmos to disable them.

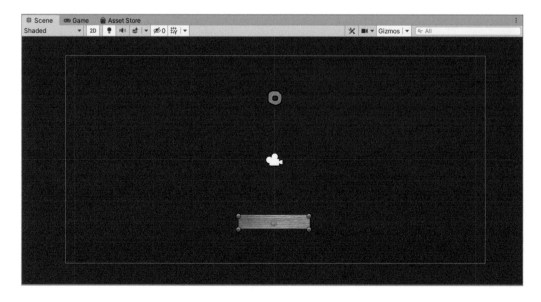

FIGURE 3.9   Donut with WoodPlank and Camera icon in Unity.

The white outline and the Camera icon have disappeared. This gives you a cleaner look of the scene, but you're going to bring them back because you like having them in the Scene view.

**<Step 7>**  Enable the Gizmos.

Now that you're oriented, you're going to add physics to the Donut:

**<Step 8>**  Select the Donut, then do Component – Physics 2D – Rigidbody 2D.

You have just added a Rigidbody 2D component to the Donut. You can see the details of this in the Inspector. The Rigidbody 2D component enables a physics simulation built into Unity. To test this out, do the following.

**<Step 9>**  Run the game by pressing the Play arrow in the top middle of the window. Watch the donut fall, then press the Play arrow again to stop running the game.

You saw that when the game was running the background turned blue. That's because Unity switched you to the Game view, which currently has a blue background. The donut fell through the wooden plank rather than bouncing on it. The following steps enable bouncing.

**<Step 10>**  Select the Donut, if necessary.

**<Step 11>**  Component – Physics 2D – Circle Collider 2D.

**<Step 12>**  Hover the mouse over the Scene view and type f to focus on the Donut.

This is a very useful keyboard shortcut. You'll be using it a lot. You now see a green circle around the donut in the Scene panel. Compare your scene with Figure 3.10. The circle is too big, so make it smaller by doing the next step.

FIGURE 3.10    Circle Collider to the donut.

**\<Step 13\>** Scroll down to the bottom of the Inspector. Hover the mouse over the Radius property in the Circle Collider 2D component of the Donut. Drag the mouse left and right to adjust the size of the green circle surrounding the Donut. Alternatively, you can type in various guesses for the radius until it looks correct. Adjust the Offset if necessary. When in doubt, make the circle a little too small.

It's tempting to run the game now, but if you do that there will be no visible change. The donut still falls through the wooden plank. You also need to add a collider for the plank as follows.

**\<Step 14\>** Select the WoodPlank object in the Hierarchy panel and do Component – Physics 2D – Box Collider 2D. Then run the game.

Well, that's better. At least the donut stops when it hits the wooden plank, but it's not bouncing! To do that you need to create a Physics Material and assign it to the Donut Circle Collider.

**\<Step 15\>** In the Project panel, click on + and then Physics Material 2D. Name it Bounce, and set the Bounciness to 1 in the Inspector.

If you're having trouble seeing Physics Material 2D in that Menu, move the mouse to the bottom of the menu where you'll see a downward pointing triangle. Watch as the menu gets much larger. Then you'll be able to see the Physics Material 2D and select it. Make sure you're selecting the 2D version, not the 3D version or the next step won't work.

**\<Step 16\>** Select the Donut, and drag the Bounce Asset to the Material slot for the Circle Collider 2D component.

You should see the name of the Material listed as Bounce.

**\<Step 17\>** Repeat the previous step for the Box Collider 2D component of WoodPlank. Then run the game.

That's more like it! The donut is now bouncing. If you watch this for a minute, you'll see that the bounciness is not exactly realistic. The donut keeps gaining altitude, which wouldn't happen in the real world. This is easy to fix.

**\<Step 18\>** Change the Bounciness of the Bounce Physics Material to 0.95.

If you run the game now, you'll see that the donut gradually loses altitude after each bounce, which is what you want in this game.

You're now going to duplicate the WoodPlank object two times, giving you three planks on the screen.

**\<Step 19\>** Make sure that you're no longer running the game.

**\<Step 20\>** Select Woodplank. Right-click and Duplicate.

**\<Step 21\>** Repeat the previous step.

You now have three planks, all on top of each other.

FIGURE 3.11    Three planks and a donut.

**\<Step 22\>**    Rearrange the positions and orientations of the planks using the Move tool and the Rotate tool. Look at Figure 3.11 for an approximate layout. Also move the Donut to the upper left of the screen. Then press the Play button.

**\<Step 23\>**    Adjust the donut starting position so it bounces on all three planks.

**\<Step 24\>**    Save the project.

Congratulations! You just made an animation in Unity. It's not interactive yet, but it's a great start. You can compare your animation with the official video available at www.franzlanzinger.com.

In the next chapter, you'll create a goal for that donut, a donut box! You'll be using the 3D program Blender to make it.

# 2D Graphics with Blender and Unity

IN THIS CHAPTER, you'll be introduced to Blender, a truly remarkable open-source application for creating 3D graphics. You'll use Blender to make a pink donut box for the Bouncing Donut game. You may ask, why is Blender even covered in a book about 2D games? The short answer is this: Blender is very useful for making 2D assets when they represent 3D objects. For example, if you want to make a 2D sprite of a sphere, then Blender is a good way to do that, especially if you're artistically challenged. Blender does the 3D calculations to make your sphere look realistic, but the sprite generated by Blender is just a rectangular pixel array that happens to look like a 3D object.

The use of 3D programs to make art for 2D games hit the big-time with the game "Donkey Kong Country" for the SNES in 1994. The developers used very expensive Silicon Graphics workstations to make the 3D models of the characters and environments. The SNES hardware could only do 2D animation, so the animations had to be rendered one frame at a time and each frame stored on the somewhat limited and expensive memory available on the SNES. It was an amazing technical and artistic achievement. We've come a long way since then. Even so, it is still instructive to look at video footage of the game, easily available online.

## INTRODUCTION TO BLENDER

Before you install Blender, take a look at the short movie "Spring" made entirely in Blender 2.8. Simply search for "Spring Blender" online and watch the seven-minute movie. This will give you an idea of what's possible using Blender. If you enjoyed Spring, search for "blender open movies." Not only are these high-quality short subject animated movies, all the sources are freely available for download and study.

If you haven't installed Blender yet, or if you have an older version of Blender installed on your system, please go to www.blender.org and follow the installation instructions for version 2.81a. This book is written for that specific version of Blender, so it is recommended that you use that version even though newer versions are available. You will need to go to a special section of blender.org to find 2.81a. Currently, older Blender releases are available for download at https://download.blender.org/release/.

If you are an experienced Blender user, it's possible for you to follow the book with a more recent version and make any necessary adjustments. But, if you're new to Blender, you should definitely use Blender 2.81a for the sake of compatibility with the printed steps.

## CREATING THE DONUT BOX IN BLENDER

Your goal is to make a pink donut box. This is an easy Blender project, perfect for getting started.

**<Step 1a>** Run Blender 2.81a.

If you're running Blender 2.81a for the first time, you'll see some setup options right at the beginning. Please use the defaults. You then get a splash screen.

**<Step 1b>** Dismiss the splash screen by clicking the mouse outside of it.

This next step is only necessary if you've used Blender before and are currently not using the Factory Settings for Blender.

**<Step 2>** File – Defaults – Load Factory Settings.

For this book, you'll be using the Factory Settings for Blender 2.81a. In the next step, you'll make the Factory Settings permanent. This way, the next time you run Blender you'll be using the Factory Settings right away.

**<Step 3>** File – Defaults – Save Startup File.

Your screen should look like Figure 4.1.

You are currently using the Blender Dark Theme. Later in this book, you'll switch to the Light Theme.

**<Step 4>** Select the Camera with the left mouse button. Look at Figure 4.2 to see the camera.

Starting with Blender 2.8 object selection is done with the left mouse button, at least when using the default setup. This was one of the many changes implemented in the release of 2.8. Before then, up through version 2.79, objects were selected using the right mouse button. If you are an experienced Blender user and if you prefer the right mouse button for selection, feel free to set up Blender like that. You can still follow along with this book, but you'll need to make the appropriate changes to the steps as needed.

When you select the camera, it will highlight in orange as shown in Figure 4.2.

FIGURE 4.1    Factory Default Scene for Blender 2.81a, Dark Theme.

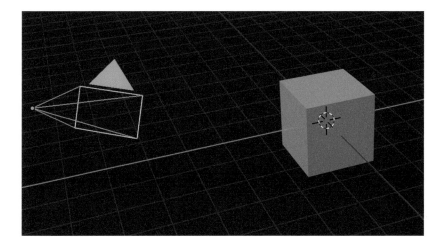

FIGURE 4.2    Camera in Blender when selected.

**\<Step 5\>**    Press the n key on your keyboard

This will bring up the properties panel on the right. The "n" is a mnemonic for "numbers". You will see the location and rotation of the camera in the properties panel. You will be changing them soon, but leave them alone for now.

**\<Step 6\>**    Select the cube.

The cube should now have an orange outline as shown in Figure 4.3.

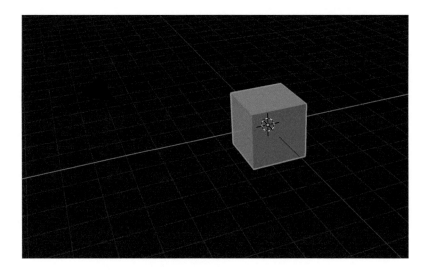

FIGURE 4.3   Cube in Blender when selected.

<Step 7> Change the location of the cube to (0m, 0m, 0.5m) and the scale to (2, 1, 0.5).
You enter these new coordinates in the properties panel. These adjustments to the scale of the cube make it look more like a donut box. The new properties panel should look like Figure 4.4.

FIGURE 4.4   Properties panel of the cube after changing the location and scale.

2D Graphics with Blender and Unity ■ 59

**<Step 8>** Double-click on "Cube" in the upper right of your window and type the new name for the cube: "donut box".

It's always a good practice to rename generic names such as "cube" to something more meaningful.

**<Step 9>** Save your work! File – Save As and use the filename donutbox.blend and the Assets folder of your Unity project.

This book will remind you to save your work at appropriate spots. Feel free to save more often if you wish.

**<Step 10>** Select the camera and change the Location to (0, −7, 4).

**<Step 11>** Change the Z rotation of the camera to 0.

**<Step 12>** Select the donut box, then do View – Cameras – Active Camera.

You should see the camera view as shown in Figure 4.5.

You'll be switching views like that very often. To make things go faster, you'll be using keyboard shortcuts for this sort of thing from now on. If you have a numeric keypad, do the following step.

**<Step 12a, numpad>** Type <numpad>0 twice.

This switches back to the user view, and then back to the camera view. <numpad> 0 toggles the active camera view on and off.

**<Step 12a, no numpad>** Edit – Preferences – Input, check Emulate Numpad. Close the pop-up. Type 0 twice.

FIGURE 4.5    Camera view of the donut box.

If you have a laptop without a numpad, or a Mac with a small keyboard, then this will allow you to use the ordinary numbers on the top of the keyboard instead of the <numpad> numbers. With this emulation enabled, whenever you are directed to type a numpad number you will be able to type the non-numpad number instead.

**<Step 13>** Left-click on the Shading Workspace selector at the middle top of your window.

The center of your screen will look similar to Figure 4.6.

Your screen just changed radically to the Shading Workspace. In the bottom center panel, you should see the Shader Editor.

**<Step 14>** Hover the mouse somewhere in the Shader Editor panel, then scroll the mouse wheel and move the mouse to see the two shader boxes as shown in Figure 4.7.

Note: if you don't have a mouse with a scroll wheel, get one! They're cheap and can be plugged in and work on any PC and any Mac.

You can see the two shader boxes. One has a green outline titled "Principled BSDF", the other a red outline with the title "Material Output". The settings in these boxes control the shading during rendering. In order to see those boxes better, you'll increase the size of the Shader Editor panel.

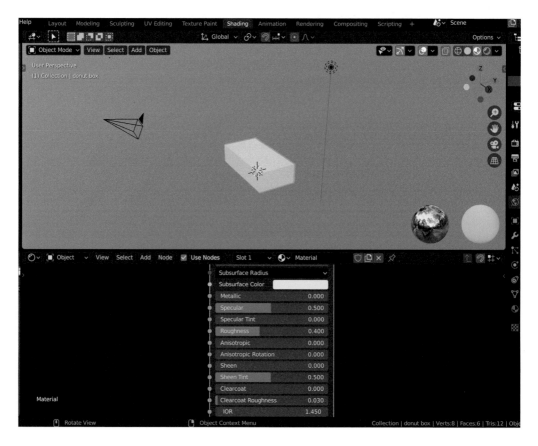

FIGURE 4.6  Shading Workspace selected.

FIGURE 4.7    Shader Editor view of the donut box.

**<Step 15>** Hover the mouse at the border between the middle two panels (the 3D panel and the Shader Editor panel) until you see the mouse icon change to a vertical double arrow. Then drag the border up to make the Shader Editor panel larger.

**<Step 16a>** Scroll the mouse wheel to zoom in on the top of the green box.

**<Step 16b>** You can pan your view by holding and dragging the Middle Mouse Button (i.e. the scroll wheel).

**<Step 17>** Select the Base Color and set it to a pink shade.
    You can experiment with this by repeatedly clicking on the color wheel and selecting the shade of pink that you like. Compare your window with Figure 4.8.

**<Step 18>** Select the Layout Workspace.
    You will once again see the donut box in the camera view, but it's gray. That's because of the viewport shading setting, which is currently set to solid. The next step will change this.

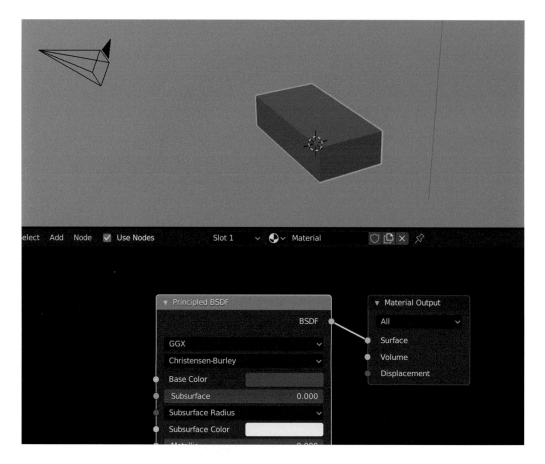

FIGURE 4.8    A pink donut box.

<Step 19> Change the viewport shading to Rendered. You do this by clicking on the fourth icon from the left in the viewport shading icon bar as shown in Figure 4.9.

If you wish you may try out all four of the viewport shading settings: Wireframe, Solid, Material Preview, and Rendered.

You should now see a pink donut box in the Layout Workspace as shown in Figure 4.10.

What you really want is an open donut box for the game. The next step will remove the top of the box.

<Step 20> Select the Modeling Workspace.

<Step 21> Press the <Tab> key on your keyboard several times.

This switches the Modeling Mode from Edit Mode to Object Mode and back. Edit Mode allows you to edit the parts of objects. Object Mode allows you to operate on objects as a whole. The upper left corner of your window shows the current Modeling Mode. You can see that the donut box is displayed differently in the two modes.

FIGURE 4.9    Viewport Shading icons.

FIGURE 4.10    A pink donut box in Blender.

**<Step 22>**  In Object Mode, select the camera, then the light and then the donut box.
Selecting the other objects was for practice. Be sure you end up with the donut box selected.

**<Step 23>**  Go into Edit Mode.

**<Step 24>**  Choose Face Select Mode by clicking on the face select icon to the right of the Edit Mode indicator as shown in Figure 4.11.
When editing 3D models, you will wish to select faces, edges, or vertices, depending on what you're trying to do. Since you're about to delete the top face, you needed to go into Face Select Mode.

FIGURE 4.11    Choosing Face Select Mode in Blender.

**<Step 25>** In turn, select the three visible faces of the donut box and observe the graphic effect of this.

As you can see, the selected face is highlighted when it is selected.

**<Step 26>** Select the top face of the donut box.

**<Step 27>** Type x, select Faces and left-click.

That's more like it. You now see an open box as shown in Figure 4.12. The box is gray in the Modeling Workspace so do the following:

**<Step 28>** Choose Rendered Viewport shading.

Compare your workspace with Figure 4.12.

**<Step 29>** Type  <numpad> 0 to look at the camera view.

You see that the box needs better lighting to become recognizable as a box.

**<Step 30>** Go to Object Mode by pressing <Tab> and then select the Light Object.

To select the Light Object, look at the Outliner panel at the top right of your window and click on Light.

**<Step 31>** Set the location of the light to (1, −1.1, 1.75).

Type n if necessary, to turn on the properties panel where you can see the light location and edit it. With the light selected, you can type g and move the

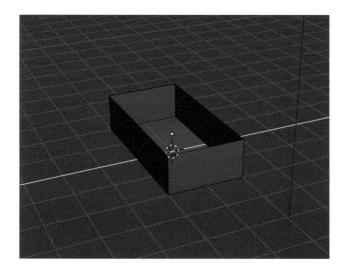

FIGURE 4.12    The donut box in the 3D viewport of Blender.

FIGURE 4.13 Donut box ready for rendering and export from Blender.

mouse to further adjust the light position if you want. This is the "final" box graphics as shown in Figure 4.13.

Before you lose all that work from those 31 steps, it's high time to save your file.

**<Step 32>** File – Save.

You're not quite finished yet. You need to make a 2D rendered image of the donut box to be used by your 2D game. If your game were a 3D game, you could directly import the .blend file into your Unity project, but for 2D projects, you need to render your objects into 2D image files which Unity can then turn into sprites.

**<Step 33a>** Render – Render Image.

This opens up a new window with the render result from your camera. Compare your render result with Figure 4.14.

We have a problem here. That gray background is not supposed to be exported to Unity. We need to make it transparent just as you did for the donut sprite.

**<Step 33b>** Type <esc> to close the render window.

**<Step 34>** Select the Rendering Workspace by choosing it at the very top of the Blender window. In the Properties Editor panel on the right, click on Film to expand the Film properties. Then check Transparent. Compare your window with Figure 4.15.

**<Step 35>** Render again and you will see that the gray background now looks like it has a checkerboard pattern.

Your new render should look like Figure 4.16.

You are finally ready to export this image to a .png file to be used in Unity.

FIGURE 4.14    Render result for donut box.

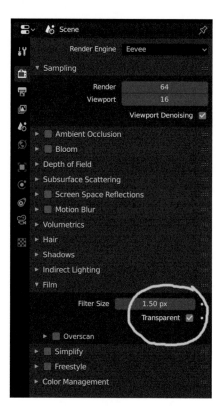

FIGURE 4.15    Setting the Film to Transparent in the Properties Editor panel.

FIGURE 4.16    The donut box rendered with a transparent background.

**<Step 36>** In the Blender Render window, do Image – Save As…, and select .png file format with RGBA Color, Color Depth 8. Use the same Assets folder as the .blend file and a filename of donutbox.png. Close the Blender Render window.

There is just one more thing. You also need to render just the front panel of the donut box. This will allow Unity to place the donut behind the front panel of the donut box but in front of the other panels.

**<Step 37>** Save the .blend file for the project by doing File – Save or <Ctrl> S (<command> S on a Mac).

You are saving the project before removing the other panels.

**<Step 38>** Go to the Modeling Workspace.

**<Step 39>** Press 0 to go back to the User Perspective view of the donut box, if necessary.

**<Step 40>** The donut box has five faces. In Object Mode, select the donut box. Then go into Edit Mode, select four faces of the donut box in turn, skipping the front face, and delete them.

**<Step 41>** Render the scene and save the image as donutbox_front.png.

**<Step 42>** Save the project as donutbox_front.blend.

Your render of the front panel of the donut box should look like Figure 4.17.

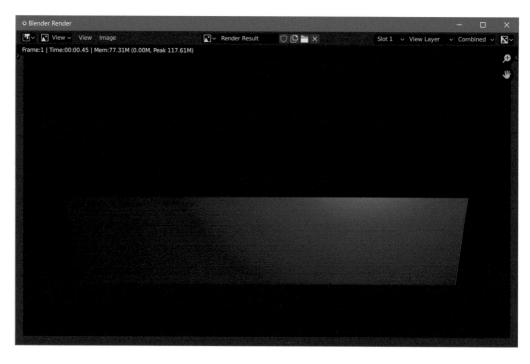

FIGURE 4.17   Front panel of the donut box.

**<Step 43>** File – Save As and use the name donutbox_front.blend.

> You are now ready to export the donut box into Unity. You've done most of that already by creating those two .png files and storing them in the assets folder of your Unity project.

**<Step 44>** Exit Blender.

## EXPORTING FROM BLENDER TO UNITY

Exporting assets to Unity is usually very easy. Just put the asset into the correct folder in the Unity project, and Unity will automatically import that asset for you the next time you run Unity. If Unity is running while you copy the asset, Unity will automatically import right then and there. In this section, you'll take the two sprites for the donut box created in Blender and export them into Blender.

**<Step 1>** In Unity, open the BouncingDonuts project.

> You might notice messages that tell you about the automatic import of the donut assets.

**<Step 2>** Press Play.

> You're simply checking to see that the game still plays. This is a good habit to cultivate when loading a somewhat older project.

<Step 3> Press Play again to stop the game. Then, change "Free Aspect" to "16:9" in the aspect ratio dropdown at the top of the Game panel.

You are fixing the aspect ratio in order to simplify your development of this small project. In a commercial project, especially one for multiple types of mobile devices, you'll need to support a variety of different aspect ratios.

<Step 4> Select the Scene panel and compare with Figure 4.18.

The thin outline surrounding your game objects indicates the game screen boundary at a 16:9 aspect ratio.

<Step 5> Move the three planks to the left to make room for the donut box on the right. Make the scene look similar to Figure 4.19.

Now take a look at the Assets folder. You should see two pink assets called donutbox and donutbox_front.

<Step 6> Drag the donutbox asset into the Hierarchy panel.

The donut box is much too large and fills the entire screen. You could adjust the position and scale of the donutbox object with the mouse, but instead you'll be typing in some numbers in the following steps.

<Step 7> Select the donutbox in the Assets panel.

<Step 8> In the Inspector, change the Pixels Per Unit to 512 and click on Apply.

<Step 9> Drag the donutbox to the bottom right of the scene. Compare with Figure 4.20.

<Step 10> With the donutbox selected, do Component – Physics 2D – Box Collider 2D.

You now see a green box surrounding the donutbox.

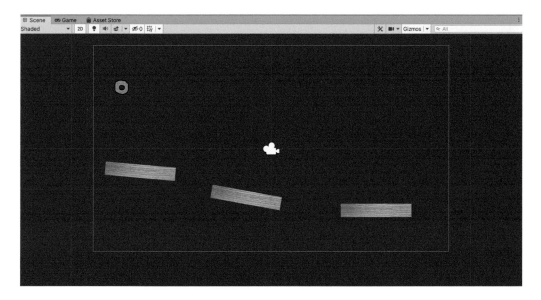

FIGURE 4.18    Scene panel set to 16:9 aspect ratio.

FIGURE 4.19   Wooden planks placed to make room for the donut box.

FIGURE 4.20   Donut box placed at the bottom right of the game screen.

**<Step 11>** Click on the icon to the right of "Edit Collider" in the Inspector. Adjust the box collider as shown in Figure 4.21.

You make the adjustment by dragging the small green squares at the midpoints of the collider rectangle. When you're satisfied with the position of the collider, click on the Edit Collider icon again. You put this collider at the floor of the donut box.

FIGURE 4.21   Adjusted box collider.

**\<Step 12\>** Press Play

The donut should bounce toward the donut box and bounce off the newly created donut box collider. You may need to adjust the positions or rotations of the wooden planks for the donut to hit the donut box rather than bounce over it.

As you can see, the donut doesn't look quite right when it overlaps with the donut box. Take a look at Figure 4.22.

It's possible that for you the donut is behind the donut box instead of in front of it. The donut and the donut box have the same Z coordinate, so the drawing priority is undefined. What you want is the donut to look like it's falling into the donut box. The next steps will do this.

**\<Step 13\>** If haven't done so already, press Play to stop running the game.

This is an important habit to get into. You do not want to be making changes the game while the game is running. While this can be useful when experimenting or debugging, all changes that you make while the game is running are only temporary and will be lost when you eventually stop running the game!

**\<Step 14\>** Select the donutbox_front icon in the Assets panel and change the Pixels Per Unit to 512 just like you did before with the donutbox. Click on Apply.

**\<Step 15\>** Drag the donutbox_front asset into the Hierarchy panel.

FIGURE 4.22   Donut overlapping the front of donut box.

**<Step 16>** Move donutbox_front to approximately overlap the donutbox.

**<Step 17>** Click on donutbox, then donutbox_front in the Hierarchy while looking at the Position coordinates. Make X and Y match exactly.

In this book, the X Position is 6.87 and the Y Position is −2.94.

**<Step 18>** Make the Z Position of the donutbox 1, the donut 0, and the donutbox_front −1.

**<Step 19>** Play the game.

**<Step 20>** Save.

The reason that the donut appears between the donut box and the front panel is the clever setting of the z coordinates. The donut has a z coordinate of zero, the donutbox one and the donutbox_front negative one. The z axis runs away from the camera, so objects with lower z coordinates have a higher drawing priority.

All you're missing now to have something resembling a game is interactivity. The next section will add code that will let you control one of the wood planks.

## BOUNCING DONUTS PROTOTYPE: FIRST GAMEPLAY!

It's now possible to make your demo into a simple game. Really simple. This will take just a few lines of code. The idea is to lay out the wooden planks so that the donut doesn't automatically reach the donut box. You then add a control that moves one of the planks in response to button presses. If the player times it just right, the donut will bounce into the donut box. There's no scoring, just one level, no music or sound, but it'll be playable.

**<Step 1>** Load the BouncingDonuts project into Unity, if necessary.

**<Step 2>** Select the Move Tool.

**<Step 3>** Move the middle WoodPlank up as shown in Figure 4.23.

**<Step 4>** With the middle WoodPlank selected, in the Inspector, click on Add Component – New Script, type the name Woodplank, and then click on Create and Add.

You may need to scroll down to see the "New Script" selection.

**<Step 5>** Replace the Update function in the Woodplank script with this:

```
void Update()
{
    if (Input.GetKey("w")) transform.Translate(0, 5 * Time.deltaTime, 0);
    if (Input.GetKey("s")) transform.Translate(0, -5 * Time.deltaTime, 0);
}
```

**<Step 6>** Play the game.

**<Step 7>** Save!

This code deserves some explanation. The GetKey function is built into Unity. It returns "true" only if the specified key is pressed down.

FIGURE 4.23   Middle WoodPlank moved up.

The `transform.Translate` function takes the parent object and moves it in the specified x, y, and z coordinates. `Time.deltaTime` is another built-in object in Unity. It returns the elapsed time, in seconds, since the last time the `Update` function was called. The 5 and −5 scale is the translation to make the object move at a speed of 5. You can experiment with other values there to see the effect.

Yes, the game is now playable. You can use the "w" and "s" keys to move the middle Woodplank object up and down. This will allow you to control whether the bouncing donut hits the donut box or not. The object moves up and down because the deltaTime variable is used for the y coordinate of the translation.

This is a major milestone. You've just created your first game in Unity with animation, physics, and pretty good 2D graphics. At this point, development could go in a variety of directions. You could make several more interesting levels, or maybe you could put in a user interface with scoring and a display of text such as "Press Start" or "Game Over". You will do those things later, but first you'll take a detour and examine Unity more closely in the next chapter.

# The Unity Interface

Y OU'VE BEEN USING UNITY for a while now. In this chapter, you'll learn even more about it. Each section explores a different aspect of Unity and lets you try out some of the related features. You'll learn about how the Unity Editor works, how to create Materials, Lights, and Cameras, and you'll explore the built-in 2D physics engine. You'll also apply what you've learned to make the Bouncing Donut game better. It's one thing to read about features, but the best way to understand them is to use them and see them in action.

Just as you did with Blender, go ahead and look at a few demo videos. Search for "Unity 2D demo reel" and watch a few of those videos. While you're at it, check out some of the 3D demos as well. Be sure to watch them in 1080p on a good monitor. If you haven't played many or even any games made with Unity, the demo videos will reference dozens of games for you to try out. If you don't have the time to play all those games, you can take the short-cut of looking at the developer websites and trailers. This can show you the astonishing things other developers are doing with Unity. It can be disheartening to look at the competition. Are you good enough to compete? Yes, you are! With dedication, creativity, and a little bit of luck, your games can find an audience.

Unity is a huge program, yet it's relatively easy to learn the basics. You already scratched the surface by using Unity to make a simple prototype game. Your next goal is to gain a better understanding of the basics. Then, you'll be ready to explore the intermediate and advanced features of Unity on your own. The Unity manual has a very large section called "Advanced Development." If you search the internet for "Unity Advanced Development Manual," you'll find that section of the manual. You can also access the manual directly inside of Unity in the Help menu. And no, don't read it unless you're actually an advanced Unity developer.

## THE UNITY EDITOR

Unity consists of the Unity Editor as well as the underlying technology to make it all work. The Unity Editor is the interface that you see when using Unity. In this section, you'll look at the layout of the various panels and buttons in the Unity Editor.

FIGURE 5.1    Unity Editor displaying the BouncingDonuts project after Chapter 4.

**<Step 1>**    Open Unity and load the BouncingDonuts project from the previous chapter. Compare your screen with Figure  5.1.

You will notice that the thin outline for the game screen is incorrect. This is a minor bug in this version of Unity. To work around it, do the following:

**<Step 2>**    Click on the Game tab, then the Scene tab.

That's better. The outline for the game screen is correct now.

Take a look at the drop-down menu in the top right corner. It should say Layout, but it may say something else if you've experimented with this earlier. The possibilities are 4 Split, Default, Tall, and Wide. You are going to make a custom layout as follows:

**<Step 3a>**    Select the Tall layout.

**<Step 3b>**    Drag the Hierarchy tab to the left and down until it is a long vertical panel.

**<Step 3c>**    Drag the Game tab straight down until the game panel is visible, similar to Figure 5.2.

**<Step 3d>**    Adjust the size of the five panels to approximately match Figure 5.2.

**<Step 3e>**    Click on Tall at the top right of the Unity window, Save Layout, and use the name 2 by 3.

From now on you'll be using this layout. Previous versions of Unity shipped with this layout, but for some reason Unity dropped it. The 2 by 3 layout shows the Scene and the Game panels at the same time, which is a good thing. Once again compare your window with Figure 5.2.

FIGURE 5.2    The 2 by 3 layout.

You might notice that the Game panel reverted to the Free Aspect setting. In your project you want the 16:9 aspect ratio, so you'll have to set that again.

**<Step 4>** In the Game panel, change Free Aspect to 16:9.

**<Step 5>** In the Scene panel, scroll the mouse wheel so you can see all of the outlines of the game screen.

**<Step 6>** Expand SampleScene in the Hierarchy panel.

You do this by clicking on the triangle immediately to the left of the SampleScene text in the Hierarchy panel.

You once again see the game objects for your scene, the Main Camera, the Donut, three planks, the donutbox, and the donutbox_front. Compare your window with Figure 5.3.

Next, you're going to explore the menus and tool buttons in the Unity Editor. It's important that you become familiar with these to the point where you know where they are and have a basic understanding of what they do.

**<Step 7>** Click on "File" in the top left corner of the window and move the mouse to the right to see the seven drop-down menus. Read all of the menu items just to get a sense of what's there. Take a look at the Help – About Unity (Unity – About Unity on Mac) and Help – Unity Manual.

You could spend days just reading and exploring these menus. Especially useful is the built-in manual, though it can be difficult for beginners. This is OK. You can still use Unity even if you only understand the basics.

In the next few steps you'll try out a few things from the main menus.

FIGURE 5.3 The BouncingDonuts project using the 2 by 3 layout and 16:9 aspect ratio.

**<Step 8>** File – Build Settings... Compare your build settings with Figure 5.4.

If you're using a Mac, you'll likely see Mac OS X as the Target Platform. It's a good idea to try to build your game early in the development process. In order to share or publish your game you'll need to do a build first. Your build settings will depend on whether you're building for a PC or a Mac target. Unity supports building your games for a myriad of devices and computers. This book covers PCs and Mac builds only.

**<Step 9>** Click on Build and Run.

**<Step 10>** Create a new folder for storing the executable files. Call it Binaries and select that folder for the build. On a Mac you'll have to make that Binaries folder a Favorite so you can select it for the build.

Be aware that you didn't put in any code for exiting the game! This can be a problem if you don't know how to stop the execution of a program.

**<Step 11, Windows>** Exit the program by pressing Ctrl+Alt+Del, running the task manager, and do an End Task for BouncingDonuts.exe.

**<Step 11, Mac>** Exit the program by pressing Command-Option-Esc, select the game and do a Force Quit.

**<Step 12>** Close the Build Settings window.

**<Step 13>** Save your Unity project and exit Unity.

**<Step 14>** Go to the Binaries folder that you just created in Step 10.

FIGURE 5.4    Build settings for BouncingDonuts.

**\<Step 15\>**  Double-click on BouncingDonuts.

 This is another way to run the game.

**\<Step 16\>**  Exit the game using the method in Step 11.

**\<Step 17\>**  Start up Unity again with the BouncingDonuts project.

 Next, you'll make the game run in windowed mode.

**\<Step 18\>**  File – Build Settings – Player Settings…

 This brings up the Project Settings dialog with the Player highlighted. This is where you control how the game is presented to your customers. You will be adjusting Settings for PC, Mac & Linux Standalone.

**\<Step 19\>**  Click on Resolution and Presentation and for Fullscreen Mode, and select Windowed. Enter a Default Screen Width of 1600 and Default Screen Height of 900. Build and Run the game in the same Binaries folder.

 When you're done playing the game you can close the window to exit the game. That's a lot easier than killing the process.

**\<Step 20\>** There is a Player setting for making the window resizable. Test out that setting.

You are getting more familiar with working with Unity, which is a good thing. You'll be trying out a few more features in the main menu in the following steps.

**\<Step 21\>** Stop running the game by closing the window.

**\<Step 22\>** In Unity, select the Donut object in the Hierarchy panel. Then do Edit – Frame Selected.

You will see that the Scene panel now zoomed in on the Donut object. This is a good way to find objects in your scene that are otherwise lost. You can use the "f" key shortcut to do the same thing as long as mouse is hovering over the scene view. Try this out on some of the WoodPlank objects and the donutbox.

**\<Step 23\>** Select the controllable WoodPlank, and do Edit – Lock View to Selected. Then click on play and watch how the camera follows the moving WoodPlank. Click on Play again to stop the game.

You can use \<Shift\> f as a shortcut for this. \<Shift\> f locks the view to the selected object. You need to hit the f key to unlock the view. Notice that those shortcuts only work when the mouse is hovering over the Scene view.

This is as good a time as any to learn more about how to customize your workspace. This is very useful and well worth the time and effort to learn about this.

**\<Step 24\>** Help – Unity Manual. Working in Unity – The Main Windows – Customizing Your Workspace. Read the beginning of that section and learn to drag tabs, detaching them, and creating new tabs.

The manual is a great resource for learning more about Unity. You may want to read all of it at some point when you become much more experienced. For now, you can use it to look things up and to maybe read the introductory sections. The manual is also available online and can be easily found by searching for it in your browser.

**\<Step 25\>** Save and Exit Unity.

In this section, you didn't really do anything worth saving except for the build settings.

## THE SCENE VIEW

The Scene View is your portal into your game. In it you can select objects, move them, rotate them, and modify them. Possible game objects include geometry, lights, cameras, audio sources, and text objects, to name a few. The Scene View is akin to having another camera looking at your scene, separate from the Main Camera object used by the game itself.

The Scene View looks at a single scene. In all but the simplest of games you'll have multiple scenes. The BouncingDonut project has just one scene called SampleScene. The scene name is listed in the Hierarchy window as well as in the Project window in the

Scenes folder. In the Hierarchy window there is a Triangle to the left of the SampleScene line. Clicking on that triangle toggles the display of the game objects in the scene.

<Step 1> Load the BouncingDonut Project in Unity. Test the triangle icon next to SampleScene in the Hierarchy.

   Currently the game objects in the SampleScene are the Main Camera, the Donut, WoodPlank, WoodPlank (1), WoodPlank (2), donutbox and donutbox_front.

<Step 2> Use the manual to read the toolbar section. It's in Working in Unity – The Main Windows – The Toolbar.

   You've been using the Play button in the middle and the Layout drop-down at the top right corner. Next, you'll learn to use the Transform Tools.

<Step 3> Select the Hand tool at the top left, and then hover the mouse over the other transform tools to see their names: The Hand Tool, the Move Tool, the Rotate Tool, the Scale Tool, the Rect Tool, Move Rotate or Scale selected objects, and Available Custom Editor Tools.

<Step 4> With the Hand tool still selected, use the mouse to pan the view. You can also use the arrow keys on your keyboard to pan the view left-right and up-down, but only after you have clicked on the Scene panel with the hand icon.

<Step 5> Zoom the view in and out by doing <Alt> RMB (right mouse button). It's <Option> – RMB on a Mac. As an alternative, you can use the scroll wheel on your mouse. The mouse must be hovering over the Scene panel for zooming to work.

   Panning and Zooming are the two main operations on the Scene panel in 2D mode. Go ahead and try 3D mode in the next step.

<Step 6> Click on the 2D icon near the top left of the scene view window. Compare your scene view with Figure 5.5.

   This gives you a 3D view of your 2D scene. Switching between 2D and 3D views is harmless and doesn't change how the game works. Originally, when Unity was first developed, there was no support for 2D at all. Unity is still, for the most part, a 3D engine, but it does have excellent 2D support. Even if you only work in 2D, it is good to know a little about the 3D features in Unity.

<Step 7> Pan and zoom the 3D view. Use <Ctrl> RMB (right mouse button) to rotate the view in 3D. When you're done experimenting with the 3D view, click on 2D again to get back to 2D mode. Adjust the view to approximately match what you had before.

   Next, you'll try out the other transform tools from the tool menu.

<Step 8> Select the Move tool and the Donut object.

   Game objects can be selected by clicking on them in the scene window, but only after you have selected a transform tool other than the Hand Tool.

FIGURE 5.5  3D Scene View.

You can always select game objects by clicking on them in the Hierarchy. When the Donut and the Move tool are selected, you see a green arrow pointing up and a red arrow pointing to the right. When you hover the mouse over an arrow, it changes color to yellow and you can then click and drag the object in along the direction of the arrow.

<Step 9> Move the Donut higher up so it no longer appears in the Game window. Play the game.

It can make sense to have the donut start off screen as you just did.

<Step 10> Select the left-most WoodPlank. Select the Rotate tool and compare with Figure 5.6.

This tool is actually a 3D tool and it works differently depending on which part of the guidelines you drag.

<Step 11> Drag the blue circle to do a 2D rotation. <Ctrl> Z to undo. (<command> Z on a Mac.)

<Step 12> Drag the red line to do a 3D rotation along the red line. <Ctrl> Z to undo.

<Step 13> Drag the yellow line to do a 3D rotation along the yellow line. Then <Ctrl> Z.

<Step 14> Click and drag inside the blue circle to do a free-form 3D rotation. <Ctrl> Z.

Next, you'll look at the Scale Tool.

<Step 15> Try out the Scale Tool with the same WoodPlank. Hit <Esc> to cancel the scales rather than letting go of the mouse button.

FIGURE 5.6   The Rotate tool selected.

There are three available scale functions: The red box, the green box, or the white center box. The center box scales along both axes, which is what you typically want to do. You can watch the effect of the scale functions in the Inspector.

Now that you get the idea, go ahead and try the remaining tools on your own.

## THE HIERARCHY WINDOW

The Hierarchy window lists the scenes and game objects in your project. In it you can create and delete scenes and game objects using one of several available menus. Notice that there is a + icon with a drop-down menu on the top left, plus a scene-specific drop-down menu with three vertical dots to the right of the SampleScene label. Also, right-clicking on game objects will bring up an object-specific pop-up menu.

<Step 1> Look at the + menu, the drop-down menu for SampleScene, and the pop-up menu for the Donut object.

You did this just to learn where those menus are. There are many more drop-downs in the Unity window. For some additional exploration, do the following step.

<Step 2> Click on all the other dropdowns with a "three vertical dot" icon.

As you can see, each panel has one of those in the top right corner. These dropdowns have a useful "Maximize" selection.

Next, you'll explore the parent–child relationship among game objects. It is possible to link objects together in a parent–child tree structure to make it easier to manipulate these objects together as groups.

FIGURE 5.7   donutbox_front is a child of donutbox.

<Step 3> Drag the donutbox_front object on top of the donutbox object in the hierarchy. Your hierarchy should now look like Figure 5.7.

The Scene View did not visibly change when you did this. The effect of making donutbox_front a child of donutbox is this: Transforming the donutbox will also apply the same transform to the child.

<Step 4> Select the move tool, then the donutbox and then move it up a little bit in the Scene panel.

As you can see, the donutbox_front object moved along for the ride. If you look at the Transform section in the Inspector, you can see that the Position coordinates of donutbox_front do not change when you move the parent object. The Position coordinates of a child are always relative to the parent rather than the scene origin. Notice, for example, that the X coordinate of donutbox_front is now 0, whereas the X coordinate used to be about 7 before you made it a child of donutbox. The Z coordinate is now −2, which is the correct relative offset from −1 to 1.

## THE PROJECT WINDOW

The project window shows the assets and packages currently available to you in your project. It does this by showing assets and packages in a hierarchical display. Figure 5.8 shows the current Project window for the BouncingDonuts project.

In the following steps you'll try out some of the menu items to help you get familiar with the Project window.

<Step 1> Open the Project panel drop-down menu by clicking on the triple-dot menu icon at the top right corner of the Project panel. This drop-down menu is shown in Figure 5.9.

<Step 2> Select the One Column Layout. Then go back to the Two Column Layout.

The One Column Layout gives you an alternate view of the Project window.

FIGURE 5.8   Project window for BouncingDonuts.

**\<Step 3\>** Select Maximize in the drop-down menu.

   This fills your entire Unity window with the Project window, a useful feature when dealing with a large number of assets.

**\<Step 4\>** With the window still maximized, slide the bottom right slider all the way to the left, and then all the way to the right. Then put the slider back to the middle.

FIGURE 5.9   Project window drop-down menu.

This size adjustment slider adjusts the size of the icons in the Assets window. When the slider is all the way to the left, the icons are replaced with lines of text.

<Step 5> Uncheck maximize.

You can learn more about navigating the Project window and how to use the search and filter features in the Unity manual in the section *Working in Unity – The Main Windows – The Project window*.

## THE INSPECTOR WINDOW

The Inspector window, usually just called the Inspector, shows all the components of the currently selected game object. In general, the Inspector allows you to examine and change the properties and settings of most items in the Unity Editor, including game objects, assets, and preferences.

<Step 1> Select the Donut game object.

You can usually do this either in the Scene window or in the Hierarchy, though right now that donut is still off-screen, so you'll need to select it in the Hierarchy. There are also two Donut icons in the Assets panel of the Project window. Those assets are not game objects and will appear differently in the Inspector. Figure 5.10 shows how the Donut game object appears in the Inspector.

You should see the following components in the Inspector for the Donut GameObject: Transform, Sprite Renderer, Rigidbody 2D, and Circle Collider 2D. Each component has a drop-down menu in the upper right corner of its panel. Below the components is a Sprites-Default section and an Add Component button. To see all this, you may need to scroll down, depending on your monitor resolution and window size.

<Step 2> Move the Donut down to make it visible in the Scene panel. Uncheck the Sprite Renderer component, and then check it again.

FIGURE 5.10  The Donut GameObject in the Inspector.

This step turns off the rendering of the sprite, but it's still operating. You can use this to create an invisible plank in your game, for example.

<Step 3> Uncheck the Sprite Renderer of the third WoodPlank and press play. Press play again to stop playing the game, and then check the Sprite Renderer to make the WoodPlank visible again.

<Step 4> With the third WoodPlank still selected, hover the mouse over the letter Y in the Position section of the Transform component. Your mouse icon should change to a double-arrow. Drag the mouse to interactively adjust the Y position of the WoodPlank game object. After you release the mouse, hit <Ctrl> Z to undo your adjustment.

All components of game objects may be removed, with the exception of the Transform component. You can undo the removal of a component as follows:

<Step 5> Remove the Sprite Renderer of the donutbox. Use the Remove Component option in the drop-down menu for the Sprite Renderer. Then type <Ctrl> Z to bring it back.

When you do this, you will still see the donutbox_front object. Notice that removing a component is permanent (unless you undo it), whereas unchecking the component merely disables it. The effect of removal vs. unchecking is the same.

<Step 6> Select the Donut asset in the Assets panel. Use the one with the icon that looks like the donut.

The Inspector shows the various import settings. Unity automatically imports graphics files such as this one. You can use the Inspector to adjust how Unity does the import. A fun experiment is to change the Pivot setting.

<Step 7> Change the Pivot from Center to Top Left. Run the game, stop running the game, then change the Pivot back to Center. Be sure to hit apply to make the Pivot change operational.

You should see the donut rotating very strangely. The Pivot point needs to sometimes be adjusted depending on the particular sprite that you're importing.

You haven't made any permanent changes to your project in this section, so there's no need to save.

<Step 8> Exit Unity without saving.

You have explored the main windows in Unity. Next, you're going to look at Rendering.

## RENDERING: MATERIALS AND SHADERS

"Rendering" is the process that Unity uses to display game objects when the game is played. Rendering uses Materials, Shaders, and Textures. This section will cover just the basics of these topics. This should not be confused with rendering in Blender, though both do very similar things: turning internal data structures into images. Rendering in Unity takes

place in real time, whereas rendering in Blender is a separate process that creates images and animations to be stored in operating system files and then viewed later using separate display programs.

First, you're going to create a Sphere object and simple lighting, so you have something with which to experiment.

<Step 1> Open the BouncingDonut project.

<Step 2> GameObject – 3D Object – Sphere.
Yes, even though this book is all about 2D, a little bit of 3D is still very useful when making 2D games. The object doesn't look like a sphere just yet. First, fix the Z coordinate.

<Step 3> In the Inspector, change the Transform Position to (0, 0, 0), if necessary. Then move the sphere with the Move Tool to avoid overlapping it with any nearby wooden planks.
When Unity creates objects the resulting transform position is somewhat unpredictable, so it's a good idea to check it and set it manually to something reasonable.

<Step 4> GameObject – Light – Directional Light. Move it away from overlapping objects.

<Step 5> Edit – Frame Selected (or type F in the Scene panel) with the Sphere selected.
The Sphere object should look like Figure 5.11.
The Sphere object now looks like a realistically rendered sphere. Your next step is to change the color of the sphere. To do this you need to create a Material.

<Step 6> In the Project window, + – Material, immediately type the new name "Blue Material" and hit the Enter key (return on Mac).

<Step 7> In the Inspector, in the Main Maps section, click on the Albedo color and make it a shade of blue of your choice.
The icon for the Blue Material now looks like a blue sphere, but the sphere in the Scene and Game windows is still white.

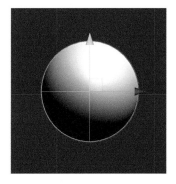

FIGURE 5.11   Sphere object with directional lighting.

**\<Step 8\>** Drag the Blue Material from the Assets panel over to the left, ending on top of the Sphere in the Hierarchy.

You now have a blue sphere in your scene. Look at the Sphere object in the Inspector. You'll see that at the bottom there is now a Blue Material component. You can also assign materials to game objects by dragging the materials on top of them in the Scene panel.

**\<Step 9\>** Zoom out your view in the Scene panel so you can see all of the game objects. Drag the Blue Material on top of the planks, the donutbox and the donut without letting go of the mouse. Then let go of the mouse when it is hovering over the background.

You will see that as you drag the material on top of these game objects, they temporarily turn a shade of blue to show you the effect of assigning the material.

There is much more to materials than changing the colors of objects. In the next steps you'll try a different shader for the Blue Material.

**\<Step 10\>** Select the Blue Material in the Assets panel of the Project window.

**\<Step 11\>** In the Inspector, change the Shader from Standard to Sprites – Default.

The Sphere is now a flat shade of blue and looks more like a disc. Also, the icon for the Blue Shader is now a blue rectangle.

**\<Step 12\>** Undo the change of shaders.

**\<Step 13\>** Save your project.

As you saw along the way, there are quite a few built-in shaders in Unity. And yes, it is possible to make your own shaders. The Unity manual has info and tutorials on how to do that. Be aware that shader coding is an interesting but advanced topic and not necessary for this book.

## LIGHTS

In the previous section, you added a directional light. Lighting can have a dramatic effect on your game. The classic 2D games from the seventies and eighties had no lighting whatsoever. The sprites were simply displayed as is. Yes, they had color look-up tables, but that's a different kettle of fish, a whole other ball of wax as it were. And, if you don't know why I'm talking about wax and fish, google ball of wax, and kettle of fish… Will my copy editor let me keep this paragraph? Somehow, I doubt it. I'm breaking at least three different rules on what not to do when writing a technical book.

In Unity, you can put one or more lights into your scene and achieve some very nice lighting effects.

**\<Step 1\>** Load the BouncingDonuts project.

**\<Step 2\>** Rename the Directional Light to "Main Light".

Renaming objects in the Hierarchy is done by selecting the object, waiting at least a half second, then clicking on the name and editing the name with the keyboard. You can also rename in the Inspector.

**\<Step 3>** Select the Rotate tool and use the mouse to adjust the rotation of the Main Light. Also, try adjusting the X and Y Rotation in the Inspector. Note the effect on the Sphere.

By adjusting the rotation of the Main Light, you can move the highlight on the Sphere.

**\<Step 4>** Adjust the Intensity of the Main Light to 0.7.

The highlight on the sphere just got smaller and less intense.

**\<Step 5>** Make the type of the light a Point. Set the Z position to −2, Range 20, Intensity 1. Then use the Move tool to move the light near the Sphere.

This gives you an idea how a point light works. Feel free to experiment with the light settings in the inspector.

Lighting can be a complex and highly technical topic when creating 3D games. For 2D games, it's relatively easy to achieve good lighting effects. In this small section, you learned how to put lights into your scene and how to make some basic adjustments to them.

In pure 2D games, where all graphics consists of sprites, lighting is done using specialized 2D lighting techniques. Unity recently introduced LWRP, the "Light Weight Rendering Pipeline" which includes 2D lights for lighting your sprites. Because this feature is very new and experimental, this book won't be covering it, but if you're interested in this topic you can attempt to learn about it and use it by searching for tutorials online to see this in action.

Collision between the Donut and the Sphere doesn't work. The next short section fixes that.

## COLLISION: DONUT VS. SPHERE

**\<Step 1>** Remove the Sphere Collider from the Sphere.

You will need to use the component drop-down menu in the Inspector to do that using the Remove Component selection. You need to select the Sphere first so you can see the Sphere Collider. The Sphere Collider was created automatically when you created the Sphere object. That collider is a 3D collider and not compatible with the 2D colliders in your game.

**\<Step 2>** Component – Physics 2D – Circle Collider 2D. Then Play the game.

The donut should now bounce realistically when it collides with the sphere.

**\<Step 3>** Save the project.

You just made the game a bit more interesting by adding a sphere to the scene.

## CAMERAS

Cameras in Unity display the scene to the player. You can have multiple cameras in a scene and quickly switch from one to another, or even display multiple cameras simultaneously. For example, in a racing game you might have an overhead map-view plus a main view from the driver's perspective and a rear-view mirror view.

In this section, you'll make some simple adjustments to the Main Camera. You'll also take a look at some of the other camera settings and experiment with them.

<Step 1> Load the BouncingDonuts project if necessary.

<Step 2> Select the Main Camera.

Notice the camera preview in the Scene window. In this project, the Game window shows the Main Camera, so the preview should match the Game window, though it is quite a bit smaller.

Compare your camera preview with Figure 5.12.

You can move the camera using the Move and Rotate tools just as any other game object. You can also type or adjust the Transform Position and Rotation in the Inspector.

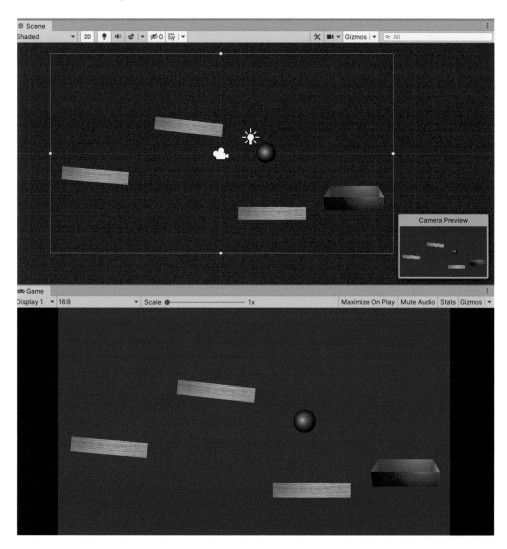

FIGURE 5.12   Camera Preview.

**\<Step 3\>** Adjust the Position, Rotation, and Scale of the Main Camera to note the effect. When you're done experimenting, set the Position to (0, 0, −10), Rotation (0, 0, 0), and Scale (1, 1, 1).

Changing the X and Y of the Position pans the camera. Changing X and Y or Rotation rotates the camera horizontally and vertically. Changing Z of the Rotation tilts the view. Changing the Scale of the camera has no effect on the view generated by the camera. In order to zoom you need to adjust the Size setting.

**\<Step 4\>** The Size setting is currently 5. Adjust the Size and watch what happens. Then return the setting to 5.

Above the Size setting is the Projection drop-down menu. You are currently using the Orthographic projection, which is what you want when working with sprites in 2D. You will be using the Perspective projection in your 3D projects when you want a realistic view of your 3D scene.

You will leave the rest of the settings at their default settings, except that you'd like to have a different background color.

**\<Step 5\>** In the Inspector, set the Background color to a dark purple.

This is just a temporary experiment to see how you can adjust the background color. Next, you'll replace the solid color with a skybox. There is a default skybox in Unity, so follow the steps below to see the skybox in action.

**\<Step 6\>** Window – Rendering – Lighting Settings. Choose the Default Skybox as the Skybox Material.

You won't see the skybox yet in the Game panel. For that you also need to change the Clear Flags for the camera.

**\<Step 7\>** In the Inspector, set the Clear Flags for the Camera to Skybox.

Compare your game view with Figure 5.13.

FIGURE 5.13   The default Skybox used in BouncingDonuts.

You can search the web for fancier skyboxes to see what those look like. This default skybox is a reasonable placeholder.

**\<Step 8\>** Save and Exit Unity.

You just got an overview of the basics of the Unity Interface. This visual interface can really help with laying out scenes, experimentation, and debugging.

# Bouncing Donuts Prototype 2

I N THIS CHAPTER, you'll develop the Bouncing Donut Prototype a bit further. You will implement a basic game structure with scoring, a title screen, and a game over screen. There will be five levels, which feels about right for an early prototype. Each level will be its own Unity scene. You'll be able to use the Unity Editor to lay out each of the levels. Along the way, you'll learn about prefabs and how to display text and numbers. This will still be a prototype, but it'll be ready to release to testers to get invaluable early feedback.

## TITLE SCREEN

Starting with something very easy, you'll create a placeholder title screen, one that has the basic functionality of the final version of the title screen, but much simpler graphics. A static, non-animated screen is fine for now. The names of games tend to change during development, so it's more efficient to spend only minimal effort in making the title screen when it's likely to get changed later on. Just as in movie production, you are considering the title "Bouncing Donuts" a working title. A working title is acceptable when releasing to a few hand-picked testers. When you get closer to a public release, you'll need to decide on the real title of the game.

The goal for this placeholder title screen is a display of the "Bouncing Donuts" text and two buttons: a "Play" button and an "Exit" button.

<Step 1> Load the BouncingDonuts project.

<Step 2> Double-click on the Scenes folder in the Assets panel.

<Step 3> In the Project window do + – Scene.

<Step 4> Name the new scene "Title".

<Step 5> Rename the SampleScene to "Game". Reload the scene when prompted.
Renaming Unity objects can be tricky for the uninitiated. You need to select the object, then single-click the name, wait about half a second, then type the

new name. When you're done setting up your two scenes your Project window should look similar to Figure 6.1.

**<Step 6>** Double-click on the Title scene in the Assets > Scenes panel.

The newly created Title scene just has the Main Camera object and nothing else.

**<Step 7>** GameObject – UI – Text.

You just created a Text object, and as a side effect a Canvas and an EventSystem.

**<Step 8>** Select the Text object in the Hierarchy and frame it by typing the "f" key while hovering the mouse in the Scene panel.

Compare your Scene and Game panels with Figure 6.2.

It's hard to see, but the New Text is very tiny and at the bottom left corner of the Game panel as well as in the upper left corner of the text box.

**<Step 9>** In the Inspector, change "New Text" to "Bouncing Donuts" with the two words on separate lines.

**<Step 10>** Select the Canvas object in the Hierarchy and frame it with the f key. Then use the Scroll wheel on your mouse to make the canvas outline larger.

**<Step 11>** Select the Text object and use the Rect tool to make the Text box larger and centered in the top half of the Canvas. Make your Scene window look similar to Figure 6.3.

The grid lines in the background may not match your screen.

**<Step 12a>** In the Inspector, change the Font Size to 60, Font Style Bold, Paragraph Alignment to centered, both horizontally and vertically.

**<Step 12b>** Adjust the Font Size by dragging the Font Size text in the Inspector.

FIGURE 6.1  Two scenes in the Project window.

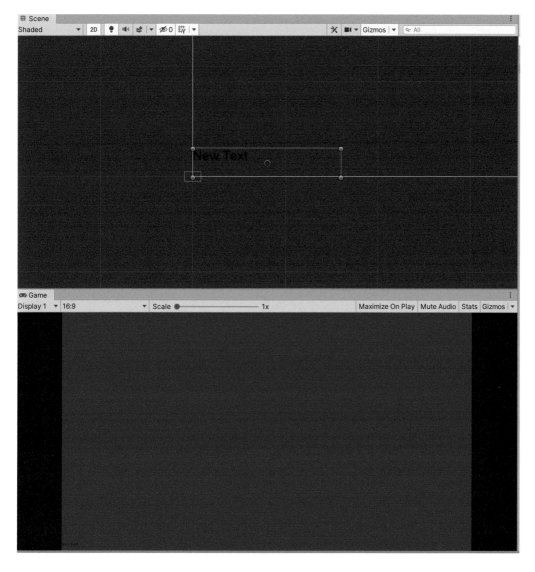

FIGURE 6.2    New Text in the Scene and Game panels.

Your goal here is to make the title large, but still inside of the Text box. So far, so good, but the dark blue background color isn't what you want.

<**Step 13**> Select the Main Camera. In the Inspector, set Clear Flags to Solid Color, Background to light pink. Compare your title in the game panel with Figure 6.4.

Next, you'll add the play button.

<**Step 14**> GameObject – UI – Button.

<**Step 15**> Move the button to the lower half of the canvas using the Move tool.

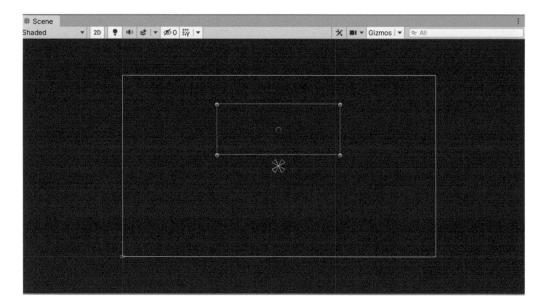

FIGURE 6.3   Text box for the "Bouncing Donuts" title.

FIGURE 6.4   "Bouncing Donuts" title in the Game window.

**<Step 16>** In the Hierarchy, expand the Button object to show the Text child object, and select Text.

**<Step 17>** In the Inspector, change the text from "Button" to "Play".

**<Step 18>** Select the Button object in the Hierarchy, and use the Rect tool to make the button somewhat larger. Compare your enlarged button with Figure 6.5.

FIGURE 6.5    Adding the Play button to the title screen.

When adjusting the button using the Rect tool, you can drag the small circle in the center and notice that it snaps to the center line, which makes it easier to keep it centered. Look at the Rect Transform Pos X coordinate. When you're centered that number is exactly 0.

The text is too small, so make it larger as shown in the following step.

**\<Step 19\>** Select the Text child object of the button in the Hierarchy, then make the font size larger and use bold for the Font Style.

**\<Step 20\>** Make another button below the Play button and give it the text "Exit", also with a larger font size and bold style.

**\<Step 21\>** Play the game. Notice what happens when you press a button.

The buttons darken when you press them. These colors and various other properties of the buttons can be adjusted in the Inspector.

The buttons don't do anything yet. To make them act like you want you'll need to write a little bit of code.

**\<Step 22\>** Save the project.

**\<Step 23a\>** Select the Canvas object in the Hierarchy.

**\<Step 23b\>** In the Inspector at the very bottom, click on Add Component – New Script. Give the script the name TitleMenu.

**\<Step 24\>** Double-click on TitleMenu in the Assets window.

Visual Studio should now open up and allow you to edit the new script. Pay close attention to the new "using statement" and the public string in the following step.

**\<Step 25\>** Edit the TitleMenu script and make it look like this:

```
using System.Collections;
using System.Collections.Generic;
using UnityEngine;
using UnityEngine.SceneManagement;

public class TitleMenu : MonoBehaviour
```

```
{
    public string GameScene;
    // Start is called before the first frame update
    void Start()
    {

    }

    // Update is called once per frame
    void Update()
    {

    }

    public void PlayGame()
    {
        SceneManager.LoadScene(GameScene);
    }

    public void ExitGame()
    {
        Application.Quit();
    }

}
```

**<Step 26>** Save your edits in Visual Studio.

You'll be doing this a lot, so learn the keyboard shortcut to save in Visual Studio: <Ctrl> S on a PC, <command> S on a Mac.

You had to add a new "using" statement for SceneManagement, as this is necessary for the `LoadScene` function call in the `PlayGame` function. The `Application.Quit()` function only works when you build your game, not when you play it inside of Unity, so you'll need to be aware of that when you're testing.

**<Step 27>** Back in Unity, click on the Canvas object in the Hierarchy, then look for the Title Menu (Script) section in the Inspector at the bottom. Type "Game" in the Game Scene text box. As always, make sure that you keep the capitalization correct. For example, "game" wouldn't work.

If you don't see a Game Scene text box you likely forgot to save your script in Visual Studio. When you save in Visual Studio, Unity automatically reloads the script and updates the Inspector text boxes.

You still haven't assigned the new functions to their respective buttons, so that's what's next. To avoid confusion, you'll need to do a bit of renaming first.

**<Step 28>** There are two buttons in the Hierarchy window, both with the name "Button". Select the first one and rename it to "PlayButton", and the other one to "ExitButton". Your Hierarchy window should look like Figure 6.6.

In general, it's a good game development practice to name your objects with meaningful identifiers. Often, tools such as Blender and Unity will create very generic identifiers for you, but you can easily get lost as soon as the project gets too large and cluttered with objects, all with the same name.

FIGURE 6.6   Hierarchy showing two renamed buttons.

<**Step 29**>   Select the PlayButton object and find the On Click() section in the Inspector. Click on the plus sign. Drag the Canvas object from the Hierarchy into the object box in the On Click() that currently says None. Replace No Function with TitleMenu.PlayGame. The On Click () section should now look like Figure 6.7.

<**Step 30**>   Select the ExitButton object, click on + and drag the Canvas object into the On Click () section as you did in the previous step. Select TitleMenu.ExitGame in the function box.

You are almost done. You need to add the Title scene to your Build Settings in order for the LoadScene function to work.

<**Step 31**>   Add the Title and Game scenes to the "Scenes in Build" section in File – Build Settings.

You need to just click on Add Open Scenes to do that.

<**Step 32**>   Make sure that the Title scene is first in the list of scenes in Build Settings. You can rearrange the order of the scenes by dragging them with the mouse.

<**Step 33**>   Double-click on the Title scene in the Assets/Scenes folder of the Project window.

This last step assures that you have the Title scene selected.

FIGURE 6.7   On Click () section for PlayButton.

**<Step 34>** Play the game, then click on the Play button. Stop playing the game.

The Play button should now be working. As mentioned earlier, the Exit button doesn't do anything here, but it should work when you build the game and run it outside of the Unity environment.

**<Step 35>** Build and test the Exit button.

**<Step 36>** Save and Exit Unity.

You are rapidly improving your Unity skills, but as you can tell from the size of this book, you're just getting started. Next, you'll put in scoring.

## SCORING

In the early years of classic arcade video games, most games had a score prominently displayed at all times, usually in the upper left-hand corner. This practice can be traced back to pinball. Pinball machines always had a score for each player and the goal of a pinball game was to get as high a score as possible.

We've come a long way since then. Scoring in modern video games varies greatly from game to game and from genre to genre. Some games have no scoring at all, while others have complex scoring with coins, points, cash, lumber, diamonds, you name it. In this Bouncing Donuts prototype, you'll keep things simple by having a display of points as you play the game. You'll award 10 points when the donut hits a plank, 100 points when a donut reaches a donut box, and 50 points for hitting the sphere.

You'll be using the Unity GUI class to display the score.

**<Step 1>** Load BouncingDonuts into Unity.

**<Step 2>** Select the Game scene.

**<Step 3>** GameObject – Create Empty.

This creates a new empty GameObject. Note that it's not really empty because it has a Transform property. This object won't be displayed directly, so the Transform won't be used.

**<Step 4>** Rename the newly created GameObject to Score.

**<Step 5>** Add a script component to Score and call the script Scoring.

**<Step 6>** Add the following code to the Scoring class and save.

```
private void OnGUI()
{
    GUI.skin.box.fontSize = 30;
    GUI.Box(new Rect(20, 20, 140, 50), "Test");
}
```

**<Step 7>** In the Unity window click on Play. Look at the upper left hand corner and compare with Figure 6.8.

This figure was produced on a 4K monitor. On a 1080p monitor, the text will be twice the size of the text in Figure 6.8. This is just a test. It doesn't look all

FIGURE 6.8   Test of GUI Box on a 4K monitor.

that great, but it's good enough for a prototype. You're now ready to display the score instead of the text "Test". Again, the size of this scoring box depends on the resolution of the game screen. The coordinates in the code are in pixels, so you may wish to adjust them as well as the font size if you find that the text is too large or too small for your monitor. Before releasing this game to the public, you will need to test on a variety of monitors to make sure that the score display is reasonable on all of the supported resolutions.

**<Step 8>**  Replace the Scoring class with this code:

```
public class Scoring : MonoBehaviour
{
    public static int gamescore;
    // Start is called before the first frame update
    void Start()
    {
        gamescore = 0;
    }

    // Update is called once per frame
    void Update()
    {
        gamescore++;
    }

    private void OnGUI()
    {
        GUI.skin.box.fontSize = 30;
        GUI.Box(new Rect(20, 20, 200, 50), "Score: " + gamescore);
    }
}
```

Before you run this code, try to understand it, and see if you can predict what it will do. You've added a public static int variable called gamescore. It's initialized to 0 in the Start function and then it is incremented in every call to Update. The display should show the text "Score: " followed by gamescore. Notice the plus sign in the Box statement. No, you're not adding the string "Score: " and game-score, you're concatenating two strings, with gamescore automatically getting converted from an int to a string before the concatenation. Concatenation is a common string operation that merely puts the two strings together, one after the other.

The size of the box is too small at a width of 140 pixels, so you increased it to 200. This is somewhat of a guessing game. Unity makes it easy to try different sizes of things until you're satisfied with the result.

**\<Step 9\>** Run the game and compare it with Figure 6.9.

As you can see the score is rapidly increasing. If you time this, you should get an increase of about 60 points every second, assuming you have a frame rate of 60. For example, if you run the game for 10 seconds with a frame rate of 60, you should get a score of about 600. The framerate on your system will likely be faster than 60 fps (frames per second). You can use the current project to estimate your framerate by running the game for some number of seconds and dividing the resulting score by the time it took to get to that score.

Your next goal is to display a meaningful score, not steadily increasing points. First, you'll remove the statement in the Update function.

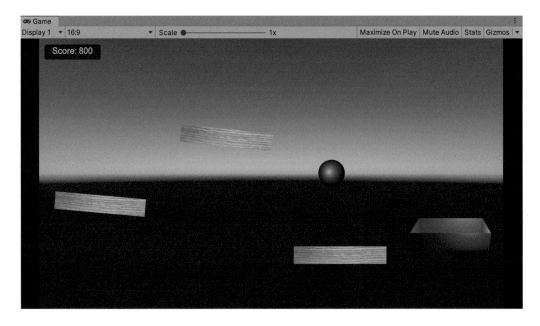

FIGURE 6.9  Testing the score display.

**<Step 10>** In Scoring.cs, remove the line gamescore++; in Update().

This will stop the automatic rapid increase of the score. Next comes the magic statement that increases the score by 10 every time the donut hits a plank.

**<Step 11a>** Add a script called donut.cs to the Donut game object.

**<Step 11b>** In donut.cs, add the following function to the donut class.

```
private void OnCollisionEnter2D(Collision2D collision)
    {
        Scoring.gamescore += 10;
    }
```

Go ahead and test this. It doesn't quite do what you want yet, because the score increases by 10 every time the donut hits anything at all, including the sphere or the donut box. By the way, the author of this book (that's me) had a typo and used a lower case d in the name of this function. Instead of 2D I had typed 2d. The result was that the function simply didn't get called because only if the function is spelled correctly will Unity find it and execute it. You don't get an error if you make this kind of mistake. You may wish to try this just to see this behavior in action.

A good way to avoid this sort of typo is to use the highly effective autocomplete in Visual Studio. When you start typing a long identifier, Visual Studio will often guess what you're trying to type. Then, rather than typing the whole thing you can just select the identifier you want from the listed choices.

Getting back to the scoring problem, in the OnCollisionEnter2D function you will need to access the object that the donut collided with and check if it's a sphere, a plank, or a donut box. You'll do this as follows:

**<Step 12>** Change the collision function in donut.cs to the following:

```
private void OnCollisionEnter2D(Collision2D collision)
{
    if (collision.gameObject.name == "WoodPlank")
        Scoring.gamescore += 10;
}
```

It's easy to overlook that there are two equal signs in the collision test statement. If you only type one equal sign there, you'll get a compiler error. Remember that two equal signs are used for testing equality, a single equal sign for assignments.

When you test this, you'll see that the score now only increments when the donut hits one of the planks. Can you guess why that is? That's right, only one of the planks has the name "WoodPlank". The other planks have different names, so fix this as follows:

**<Step 13>** Change the names of the other WoodPlank objects to have the name "WoodPlank".

In case you hadn't noticed before, names of GameObjects need not be unique. Now you just need to add additional if statements for collisions with the Sphere and the donut box.

**\<Step 14\>** Change the collision function in donut.cs to the following:

```
private void OnCollisionEnter2D(Collision2D collision)
{
    if (collision.gameObject.name == "WoodPlank")
        Scoring.gamescore += 10;
    if (collision.gameObject.name == "Sphere")
        Scoring.gamescore += 50;
    if (collision.gameObject.name == "donutbox")
        Scoring.gamescore += 100;
}
```

As usual, test this right away before moving on. This incremental method of software development is far superior to the alternative approach of writing all the code and then testing it.

You should note that the reference to the gamescore variable in this code needed to use the full name of `Scoring.gamescore`. This is one way to access variables in one class from another. In this case, you referred to the gamescore variable, which resides in the Scoring class, from the donut class.

If you're an experienced C# coder, you probably objected to the poor coding style of this function. The if statements should have braces. You're going to fix this right now.

**\<Step 15\>** Add braces to the if statements as follows:

```
private void OnCollisionEnter2D(Collision2D collision)
{
    if (collision.gameObject.name == "WoodPlank")
    {
        Scoring.gamescore += 10;
    }
    if (collision.gameObject.name == "Sphere")
    {
        Scoring.gamescore += 50;
    }
    if (collision.gameObject.name == "donutbox")
    {
        Scoring.gamescore += 100;
    }
}
```

You may wonder why this is better. After all, this takes up more real estate. The reason is this: this code is much easier to read and maintain. When you use an incremental approach to software development, your code will change over time. If you're on a team of many coders, the changes might be made by someone else.

This brings up the larger topic of *coding standards*. A coding standard is a collection of rules that aim to make your code more readable and maintainable. The coding standard for this book is in Appendix V. It is up to you if you wish to follow that standard, follow another standard, or just wing it. Be aware that many professional software teams have coding standards that must be adhered to religiously if the team members want to keep their job.

## GAME OVER

The traditional way of telling your players that the game is over is to have the words "Game Over" prominently displayed on screen with sad music in the background, followed by a chance to play again by going to the main game menu. During the "Game Over" message, the player can no longer play the game, but the scene is still on display to allow the player to see what just happened. To implement this, you'll introduce a game state variable. Keeping it simple, there will be just two game states: gameplay and game over.

**\<Step 1\>** GameObject – Create Empty and rename it to GameState.

**\<Step 2\>** Create a new script for the GameState object and call it GameState with the following code:

```
using System.Collections;
using System.Collections.Generic;
using UnityEngine;

public class GameState : MonoBehaviour
{
    public static int state;
    public const int gamePlay = 1;
    public const int gameOver = 2;

    // Start is called before the first frame update
    void Start()
    {
        state = gamePlay;
    }
}
```

The two states are integers, and the particular values for them don't really matter as long as they differ from one another. The Start function initializes the state to gamePlay. You removed the default Update function because you know you won't be needing it for this class. Next, you will change the state to gameOver when the donut hits the donutbox.

**\<Step 3\>** Replace the `OnCollisionEnter2D` function in donut.cs with this:

```
private void OnCollisionEnter2D(Collision2D collision)
{
    if (collision.gameObject.name == "WoodPlank")
    {
        Scoring.gamescore += 10;
    }
    if (collision.gameObject.name == "Sphere")
    {
        Scoring.gamescore += 50;
    }
    if (collision.gameObject.name == "donutbox")
    {
        Scoring.gamescore += 100;
        GameState.state = GameState.gameOver;
    }
}
```

You added a single line that changes the state to gameOver when the donut collides with the donutbox. You couldn't just say state=gameOver because you're now in a different class.

So far, the state has no effect on the game, so if you test the game right now you will see no visible change. The next step turns off player control during the gameOver state.

**<Step 4>** In woodplank.cs, change the Update function to this:

```
void Update()
    {
        if (GameState.state == GameState.gamePlay)
        {
            if (Input.GetKey("w"))
            {
                transform.Translate(0, 5 * Time.deltaTime, 0);
            }
            if (Input.GetKey("s"))
            {
                transform.Translate(0, -5 * Time.deltaTime, 0);
            }
        }
    }
```

You are testing to see if the state is gamePlay before executing the control code. Now, when you test the game and the donut hits the donutbox, the w and s keys no longer control the plank.

It's time to test this. To make testing easier, do the following:

**<Step 5>** Move the donutbox to the left to make the game very easy.

You might wish to have a layout like Figure 6.10.

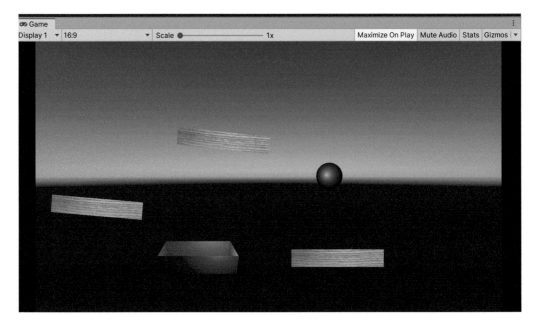

FIGURE 6.10    Donut box on the left for testing.

<Step 6> Test the game.

> When the donut hits the donutbox, your control of the WoodPlank should turn off.
>
> Of course, there is still more to do. The donut should stop moving when it collides with the donut box. The following code does that, and more:

<Step 7> In donut.cs, replace the Update function with this:

```
void Update()
{
    if (GameState.state == GameState.gameOver)
    {
        gameObject.SetActive(false);
    }
}
```

<Step 8> Test the game again.

> Not only does this stop the donut from moving, it makes it disappear! As luck would have it, this actually looks pretty good. You could have also just put the SetActive function call into the collision code, but this way works also.
>
> Rather than leaving well enough alone you're going to do what you originally intended, which is to stop the motion of the donut.

<Step 9> Comment out the SetActive function call. Your new update function will look like this:

```
void Update()
{
    if (GameState.state == GameState.gameOver)
    {
        //          gameObject.SetActive(false);
    }
}
```

> When you test this, you once again have the donut bounce out of the donut box. The phrase "comment out" means that you put the affected code inside of a comment, thus allowing you to bring back the code easily in the future, if you wish.

<Step 10> Add the following line to the donut class:

```
public Rigidbody2D rb;
```

Put this line immediately after the opening brace of the class, before the Start method.

<Step 11> Change the Start method to this:

```
void Start()
{
    rb = GetComponent<Rigidbody2D>();
}
```

This initializes the rb local variable to the RigidBody2D component of the donut GameObject. Take care to type the angled brackets as well as the round braces. This is necessary to access the velocity property of the donut.

**<Step 12>** Change the Update method to this:

```
void Update()
{
    if (GameState.state == GameState.gameOver)
    {
        //          gameObject.SetActive(false);
        rb.velocity = Vector2.zero;
    }
}
```

This code continually sets the velocity vector for the donut to zero during the gameOver state. When you test this, the donut freezes if and when it collides with the donut box.

**<Step 13>** Compare your gameOver state with Figure 6.11.

It's a little bit strange that the donut bounces with perfect elasticity when hitting the wooden planks but not when it hits the donut box. You're going to live with that because, well, this is a prototype game and it doesn't need to be perfectly realistic, just somewhat believable. The donut does continue to spin for a while when it freezes its motion, which looks pretty good, even if that violates physics too.

You do have a bug here, and you might or might not have encountered it. If the donut hits on the edge of the donut box, it doesn't look right. Look at Figure 6.12 to see this bug.

This is one of those bugs that can be fixed at some time in the future. The bug may go away on its own if you change the donut box graphics, or the donut graphics, or both. It is probably not acceptable to release the game to the public with this bug, so this needs to be added to the bug list so you don't forget about it.

FIGURE 6.11   Frozen Donut during gameOver.

FIGURE 6.12    Bug in donut vs. donut box collision.

**<Step 14>** Create a bug list, and put the donut vs. donut box bug in it.

A good way to do this is to create a Docs folder in Assets, then use your OS to create a text file with the following in it:

donut vs. donut box collision not working properly
    Priority: medium
    shippable: no

You can, of course add other info, such as when the bug was discovered, when it was fixed, etc.

Using a spreadsheet instead of a text file might work for you if you like using spreadsheets. On larger projects with many developers, you will end up using bug tracking software. Remember, though, that the best way to deal with bug tracking is to limit the number of active bugs to begin with! Projects with hundreds or even thousands of bugs tend to crash and burn, so try not to let that happen to your project if you can help it.

You're still not done with the game over implementation. The game needs to display the game over text when in the game over state.

**<Step 15>** In Scoring.cs, replace OnGUI with this:

```
private void OnGUI()
{
    GUI.skin.box.fontSize = 30;
    GUI.Box(new Rect(20, 20, 200, 50), "Score: " + gamescore);
    if (GameState.state == GameState.gameOver)
    {
        GUI.skin.box.fontSize = 60;
        GUI.Box(new Rect(
            Screen.width/2 - 200,
            Screen.height/2 - 50,
            400,
            100),
            "Game Over");
    }
}
```

The GUI.Box call refers to the screen width and height to place the Game Over message near the center of the screen. The font size settings are there to make the text a bit larger. Dealing with fonts and font sizes can be a big job when you go into production, especially when you need to support a number of different devices, resolutions, and languages. Right now, you're only supporting English and the particular computer that you're using for developing the prototype.

## IMPROVED DONUT BOX COLLISION

As luck would have it, some time has passed, and you thought of a simple way to fix the collision bug between the donut and the donut box. You will create two box colliders that line up with the left and right sides of the donut box. At first glance, you may be tempted to add those two colliders to the donut box object. This, however, doesn't work. Can you guess why? Try to think of why that doesn't work before reading on.

That's right, the game over state gets triggered as soon as the donut hits one of those colliders. So instead, you'll create two invisible barrier objects as follows:

**<Step 1>** GameObject – Create Empty and name it DonutBoxLeftWall.

**<Step 2>** Add a Box Collider 2D component and make it look like Figure 6.13.

**<Step 3>** Repeat Steps 1 and 2 for the right wall, and test.
When testing, try to get the donut to bounce off a wall.

**<Step 4>** In the Hierarchy, drag the wall objects onto the donutbox object.
This makes the walls children of the donutbox object, which makes it easier to do the next step. The donutbox_front object is also a child of donutbox, so now donutbox has three children.

**<Step 5>** Duplicate the donutbox object, move it to the right so it no longer overlaps, and change the name from donutbox (1) to donutbox. Test this.

FIGURE 6.13   Donut box left wall collider.

You now have two donut boxes. If the donut comes to rest at either of the donut boxes, you should have a game over state.

You are improving your basic Unity skills, so some of the step descriptions aren't quite as explicit as in earlier chapters.

## PREFABS

Prefabs are templates for GameObjects. So far, when you wanted several GameObjects with identical properties, except for their locations, you duplicated and moved them. This works well, but if you wish to make a change to all of the copies you would then have to select each of the copies and make the change, which could be very tedious. If you use prefabs instead you can make the change to the prefab just once and all the instances of the prefab will immediately exhibit your change. In this section, you'll make a prefab for the donut box and then use it to put multiple donut boxes into the scene.

The Unity Manual has a good section about prefabs.

**<Step 1>** Find the Prefabs section in the Unity Manual and read the introduction and Creating Prefabs sections.

**<Step 2>** Save your project.

This is just a reminder that you need to save your work often. It is easy to make mistakes during development, and sometimes the best way to fix mystery mistakes is to start over from your last save.

Making prefabs is very easy. You just drag objects from the Hierarchy into the Assets folder.

**<Step 3>** Drag one of the donutbox objects from the Hierarchy to the Assets folder.

You now have a prefab in the Assets folder.

**<Step 4>** Delete the other donut box in the Hierarchy.

You need to do that because that donut box isn't connected to the prefab.

**<Step 5>** Recreate the just deleted donut box by dragging the donut prefab back into the Scene, placing it where it was before.

**<Step 6>** Rename donutbox (1) to donutbox in the Hierarchy.

This step is necessary because your collision code requires that the name of the donutbox is "donutbox" rather than "donutbox (1)".

You now have both donut boxes connected to the prefab in the Asset folder.

**<Step 7>** Test and save.

This didn't really accomplish anything visible or testable by the player. The game behaves exactly as before. The advantage is that now, you can easily add more donut boxes by dragging the prefab into the Scene. You do need to remember to do a rename as well so that the collision code works. Furthermore, you can make changes to the prefab and the changes will affect all the prefab instances.

## REFACTORING

*Refactoring* is a fancy word for changing your code without changing its behavior. The goal of refactoring is to make code easier to read and/or easier to maintain. Sometimes, refactoring can have an effect on performance, but that's usually not the intention. If you wish to make your code perform faster or take less memory, that process is called *optimization*. We only touch briefly upon optimization as it is unnecessary for the projects in this book.

In the previous section, you refactored the donut box objects to use prefabs instead of creating the donut boxes as independent GameObjects. In this section, you'll continue to refactor in order to make the code organization easier to deal with. You probably noticed that the assets folder has gotten cluttered with a lot of items. You'll start with reorganizing all those assets into separate folders.

<Step 1> Back up your project!

Yes, the time has come to back it up. The next step is a little bit dangerous, so having a backup is cheap insurance in case something goes awry. Find a good cloud service to back up to, or use a separate storage device.

<Step 2> Create the following four folders in the Project panel: Prefabs, Materials, Scripts, and Sprites. Then move assets into their appropriate folders by dragging and dropping within the Unity Editor.

In addition to those new folders, you also have the Docs and Scenes folders for a total of six folders in the Assets panel. Be sure to move these assets within the Unity Editor rather than the OS so that Unity can find them when the game runs. It is your intention to maintain this folder structure as the project evolves. This makes things a bit more complex, but that's much better than having all of your files at the top level.

<Step 3> Test it!

Yes, theoretically testing is unnecessary here. In practice, however, things can go very wrong when you start moving files around, so it's a really good idea to at least see if the game still runs without complaining about a missing file or a compiler error somewhere.

Our next refactor is to change the name of the donutbox object and prefab to DonutBox. This may seem like an unnecessary complication, but it's a good exercise, and it makes your project compliant with the coding standard in Appendix V. You're making the name use PascalCasing. PascalCasing is a naming convention that uses a single capital letter for each word and concatenates the words together without spaces or underscores in between.

<Step 4a> Change the name of the donutbox prefab to DonutBox.

Unfortunately, this only changes the prefab, not the dependent objects.

<Step 4b> Change the names of all the donutbox objects (all two of them) in the Hierarchy to DonutBox.

**<Step 5>** In donut.cs, change "donutbox" to "DonutBox" in the collision code near the end of the file.

If you forget this last step, the collision code will no longer generate a game over state.

**<Step 6>** Test again. Try to get the "Game Over" text to appear.

The game should behave exactly as before, but you now have a nicer looking Hierarchy panel with all objects starting with a capital letter. It is this kind of obsessive attention to detail that can make your project less error prone and easier to maintain.

Next, you're going to change the name of a local variable in donut.cs using the built-in refactor feature of Visual Studio.

**<Step 7>** Open donut.cs by finding the script in your new Scripts folder and double clicking on it.

You might have noticed that in the heat of battle, you used a rather cryptic variable name, rb, when you really should have used something like rigidBody.

**<Step 8>** Select rb on line 7 with a single click.

The variable should highlight when you do that.

**<Step 9>** In Visual Studio, do Edit – Refactor – Rename (Edit – Rename on Mac). If you get a popup window, don't change the settings in the popup. Don't click on Apply just yet.

**<Step 10>** Change the rb to rigidBody at one of the three locations in the file.

**<Step 11>** Click on Apply in the aforementioned popup window. On Mac, type <return> instead.

**<Step 12>** Save and test.

Visual Studio makes it easy to do a refactor name change, even when the names appear in multiple files.

You'll finish this section with just one more refactor: turning the wood planks into prefabs. This is a little bit more difficult because only one wood plank has a script, the other two do not.

**<Step 13>** Create a prefab using the rightmost plank, a plank without a script.

**<Step 14>** Delete the other two planks.

**<Step 15>** Recreate the deleted planks using the prefab.

You do this by dragging them into the Scene, rotating the left one, and dragging the woodplank script onto the middle plank.

**<Step 16>** Rename the newly created WoodPlanks so all three have the same "WoodPlank" name.

**<Step 17>** Test and save.

Refactoring can be much more than just name changes, moving files around or adding prefabs. If your code gets unwieldy, too long, or just plain ugly, it's time to refactor.

## A SECOND LEVEL

You wish to add another level, and then several more. The refactoring in the previous section will make this a bit easier. Each level will be its own scene. You'll start by copying the Game scene.

<Step 1> Click on the Scenes folder in the Unity Project panel.
You should still have the same two scenes, Title and Game.

<Step 2> Click on the Game scene icon.
This highlights the name with a blue rounded box.

<Step 3> Edit – Duplicate.
You now have a third scene called "Game 1".

<Step 4> Rename the new scene to "Level 2".
There are two ways to rename a scene. You can right-click on the icon to get a pop-up menu, select Rename, and then type the new name followed by Enter. You can also carefully left-click on the name, wait about half a second, and then type the new name. Just because you did this, that doesn't mean that your newly duplicated scene is the active scene. At the top of the Hierarchy panel, you can see that "Game" is still the active scene.

<Step 5> Double-click on Level 2 in the Scenes folder.
Level 2 is now the active scene. Move some of the planks around to make a slightly different level.

<Step 6> Test Level 2.
You're making sure that the new level is still playable. If it isn't, adjust the WoodPlank objects some more and try again. It doesn't have to be a good level yet, or even fun, just playable so you can get that donut to its goal.
Currently, your game enters the game over state when you complete the first level. You're about to create a new state, called the "level complete" state, so that the player completes level after level and only get to the "game over" state when the donut reaches the last donut box on the last level. This game also doesn't handle the case of the donut leaving the screen, never to return. You should also have a "game over" when that happens. This seems severe, but for now your player is only going to get one life. Later on, you'll support multiple lives.

<Step 7> File – Save.

<Step 8> Click on the Scripts folder, then edit the GameState script.

<Step 9> Insert the following line immediately after the gameOver declaration:

```
public const int levelComplete = 3;
```

The idea is this: when the donut reaches the donut box, you show a "Level Complete" message to the player for a short while, and then you either move on to the next level or enter the gameOver state. The code to do this will be in the donut file.

**\<Step 10\>** Edit the donut.cs file to match the following:

```
using System.Collections;
using System.Collections.Generic;
using UnityEngine;

public class donut : MonoBehaviour
{
    public Rigidbody2D rigidBody;
    float levelCompleteTimer;
    // Start is called before the first frame update
    void Start()
    {
        levelCompleteTimer = 5.0f;
        rigidBody = GetComponent<Rigidbody2D>();
    }

    // Update is called once per frame
    void Update()
    {
        if (GameState.state == GameState.levelComplete)
        {
            //          gameObject.SetActive(false);
            rigidBody.velocity = Vector2.zero;
            levelCompleteTimer -= Time.deltaTime;
            if (levelCompleteTimer < 0.0f)
            {
                GameState.state = GameState.gameOver;
            }
        }

    }

    private void OnCollisionEnter2D(Collision2D collision)
    {
        if (collision.gameObject.name == "WoodPlank")
        {
            Scoring.gamescore += 10;
        }
        if (collision.gameObject.name == "Sphere")
        {
            Scoring.gamescore += 50;
        }
        if (collision.gameObject.name == "DonutBox")
        {
            Scoring.gamescore += 100;
            GameState.state = GameState.levelComplete;
        }
    }

}
```

That's quite a long file now. Here is a summary of the changes from the previous version. You added a variable called `levelCompleteTimer` and declared it to be a float. You initialized it to 5.0f in the `Start` function. In the `Update` function you are reducing this variable by the Time.deltaTime built-in variable

to have the timer count down five seconds worth. When the timer hits 0 or below, the state goes to gameOver. At the bottom of the file you enter the levelComplete state when the donut collides with the DonutBox object.

**<Step 11>** Test and save.

You haven't put the "Level Complete" message into your project yet, so the game plays as before, except that there's a five second delay before the "Game Over" message displays.

**<Step 12>** Replace the OnGUI() function in Scoring with this code:

```
private void OnGUI()
{
    GUI.skin.box.fontSize = 30;
    GUI.Box(new Rect(20, 20, 200, 50), "Score: " + gamescore);
    if (GameState.state == GameState.gameOver)
    {
        GUI.skin.box.fontSize = 60;
        GUI.Box(new Rect(
            Screen.width/2 - 200,
            Screen.height/2 - 50,
            400,
            100),
            "Game Over");
    }
    if (GameState.state == GameState.levelComplete)
    {
        GUI.skin.box.fontSize = 60;
        GUI.Box(new Rect(
            Screen.width / 2 - 200,
            Screen.height / 2 - 50,
            400,
            100),
            "Level Complete");
    }

}
```

The fast way to do this editing is to copy and paste the Game Over section and then make the changes.

**<Step 13>** Test.

As you can see, the box surrounding the "Level Complete" display is too small.

**<Step 14>** Enlarge the box for the "Level Complete" box in Scoring.cs.

Changing the 400 to 500 will do that. To center the box, change the −200 to −250.

**<Step 15>** Test and Save.

Next, you'll handle the case when the donut falls off the bottom:

**<Step 16>** Add the following code at the beginning of the Update function in donut.cs:

```
if (GameState.state == GameState.gamePlay)
{
    if (transform.position.y < -10.0f)
    {
        GameState.state = GameState.gameOver;
```

```
        }
    }
```

This code checks the y position of the donut and if it's less than 10.0f units the game goes into the gameOver state.

**<Step 17>** Test this by running the game and having the donut fall through the bottom of the screen.

Next, you will add code which will go to Level 2 rather than game over when the levelCompleteTimer goes negative. First, you'll add a level variable to GameState.cs.

**<Step 18>** Insert the following code to GameState.cs:

```
public static int level = 1;
```

This line of code goes after the state variable declaration.

You need to add the Level 2 scene to the Build Settings.

**<Step 19>** Select the Level 2 scene by double-clicking on it in the Scenes folder, and then do File – Build Settings… and click on "Add Open Scenes".

**<Step 20>** Replace the Update function in donut.cs with this:

```
void Update()
{
    if (GameState.state == GameState.gamePlay)
    {
        if (transform.position.y < -10.0f)
        {
            GameState.state = GameState.gameOver;
        }
    }
    if (GameState.state == GameState.levelComplete)
    {
        //          gameObject.SetActive(false);
        rigidBody.velocity = Vector2.zero;
        levelCompleteTimer -= Time.deltaTime;
        if (levelCompleteTimer < 0.0f)
        {
            if (GameState.level == 1)
            {
                GameState.level = 2;
                SceneManager.LoadScene("Scenes/Level 2");
            }
            else
            {
                GameState.state = GameState.gameOver;
            }
        }
    }

}
```

This code will load Level 2 rather than go into the gameOver state. It does this by checking to see if the current level is 1, and if it is, it sets the level variable to 2 and then loads Level 2.

For this to work, you also need to modify the "using" section at the top of the file:

**<Step 21>** Make the top of the file look like this:

```
using System.Collections;
using System.Collections.Generic;
using UnityEngine;
using UnityEngine.SceneManagement;
```

Just as in the TitleMenu script you needed to add access to SceneManagement.

**<Step 22>** Select the Game scene and Test.

And, well, it's a start. You can go from Level 1 to Level 2, but then the score gets reset, which is probably not what you want. The problem is that when you load Level 2 everything gets reinitialized, so the code thinks it's at Level 1 with a score of 0. The following steps fix this.

**<Step 23>** Insert the following function into GameState.cs before the Start function:

```
private void Awake()
{
    DontDestroyOnLoad(gameObject);
}
```

Awake is a built-in Unity function that is called when its scene is initialized. This function preserves the state and level variables when a new scene is loaded. The score is still getting reset, so do the next step.

**<Step 24>** Insert the same Awake function into Scoring.cs. Also, move the initialization of gamescore to the declaration, just as you did with the level variable in GameState.cs.

**<Step 25>** Test and save.

Wow, you did it! The game is looking and playing more and more like a real video game. There's just one major problem. The game is way too small. In the next section, you'll add some more levels and rework the first two levels.

## FIVE LEVELS

The first two levels are experiments, meant to test out the basic software that's running the game. You'll continue to expand the game and add features in this section. First, it would be good to display the current level number. This not only helps the players but also helps you with development and testing.

**<Step 1>** In Scoring.cs, insert the following code after the first GUI.Box call in OnGUI:

```
GUI.Box(new Rect(Screen.width - 200, 20, 200, 50),
        "Level " + GameState.level);
```

Even though it's two lines of code, it's really just a single statement.

**<Step 2>** Test.

The level is now shown in the upper right corner, though it's a bit too far to the right.

**\<Step 3\>** Change the −200 to −220, and test again.

This moves the box 20 pixels to the left of the screen border, which achieves symmetry with the score box.

This code contains *magic numbers*, which really ought to be avoided. A magic number, in the context of computer programming, is a literal number, inserted directly into code without explanation. When creating prototype code, it is acceptable to have magic numbers, but be aware that you plan to go through your code and replace most magic numbers with constants during production coding.

Now, you're going to set yourself up for five levels. You'll create the three additional levels all at once and worry about making them interesting later.

**\<Step 4\>** Select the Level 2 Scene in the Assets > Scenes panel and do Edit – Duplicate three times.

Amazingly, Unity automatically named the new Scenes Level 3, Level 4, and Level 5, just what you wanted.

**\<Step 5\>** Go to the Build Settings and add the new level scenes.

You do this by opening the scenes one by one and doing an Add Open Scenes for each one. Your Build Settings should now have six scenes: Title, Game, Level 2, Level 3, Level 4, and Level 5. This is a bit ugly, so you're going to rename the Game scene to Level 1:

**\<Step 6\>** In the Scenes panel, rename the Game scene to Level 1.

Unfortunately, Unity doesn't automatically update your code when you do this sort of rename. You might recall that the TitleMenu code loads the GameScene string, which, in turn, refers to the first level.

**\<Step 7\>** Replace TitleMenu.cs with this code:

```
using System.Collections;
using System.Collections.Generic;
using UnityEngine;
using UnityEngine.SceneManagement;

public class TitleMenu : MonoBehaviour
{
    public void PlayGame()
    {
        SceneManager.LoadScene("Scenes/Level 1");
    }

    public void ExitGame()
    {
        Application.Quit();
    }
}
```

You made the LoadScene call compatible with the other places in your code where you load scenes. More importantly, you should now be able to test the game.

**<Step 8>** Make Title the active scene, and test.

Just because you added those additional levels doesn't mean they are accessible to your game just yet. First, though it's a good idea to make the different levels visually different.

**<Step 9>** Make Level 3, Level 4, and Level 5 different by moving the planks or the Sphere in each of them. You can also add more Spheres or more DonutBoxes.

You'll be editing each of these levels more extensively later. For now, it's good enough to just make them differ from one another.

**<Step 10>** In donut.cs, replace the levelCompleteTimer section with this:

```
if (levelCompleteTimer < 0.0f)
{
    if (GameState.level == 1)
    {
        GameState.level = 2;
        SceneManager.LoadScene("Scenes/Level 2");
    }
    else if (GameState.level == 2)
    {
        GameState.level = 3;
        SceneManager.LoadScene("Scenes/Level 3");
    }
    else if (GameState.level == 3)
    {
        GameState.level = 4;
        SceneManager.LoadScene("Scenes/Level 4");
    }
    else if (GameState.level == 4)
    {
        GameState.level = 5;
        SceneManager.LoadScene("Scenes/Level 5");
    }
    else
    {
        GameState.state = GameState.gameOver;
    }
}
```

This code isn't the prettiest, but it gets the job done. It's a good exercise in the use of `if` and `else` in C#. Be sure to read this code and try to understand the logic behind it. It basically checks the current level, increments it, and then loads the next level. Can you think of a better way to write this code? For now, you'll leave it as is and test it.

**<Step 11>** Double-click on the Title scene in the Scenes folder and test.

This may be easier said than done. You need to play all five levels and get the donut into a donut box on each level. If you have trouble, simply move the donut to a position just above one of the donut boxes. This will make the level much too easy, but for now you're just testing to see if you can get through the five levels and end up with a valid score and a game over message at the end of the game.

**<Step 12>** Save.

You're now going to improve the five levels and make them more fun and ramp the difficulty gradually from Level 1 to Level 5. The first level should be super easy. There are, of course, many ways to do this.

<Step 13> Select the Level 1 Scene and make it look like Figure 6.14.
You now have just two planks and a donut box. You removed the sphere and arranged the planks so that the following happens: If the player does nothing the donut misses the donut box and you get "game over" soon after. If the player moves the plank up somewhat, then the donut will bounce into the donut box and the player moves on to Level 2.

Your goal is to send this game to friends and family and have them play the game without your help. This implies that the game needs to explain the controls somewhere. The days of printed manuals are history, so it's up to you to have the game explain the controls to the players. The controls will be easier to explain if they use the keyboard arrow keys.

<Step 14> In woodplank.cs, change "w" to "up" and "s" to "down". Test this.
That was easy. Explaining this to the players is almost as easy.

<Step 15> Select the Title scene and make it look like Figure 6.15.
To do this, create a new UI Text object, enter the text "Use arrow keys to guide the donut to the donut box" and adjust the layout and font sizes to make it all fit onto the title screen.

A better design would be to have the playing instructions on its own scene, but that can be done later. For a small prototype, this is good enough.

FIGURE 6.14   New and improved Level 1.

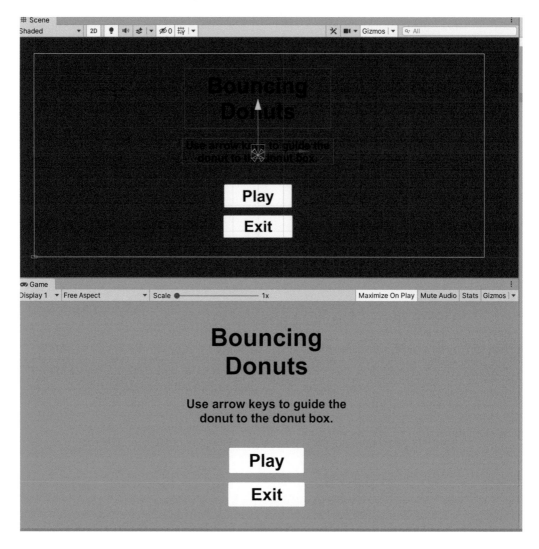

FIGURE 6.15    Title scene with instructions for the player.

**<Step 16>** Test the game, and pretend you haven't seen the game before.

Let's hope the player can click on Play or Exit with the mouse without being told to use the mouse. This game doesn't need the mouse at this point, so maybe it would be good to support players who only use the keyboard.

**<Step 17>** Add a note at the bottom of the BugList document: Support keyboard only on Title scene. Priority: low. Shippable: yes.

This is just a reminder. As you can see, as bugs accumulate you may wish to have a better system than a mere text file. You'll revisit this topic later.

When you're playing the game, you notice a very serious issue, one that was there right from the beginning. The game gets stuck in the Game Over state. It's time to fix this. You'll handle this the same way as the level complete state. You'll use a timer.

**<Step 18>** In donut.cs, add a declaration for `gameOverTimer`.

You do that immediately after the `levelCompleteTimer` declaration.

**<Step 19>** Initialize the timer to `5.0f`.

This one you do in the `Start` function.

**<Step 20>** Insert the following code at the end of the `Update` function after the `levelComplete` section:

```
if (GameState.state == GameState.gameOver)
{
    gameOverTimer -= Time.deltaTime;
    if (gameOverTimer < 0.0f)
    {
        SceneManager.LoadScene("Scenes/Title");
    }
}
```

This is straightforward. If you're in the `gameOver` state, you update the `gameOverTimer` and when it goes negative you load the Title scene.

**<Step 21>** Test it!

Well, that works, except that the game over message is still on the screen and the score doesn't get reset when you play again.

**<Step 22>** Insert the following line before you load the Title scene in donut.cs:

```
GameState.state = GameState.gamePlay;
```

**<Step 23>** In TitleMenu.cs, insert the following lines before loading Level 1.

```
Scoring.gamescore = 0;
GameState.level = 1;
```

**<Step 24>** Test it again and save!

Wow, it feels like a real game now. Of course, there's still no audio, and only the first level is the way you want it. You can finally develop Levels 2 through 5.

These first five levels are intended to be simple, ranging in difficulty from very easy to somewhat easy.

**<Step 25>** Make Level 2 look like Figure 6.16. Give that first plank a z-rotation of −10. Then test the game.

Level 2 is slightly more difficult than Level 1 and introduces a third plank. The angle of the first plank is critical. If it's too steep, the donut moves through the level too quickly. If it's too shallow it's too slow. A z-rotation of −10 or so works well.

Next you want to introduce the Sphere in Level 3. You may no longer have a Sphere object there, so just in case, make the Sphere object into a prefab as follows.

**<Step 26>** Find a Scene with a Sphere in it. Drag the Sphere into the Prefabs folder.

**<Step 27>** Make Level 3 look like Figure 6.17.

FIGURE 6.16    Bouncing Donuts Level 2.

FIGURE 6.17    Bouncing Donuts Level 3.

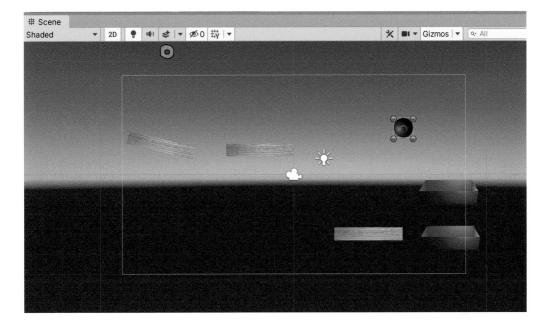

FIGURE 6.18    Bouncing Donuts Level 4.

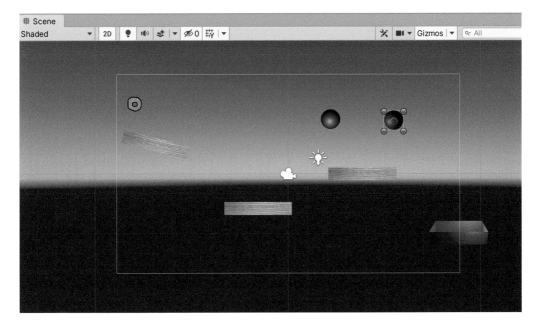

FIGURE 6.19    Bouncing Donuts Level 5.

Feel free to experiment with the Y location of the Sphere. The Sphere acts as a barrier in this level.

If it's too low it'll be easy to bounce the donut over it. If it's too high the donut will bounce below it.

<Step 28> Make Levels 4 and 5 appear like Figures 6.18 and 6.19. Test and save.

Level 4 introduces the second donut box, and Level 5 is a more difficult challenge.

As you're testing these levels make sure that you can get through them consistently. If not, make small adjustments to the positions of the game objects to make the level easier, but not too easy.

The game is almost ready for release to your early testers.

## RELEASE: BOUNCING DONUTS PROTOTYPE 2

In this release, you will ask friends and family to play the game and give you much needed feedback. Before you do this, you'll need to fix any obvious problems that would make testing difficult for your testers. You also need to find a way to transmit the game to your testers.

Your fist prototype didn't get released to anyone. It was just created for your own benefit. It was simply too early for release, even to testers. Your goal now is to actually send the game to your testers in a manner similar to having them acquire a real product. You don't want to assume that they have Unity installed, nor is it reasonable to have them install Unity. A good first step toward releasing is to build the game and then copy the build to another computer.

For this section, this book assumes that you're using a Windows PC rather than a Mac. If you're using a Mac for development, you'll likely want to target Windows PC's in addition to Macs. The reality is that Windows has a 90% market share for desktop gaming, so you'll reach many more players if you release for Windows, not just Mac. You can still follow the steps in this section on a Mac, but you might need to make some adjustments.

<Step 1> Verify that the aspect ratio is 16:9.

You do this in the Game panel. You're going to assume that your testers can handle a 16:9 aspect ratio with their monitors.

<Step 2> File – Build Settings …

This brings up the Build Settings window.

<Step 3> Check and make sure that your six scenes are all in the "Scenes in Build".

<Step 4> Select the "PC, Mac & Linux Standalone" Platform.

<Step 5> Target Platform windows or Mac OS X, depending on what you installed.

<Step 6> For Windows, select Architecture x86

This setting makes the game runnable on older 32-bit PCs. This game is fairly simple and won't ever be large enough to require a 64-bit computer. At least that's the theory. You may wish to revisit this setting before you do a wide release.

**<Step 7>** Click on Player Settings and review those settings.

       The author chose Windowed mode with a default Width of 1600, Height of 900.

**<Step 8>** Close the Player Settings window and click on Build.

**<Step 9>** Create a new folder with the name TestRelease.

**<Step 10>** Select the TestRelease folder.

       This selection triggers the build. It should take a minute or two to do the build, depending on the speed of your computer.

**<Step 11>** Play the game by double-clicking on the BouncingDonuts file in the TestRelease folder. Keep playing it for a while and take notes.

       You will likely find many comments and flaws yourself, even before release. This is normal and common. Make a note of what you'd like to see improved. It's tempting to fix those things right now, but unless the game is completely unplayable you might as well release right now to just a few testers. You're not just testing the game per se, but also the manner of distribution to your testers.

       This brings up the issue of sending the TestRelease folder to another computer. There are many ways to do this. The following steps are just one way.

**<Step 12>** Create a zip file from the TestRelease folder. Rename it BouncingDonutsTest.zip.

       You probably already know how to make zip files. This is built into both Windows 10 and Mac OSX. If you don't know about zip files, search the web for a tutorial on how to make zip files.

       You might find that emailing zip files is a bad idea because email systems tend not to allow them. Also, these zip files can get quite large, so email is not the way.

**<Step 13>** Use your favorite cloud storage service to make the zip file accessible to the public.

       Some examples of cloud storage would be Dropbox, Google Drive, and Microsoft OneDrive. All of these are free to use up to an adequate storage limit.

**<Step 14>** Email the link to another one of your computers, and test the game on that computer.

       You might have a laptop that's not as powerful as your development system. That would be a good first choice. If you have easy access to several computers, test on all of them.

**<Step 15>** Email a link to just one tester, together with some instructions.

       It's up to you to write instructions to your testers. Below is the slightly edited email that the author used during the production of this book for a Windows user.

Hi Susan,

Thank you for volunteering to test Bouncing Donuts. At the bottom of this email is a link to a zip file. Create a folder for this game, any name you wish, put the zip file into it, and then extract. You should see an extract box at the top of your Windows explorer window when you select the zip file.

Once the game is extracted, run the BouncingDonuts.exe file and try to play the game. Please make notes about your experience, any technical issues you might have, and anything else you'd like to tell me.

This version has no audio. The game shouldn't crash or hang, but if it does, please write down what you did before the crash, then reboot your system. Then try to duplicate the crash, if possible.

This will likely not be a commercial game, but rather part of a tutorial for my new book about game development.

Please tell me about the computer you're using. I'd like the following info:

Operating system version (probably Windows 10)
Screen resolution: for example, 1920×1080
Graphics card or graphics processor.

Thanks. There's no rush with this, so take your time. There are five levels, and the game will go to game over if you manage to complete all five levels. You only get one life, which I plan to fix very soon, especially once there's more levels.

The instructions at the beginning should say "Use the up and down arrow keys ... " The left-right arrow keys do nothing.

There is scoring, but it's not quite the way I want, so you can safely ignore the score.
: <insert link here>

This is one of the most exciting parts of game development. You're finally revealing your masterpiece to an unsuspecting guinea pig. It's important to reveal very little about the game to your testers. It's OK to say that it's a bouncing donut game, that it's a puzzle game, and that it's an early prototype. Don't make excuses for how bad or incomplete the game is. Simply ask people to play it and solicit honest feedback. You'll get better feedback from strangers, but you're not quite ready for that yet because the game is, after all, just a prototype.

You'll want to release to just one tester first to make sure there are no serious problems with your distribution method.

**<Step 16>** Send the game to some additional testers. Five testers would be a good number. Once you get feedback from people, you'll need to thank them for their help and politely tell them that you'll consider their feedback during your further development. At the very least, make a note of who they are and remember to send them a free copy of the final game when it's released.

While you're waiting for feedback from your testers you plan to work on audio, a glaring omission so far.

# Sound Effects with Audacity

I N THIS CHAPTER, you'll learn to use Audacity to make sound effects for your games. You will then import some sound effects into the Bouncing Donuts Unity project and write C# code to play them.

## INTRODUCTION TO SOUND IN GAMES

Sound is an often overlooked part of game development, mainly because it's easy to make a prototype without sound and put it in as an afterthought toward the end of the project. Sound can have a large impact on the feel and mood of your game, but for many games, sound doesn't directly affect gameplay. Commercial projects will use professional sound designers and composers to create custom sound and music. Regardless of your budget or the size of your team, it's a good idea to learn how to make your own sound effects and music. That way you can gain an understanding of how sound works and how to talk with the sound pros who work with you.

Sound in most modern video games is stored using some sound format such as .mp3 or .wav and then played back during game execution. Unity, for example, supports .wav, .aif, .mp3, and .ogg sound formats. In your current project, you will create short sound effects and store them in .wav files. For music, you'll use .mp3 format instead. Wav files are uncompressed and thus use up much more space, but they have better quality. For music, mp3 format is a good choice in order to save on memory usage.

For your simple puzzle game, Bouncing Donuts, the sound design is fairly simple. You'll create an effect for when the donut collides with the wooden planks, another for colliding with the sphere, and a donut box collision sound. In the next chapter, you'll compose short pieces of music for the end of level, game over, and the game ending. You'll also compose two longer pieces of music: the background music and the menu music.

## INSTALLING AUDACITY

Audacity is free, open-source, cross-platform audio software. It is a multi-track audio editor and recorder for Windows, Mac OSX, and other operating systems. You can get the latest version of Audacity at www.audacityteam.org. The version of Audacity used in this

book is 2.3.0. If you wish to follow along with the steps in this chapter, you should also use version 2.3.0 in order to assure compatibility. Audacity has been stable for many years, so it is likely that later versions of Audacity would also be compatible, though the menu structure might be different.

Special Note for Mac Users: Audacity 2.3.0 will not run under the Catalina version of Mac OS because it is a 32-bit application, and Catalina doesn't support those. Your best option is to use Audacity 2.3.3 instead. Even then, recording from a microphone needs a workaround. If you're interested, you can find this workaround online, but you won't be recording directly into Audacity for this book, so you can ignore that issue for now. The author has tested this book on a Mac running Catalina and Audacity 2.3.3, as well as on Windows 10 with Audacity 2.3.0.

In addition to the main purpose of Audacity as an audio editor, it also includes a wealth of ways to generate sound effects from scratch.

When it comes to sound effects, there are two basic technologies to create them: using synthetic sound generation software such as Audacity, or using a sound recorder to record real-world sounds. You will be mostly using the synthetic method for Bouncing Donuts. Because Bouncing Donuts is a fairly abstract game, it's not all that important to have realistic sounds for it. Most anything could work.

## MAKING SOUND EFFECTS IN AUDACITY

There is a multitude of ways to put sound effects into your games. For example, you can record the effects yourself, use a sound effects library, or create sound effects using sound creation software such as Audacity. In the next three sections, you'll try out those three methods. You'll also use Audacity to post process the sound effects, if necessary, and convert them to .wav format. First, you'll use Audacity directly to make a boing sound. You'll use this sound when the donut bounces on something.

<Step 1> Create an Audio subfolder in the Assets folder for Bouncing Donuts.
This is where you'll put all of your audio files, both sound effects and music.

<Step 2> Open Audacity.

<Step 3> File – Save Project – Save Project As … and store it in your newly created Audio folder with the name BoingA.
It may seem silly to save the project before you've even done anything. Nevertheless, this is a good habit to get into. This way you won't save your work in the wrong location later on.

<Step 4> Tracks – Add New – Mono Track.
This sound effect doesn't need to be in stereo because it is localized at the spot where the donut collision happens. Unity will generate the stereo location for you automatically. This saves you a little bit of storage compared to using stereo at this point of the process.

FIGURE 7.1    Audacity showing a Pluck sound.

**<Step 5>** Generate – Pluck… with Pluck Midi Pitch of 40, Fade-out type gradual, Duration 1.0 seconds. If you have two Plucks in the menu, be sure to use the first of the two Plucks in the menu.

You'll see the wave form of the pluck sound in the track panel. Your Audacity window should look like Figure 7.1.

**<Step 6>** Press the green play icon, or hit the <space> bar to play the sound. If you don't hear anything, test your computer to make sure that you have sound output enabled.

A good way to test for sound is to play an online music video. Make sure your speakers are turned on, or your headphones plugged in, and it's good to know where your volume controls are for your computer.

If you want the sound to loop, you can press <Shift> <space> to start looping, space to stop.

**<Step 7>** Effect – Phaser… Click on Manage – Factory Presets – Defaults.

The Factory Default step may be unnecessary, but it's a good one to learn because Audacity will remember any changes you make to these settings, even if you changed them years ago. So, if you want to start out with reasonable settings, it's a good idea to start with the factory defaults.

**<Step 8>** Apply and Close.

The waveform has changed, and the sound is a bit different.

**<Step 9>** Undo the Phaser command, listen to the old sound, and then redo the Phaser command.

You do this by using Edit – Undo Phaser, Play, and Edit – Redo Phaser. You can also do this with the keyboard shortcuts, <Ctrl> Z, <space>, <Ctrl> Y.

Try both methods. It's useful to know these keyboard shortcuts, especially since they also work in Unity, Blender, and GIMP! To make things complicated for Mac users, on Macs in Audacity it's <command>Z and <shift><command>Z instead. For the rest of this section, if you're a Mac user, please change the keyboard shortcuts by replacing <Ctrl> with <command>.

<Step 10> With the mouse, select the tail of the waveform from 0.4 seconds to the end, and press the delete key.

This makes the effect shorter. To see the waveform again, you need to do the following:

<Step 11> Select – All (<Ctrl>A) and View – Zoom – Zoom to Selection (<Ctrl>E).

<Step 12> Effect – WahWah…, Manage – Factory Presets – Defaults, Apply, Close.

<Step 13> Effect – Normalize… – OK.

Compare your waveform with Figure 7.2.

You now have a funny boing sound, created entirely within Audacity. You did a Normalize at the very end of the creation process. With the default settings, Normalize is an Audacity effect that adjusts the volume of a selection so that the peak amplitude is set to a good value just below clipping. You will be doing that to most of your sound effects. You will then have a chance to adjust the relative volumes of your sound effects within Unity later on. Unity can also normalize for you, but you prefer to do that in Audacity so you can test your sound effects at full volume inside of Audacity.

<Step 14> Export to BoingA.wav, use 16-bit signed PCM, and enter the metadata of your choice. Use the same Audio folder that you created in Step 1.

FIGURE 7.2 Boing sound waveform.

The metadata settings allow you to include your name or your company's name within the wav file, as well as other information that you wish to have there. The metadata exists for the purpose of documentation and doesn't affect how the sound file sounds during playback.

**<Step 15>**  Save the project.

The project file with extension .aup allows you to continue the project at a future time. It isn't used by Unity, but the file does show up in the Assets panel. This is similar to GIMP and Blender where the project files serve the same function.

You're now going to create another boing sound by using a recording device of your choice to record a boing and then bring it into Audacity for post processing. This is easier said than done, but it can be a lot of fun.

## RECORDING SOUND EFFECTS

To record sound effects, you'll need some kind of recording device. If you're serious about sound quality, you'll need to use a field recorder, available for a reasonable cost online. You can also just use your cell-phone. Just be sure to use an app that generates mp3 or wav files so that your recording can be easily imported into Audacity. Another method would be to use a microphone connected to your computer.

This section is optional, so if you prefer, you can just make a slightly different Audacity boing sound using the techniques of the previous section.

**<Step 1>**  Grab your portable recording device. Then walk around someplace and record short sounds as you open and close doors, rattle kitchen utensils, tap your fingers on a desk, etc.

You could spend hours doing this, but please, restrain yourself and record just a minute or two of some random short sounds. You can always redo this later on.

**<Step 2>**  In the Audio folder, create a subfolder called MySoundEffectsLibrary.

You have decided to create your very own sound effects library. All the sounds and the source materials for those sounds will reside in this newly created folder.

**<Step 3>**  Move the BoingA.aup file and the BoingA_Data folder to the library.

**<Step 4>**  Copy the BoingA.wav file to the library.

Your intention is to have the wav files appear in two places: in the Audio folder and in the library. The supporting files, such as the .aup files, will be just in the library.

**<Step 5>**  Copy your recording to the library.

Be sure to have your recording in a format that Audacity can import. Mp3 and Wav are OK. If your recording comes directly from the iPhone voice

recorder, for example, it may be in an incompatible format such as m4a. You would have to convert this file or better yet, find an app that can directly record to mp3 or wav sound format.

<Step 6> Open Audacity and import your recording.

<Step 7> Select one of the sound effects with the mouse.
You may need to zoom in and scroll before making the selection.

<Step 8> Effects – Normalize and listen to the sound effect. If you don't like it, go back to step 7 and repeat.

<Step 9> File – Export – Export Selected Audio …
Use the .wav file format and give it a name of BoingB in the sound effects library folder.

<Step 10> Save the project using the name BoingB.aup in the sound effects library folder.

<Step 11> Exit Audacity and copy the .wav file from the library to the Audio folder.
Your sound may not sound much like a boing, but that's OK, it's just a name after all. Making your own recordings of sound effects can be a time-consuming but fun process. Once the game is farther along you may wish to rerecord some of the sound effects.

## USING SOUND EFFECTS FROM THE INTERNET

A relatively easy way to obtain sound effects for your games is to obtain them from the internet. Whether your budget is large, small, or non-existent, the internet has you covered. A good place to start is freesound.org. All sounds on that website are CC (creative commons) licensed sounds. Odds are good that the sound effect you're looking for is already available there. As an exercise you'll get a sound effect from freesound.org, import it into Audacity, normalize and trim it, and then make it available for your game project.

<Step 1> Go to freesound.org.

<Step 2> Search for "boing".

<Step 3> Listen to several of the sounds, then choose jawharp_boing.wav.

<Step 4> Follow the download instructions. You will need to create a freesound.org account.

<Step 5> Copy the file to your assets/MySoundEffectsLibrary folder. The name of the file in your download folder is `188869 __ plingativator __ jawharp-boing.wav`. This sound has been downloaded 28074 times as of May 3, 2020. You are not alone!

<Step 6> Open Audacity and import the .wav file.

<Step 7> Save the project with the name BoingC.

FIGURE 7.3    Selecting the fifth Boing.

**<Step 8>** Pick the fifth boing, select it using your mouse. You may choose one of the other ones if you prefer.

Compare your screen with Figure 7.3.

**<Step 9>** Effect – Normalize... and click on OK.

**<Step 10>** File – Export Selected Audio... and use the name BoingC.wav, library folder.

**<Step 11a>** Save the project in the library folder.

**<Step 11b>** Copy BoingC.wav from the library to the top level of the Audio folder.

Before you move on, you need to check the licensing on this sound. It is made available using the CC Attribution license. This means that you must give appropriate credit, provide a link to the license, and indicate if changes were made. You did, in fact, make some small changes by doing a normalize and trimming the sound effect.

**<Step 13>** In the bug list, enter the relevant information about attributing this sound effect upon release.

You will need to make a note of the link to the license: https://creativecommons.org/licenses/by/3.0/

Under the terms of this license you need to have a copyright notice, a license notice, a disclaimer notice, name of the creators, and a list of changes. The freesound.org website claims that credit isn't required, so you can skip that, if you wish.

This is a small downside of using assets from the internet, even free ones. It can be a burden to keep track of the licenses for all of those assets. Even if it's not required it does feel good to credit your fellow creators by giving credit where credit is due.

You have just successfully created three different collision sounds using three different methods. You're now ready to import the sounds into your game project.

## SOUND EFFECTS PROGRAMMING IN UNITY

It's not enough to create the sound effects for your game and store them in the Assets folder. You also need to tell the game when and under what conditions to play them. Unity makes this fairly easy.

<Step 1> Open the BouncingDonuts project in Unity.

You may notice that it takes an unusually long time to open the project this time. Why is that? If you were paying attention, you saw that during the loading process, there were messages such as in Figure 7.4. It turns out that MySoundLibrary has quite a few large files in it. Unity processes all those files when it first encounters them and makes .meta files for them. You may wish to rethink this folder layout in the future.

<Step 2> Select Assets>Audio in the Project panel.

You should see four items as shown in Figure 7.5.

<Step 3> Select BoingA by clicking on it.

<Step 4> Listen to the sound effect as follows: Open the waveform panel at the very bottom of the inspector by moving the mouse to the bottom until the mouse cursor changes shape to vertical arrows, then clicking.

The waveform for BoingA in the Inspector should look like Figure 7.6.

<Step 5> Click on the waveform in order to play it. Check that it sounds like BoingA inside of Audacity.

You can also play it by clicking on the Play icon near the top right of the panel.

FIGURE 7.4   Unity loading MySoundEffectsLibrary.

FIGURE 7.5 Three sound effects and the Sound Library folder in Assets>Audio.

FIGURE 7.6 BoingA waveform panel in the Unity Inspector.

**\<Step 6\>** Click on BoingB and BoingC in the Assets > Audio panel.

Once you have the waveform panel set up, clicking on other sound files in the Assets folder immediately plays them. You can experiment with this by going into the MySoundEffectsLibrary folder and clicking on some of the other sound files in there, such as the original recording you made, or the audio file that you downloaded from the web.

Next, you'll trigger these sound effects by adding three Audio Source components to the Donut game object. The donut.cs script will then play the appropriate Audio Source when the donut collides with something.

Before you do all that, you need to see that the Donut objects in your levels aren't prefabs. You have five Donut objects in five different scenes. You could

add three Audio Sources to each of the five Donuts, but it'll be better to bite the bullet, so to speak, and create a Donut prefab first, and then make all five donuts instances of that prefab.

<**Step 7**> Save your project and scene.

<**Step 8**> Make Level 1 the current scene.

<**Step 9**> Drag the Donut to the prefabs panel.

You now have a Donut prefab, and the Donut in Level 1 is an instance of it. Unfortunately, this leaves the Donuts in Levels 2 through 5 as standalone objects rather than instances of the Donut prefab.

<**Step 10**> Save Level 1.

<**Step 11**> Make Level 2 your current scene.

<**Step 12**> Drag the Donut prefab on top of the Donut object in the Scene panel.

You'll notice that you now have two donuts in your scene, Donut and Donut (1). Your plan is to delete the Donut object and rename the Donut (1) object to Donut. In order to preserve the location of your donut, do the following.

<**Step 13**> Make a note of the X and Y position of the Donut object.

<**Step 14**> Set the X and Y position of Donut (1) to match the position of the Donut object.

<**Step 15**> Delete Donut.

<**Step 16**> Rename the Donut (1) object to Donut.

Phew. That was a bit tedious, but it's worth it. Your Donut is now an instance of the Donut prefab, just as you wanted.

<**Step 17**> Repeat for levels 3, 4, and 5.

It's about time that you test all this.

<**Step 18a**> Test your game, and make sure all the levels still work.

<**Step 18b**> File – Save Project.

You can now make changes to the Donut prefab and have those changes reflected in all five instances in the five different scenes.

<**Step 19**> Select the Donut prefab.

<**Step 20**> Click on Open Prefab.

<**Step 21**> Component – Audio – Audio Source.

<**Step 22**> In the Inspector, scroll down to see the Audio Source section.

The Audio Source section looks like Figure 7.7.

As you can see, there are quite a few settings for Audio Sources. You will experiment with these settings later on. For now, the default settings are a good choice.

FIGURE 7.7   Audio Source section for Donut prefab.

**\<Step 23\>** Select the Audio folder in Assets and drag BoingA into the AudioClip text entry box.

Because the "Play on Awake" checkbox is enabled, you would hear the BoingA sound every time a Donut instance is woken up, typically at the beginning of a level. This is good for testing purposes, or for music clips, but for our sound effects, we need to disable it.

**\<Step 24\>** Uncheck "Play on Awake".

**\<Step 25\>** Repeat Steps 21–24 for BoingB and BoingC.

When you're all done, you should have three Audio Source components for the Donut prefab. Next, you'll change the code in donut.cs to actually play the sound effects.

**\<Step 26\>** Select the Scripts folder and double-click on donut.

**\<Step 27\>** Insert the following three lines after the `gameOverTimer` declaration near the top of the file.

```
AudioSource boingA;
AudioSource boingB;
AudioSource boingC;
```

**\<Step 28\>** Insert the following lines at the end of the `Start` function:

```
AudioSource[] audios = GetComponents<AudioSource>();
boingA = audios[0];
boingB = audios[1];
boingC = audios[2];
```

The `audios` variable is a one-dimensional array of `AudioSource` objects, handed to you by the built-in `GetComponents`. Here you initialized the three sounds, which only needs to be done once in `Start`.

Next, you'll put in code to play these sounds depending on the type of collision.

**\<Step 29\>** Insert three `.Play` calls in `OnCollisionEnter2D` as follows:

```
private void OnCollisionEnter2D(Collision2D collision)
{
    if (collision.gameObject.name == "WoodPlank")
    {
        Scoring.gamescore += 10;
        boingA.Play();
    }
    if (collision.gameObject.name == "Sphere")
    {
        Scoring.gamescore += 50;
        boingC.Play();
    }
    if (collision.gameObject.name == "DonutBox")
    {
        Scoring.gamescore += 100;
        boingB.Play();
        GameState.state = GameState.levelComplete;
    }
}
```

Notice that you're using BoingA for the WoodPlank collision, BoingC for the Sphere, and BoingB for the DonutBox.

**\<Step 30a\>** Save the code in Visual C.

**\<Step 30b\>** Play the game, and listen to the sound effects.

**\<Step 31\>** Save the project.

You now know enough to add additional sound effects to the game using the same techniques as demonstrated in the steps of this section. For example, it would be good to have a sound effect when the donut hits the DonutBox but doesn't come to rest inside of it. It might also be fun to have sound effects happening when you are moving a wooden plank with the keyboard. This is still just a prototype, so it's best to leave these ideas for a later time and move on to adding background music.

# Music with MuseScore

IN THIS CHAPTER, you'll explore music in video games. In particular, you'll use MuseScore to create a short composition and export it into your Unity project. Music has become as important in video games as it is in film and television. It is unusual to not have music in a film, and the same holds true for video games. Music is an essential part of the atmosphere and feeling of a game, though for most games the game is playable without hearing the music. Especially in mobile games, the music is not heard by the players when they are playing in a noisy environment without access to headphones.

You will need some musical training to fully understand this chapter. If you are not musically inclined or don't have musical training, you may skip most of this chapter and simply download the music file instead of creating it yourself. You will still need to put in the code that plays the music. That is explained in the last section.

## INTRODUCTION TO MUSIC IN VIDEO GAMES

Video game music is typically used as background for title and menu screens, cut scenes, as well as during gameplay. In some games, the music adapts to actions during gameplay. Video game music can be licensed, adapted from public domain music, or written for the game.

The history of music in video games starts in the 1980s when video game music was usually produced by inexpensive sound synthesizers available at the time. As technology advanced in the following decades, video game music evolved into the full orchestra arrangements and full fidelity recordings of popular music. A very good and detailed history of video game music can be found on Wikipedia.

The technology used to produce video game music was, in the early days, nothing more than typing in the notes for each track, assigning instruments and setting the volume. We've come a long way since then. In modern games, music production uses, for the most part, the same tools and techniques of film and television scoring, with a few adaptive techniques thrown in.

An example of an adaptive video game music technique would be *vertical re-orchestration* where the mix of the separate tracks is dynamically changed in response

to player actions. Even simpler would be to simply increase the volume and the tempo of the background music during a climactic battle scene.

In this chapter, you're going to use MuseScore to create a short, original background music loop and then integrate it into your game. A part of this chapter assumes musical training, but you have the option to simply skip the starred sections if you're not interested in creating your own music.

## INSTALLING MUSESCORE

MuseScore is a score writer for Windows, macOS, and Linux. Like so many of the tools used in this book, MuseScore is open source and entirely free. You can download the latest version of MuseScore for your system at musescore.org.

&lt;Step 1&gt;  Go to musescore.org using your favorite browser.

&lt;Step 2&gt;  Download the most recent version of MuseScore.

This book uses MuseScore 3.2.3. You will most likely be able to use a more recent version without issues, but be aware that the screenshots in this chapter may not match your screen if you use another version of MuseScore. The MuseScore website should have a link to version 3.2.3, or a very similar version if you want to follow along with the steps in this chapter exactly as written.

&lt;Step 3&gt;  Create a MuseScore account at musescore.org.

This free account will give you access to thousands of scores which you could possibly use in your games.

Be aware that the music on MuseScore may not be in the public domain, so be sure to check the licensing situation for any music that you obtain from musescore.org, or any other website for that matter. There are people whose full-time job is to clear music for use in films, TV, and video games. If you are working for a game company, this would be a good time to ask management about your company's music clearance policy. If you're an indie, you probably won't be able to afford music licensing of popular songs, so you should probably just hire a composer to write original music and performers to perform it. If you have a really low budget, look for public domain music and/or public domain recordings of public domain music. If you play the 200-year-old Beethoven's Moonlight Sonata on a piano and record yourself doing that, you're free to use that recording.

Even if you're not a professional musician, a little bit of musical training can go a long way. Don't be afraid to dive in and make your own music.

## CREATING YOUR OWN SCORE*

In this section, you'll create a short eight measure score. The * after the title of this section indicates that this section is optional, and you can skip it if you wish. This section assumes that you know some basic music theory. If you've taken a couple of years of piano lessons, you're good to go.

<**Step 1**>  Open MuseScore.

You will see two windows, the Start Center and the main MuseScore window. Compare your view of the main window with Figure 8.1.

You won't be able to access the main window right away. First you need to decide what to do in the Start Center.

<**Step 2**>  In the Start Center, click on Create New Score…

This is the first of possibly several rectangles in the center panel.

<**Step 3**>  Enter the title of this song "Donut Theme". You can leave the Subtitle blank.

<**Step 4**>  Enter the composer. Use your own name!

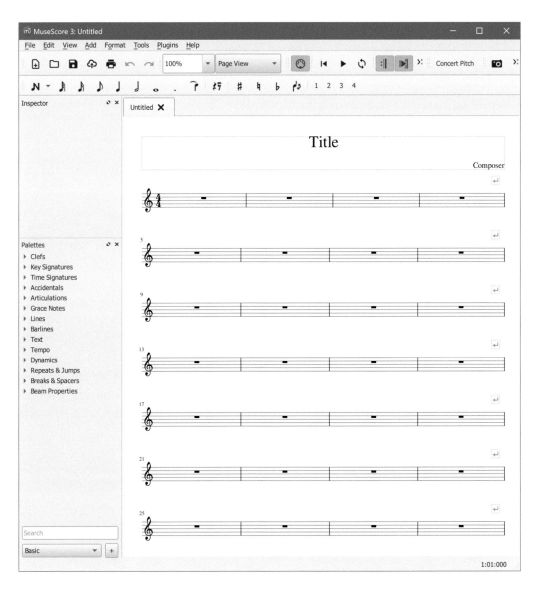

FIGURE 8.1    Main MuseScore window at startup.

**\<Step 5\>** Enter the copyright. Type in your name and the current year.

**\<Step 6\>** Next >

**\<Step 7\>** Double click on Choose Instruments.

**\<Step 8\>** Keyboards – Piano.

**\<Step 9\>** Add.

**\<Step 10\>** Next >

**\<Step 11\>** Leave the key signature at C major.

**\<Step 12\>** Check the Tempo box and leave the tempo at 120.
The 120 sets the tempo at 120 beats per minute. You can later change that to slow down or speed up the music playback.

**\<Step 13\>** Next >

**\<Step 14\>** Change the number of measures to 4.

**\<Step 15\>** Finish.
Compare your score with Figure 8.2.
You should have your own name on the right side at the top rather than my name.

**\<Step 16\>** In BouncingDonuts/Assets/Audio, create a folder called Music.

**\<Step 17\>** File – Save As… and use the name Donut Theme.mscz in the newly created Music folder.
You're now ready to enter the notes for your composition. Composing music can be a career requiring years of training. Your composition may not be as good as one created by a pro, but it'll be your own, which can be very satisfying. Keep in mind that there are plenty of examples of novice composers who created hit songs.
You still don't have any notes in your composition, so as a way to learn how to do that you'll enter the notes of a composition called "Bouncing Through" by Wilder White. Wilder is one of my piano students. Wilder wrote this song

FIGURE 8.2 "Donut Theme" in MuseScore Initial Setup.

in 2019 as a short composition exercise. Take a look at Figure 8.3 to see this four measure composition.

Your goal is to enter this composition without changes to your MuseScore file.

**\<Step 18\>** File – Save As… with the name "Bouncing Through".

**\<Step 19\>** Double Click on the composer name and change it to "Wilder White".

**\<Step 20\>** Double Click on the song title and change it to "Bouncing Through".
Next, you'll enter the notes in the bass clef (the bottom line).

**\<Step 21\>** Click on the first measure in the bass clef.
Your screen should look like Figure 8.4.

**\<Step 22\>** Type the following characters: n7dcdc\<Esc\>
You entered note entry mode, selected whole notes for the note duration (7) and then entered four notes, DCDC. You also were able to hear the notes as you entered them. The \<Esc\> exited you out of note entry mode. As you can see the C's are one octave too low. Compare your screen with Figure 8.5.
You'll now adjust the C's by moving them up.

**\<Step 23\>** Click on the C in the second measure, then hit the up arrow 12 times.
As you do this, you'll hear a piano playing a chromatic scale as the note is moved up to its intended position, middle C.

FIGURE 8.3 "Bouncing Through" by Wilder White.

FIGURE 8.4 First measure of bass clef selected.

FIGURE 8.5    Bass notes entered with C's too low.

**<Step 24>**    Repeat the previous step for measure 4.

Your base line should match the original score. You'll next enter the treble clef notes.

**<Step 25>**    Select the first measure in the treble clef.

The measure should be outlined with a blue box, just as when you selected the first measure in the bass clef earlier.

**<Step 26>**    Type n400agfe5d

You just entered the notes for the first measure.

**<Step 27>**    Type 4ee5ded

The digit 4 selects eighth notes, 5 selects quarter notes. The letters are the names of the notes.

**<Step 28>**    Type 4a

The a is entered one octave too low. You can quickly adjust this as follows:

**<Step 29>**    <Ctrl><up arrow>

You hold the Control key (command key on a mac) and while holding, press the up arrow key. This should have moved your note up by one octave.

**<Step 30>**    Type gfe5d3eee0

It got a little more difficult, but you entered the notes for the third measure. Here comes the last one:

**<Step 31>**    Type 0d4dc<Ctrl><up arrow>6c4d<esc>

Use <command> instead of <Ctrl> on a Mac. You are done!

**<Step 32>**    Play it by clicking on the play icon, or just pressing the space bar.

Oh, you forgot to put in the repeat.

**<Step 33>**    Select the last measure, either clef.

**<Step 34>**    Click on Repeats & Jumps in the palette on the left. Double-click on the repeat sign at the bottom left (the two dots followed by a double bar).

You should now have an exact copy of Wilder White's composition.

**\<Step 35\>** Save the file.

Next, you need to export to a format that Unity is able to use. You will be using mp3 format which is well suited for music in games. Earlier you used .wav format for sound effects because that format produces clean sound for sound effects at the cost of having larger files.

**\<Step 36\>** File – Export. Use the mp3 format and save to the Music folder. This may take about ten seconds on your system. During the export, MuseScore can't do anything else, so you just have to wait for the process to finish.

This particular composition is published in this book under a Creative Commons Attribution 3.0 License. This means that if you use this composition in one of your projects, you need to remember to give credit to Wilder White where convenient. For more information about this license, go to creativecommons.org.

**\<Step 37\>** Exit MuseScore.

**\<Step 38\>** Run MuseScore and select the Donut Theme file that you saved earlier.

Once again you have a blank composition. This time, you're going to make your own song.

**\<Step 39\>** Follow the steps that you used to make "Bouncing Through", but change a few notes and rests along the way. Experiment until you have something you like, make up a name for it and save your composition in the Music folder.

Here are some hints for making your own short compositions:

- Keep the notes in the bass clef the same or similar to "Bouncing Through".

- In the melody line, use the notes DEFGA in any order.

- Use only quarter and eighth notes in the melody line.

- Watch some introductory MuseScore tutorial videos online for more ideas.

Now that you've gotten a taste of what it's like to compose music, it's time to look at alternatives. As you can see, it's a lot of work to make even a very simple melody with an even simpler baseline accompaniment using just a piano. Imagine trying to compose for a full orchestra! It's not easy, and it takes years of training and musical talent to learn how to create appealing complex compositions. Fortunately, the internet is your friend. In the next section, you'll try out obtaining third-party music.

## USING THIRD-PARTY MUSIC

You're going to keep things simple and search freesound.org for free music. There are plenty of other websites with free and low-cost music tracks available. Freesound.org is a good place to start your search, especially since you already have an account there.

<Step 1> Go to freesound.org and log in, if necessary.

If you recently logged in there for your sound effects, then freesound.org will remember that and still have you logged in.

<Step 2> Search for video game music.

You'll get hundreds of hits, so there's more than enough to choose from. To make your life a bit easier, choose the Creative Commons 0 license, which reduces the number of available tracks to about 70.

<Step 3> Choose Playground Runaround, listen to it, and download it.

This is a fairly long mp3 file and uses about 5.5 megabytes of storage. It's good to be aware of the size of these files in case you wish to limit the size of your game.

<Step 4> Listen to some of the other music, and download one or two more tracks that you like.

As you can see, this is a piece of cake. Of course, as this is just a prototype, the music can easily be replaced with something else later on in development.

<Step 5> Move your downloaded files to the Music directory of your project.

## IMPORTING MUSIC INTO UNITY

Simply by storing your music files inside of the Assets folder of your Unity project makes the music available to use in your game. Don't forget to keep track of licensing if you obtained your music files by downloading them from the web.

In the following steps, you'll import the Bouncing Through track and the Playground Runaround track. You'll also set up your Unity project to play these tracks where appropriate. Feel free to use other tracks instead, preferably your own compositions.

<Step 1> Open Unity and load the Bouncing Donuts Project.

<Step 2> Go to the Music folder in the Assets panel and test the two music tracks you wish to use.

<Step 3> Select the Title Scene, if not already selected.

You can tell which scene is the current one by looking at the top of the Hierarchy panel.

<Step 4> Add an Audio Source Component to the Main Camera.

<Step 5> Drag the Bouncing Through mp3 file to the AudioClip text entry box in the Inspector.

The Audio Source section in the Inspector should look like Figure 8.6.

Notice that Play on Awake is checked, and the Loop is unchecked. This is the default.

FIGURE 8.6   Audio Source section for Main Camera in Title Scene.

**<Step 6>**   Check the Loop checkmark. Play the game, stay on the title screen and listen.
     You want this music looping while the menu is active. You will hear that the four measure theme plays twice, followed by a short pause, and then it loops back. This is a bit awkward, so you should probably trim the mp3 file, but for now it's good enough. You can do the trim in Audacity.

**<Step 7>**   Select the Level 1 scene by double-clicking it in the Scenes folder.
     Because you didn't save the changes for the Title Scene, Unity reminds you to do the save.

**<Step 8>**   Add an audio source component to the Main Camera.

**<Step 9a>**   Click on the small circle icon to the right of the text box for the AudioClip.
     This opens a pop-up window with all of the available playable audio clips.

**<Step 9b>**   Select the Playground Runaround clip that you downloaded in the previous section.
     This starts playback of the track. You can stop that by closing the popup.

**<Step 10>**   Test the audio on Level 1.
     The sound effects and the background music should both be audible while you're playing Level 1. The sound effects don't really mesh well with this background music, but this can be polished later on. The problem is that the pitches of the sound effects should be in harmony with the music, and right now they aren't. For a prototype, the current sounds are good enough.

**<Step 11>** Repeat Steps 7–10 for Levels 2–5.

This is a bit tedious, but it's easier than making a prefab for the camera.

You now have two music tracks and a few sound effects, which is a good start. You're planning to improve and add to the sound later on in the project.

You just learned the basics of creating music tracks for Unity projects. You tried composing your own music and learned how to find free music online. In the game itself, you simply chose to start a background music track at the beginning of each level. In a more complex game, you would change tracks within a level and possibly adjust the music depending on the actions in the level. You will revisit these topics in Part II of this book.

# Bouncing Donuts 1.0

I N THIS CHAPTER, you will finish this small prototype project. You'll start by responding to the feedback from the testers. Then, as with all prototypes, you need to decide whether to continue development of the prototype, start production, or shelve it. Spoiler Alert: you're going to shelve it. This isn't much of a spoiler since almost all prototypes are destined for the shelf. Most professional game developers will toss everything from their prototypes and start over with brand new code and assets when they start production. Shelved prototypes have the potential to inspire production projects, even years later. Very occasionally, prototypes are released to the public as is, with typically poor results, though of course there are exceptions, such as Flappy Bird.

## BUG FIXES

Your testers have responded, and you have received some comments, suggestions for improvement and bug reports. The biggest problems are that the game is much too short, and that the player gets just one life, which makes it pretty frustrating to play. There is also a bug with the donut box collision. If the donut hits the bottom of the donut box from below the box, the code thinks that the donut is inside of the box and finishes the level.

In this section, you'll fix the collision bug. You may ask, if you're going to shelve the project, is it worthwhile to fix these bugs? Well, maybe. You're viewing this prototype as a learning experience. It's worth it to fix a simple bug or two, and maybe try out just a few more ideas. If you then shelve it, you can at least be satisfied that you gave it your best effort.

Fixing the collision bug is pretty easy and interesting. You'll put in an invisible barrier at the bottom of the donut box prototype.

<Step 1>  Open the Bouncing Donuts Project.

<Step 2>  Select the Level 1 Scene.

<Step 3>  In Assets/Prefabs, double-click on DonutBox.
　　　　　This opens the DonutBox asset. It's the same thing as single-clicking on it and then clicking on Open Prefab in the Inspector.

**\<Step 4\>** Click on DonutBoxRightWall, Right-click to bring up the popup menu, click on Copy.

**\<Step 5\>** Right-click in the Hierarchy panel and click on Paste.

**\<Step 6\>** Rename DonutBoxRightWall (1) to DonutBoxBottom.

**\<Step 7\>** In the Inspector, click on the Edit Collider icon.

**\<Step 8\>** In the Scene panel, adjust the collider to match Figure 9.1.

**\<Step 9\>** Test it.

       The best way to test this is to temporarily move the donut box on Level 1 as shown in Figure 9.2.

FIGURE 9.1    Adjusting the Bottom Donut Box Blocker.

FIGURE 9.2    Testing the Donut Box collision bug fix.

This may take you a few tries to put the DonutBox at a location where the Donut barely misses the DonutBox and then hits it after bouncing. You can duplicate the bug by disabling the DonutBoxBottom game object.

Make sure that you've replaced the DonutBox on Level 1.

**<Step 10>** Save your work.

It's tempting to now add more levels, implement a lives system, and continue development, but before you do that, it's time to review what has happened so far.

## SHELVE OR GO ON?

In game development, as in any creative endeavor, you are always faced with the possibility of dropping everything and doing on to some other project. Frequently, at game studios large and small, projects get canceled for various reasons. It is particularly tragic when very good games get canceled by upper management for financial or business reasons. If you're an indie developer, you may not have the resources of a large studio, but at least you get to make that go or no go decision all by yourself.

All prototypes should follow the first rule of prototyping: Have a question that the prototype will answer quickly and cheaply. When you have your answer, you stop and move on. So, what is the question to be answered by this prototype? How about this one: Is it fun to make a donut bounce into a donut box while controlling environmental elements but not the donut itself? This is, of course, a very subjective question. Ultimately, it's your impression of the game and your call. For a prototype, it's an OK game, but it's very short and only hints at some possible future potential. The truly good prototypes are so much fun to play that you stop working on the game and instead play it for hours and hours. This didn't happen here, so as painful as it may seem, it's time to shelve it.

This isn't a total loss. Quite the contrary! You created a game in Unity with many of the features present in real commercial games. You learned quite a bit about sound effects, music, 2D, and even a little bit of 3D graphics. You did some actual C# coding and you experienced firsthand what it's like to create a video game.

To change the subject, there is a problem with the name "Bouncing Donuts." It's in use. There is a free indie game called "Bouncing Donut" on the Apple App Store by Paolo Bottigliero. No, it's not OK to just add an s to an existing product and claim that it's different.

The name problem is fairly easy to fix. Prototypes are supposed to have working titles, though often the working titles end up being the real thing. Of course, if you're not releasing the game, then you might as well keep the name for your own purposes. Just remember that you'll need to change the name if you ever do take this game into production.

It's one thing to shelve a project, and quite another to abandon it. You really don't want to abandon this project considering the time and effort you put into it. In the next section, you'll release the game, unfixed problems and all, to yourself! That's right, you won't be releasing this game to the public, but you might wish to have it in some kind of releasable form so you can show it to friends, family, or potential employers.

## RELEASE: BOUNCING DONUTS 1.0

The release of this game is somewhat of a misnomer because, well, you're not really releasing it to the public. Still, it's a good idea to go through some of the technical aspects of releasing this game, just as an exercise. You might learn something which will prove useful when you release your next game. First, you need to test the game one more time, just by yourself.

**<Step 1>** Play the game inside of Unity, from beginning to end after Level 5.

It's easy to break things when you're testing or fixing bugs. For example, you might have forgotten to put the DonutBox back to its original position when you were testing for that DonutBox bug.

**<Step 2>** Fix any known bugs or else document them. Then test the game again.

**<Step 3>** Build the game, and store the build in a Release folder, rather than in the TestRelease folder.

**<Step 4>** Make a note of the names of all the people that helped you.

This is important for a future release when you will have credits.

**<Step 5>** Make a list of all the assets that you didn't create yourself: the boing sound effect that you found on freesound.org, or the playground music, also from freesound.org.

**<Step 6>** Make a list of essential parts of the game that still need to be done before you release it to the public.

This would be things like a copyright notice, the title of the released version of the game, and a webpage or website for the game. Also, an installer, and a list of possible target platforms, such as PC, Mac, Linux, WebGL, consoles.

In the next section, you'll do a postmortem. Postmortems are an important part of learning your craft as a game developer.

## POSTMORTEM

A postmortem is a review of the game development process, usually produced by the development team after release. At the very least you need to review what went right and what went wrong during the process. What did you learn, and how can you improve things the next time?

The word postmortem originated from the Latin "post" meaning after, and "mortem" meaning death. Physicians often review the treatment of a patient who died to try to understand what happened and if mistakes were made.

For this project, your goal was to make a small, playable game using Unity together with a host of other graphics and audio tools. You definitely succeeded and can be happy with the result, even though you've decided to shelve it. The game looks pretty good, for a prototype. It's fun to play but the gameplay isn't very deep in those five levels.

The game is definitely frustrating at times. Players really shouldn't have to replay the earlier levels once they got through them. This means that the progress of the player needs to be saved. You didn't implement this feature yet because you can start at any level inside of Unity as a developer.

A real postmortem for a commercial game would be much more detailed and larger. For this small prototype, this section gives you a flavor of what a postmortem is like. You might find it interesting to watch some "Classic Game Postmortem" videos online. There are many to choose from, courtesy of the Game Developer Conference. The author of this book did one in 2012 about his very own "Crystal Castles," published by Atari in 1983.

You're now ready to go on and start your next project.

# II

## 2D Game Development from Concept to Release

Part I of this book introduced you to the basics of game development by helping you take your first steps with a variety of tools including Unity, Blender, GIMP, Audacity, and MuseScore. You created a prototype of a 2D game with the working title "Bouncing Donuts." You decided to shelve that game and move on to another project.

You will, once again, use the same software tools from Part I to build a much larger game with animated sprites, tilemaps, particle systems and, of course, sound and music. You can skim ahead in this book to get a flavor of what it'll look like. But, try not to cheat too much. It's more fun and realistic to take the steps one by one and experience the trials and tribulations of building this game without knowing much about the end result.

Your new project won't start until Chapter 11. First, you'll take a deeper look into Unity's 2D tools.

# 2D Tools in Unity

D URING THE EARLY YEARS OF UNITY, it was called Unity3D and was designed to make 3D games. Even with the original Unity3D, it was possible to make 2D games, but the process became much easier in 2013 when Unity released an updated 2D toolset. Since then, Unity has continued to add 2D tools and support, including a 2D physics engine, tilemaps, and 2D animation features.

Your goal in Part II is to create a 2D maze game inspired by the mostly 2D arcade maze games of the early 1980s. Those early maze games used what was then called stamp hardware to display playfields. The stamps of the 1980s are now more commonly called tiles. Tiles are fixed-size rectangular graphical elements laid out in a grid. In contrast to tiles, moving characters were displayed using motion object hardware, now called sprites. Today, the hardware is quite different and mostly hidden behind several software layers. Developers can just use the game engine and don't have to even know about the hardware. The logical concepts of tiles and sprites are still available via the game engine.

Before diving in and designing your new game, you're going to experiment with Unity's 2D features and tools to gain a better understanding of what's possible with tiles and sprites.

## UNITY 2D SETTINGS

You briefly tried out the 3D Scene view earlier in this book in Chapter 5. Ever since then you used only the 2D Scene view. It's important to understand the 2D and 3D settings in Unity. It can be confusing to the uninitiated that there are, in fact, two independent 2D settings in Unity: the project setting and the Scene view setting. In the following steps, you'll experiment with these settings.

&lt;**Step 1**&gt;  Open the Unity Hub.

&lt;**Step 2**&gt;  Click on New and select 2019.3.0f6.
        Here is where you select which version of Unity you'll be using for your new project.

**\<Step 3\>** Select the 2D template.

> This is where you put your project into 2D mode. This setting is mostly separate from the 2D setting for the Scene view. This will be explained in more detail below.

**\<Step 4\>** Use the Project Name "2Dvs3Dsettings".

> The project for this section is an experiment to help you learn the effect of the 2D and 3D settings.

**\<Step 5\>** Create.

> After a minute or so, the new project is created in a separate window.
>
> You just created a new project using 2D template. This put your project into 2D mode.

**\<Step 6\>** In the new project, do Help – Unity Manual.

> The manual should appear in a separate window.

**\<Step 7\>** In the manual window, search for "2D and 3D mode settings".

> You should now see the manual section that describes the differences between 2D project mode and 3D project mode.

**\<Step 8\>** RTFM.

> OK, this is an old one. Read the Freaking Manual. And yes, that's the censored version for this acronym. Decades ago, before YouTube video tutorials, and before really good books such as this one, programmers had two resources to help them: coworkers and the manual. If you asked a coworker a question that was easily answered by reading the manual, your coworker would simply smile and say RTFM.
>
> In the 21st century, this is generally not the best advice, but the Unity Manual is definitely worth reading as you get more experienced.
>
> You are likely not ready to read all of the manual just yet, but please read the section on 2D vs. 3D mode settings.
>
> You're now going to test some of the most important differences yourself.

**\<Step 9\>** In the Hierarchy panel, click on SampleScene.

**\<Step 10\>** Click on Main Camera in the Hierarchy panel.

> You now see the Main Camera in the Inspector.

**\<Step 11\>** For the Main Camera, check that the Size is 5, and that the Position is (0, 0, −10).

**\<Step 12\>** Check that the camera is set to be Orthographic.

> Orthographic means that objects do not change size regardless of their z coordinates.

**\<Step 13\>** Take a close look at the 2D icon at the top of the Scene view. It should be highlighted.

This means that you are using the 2D Scene view, in addition to being in 2D project mode.

<Step 14> Click on the 2D icon.

You immediately see an entirely different Scene view. Your project is still in 2D project mode, but the Scene view is set to 3D. Notice that the camera hasn't changed at all and it's still using an Orthographic Projection. The 2D icon is no longer highlighted.

<Step 15> Click on the 2D icon again.

You are now back to using the 2D Scene view.

You may be surprised to find out that you can change the project mode to 3D and back to 2D at any time. You're going to try that out now. You'll be following the instructions from the manual in the following steps.

<Step 16> Edit – Project Settings…

<Step 17> Select the Editor panel in the Project Settings panel.

<Step 18> Default Behaviour Mode – 3D

Well, your project is now in 3D mode. Note that the Scene view is still in 2D mode and that the Main Camera didn't change at all. That's because changing the Default Behaviour mode only affects cameras and the Scene view mode when they are created.

<Step 19> File – New Scene.

You now see a new scene in the Scene panel, complete with a Skybox. In 3D mode, new scenes get a default skybox. The Scene view is still in 2D mode, however.

<Step 20> Click on the 2D icon to disable 2D mode.

<Step 21> Select the Main Camera and look at it in the Inspector.

You can see that this is a Perspective camera, just as you would expect in 3D project mode.

On a different subject, in the Hierarchy, you see that there is a Directional Light object. That light gets created by default in 3D project mode when you create a new scene.

<Step 22> In the Project panel, double-click on the Scenes folder, then the SampleScene.

You are now back in your original 2D scene. The Scene view is still in 3D, however. The New Scene that you created in Step 19 has disappeared. Unity didn't warn you about losing that scene because you didn't change anything in that scene.

If this all seems a bit confusing at first, go and repeat these steps. It helps to know at least a little bit about the 2D and 3D settings even if you intend to stick with 2D for your project. Many 2D projects start out in 2D but eventually

migrate to using 3D technology in order to get better lighting and a more realistic perspective, even if the gameplay is still in 2D.

**<Step 23>** Save the project.

You may wish to, on your own, create some game objects, sprites, and lights and do some further experimentation with the 2D and 3D settings.

## SPRITES

Sprites are rectangular 2D graphic objects. You can think of a sprite as a matrix of pixels. Each pixel has a color and, optionally, an alpha value that controls the transparency of the pixel. Sprites were called motion objects internally at Atari in the 1970s and 1980s. This is a good alternative name for a sprite. The purpose of sprites is to move relative to the background and the other sprites in the scene.

Sprites in Unity are textures with special techniques and tools for managing them efficiently. In this section, you will try out the Sprite Creator and the Sprite Editor, two of the built-in tools especially suited for sprites in Unity. You will also explore the Sprite Renderer and learn about sprite packing.

**<Step 1>** Use the Unity Hub to create a 2D project in Unity with the name "SpriteTest".

**<Step 2>** Select the Default Layout.

Rather than the 2 by 3 layout, you'll be using the Default Layout.

**<Step 3>** In the Project panel, + – Sprites – Square.

**<Step 4>** Hit the Enter key to finish creating the square.

**<Step 5>** Drag the square into the Scene panel.

**<Step 6>** Carefully look at the sprite in the Inspector.

This is a good time to learn about some of the settings in the Inspector. Developers can go years without learning about some of the very useful features of Unity that are right in front of them all that time.

**<Step 7>** Below the Inspector tab, there is a perspective drawing of a cube with a little triangle at the bottom. Click on it.

This allows you to attach an icon to your Sprite when it is displayed in the Scene panel.

**<Step 8>** Select the red oval icon. Then click elsewhere in the inspector to close the icon pop-up panel.

**<Step 9>** Select the Move tool and move the Square around a bit using the handles as well as with the yellow square, but not the oval.

As you can see, the icon moves with the sprite, and you can see the name of the sprite. This can be very useful when debugging a complex scene.

**<Step 10>** Create a circle sprite and drag it into the scene as well.

<Step 11> Select a small green circular icon for the circle sprite.

<Step 12> Make the circle yellow.

You do this by setting the color for the Sprite Renderer in the Inspector.

<Step 13> Drag the circle so that it overlaps with the square.

Compare your Scene panel with Figure 10.1

As you can see, the circle is behind the square. The order of drawing for sprites is determined by three things: the Z coordinate, the sorting layer, and the sorting order. You will typically have the Z coordinate at 0 or some other constant value for all of your sprites. You can set up named Sorting Layers so that, for example, all of your enemies are in one layer and all the bullets are in another. You can then rearrange the layers to suit your sorting needs.

<Step 14> Create sorting layers named Circles and Squares.

In the Inspector under Additional Settings, click on the Sorting Layer drop-down to select Add Sorting Layer... Then click on + to add the two new sorting layers. When you're finished, click on the Circle in the Scene panel to exit the Sorting Layer dialog.

<Step 15> Assign the Circles sorting layer to the Circle, and the Squares sorting layer to the square.

<Step 16> Rearrange the order of the Circles and the Squares sorting layers.

You do this by clicking on Add Sorting Layer... to get the Sorting Layer panel, then grab the layers with the mouse and drag them up or down as needed. As you switch the order of the sorting layers you can see the effect in real time in the Scene panel.

You can affect the sorting order within a sorting layer using the "Order in Layer" setting.

Next, you're going to use the Sprite Editor just so you know how to find it.

FIGURE 10.1    Circle and Square in the Scene panel.

**<Step 17>** Click on the Circle in the Assets panel. Notice that the Inspector for that Circle looks quite a bit different.

**<Step 18>** Click on Sprite Editor in the Inspector.

**<Step 19>** Change the number of sides to 16.

**<Step 20>** Click on Apply and close the window.

**<Step 21>** Select the circle in the Scene view and type the f key to focus on it. And notice that it's not quite a circle anymore but rather a 16-sided polygon. That's because you changed the number of sides to 16, which still looks like a circle when it's small. The sprite creator tool is a quick way to make sprites for a prototype project, but it is fairly limited in that it can only make solid-colored polygons with 3–128 equal length sides.

**<Step 22>** Save and Exit Unity.

Feel free to look at the description in the Unity manual for the Sprite Editor. It is mainly used for identifying multiple sprites contained in a single image. You can safely skip learning the details of that for now.

## TILES

In this section, you'll learn about tiles. Tiles were sometimes called stamps in the early days of arcade development in the 1980s. As those names imply, tiles don't overlap and are adjacent to one another, just like the tiles on a tile floor, or the stamps on a sheet of postage stamps. As far as Unity is concerned, tiles are really just sprites with the extra provision that they are laid out in a grid or several overlapping grids.

Keeping it simple, you're going to make just nine tiles for a patch of grass surrounded by dirt. You'll use GIMP to create the tiles and then use Unity to lay out the tiles to make a larger patch of grass.

**<Step 1>** Open GIMP.

**<Step 2>** Make the background color brown and the foreground color black.

To set the colors, look for two overlapping rectangles below the toolbox, and click on the lower rectangle. You can then use the color picker panel to select the background color. Then, repeat for the other rectangle. The result should look like Figure 10.2.

**<Step 3a>** Edit – Preferences – Default Grid. Set the Spacing to 32×32 pixels. Line Style Solid.

**<Step 3b>** Click on OK. Exit GIMP and start GIMP again.

This is necessary to save the Default Grid Spacing in GIMP 2.10.14. This may be a bug in that version, so if you're using another version of GIMP, this step may be unnecessary.

You're now ready to create your tiles.

FIGURE 10.2   Black foreground and brown background colors in GIMP.

**\<Step 4\>**   File – New and set the image size to 128×128 pixels.

Take extra care with typing in the dimensions of this image. They must be exactly 128 by 128.

**\<Step 5\>**   View –Zoom – 400%.

You may wish to zoom in even more, depending on the resolution of your monitor. A quick way to zoom in and out is to use the+and – keys on the numpad. You can see the current zoom level displayed at the bottom of the GIMP window.

**\<Step 6\>**   View – Show Grid.

You should see 16 brown boxes with thin black grid lines separating them. The grid lines aren't actually part of your image. They are there to help guide your drawing so you know how the tiles will be sliced later on. Compare with Figure 10.3.

You're now set up to draw your tiles.

FIGURE 10.3   Sixteen tiles in GIMP.

<Step 7> Use a Pencil and set the Brush Size to 3.

<Step 8> Draw an oval as shown in Figure 10.4.

<Step 9> Make the foreground color green.
Any shade of green is fine.

<Step 10> Fill the inside of the oval with the green foreground color.
As you probably know, you do this by selecting the Paint Bucket and click anywhere inside the oval to do the fill. The result should look like Figure 10.5. Yes, you just created a very small tile set in GIMP.

<Step 11> Minimize GIMP and create a new 2D Unity project with name MyUnityTiles.
You really should have created the Unity project before doing this GIMP work, but you can quickly make up for that by temporarily suspending GIMP and then save your work in the newly created Assets folder after the Unity project is created.

FIGURE 10.4  Oval line drawing in GIMP.

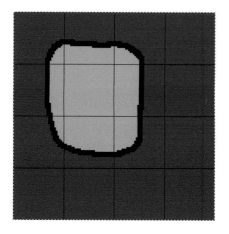

FIGURE 10.5  Simple tiles created in GIMP.

**<Step 12>** In the GIMP window, save your project in the Assets folder of the MyUnityTiles project. Use the name MyTiles.xcf.

**<Step 13>** Export the GIMP image as MyTiles.png, also into the Assets folder.

**<Step 14>** Close the GIMP window.

**<Step 15>** Use the Default Layout in Unity.

**<Step 16>** Select MyUnityTiles in the Assets panel.

There are two MyTiles icons in the Assets panel. As usual, you will choose the icon with the preview graphics, not the GIMP project icon. You want the .png file, not the .xcf file.

**<Step 17>** In the Inspector, select Multiple Sprite Mode and 32 Pixels Per Unit.

**<Step 18a>** Click on Sprite Editor.

You will get a warning that you have unapplied import settings. That's because you made changes in the Inspector but didn't apply them. Go ahead and click on Apply to remedy this omission.

The Sprite Editor should show your tile set in a very large pop-up window like Figure 10.6.

Well, you have a small problem. There are some stray pixels at the border of your green blob. Where did those come from? It's not obvious, but the culprit is the compression done by Unity during Import. In the Inspector, you can see that Compression is set to Normal Quality.

**<Step 18b>** Set Compression to None, and Apply.

Magically, the stray pixels are removed. It pays to be aware of this issue. If you're aiming for a clean pixelated look in your graphics, turn off compression. It turns out that in this case, High Quality Compression also gives you perfect graphics fidelity, so you can use that if you want to save some memory.

FIGURE 10.6    MyTiles in the Sprite Editor.

**<Step 18c>** Set Compression to High Quality, Apply.

You're now ready to slice up your tile set.

**<Step 19>** In the Sprite Editor, click on Slice and select Type: Grid by Cell Size.

**<Step 20>** Set the Pixel Size to 32 by 32, then click on Slice.

This should give you 16 tiles, each 32 by 32 pixels.

**<Step 21>** Click on Apply in the Sprite Editor and then close the Sprite Editor.

**<Step 22>** Expand MyUnityTiles in the Assets panel.

You do the expansion by clicking on the small triangle on the right side of the MyUnityTiles icon. You should see 16 tiles as shown in Figure 10.7.

You just wanted nine tiles, but the extra seven blank tiles came along for the ride, which doesn't do any harm other than using up a little bit of extra memory.

Next, you're going to build a Tile Palette which you can then use to paint into your tile map.

**<Step 23>** Window – 2D – Tile Palette.

This creates a separate floating window. This is a good time to learn or review how to dock windows. Grab the Tile Palette window by the tab with the mouse and drag it into the Scene panel until it is laid out on the right side of the Scene panel. Your window should look like Figure 10.8.

This layout will allow you to quickly draw tiles into the scene by having the palette next to it.

FIGURE 10.7   Result of slicing tiles.

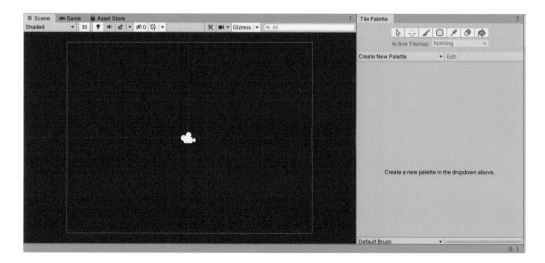

FIGURE 10.8   Tile Palette docked next to the Scene panel in Unity.

<Step 24> In the Tile Palette panel, click on Create New Palette.

<Step 25> Name the Palette MyPalette, Cell Size Automatic, then click Create.

<Step 26> You are asked to select a folder to store the palette. Create a new subfolder in Assets called Tiles and use that folder.

<Step 27> Drag MyUnityTiles from the Assets panel into the Tile Palette. When asked, choose the Tiles folder again.

> Compare your Tile Palette window with Figure 10.9.
> Next, you'll create the Tilemap.

<Step 28> Select the SampleScene in the Hierarchy.

<Step 29> GameObject – 2D Object – Tilemap.

> This creates the Tilemap GameObject in the scene. It's not showing up yet in the Hierarchy though because the SampleScene isn't expanded.

<Step 30> Expand SampleScene, then Grid in the Hierarchy panel. Select the Grid. Focus on it with the f key.

> You now see the grid in the Scene panel as shown in Figure 10.10.
> You have a Tilemap, so next, you'll populate the Tile Palette with tiles.

<Step 31> Experiment with drawing tiles as follows: Look at the toolbar at the top of the Tile Palette. You can use those tools to draw into the Grid in the Scene panel.

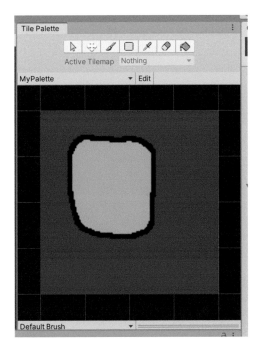

FIGURE 10.9    Tile Palette window with 16 tiles.

FIGURE 10.10   Tilemap in the Scene panel.

Select the Paintbrush, then click on a tile in the Tile Palette, then hover the mouse in the Scene panel.

Pressing the mouse draws the current tile. You can undo with <Ctrl> Z (<command> Z on Mac).

**<Step 32>** Draw a large rectangular area as shown in Figure 10.11.

The bottom edge has gaps in the black line. In a real project, you would now want to go back into GIMP and redraw the bottom of the oval to improve the look of this.

You can try out the other tools in the toolbar on your own.

**<Step 33>** Run the game.

That's right, there's a game in there too. Of course, this game doesn't do anything other than display the Tilemap superimposed on a solid blue background.

Creating the background for a representative level of your game is often the first step in developing a new game.

**<Step 34>** Stop running the game, save, and quit Unity.

FIGURE 10.11   Using the Tile Palette to draw a large grass area.

## 2D SPRITE SHEET ANIMATION

There are at least three main ways of creating 2D animations in Unity:

- Traditional hand-drawn sprite sheet animation.

- Sprite sheets generated by a 3D program such as Blender.

- Skeletal animation.

In this section, you'll try out sprite sheet animation with a very simple animation created in GIMP. Skeletal animation is briefly discussed in the following section. The process for creating sprite sheets using Blender will be covered in a later chapter.

It's important to distinguish between animating a sprite and moving it. The bouncing donut, for example, wasn't really animated because you just drew a single frame. You were still able to move that sprite using Unity, and the physics engine created a rotation animation for you automatically.

You'll start by using GIMP to sketch several frames of a walking character. This time you remembered to set up your project in Unity first.

**<Step 1>** Use the Unity Hub to create a new 2D project with the name SpriteSheetTest.

**<Step 2>** Use the Default Layout.

**<Step 3>** Minimize the window, or move it to another monitor, while you work in GIMP.

**<Step 4>** Open GIMP.

**<Step 5>** File – New… and set the width to 256, height to 32.
You forgot to set the background color to transparency, and you don't want 256 as the width after all, so you'll try again.

**<Step 6>** File – Close View.
This closes the current view. You no longer need this image. An alternative way to remove images is to click on the tiny X next to the small preview image at the top of the main panel.

**<Step 7>** File – New… width 128, height 32, Advanced Options: Fill background with transparency. Click on OK to create the new image.

**<Step 8>** Zoom in on the image to fill your window. Use the numpad+key to do this.
Your GIMP window should look similar to Figure 10.12.

**<Step 9>** Turn on the grid and adjust the size if necessary, just as you did in the previous section.
You now see four transparent squares.

**<Step 10>** Use a pencil with a width Size of 3, black foreground color, and draw four circular blobs into the four squares.
Your image will look something like Figure 10.13.

FIGURE 10.12    GIMP set up to make four frames of animation.

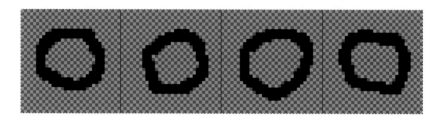

FIGURE 10.13    Four hand-drawn blobs.

**<Step 11>** Save into the Assets folder of the SpriteSheetTest Unity project. Use the name Blob.

> You really should have done that earlier. You're now set up to work on your animation and save it into the correct folder.

**<Step 12>** Fill the interiors of the blobs with slightly different shades of red.

> Your animation is complete and should look about like Figure 10.14.

**<Step 13>** Export with the name Blob.png. File – Save.

**<Step 14>** Exit GIMP.

**<Step 15>** Look at the Unity window that you minimized earlier.

> You now have the Blob ready to go in the Assets panel.

**<Step 16>** Drag the Blob into the Scene panel and focus on it. It should look like Figure 10.15.

> This is not what you want. You're seeing four blobs, not a single animated blob. Fortunately, Unity makes it easy to convert the four blobs into an animation.

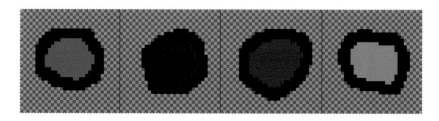

FIGURE 10.14    Animated blob created as a test in GIMP.

FIGURE 10.15    The Blob in Unity.

<Step 17>  Click on the Blob asset in the Assets panel.
You will now adjust the import settings in the Inspector.

<Step 18>  Set the Sprite Mode in the Inspector to Multiple.

<Step 19>  Change the Pixels Per Unit to 32.

<Step 20>  Change the Filter Mode to Point (no filter).
You are creating pixel art, so you don't want to filter the pixels, which would result in a blurry image. Feel free to experiment with this setting to see for yourself what the different filters look like.

<Step 21>  Click on Apply.
The Blob GameObject is no longer operational, so you might as well delete it as follows.

<Step 22>  In the Hierarchy, delete the Blob GameObject.

<Step 23>  Use the Sprite Editor to Slice the Sprite into four tiles.
Look at the previous section for details on how to do this. Use 32 by 32.

<Step 24>  Drag the Blob from the Assets panel to the Scene panel just as you did earlier.
This time Unity asks you for a location to store an animation.

<Step 25>  When Unity asks for a file to store the Blob animation, create an Animations folder in the Assets folder, then use the name BlobAnim.anim for your new animation. Believe it or not, you now have a working animation.

<Step 26>  Click on the Play icon to play the game. Observe the animation and then stop the game.
You have observed a very simple animation, cycling through the four frames that you created in GIMP. Next, you'll adjust the animation and slow it down.

FIGURE 10.16    Animation window in Unity.

**<Step 27>** Double-click on the BlobAnim animation in the Animations folder.

You should see an Animation window pop-up. Compare that to Figure 10.16

This window lets you adjust the animation you just created. You have four Frames laid out in sequence on what's called a dopesheet.

**<Step 28>** Click on the three-dot menu icon at the top right, next to the 4.

There are two three-dot menu icons in this pop-up, and both are at the top right of the window. Pick the one that's immediately below the X at the corner.

**<Step 29>** Select Frames and set the Sample Rate to 60.

**<Step 30>** Click on the arrow to the left of Sprite, above the Add Property button.

**<Step 31>** Enter 40 in the text box that has 0 in it right now.

This moves the current frame to 40. You may need to scroll the mouse wheel to zoom out your view and see all the frames.

**<Step 32>** Click on the Add a Keyframe icon.

**<Step 33>** Move the existing keyframes so that they are at frames 0, 10, 20, 30, and 40.

**<Step 34>** Test all this by playing the game, then stopping it.

As you can see, this slowed down your animation by creating 40 frames spread out over 2/3 of a second. If you set the Sample Rate to a lower value, say to 30, the animation plays even slower. This short exercise showed you how to make simple sprite sheet animation using GIMP to create the sprites and Unity to display and adjust the resulting animation.

**<Step 35>** Save.

## 2D SKELETAL ANIMATION*

In this optional section, you'll briefly explore 2D skeletal animation in Unity. 2D skeletal animation is a fairly recent addition to Unity. This feature lets you assign bones to various parts of an animated object and then move the bones to create animations. Typically, skeletal animations are easier to create than drawing each frame individually as you would do for sprite sheet animation. For example, you might have bones for the legs and the arms of a character, and by simply moving the leg bones you can quickly create a walk animation.

We do have a problem here though. 2D skeletal animation in Unity is not for the faint of heart, and it's not all that easy to use for beginners. So, the best course of action here is to take a glance at some tutorial videos to see what can be done, and then to move on.

<Step 1> Search the web for "Skeletal Animation Unity" and watch the beginning of a few of them.

This will give you a good overview of what this looks like and how you might use it in the future.

<Step 2> If you are so inclined, try to follow along with one or two of the tutorial videos. Don't worry if you get stuck or if the video isn't compatible with your version of Unity. You're not actually going to use this technique in this book, so this is really just an optional exercise just in case you would like to use this in one of your future projects. 3D skeletal animation works in a very similar manner, the only difference being that the bones and the geometry are 3D rather than 2D.

Now that you have a better grasp of the basics of the Unity interface, you're ready to start your project.

# Designing a 2D Maze Game

D EVELOPING A GAME is much like writing a novel or a screenplay. It starts with a blank page, or in the case of a game, an empty folder. You can stare at it all you want. It's not going to write itself. Nevertheless, after you get going, after a while it may seem that way on a good day.

Where do your game ideas come from? Game developers get that a lot. It's a tough question. As usual, when in doubt, google it! You'll instantly find several links to websites, papers, and random pieces of advice on how to generate game ideas. The idea is the easy part. Your success will stem mostly from what you do with that idea when you and your team get down to it and make the game.

Because this book is about 2D games, a good first logical step is to look at the main 2D game genres and pick one. An incomplete list might look like this:

- Match 3

- Platformer

- Maze

- Scrolling Shooter

- RPG

- Tower defense

- Puzzle

- Hidden Object.

Each of these genres encompasses hundreds of commercially successful games to look at and study. For the purposes of this book, the maze game category stands out as a rich and varied starting point for covering many of the basic 2D game development techniques. Games such as Pac-man, Mr. Do, Bomber Man, Donkey Kong, and the Legend of Zelda provide enough inspiration to get started with making your own maze game.

So, the initial concept for your new game is this: Make a 2D Maze Game, inspired by arcade maze games from the 1980s and 1990s. You'll also look at remakes and sequels. You won't be copying them, or remaking them, but rather creating an original game using Unity, Visual Studio, GIMP, Blender, Audacity, and MuseScore. You'll be open to breaking new ground, so when you're done, the game may not even look like a maze game.

## FAMOUS MAZE GAMES

Maze games were absolutely hugely popular in the 1980s, getting their start with Pac-man. Pac-man was so successful that sequels and remakes have dotted the gaming landscape ever since (pun intended). It's really the first example of a gaming dynasty. Smart publishers know that a truly great game deserves to be supported indefinitely. Good games are timeless, just as Shakespeare's plays and Beethoven's symphonies.

The best way for you to educate yourself on maze games, next to owning and playing them, is to search for videos and watching them. Searching for "maze games" won't get you what you want. Try "arcade maze games."

The original Pac-man is extremely simple: just a single maze, a few frames of animation for each of the five animated characters, and some non-animated fruit sprites. And yes, there are some additional animations for the three cutscenes.

Another fantastic resource for researching maze games is *evolution* videos. For example, look for a video about the evolution of Bomberman. You'll find boss-battles as well as copious examples of 2D sprites and animation techniques.

To go deep into a game, search for "gameplay" + "insert name of game here." For example, "Bomberman NES gameplay" will lead you to a video of the basic gameplay of the original Bomberman on the NES.

It's particularly educational to look at The Legend of Zelda for the NES. It's not really a maze game, but fairly close. In that game, you have room after room of mini-games, tied together with an elaborate story and inventory system. Maybe you could do something like that in your game.

## SETTING UP THE PROJECT

It's time to start the project. The scope of the game is limited by the size of this book and the time you're willing to invest. You will aim for a relatively small game with just a few levels, some gameplay variety, and difficult ramping. You'll polish the game somewhat to make it look good and feel good. You yourself will want to play the game and really enjoy the experience. You'll test the game with strangers, friends, and family, and if at least some of them like the game you'll release it to the general public.

You'll need a working title, so pick a bad one so you're not tempted to keep it when you release. How about DotGame? The Dot refers to the name of the main character, who will be a dot. Upon further reflection, this title isn't all that bad, but this isn't the time to worry about the title.

&lt;Step 1&gt; Use the Unity Hub to create a 2019.3.0f6 2D Unity project with the name DotGame.

You may get a pop-up warning that a newer version of Unity is available. Please stay with 2019.3.06f in order to follow along with the steps in this book.

If you're building this game a second time, feel free to use the latest version of Unity. By the way, the method of going through technical books several times is a really good way to really learn the material. The best way: write the book, and then go through it several times.

**<Step 2>** In Assets, you have a single folder, Scenes. Add the folders prefabs, sound, art, animations, tilemaps, and scripts.

**<Step 3>** Save and exit.

As you progress with this project, other folders will be added, so this is just a way to get started. You now have a place to store the assets for this game. Your development plan is to create some assets first before you make the game playable. This approach is somewhat dangerous if the game turns out to be unfun. For this game, you're willing to take that chance because you're not planning on doing truly revolutionary gameplay, just a good-looking, original maze game. Of course, you won't be creating a ton of assets right away. Rather, you'll create just enough to see what the game might look like and to build your first level or two.

## PLAYER CHARACTER: DOTTIMA DOT

First things first: you need a player character. You will begin with some simple sketches on paper. Your goal is a character that looks like Figure 11.1.

The name is Dottima Dot. There's a chance that this name will change, but that's it for now. Eventually, you'll animate the eyes and the mouth to give expression to the character. It fits well into a square, which is really good for a maze game.

**<Step 1>** Draw your own sketch of Dottima Dot on a piece of paper.

**<Step 2>** Take a photo with your phone and email it to yourself on your development system.

**<Step 3>** Store the photo in the art assets folder of DotGame.

FIGURE 11.1   Dottima Dot.

<Step 4> Rename it to DottimaSketch.jpg.

You won't be using this photo file directly in DotGame. This is a reference image that you'll use to draw the real thing in GIMP.

<Step 5> Get a manila folder, write the title "DotGame" on its tab, and put the paper sketch into the folder.

<Step 6> File your physical manila folder in a file cabinet so you can find it in the future.

OK, this isn't really necessary, but you'll be glad that you have a place to store physical assets for your project. If you don't do this, you might regret it later when you can't find your very first sketch for one of your very first games.

<Step 7> Back up your work every day!

It's up to you how you do your backups. Whatever you do, don't rely on our computer to always be there and work. Ask yourself this: What would I do if my computer were broken beyond repair, or lost somehow? If you were to lose more than a day's development in such a situation, you're doing it wrong.

Next, you're going to draw Dottima Dot in GIMP on a 1024×1024 canvas. Why so big? Well, characters sometimes get displayed in very large contexts, such as on a title screen, so it's better to start with high resolution and scale down if needed. Scaling down is always easier and looks better than scaling up. You don't need to follow this book exactly as long as your character fits nicely into a square and is basically a face with eyes and maybe a mouth. The next few steps will show you one way to draw Dottima in GIMP using some of the tools built into GIMP.

<Step 8> Create a new file in GIMP with a transparent background, size 1024×1024, name DottimaFace.xcf. Store the file in the art folder.

<Step 9> Click on the Ellipse Select tool.

<Step 10> Check Fixed in the Tool Options panel.

<Step 11> Draw a large circle in your image, filling most of it.

You will see a faint outline of a circle plus a faint outline of a square surrounding the circle.

<Step 12> Select the Pencil tool and give it a size of 15.

<Step 13> Make the Foreground Color black.

<Step 14> Edit – Stroke Selection.

<Step 15> Select Edit with Paint tool and select the Pencil tool.

<Step 16> Click on Stroke.

You should now see a circle drawn with the Pencil tool, similar to Figure 11.2.

<Step 17> Draw the eyes, nose, and mouth with the mouse and the Pencil tool.

Your face should look similar to Figure 11.3.

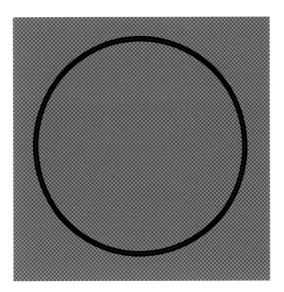

FIGURE 11.2 Circle drawn in GIMP.

FIGURE 11.3 Dottima Face sketched in GIMP.

FIGURE 11.4  Dottima Face in GIMP with filled colors.

**<Step 18>** Choose a light blue color for the face and make it the foreground color.

**<Step 19>** Select the Bucket Fill tool.

**<Step 20>** Check Fill transparent areas and Sample Merged in the Fill tool options. Also, click on FG color fill for the Fill Type.

**<Step 21>** Increase the Threshold to about 55.

**<Step 22>** Click on the face. If it didn't fill, increase the threshold.

**<Step 23>** Fill the eyes with a yellow color.
> Your final version of Dottima Dot, at least for now, is shown in Figure 11.4.
> You'll be doing much more with this character, but for now, you have something to work with.

**<Step 24>** Export to DottimaFace.png in the art folder.

**<Step 25>** Save the project.

## MAZES AND BACKGROUNDS

The mazes in maze games of the 1980s are typically simple grids filled with square tiles. More modern maze games go beyond that limitation, allowing for animated tiles, tiles of varying rectangular sizes, and even sprite-based mazes. In DotGame, you'll start out with simple square tiles, allow for scrolling, but otherwise you'll keep it simple. You might make one or more layers of backgrounds behind the maze. Those backgrounds would be there mostly for decoration.

As you progress in the development of the game, you could experiment with other types of mazes, or even environments that aren't mazes at all, such levels, or mini-games where Dottima flies and shoots rather than exploring mazes. This is all rather vague, but sometimes you need to start building your game before you can get more specific about the design.

## THE STORY

Stories weren't really common in early maze games. A few cutscenes here and there was usually all you got to see. In a typical three-minute arcade game, there really wasn't time to tell a story. As digital games evolved and moved to the home, elaborate stories in games became common and even expected by the players.

Storytelling in games is a specialized skill, much like composing the music or 3D modeling and animation. It is beyond the scope of this book to teach you how to write, draw, or compose. Writing fiction is one of those skills that everyone thinks they can do, but when they sit down to write a novel or screenplay, they find out the hard truth that it's not that easy. That said, you're still going to write the story for your game, just to learn the process and the technical aspects of getting text and speech into your game. You also need to consider localization for different languages and cultures. And, with a little bit of luck and a dash of writing talent, you might just have a good story for this game.

The story for DotGame will be quite simple. Dottima is just a dot in a book, the period at the end of the last chapter. Mysteriously, Dottima is transported to the beginning of the book, so she thought it would be good to move through the book to get to the end where she belongs. It's a strange, original concept, perfect for your purposes.

It can be quite helpful for the design of a game to write out a short synopsis of the story, even a very simple one. You can then think about what the different levels might be, for example, chapters in the book. Some very natural questions arise. What is the book about? Who are the characters in the book? Is it just plain text, or are there illustrations? What's the title of the book? Who is the author?

Before even attempting to answer those questions, you realize that you don't know the first thing about how you're going to tell this story. A simple way is to show some text screens, together with some static illustrations. Telling the story in that form would be appropriate for this game.

It's not too early to think about speech and localization. Given your limited budget, you won't hire voice actors to read the story, especially if you want your game to go for worldwide distribution. Simple text is good enough, and you'll make sure that there's plenty of extra space for translations into other languages.

One weird aspect of this story is that the period doesn't work the same way in Japanese, Chinese, and Arabic, for instance. The story will have to be adapted for those languages. The shape of a period in Japanese, for example, is a small hollow circle, not a filled-in dot. This is a great example of the advantage of thinking about cultural and language differences around the world before even starting to develop your game.

## ENEMIES: ROBOTS AND QUESTION MARKS

It occurs to you that you'd like to have other punctuation marks as NPCs (non-player characters). That would require some additional care regarding languages other than English. As a way to deal with your international audience, you'll include a variety of punctuation marks from different languages, and you'll just stipulate that Dottima originated in an English book.

As you can see, a theme is emerging in this game. This game will be about letters, characters, books, and related objects such as pencils, erasers, pens, paper, etc. To make the game a bit more interesting, you'll add robots to the character mix. Why robots? Well, they're easy to draw and model in Blender. That's the real reason. Now you just have to weave the robots into the story.

## GAME DESIGN DOCUMENT

Game design documents (GDDs) are detailed, living documents that keep track of a game design before and during development. They were very popular up until about 2010, especially for larger game development teams. Unfortunately, it's very difficult to capture a game design in a document before actually playing the game. Keeping track of changes in the GDD is next to impossible when you're busy making the game and changing it by the minute. So, what to do?

A traditional GDD would be on the order of 100 pages for a team of ten or more developers. A good, though somewhat dated description is in this Gamasutra article from 1999 by Tim Ryan: https://www.gamasutra.com/view/feature/3384/the_anatomy_of_a_design_document_.php

Ten years later, Tim Ryan realized that GDDs are being replaced by wikis: https://www.gamasutra.com/view/feature/132483/learning_the_ways_of_the_game_.php

Currently, game development teams tend to use web-based tools with support for mobile devices. So, in short, GDDs are obsolete for medium to large projects. For the purposes of DotGame, a small game where you're the only developer, you'll stick with a text-based GDD of a page or two. It's definitely a good idea to write down the main concept and the scope of the project. You should periodically read that document and update it. Here is the text of your GDD for DotGame:

> DotGame is a maze game inspired by the popular arcade maze games of the 1980s. The main character, Dottima Dot, is the period from a book comes to life in a series of maze-like levels. Each level poses new challenges for Dottima as she tries to find her way back to the book she came from. Along the way, she encounters doors with locks and keys, question marks, semicolons, and evil robots just to name a few of the possible enemies.
>
> This is a 2D Unity game using scrolling tiles for the mazes and animated sprites for the characters. There are occasional cutscenes and text screens to tell the story. The text screens will be translated to several languages, but at first, only English is supported. There will be some kind of scoring system similar to three stars per level and an economy with coins and pencils as resources. The economy and scoring systems are closer to what's found in modern match-three games rather than the simple single score found in 80s arcade games.
>
> The development plan is to first make a single level featuring Dottima moving from a start position to an exit without enemy interference. Then add an enemy or two, scoring, sound, and music. Then build a title screen and start to tell the story using a text screen. Additional levels, at least ten, will be built after that. New levels, environments, and characters are gradually introduced using the story screens. Add cutscenes where appropriate every few levels. Develop an ending with credits.
>
> The game is aimed for release on PC and Mac using Unity, with possible mobile versions in the future.

As you can see, this is a far cry from a detailed GDD of 100 pages, but some of the main points are covered. You'll be pleasantly surprised if the final game resembles your initial thoughts put forth in this document. This isn't a contract but rather a launchpad.

<**Step 1**> Create a Docs folder in assets.

    You'll store game-related documents in this folder.

<**Step 2**> Find the GDD at franzlanzinger.com, copy it into a text file and save it in your Docs folder with the name DotGameGDD_Ver1.txt.

    At franzlanzinger.com, you'll find other helpful resources for this book.

    In order to preserve the history of development of the game, you plan to update this document periodically (period, get it?) and save the updated version using a new name, such as DotGameGDD_Ver2.txt.

# Building the Level 1 Maze

Tᴴɪs ᴄʜᴀᴘᴛᴇʀ ᴄᴏᴠᴇʀs the creation of the maze for Level 1 of DotGame. You'll start by drawing tiles in GIMP, followed by importing them into the Unity project for DotGame. You'll then test them by building a maze using your tiles and a placeholder character around in the maze. You won't have real gameplay yet. Instead, you'll develop the initial look and feel of the game.

## USING GIMP TO MAKE TILES FOR LEVEL 1

You learned how to make tiles in the previous chapter. Now you'll put this knowledge to use by creating the tiles for a simple maze for Level 1. This isn't necessarily going to be the first level in the final game but just a simple level to get you started.

Your theme, in general, is books, words, libraries, and bookstores. After searching online for some inspiration, you decided that you can make some tiles out of book spines. Book spines aren't square, however, so you'll make your tiles so that a single book spine will be composed of three or four square tiles arranged next to each other.

Your first order of business is to find an image of a book spine that you can use. This is easier said than done because you don't want to pay for this image. In order to avoid a copyright violation, you'll want the book to be in the public domain as well as the image of the book. Even if you purchase a physical book that doesn't give you the right to take a photo of it and use it in your game.

Fortunately, the internet has free images of old book spines.

<Step 1> Go to pixabay.com and search for "books spine leather old".

<Step 2> Pick the image with seven green books by Karl May and download the 1920 × 1284 version.

Figure 12.1 shows this image.

You could download the even larger version, but 1920 × 1284 is plenty detailed enough for your purposes. Pixabay images are free to use for commercial or other purposes, so you're OK to use this image. It's a good policy to

FIGURE 12.1    Image of seven book spines, downloaded from Pixabay.

always check ownership of anything you copy from the internet before using it in your game, even if you intend to replace or heavily modify the asset.

By the way, Karl May lived until 1912, so there's likely no copyright problem with this image of the spines of those books. The photographer has released the image using a CC0 license. You are going to trust that license and use the image. The contents of Karl May's books are all in the public domain because of their age. That doesn't really matter though because you're not using the text of the books, just the graphics from the spines. And, since you're probably curious, Karl May was a best-selling German author of adventure novels set in the Old American West and other exotic locations.

**<Step 3>**  Copy the image in your Assets/art folder. The name is likely spine-527991_1920. jpg.

Your plan is to cut out some of those book spines, make them into 32 × 128 strips, and colorize them so they have different colors. You'll also make horizontal versions to give you more flexibility when drawing the mazes.

**<Step 4>**  Load the book spine image into GIMP.

**<Step 5>**  Use the Rectangle Select tool to select one of the books.

**<Step 6>**  Edit – Copy.

**<Step 7>**  Edit – Paste As – New Image.

Figure 12.2 shows GIMP displaying the new image.

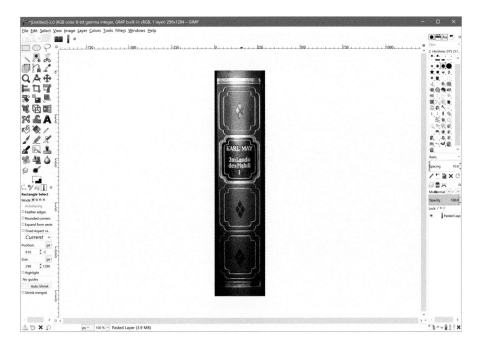

FIGURE 12.2    GIMP displaying the cut-out book spine.

**<Step 8>** Image – Scale Image…

**<Step 9>** Change the units to Pixels (px) if necessary.

**<Step 10>** Click on the chain to break it.

**<Step 11>** Enter Width: 128 Height: 512.
  To do this you needed to click on the chain icon to allow for the slight change in aspect ratio. The book will now look smaller and stretched horizontally by a little bit. You did this change in aspect ratio to get powers of two for the dimensions. By default, the chain is intact, which means that the original aspect ratio is preserved when you change dimensions.

**<Step 12>** Verify that you are scaling to $128 \times 512$ pixels, then click on Scale.

**<Step 13>** File – Export As book1.png.

**<Step 14>** Colors – Hue Saturation.

**<Step 15>** Change the Hue to about 80. Click on OK.
  The book is now a dark blue.

**<Step 16>** File – Export As book2.png.

**<Step 17>** Using different hues, repeat Steps 14–16 two times to get book3.png and book4.png.
  You now have four book images with different hues.

You're also going to need rotated versions of these four books, so you'll do that in GIMP as follows.

**<Step 18>** Load book1.png into GIMP.

**<Step 19>** Image – Transform – Rotate 90 degrees counter-clockwise.

**<Step 20>** Export as book1r.png.

**<Step 21>** Repeat Steps 18–20 for books 2–4.

You now have eight sprites of book spines, ready to be turned into tiles.

In the next section, you'll import these sprites into Unity and arrange them into a small maze.

## MAZE LAYOUT IN UNITY

**<Step 1>** Open the DotGame project in Unity.

Your goal is to make a maze where the walls look like spines of books. In the art folder of the Assets panel, you should see, among other things, the eight book spines that you created in the previous section using GIMP.

**<Step 2>** Select book1 in the art folder.

In the Inspector panel, you should see the book1 Import Settings.

**<Step 3>** In the Inspector, change the Sprite Mode for book1 to Multiple and click on Apply.

**<Step 4>** Click on the Sprite Editor button.

**<Step 5>** Change the Slice Type to Grid by Cell Size.

**<Step 6>** Change the Cell Size to 128 by 128.

**<Step 7>** Click on the Slice button.

Your book now consists of four 128 × 128 tiles, stacked vertically.

**<Step 8>** Apply and Exit the Sprite Editor.

The book1 asset now has a small arrow associated with it.

**<Step 9>** Click on the arrow for book1 and verify that you now have four slices named book1_0, book1_1, book1_2, and book1_3.

These slices don't exist as separate png files. Rather, they are kept track of internally by Unity.

**<Step 10>** Repeat Steps 3–9 for the other seven books. Then save your work.

This is fairly straightforward, but take care to do all the steps exactly as described above. Unity will remember the Slice settings, so this can go pretty quickly. You are now ready to create your Tile Palette for painting your maze.

**<Step 11>** GameObject – 2D Object – Tilemap.

**\<Step 12\>** Select Grid in the Hierarchy. In the Inspector, rename the new object from "Grid" to "Maze1 Grid".

**\<Step 13\>** Window – 2D – Tile Palette.

**\<Step 14\>** Create New Palette. Name this Tile Palette BooksPalette and create a folder with the same name when prompted.

**\<Step 15\>** Drag the eight books into the Tile Palette one at a time. Use the BooksPalette folder when prompted for a folder. Use a layout similar to Figure 12.3.

It's up to you how you lay out this Tile Palette. It won't be displayed directly in the game, but it's just a tool to help you create your levels.

**\<Step 16\>** In the Tile Palette, select the Paintbrush tool.

This is the third tool from the left with the designation "Paint with active brush (B)".

**\<Step 17\>** Use the mouse to select the four tiles that make up the vertical green book.

**\<Step 18\>** Select Maze1 Grid in the Hierarchy panel, hover the mouse over the Scene panel, and type f to focus on the grid.

**\<Step 19\>** Scroll the mouse wheel to zoom in on the central portion of the grid.

**\<Step 20\>** Click the left mouse button to draw the green vertical book into the grid, similar to Figure 12.4.

FIGURE 12.3   Tile Palette containing eight book spines.

FIGURE 12.4   Green vertical book in Maze1 Grid.

As you can see, the book doesn't align with the grid lines. The following step fixes this.

**<Step 21>** In the Inspector, you should still display the properties Maze1 Grid. If not, click on that game object in the Hierarchy. In the Inspector, change the Cell Size X and Y to 1.28.

The book now aligns perfectly with the grid lines. The 1.28 adjustment is necessary because the tiles are 128 × 128 pixels, and the import setting for the tile is set to 100 pixels per unit.

It's time to think about the screen aspect ratio of your game. This depends somewhat on your target game system. These days, most modern desktop computers use horizontal monitors with an aspect ratio of 16 × 10 or 16 × 9. A typical resolution is 1920 × 1080, which corresponds to a 16 × 9 aspect ratio. This is also the resolution of 1080p and 1080i television screens. So, for now, you're going to select a 16 × 9 aspect ratio. This also covers 4K monitors that have 3840 × 2160 resolution.

**<Step 22>** Select the Game panel and change the aspect ratio to 16 × 9.

The Game panel should look like Figure 12.5.

**<Step 23>** Select the Scene panel and draw a maze similar to Figure 12.6.

**<Step 24>** Look at the Maze in the Game panel as well.

You now have a pretty good initial maze. It's not very complex, but it will let you test out moving your character around. Notice that you left a gap in

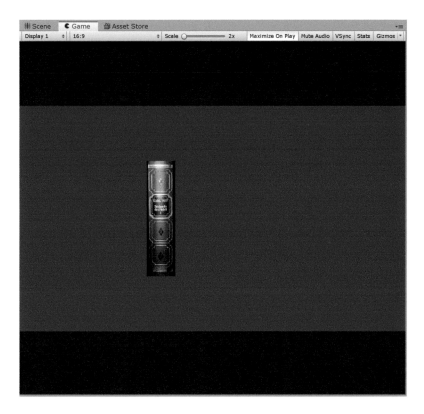

FIGURE 12.5    16 × 9 aspect ratio in the Game panel.

FIGURE 12.6    Maze 1 in the Scene panel.

the upper right corner. You also have a natural starting point in the lower left corner.

Graphically, it looks pretty good except for the blue background. The next step does a quick fix.

**<Step 25>** Select the Main Camera object in the Hierarchy.

**<Step 26>** In the Inspector, change the background color to a pale yellow.

The pale yellow goes well with the book spine colors. It's certainly better than the default blue color. Next, you're going to test what things look like when you actually run the game.

**<Step 27>** Play the game inside Unity.

It's not much of a game just yet. You see the maze and that's it. Your next goal will be to have the main character (that's Dottima Dot) move through the maze from its starting point until it gets to the exit. This still won't be a game, but you're following the tried and true method of taking small steps during development. Before you bring in Dottima, there's just one more thing to do: building the project. You should periodically build your projects during development, even though it's theoretically unnecessary. It's helpful to see how your players will experience that game, and the only way to do that is to do a build.

**<Step 28>** File – Build and Run. Select a new folder called Binaries as your location.

Again, the game just sits there and shows the maze. Exiting this game is easiest by closing the window using your operating system. In Windows, that's Ctrl+Alt+Del and then close the task with the name DotGame. On a Mac, it's <command> <option> <esc>. You're going to have to add an easier way to leave your game via a menu.

You've reached a good stopping point, so do this:

**<Step 29>** Save the project and the scene.

This is as good a time as any to take a side trip in your development journey and get started with source control. You've gone long enough without source control, so the next chapter will get you started with that. After that you'll take another side trip and add menus in order to control your screen resolution.

# Source Control

I N THIS CHAPTER, you'll learn how to use source control for your Unity projects. Source control is an important technology that allows developers to keep track of their development history, back up their work, and collaborate effectively. Source control is sometimes called revision control or version control. A source control system stores a history of changes that occurred during development, thus allowing developers to go back in time before things went awry, or when an experiment didn't work. Source control also allows developers to merge changes when two or more of them worked on the same project or even the same files.

For DotGame, you will be the only developer, so you're mainly interested in the change tracking features of source control. You will use source control as a convenient way to back up your work online. If you're developing for both PC and Mac, source control can give you a way to organize your PC and Mac versions on your two systems. You'll be using Sourcetree, Git, and BitBucket for your source control software and repository storage. The main reason for these choices is that they work well for relatively small projects and are completely free and private for up to five users. As you become more experienced, you might encounter other source control systems, but they all work more or less the same way.

## INSTALLING SOURCETREE, GIT, AND BITBUCKET

Git will be the source control software running on your system. It is free and open source. Sourcetree is a free Windows and Mac client for Git. Sourcetree makes using Git somewhat easier, though strictly speaking it's not necessary. As a beginner, you'll find that Sourcetree also makes learning Git easier. Bitbucket is an online service by Atlassian, a software company based in Sydney, Australia, with offices worldwide and 150,000 customers. Bitbucket is free to use for teams of five or fewer users. Bitbucket will allow you to store your source code repositories online. To get started, you will need to install Sourcetree, which automatically installs Git for you, and then create a Bitbucket account. A popular alternative to Bitbucket is GitHub which is free to use for up to three users as of January 2020. The terms of use for Bitbucket and GitHub (or any other online service for

that matter), are subject to change, so be sure to check out the respective websites for the current details and limitations.

<Step 1> Go to sourcetreeapp.com and follow the instructions to install Sourcetree and Git on your computer.

<Step 2> Enter your Author name and Author email address.

This information is entered for documentation purposes to help other people on your team identify who is responsible for changes in your project.

<Step 3> Go to bitbucket.com and create an account.

Make a note of your chosen username and password.

You are now set up to start using Sourcetree, Git, and Bitbucket.

## SOURCE CONTROL WITH SOURCETREE AND GIT

Now that you have installed Sourcetree and Git and created a Bitbucket account, you'll test out the very basic features of Sourcetree. In this section, you will only work locally, so Bitbucket won't be used. First, you simply create a folder on your computer and create a small text file in that folder.

<Step 1> On your desktop, create a folder and call it GitTestFolder.

You can put your test folder anywhere on your system, but you're putting it on the desktop for easy reference.

<Step 2> Create a text file in this folder and call it ReadMe.txt.

<Step 3> Put the following text into ReadMe.txt:

This is a test folder to try out Sourcetree and Git.

<Step 4> Run Sourcetree.

You should have a Sourcetree icon on your desktop. Click on that to run Sourcetree.

<Step 5> File – Clone/New.

<Step 6> Click on Create.

<Step 7> Browse and find GitTestFolder on the Desktop.

You should see C:\Users\user\Desktop\GitTestFolder as the location of the repository. The name of the repository is GitTestFolder. Choose Git, not Mercurial. Leave the Create Repository on Account unchecked.

<Step 8> Click on the big Create button at the bottom. You'll get a pop-up warning that the GitTestFolder exists already. Click on Yes.

After a short wait, you'll have the repository created. If you look at the GitTestFolder contents using your operating system, you may see the hidden

.git subfolder. If it's not visible, your system settings may not be configured to show hidden files and folders.

<Step 9>  Search for "Show hidden files" in the Windows search box. Turn on this setting if it's not set already. On a Mac, press Command+Shift+Dot to toggle display of hidden files.

As a software developer, you often want to see hidden files and folders. After all, they're there, and you may need to look at them in the course of development. Of course, hidden files are hidden for a reason! The danger is that if you should happen to accidentally delete or alter the .git folder, for instance, you would then break the repository, so proceed with extra caution.

<Step 10>  In Sourcetree, select File Status.

<Step 11>  Above the Staged Files panel, there is a drop-down menu. Choose All in the Show Only section.

The drop-down menu now has the label "All files, sorted by file status". The Staged files panel is empty and the Unstaged files panel has the ReadMe. txt file in it.

<Step 12>  Click on Stage All.

The ReadMe.txt file now appears in the Staged files section. You would think that it would now disappear in the Unstaged files panel, but it's still there.

<Step 13>  In the commit text box at the bottom, type "Initial commit, ReadMe.txt".

You are about to commit your new file, so before you do that it is required that you describe your commit. Git doesn't care what you write, just that you write something. It's a very good idea to write descriptive commit messages because you'll be dealing with dozens or even thousands of commits, so you need to describe them to make sense of it all in the future.

<Step 14>  Press the Commit button.

<Step 15>  Click on the master branch in the BRANCHES section.

You now see the master branch with its single node. As you perform additional commits, you will add more nodes.

Next, you'll edit the ReadMe file and create another file. Then you'll commit the changes.

<Step 16>  Edit the ReadMe file and add a second line with the text "Second line in ReadMe file".

<Step 17>  Create the file testfile.txt with the line "test file line 1" in the file.

<Step 18>  In Sourcetree, click on File Status.

You now see an orange icon next to ReadMe.txt, indicating that it's been changed, and a purple question mark next to the new testfile.

**<Step 19>** Stage All.

**<Step 20>** Type your commit message: Add testfile.txt, modify readme

Notice that the commit message uses "Add" rather than "Added". This is the conventional way of writing commit messages. Another convention is to not have a period at the end if it's just a one-liner.

**<Step 21>** Commit.

You now have green checkmarks next to the files in the Unstaged files panel.

**<Step 22>** Click on History.

You could also have just clicked on the master branch to get to this display. You now see your master branch with two nodes, the initial commit and the node that you just added with your latest commit.

Now, you're finally going to see why source control is useful.

**<Step 23>** Double-click on the Initial Commit node. Click on OK.

You just destroyed the changes in the latest commit and are back to where you were after the initial commit. Take a look in the folder to verify this. The file "testfile.txt" is gone, and ReadMe.txt has its original contents.

**<Step 24>** Double-click on the top node.

You just got back the second commit. The file "testfile.txt" is back, and the ReadMe file is restored to two lines.

From now on you will periodically stage and commit your projects so that you can go back in time to any of the commits. This can really be helpful when you break your code badly enough that you don't know how to undo the changes. This *will* happen to you, so source control is an essential tool to make your life as a game developer much easier.

Of course, you can have subfolders in your project.

**<Step 25>** Create a subfolder named Assets.

**<Step 26>** Create an image with the name testimage.bmp in Assets.

You can use GIMP for this, for example.

**<Step 27>** Stage all and commit.

**<Step 28>** Revert to an earlier version, check that the image is gone, then bring it back.

It helps to know that binary files such as images can be problematic when under source control. If you put large binary files under source control, and if you then make a lot of changes to these files, the repository can become unwieldy and possibly too large. The way to deal with this problem is to use Git Large File Storage (LFS). You will learn how to set that up later on when your files become large enough for this to matter.

You have just learned the very basics of source control with Sourcetree and Git. There is much more to learn about this, but you know enough to use it. In the next section, you'll learn how to use a remote repository hosted by Bitbucket.

## REPOSITORIES ON BITBUCKET

Using Sourcetree only locally is a perfectly fine way to develop a solo project. Even then, it can be beneficial to back up your repository (also called *repo* for short) elsewhere. In the unlikely event that your local storage fails, you can get your project back by *cloning* your repo to another system.

You will now back up your GitTestFolder project to Bitbucket.

<Step 1> Go to bitbucket.com in your browser, and log in.

You may get logged in automatically. If that is so, make sure that you still know your username and password, or have a way to find them.

<Step 2> Click on the plus icon, the create icon.

<Step 3> Create a new repository with the name GitTestFolder, Access level private, no README, Version control Git.

Don't forget to remove the README file. You need a blank repo without the README file for the Push step to work.

<Step 4> Click on Create repository.

<Step 5> In Sourcetree, click on Remote then Settings on the popup.

This will take you to the Repository Settings dialog.

<Step 6> Click on Add.

<Step 7> In the Remote Details popup, check Default remote. This chooses origin as the name.

<Step 8> Copy and paste the URL from bitbucket to URL/Path.

The URL can be found in the GitTestFolder panel of bitbucket near the top, after git clone.

<Step 9> In Remote Account, select your own account rather than the Generic Account.

<Step 10> Click on OK.

If all that worked, you are now ready to do a Push from your local repo to the remote repo at bitbucket.org.

<Step 11> Click on Push. Check master, then click on Push at the bottom.

All this may seem a bit overwhelming at first, but as you get used to it, it'll become fairly easy.

<Step 12> Click on Remote.

You should now be looking at your repo stored safely at bitbucket.org in your browser window.

<Step 13> Try to clone the repo to another location.

You can do this on another system with Sourcetree installed and internet access, or the same system.

You're done trying out the basics of source control with Sourcetree, Git, and Bitbucket. Next, you'll see if you can get this to work using a Unity project. Unity projects have more files, and Unity needs to be configured correctly, but other than that you're ready to dive in.

## USING SOURCETREE WITH UNITY

Now that you know how to use the basics of source control using Sourcetree and Bitbucket, you'll next wish to apply this knowledge to your Unity projects. First, you'll create a small test project in Unity.

**<Step 1>** Open Unity Hub.

**<Step 2>** Click on New, 2D, name UnityGitTest in location of your choice.

**<Step 3>** Click on CREATE.

**<Step 4>** Assets – Create – Sprites – Hexagon.

**<Step 5>** Drag the Hexagon from the Assets folder to the Scene panel.

**<Step 6>** Give it an orange color.
OK, that's enough. You just created something very simple, perfect for testing source control.

**<Step 7>** Edit – Project Settings… – Editor.

**<Step 8>** Version Control Mode: Visible Meta Files.

**<Step 9>** Asset Serialization: Force Text.

**<Step 10>** Save and exit Unity.
You're now ready to put this project under version control.

**<Step 11>** In Bitbucket, create a repository with name UnityGitTest, private, no README, type Git.

**<Step 12>** Create repo in Sourcetree for the test project.
You'll see that there are a lot of unstaged files. Most of those files don't need to be under source control. The simple way to fix this is to add a special .gitignore file.

**<Step 13>** Find a recent .gitignore file online and place it to the top level of your project file before staging anything.
You can also type it into a text editor. Here is the .gitignore file recommended by Github.

```
# This .gitignore file should be placed at the root of your Unity project directory
#
#from https://github.com/github/gitignore/blob/master/Unity.gitignore
#
/[Ll]ibrary/
```

```
/[Tt]emp/
/[Oo]bj/
/[Bb]uild/
/[Bb]uilds/
/[Ll]ogs/
/[Mm]emoryCaptures/

# Never ignore Asset meta data
![Aa]ssets/**/*.meta

# Uncomment this line if you wish to ignore the asset store tools plugin
# /[Aa]ssets/AssetStoreTools*

# Autogenerated Jetbrains Rider plugin
[Aa]ssets/Plugins/Editor/JetBrains*

# Visual Studio cache directory
.vs/

# Gradle cache directory
.gradle/

# Autogenerated VS/MD/Consulo solution and project files
ExportedObj/
.consulo/
*.csproj
*.unityproj
*.sln
*.suo
*.tmp
*.user
*.userprefs
*.pidb
*.booproj
*.svd
*.pdb
*.mdb
*.opendb
*.VC.db

# Unity3D generated meta files
*.pidb.meta
*.pdb.meta
*.mdb.meta

# Unity3D generated file on crash reports
sysinfo.txt

# Builds
*.apk
*.unitypackage

# Crashlytics generated file
crashlytics-build.properties
```

You may wish to first create this file with the name gitignore.txt, and then rename it to .gitignore. If you did this correctly, you should have about 28 unstaged files.

**\<Step 14\>** Stage All. Then Commit with "initial commit" message.

**\<Step 15\>** Look at the project and verify that it has a .git folder.

**\<Step 16\>** Set up the Remote as you did in the previous section, and then Push.

**\<Step 17\>** Verify that bitbucket has a populated repository with the name UnityGitTest.

**\<Step 18\>** Clone this repo to another location and test it there.

Finally, it's time to test what happens when you make changes to your project.

**\<Step 19\>** In Unity, move the hexagon and change its color.

**\<Step 20\>** Save and exit Unity.

In Sourcetree, you'll see that just one file changed, SampleScene.unity.

**\<Step 21\>** In Sourcetree stage all, commit, and push.

**\<Step 22\>** In Sourcetree, check out the initial commit.

**\<Step 23\>** Open Unity and load the project.

You should see the hexagon in its original position and with its original color.

**\<Step 24\>** Check out the latest commit and test it in Unity.

That's it. It's not particularly easy to set up, but it's worth the effort except maybe for small experimental projects.

One more note: Git allows you to work locally when you don't have an internet connection. You can do everything except push and pull. When you have an internet connection again in the future, you can update your remote repo by doing pushes of the local repos.

# Menus

THIS CHAPTER COVERS THE CREATION OF MENUS using the Unity UI system. You will create a main menu and an options menu. This will allow you to control the screen resolution of your game, and to select fullscreen versus windowed mode. Before all that you'll set up source control for your game.

## SOURCE CONTROL SETUP

Before starting with menus, you'll set up your game with source control as you just learned in the previous chapter. This section is optional, so if you don't wish to do source control on this project, or if you want to delay setting this up until later, that's OK.

<Step 1> Open the DotGame project in Unity.

<Step 2> Edit – Project Settings… – Editor.

<Step 3> Version Control Mode: Visible Meta Files.
This is likely set up already, but it's good to check for this.

<Step 4> Asset Serialization Mode: Force Text.
If this is set up already, you can just leave it.

<Step 5> Save and exit Unity.

<Step 6> Log into Bitbucket as you did in the previous chapter.

<Step 7> Create a repository with name DotGame, private, no README, type Git.

<Step 8> Copy the .gitignore file from the test project of the previous chapter.

<Step 9> Stage All. Then Commit with "initial commit" message.

<Step 10> Look at the project in your operating system and check that you have a .git folder.

<Step 11> Set up the Remote as described in the previous chapter, and then Push.

**<Step 12>** Verify that Bitbucket has a populated repository with the name DotGame.

It would now be a good idea to clone this repository at another location on your system or even another system such as your laptop and test it there. Be sure to not include your builds in your repository. The folder "Builds" is listed in the .gitignore file, so any builds in that folder are excluded.

You're now ready to continue development on your game. In the future, you would likely set up source control somewhat earlier in your project development.

## MAIN MENU LAYOUT

The goal in this section is to create the layout for the main menu scene. Eventually, DotGame will start with a splash screen and then go into the main menu scene. The main menu will look like Figure 14.1.

This is as simple as it gets, just three buttons. The "Play DotGame" button simply starts the game. The "Settings" button moves the user to the Settings menu. The Exit button quits the application. You're going to spend some effort to make this menu look good.

Unity has two competing user interface systems, the standard UI system and TextMeshPro. You will be using the TextMeshPro system in this project because it has features that make your text and the associated menus look quite a bit better than the ordinary built-in UI. You'll start by making a new scene for the menus.

**<Step 1>** Open the DotGame project and select the Assets/Scenes panel.

**<Step 2>** In the Project panel, click on +, select Scene with name Menus, and change the name from New Scene to Menus.

**<Step 3a>** Double-click on Menus to select it.

**<Step 3b>** Select the Scene panel.

Your Scene panel should be empty.

**<Step 4>** Hierarchy – + – UI – Panel.

FIGURE 14.1   MainMenu for DotGame.

FIGURE 14.2  Menus Canvas and Panel.

This creates a Canvas and below it in the Hierarchy the Panel as shown in Figure 14.2.

Next, you will get a background image for the menu scenes. A single background image is OK for now.

**<Step 5>** Go to pixabay.com and search for "book blurred". Most anyof the possible images would work. Choose one that you like and download it into the Assets/art folder.

This book uses the 1920×1278 image of a single book with a blurred, lightly colored tan background. The name is blur-1283865_1920.jpg. You want the players to look at the superimposed menu text and not get distracted by the background image. You've chosen a simple background image with a color palette of mainly light brown colors.

**<Step 6a>** Drag the image from the Assets/art folder into the Source Image slot of the Inspector.

Be sure that the Panel is selected before you do this. You're not seeing the entire panel, so do this:

**<Step 6b>** Focus on the Panel game object in the Scene.

**<Step 6c>** Zoom in to enlarge it somewhat with the scroll wheel.

Your Scene panel should look like Figure 14.3.

You notice that the image is washed out. You don't want that, so the next step fixes that.

**<Step 7>** Select the Color below the Source Image slot in the Inspector.

You should see a color dialog.

**<Step 8>** Drag the Alpha channel to the maximum of 255.

As you drag the Alpha channel slider, notice the following: The image is getting brighter. Also, the Color slot in the Inspector has a slider as well, and it is changing. That slider is there to show the current alpha value associated with the color, but it can't be dragged with the mouse.

**<Step 9>** Close the color dialog.

You now have a reasonable background for your menu.

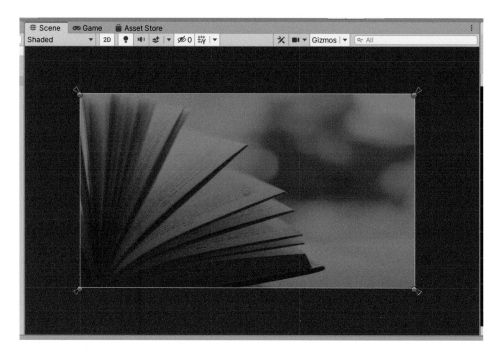

FIGURE 14.3    Washed out background for menu.

**<Step 10>**    Check the "Preserve Aspect" box in the Inspector. Then uncheck it.

The effect of the Aspect box is minor, so you're going to leave it alone for now. Dealing with aspect ratios can be very tricky in 2D games on computer monitors, TVs, phones, and tablets because of the wide variety of available resolutions and aspect ratios. In this case, you are stretching the original photo a bit, which is OK for the purpose of providing a backdrop for your menus.

**<Step 11>**    Rename the Panel to Background.

It is a good habit to rename generic objects with more meaningful names.

**<Step 12>**    Hierarchy – + – UI – Text – TextMeshPro.

If this is the first time that you're accessing TextMeshPro, which is likely, then you'll get a pop-up dialog as shown in Figure 14.4.

Within that pop-up, click on the "Import TMP Essentials" to enable TMP. When that import is completed, you can close the pop-up. There is no need to import the TMP Examples and Extras package at this time.

**<Step 13>**    Change the Position in the Inspector to (0, 0, 0).

This last step may not be necessary depending on your previous usage of Unity.

You should see a small, white text object with the text "New Text" near the center of the Canvas. The object in the Hierarchy has the name "Text (TMP)", which is a bit strange. The TMP is a reminder that this is a TextMeshPro object. We'll rename this a bit later in this section.

FIGURE 14.4    TextMeshPro (TMP) first-time user dialog.

<Step 14>    Select the Rect tool from the tool bar, the fifth icon from the left.
             You may have this selected already, in which case, never mind.

<Step 15>    Change the Font Size to 72.
             This makes the text too large, so you'll adjust the bounding box as follows.

<Step 16>    Hover the mouse over the lower right corner of the bounding box.

<Step 17>    Hold down the left mouse button, then press and hold Alt, then scale the box to make it large enough for the text to be contained within the box.

<Step 18>    In the Inspector, change the Alignment to Center horizontally and Middle vertically.

<Step 19>    Change the text to "PLAY DOTGAME".
             You may need to change the containing box again so that this somewhat longer text fits. Be sure to use the Alt key to keep the text box centered correctly.

<Step 20>    Change the Font Style to B, which stands for Bold.
             Since you're here, it'll be fun to change some of the other text settings.

<Step 21>    In the Outline section, click on – Click to Expand –

<Step 22>    Enable, if necessary, and choose a yellow color for the Outline, Thickness of 0.3.

<Step 23>    In the Underlay section, click on – Click to Expand –

<Step 24>    Again, enable if necessary. Then set Offset X to 1, Offset Y to −1, Softness to 0.3.
             This is, of course, just one of the many ways you can adjust the TextMeshPro settings. As you made these changes to the settings, you were able to watch the effects in the Scene panel. Your menu looks like Figure 14.5.
             So far you have a text box which won't do anything, which is not what you want. You will create a Button and then use this text for it.

FIGURE 14.5    Yellow text for the main menu.

**<Step 25>**  Select the Canvas in the Hierarchy.

**<Step 26>**  In the Hierarchy, do + – UI – Button – TextMeshPro.

**<Step 27>**  In the Inspector, change the position to (0, 0, 0) if necessary.

**<Step 28>**  Select the Move tool.

**<Step 29>**  Drag the Button using the green up arrow to the top section of the Canvas.
Your Scene panel should look like Figure 14.6.

**<Step 30>**  Select the Rect tool.

**<Step 31>**  Scale the white rectangle to be large enough for the PLAY DOTGAME text.
Your Scene panel should now look like Figure 14.7.

**<Step 32>**  Uncheck Image in the Inspector.
This makes the white background disappear, but you still have the surrounding box for the button.

**<Step 33>**  Expand the Button object in the Hierarchy.
You now see that there is a Text object below the Button object. This is where the "Button" text resides. You will replace this text with the PLAY DOTGAME text as follows:

**<Step 34>**  Select the Text (TMP) object below the Button object in the Hierarchy.

**<Step 35>**  Right-click and delete this object.

FIGURE 14.6    Scene panel while creating a button.

FIGURE 14.7    Scene panel with large white button.

FIGURE 14.8 Play button in the Hierarchy.

**<Step 36>** Rename the Button object to "PlayButton".

**<Step 37>** Drag the Text (TMP) object on top of the PlayButton in the Hierarchy.
The Hierarchy should now look like Figure 14.8.

**<Step 38>** Select the Text (TMP) object in the Hierarchy.

**<Step 39>** In the Inspector, look for the Rect Transform section. Then find the funny looking icon below it with the horizontal and vertical text "middle" and "center". This is the anchor preset icon.

**<Step 40>** Click on the anchor preset icon, hold down Alt, and select the bottom right box.
This last step magically moves the PLAY DOTGAME text into the PlayButton text box and centers it.

**<Step 41>** Select the PlayButton.

**<Step 42>** Enable Image in the Inspector.

**<Step 43>** Change the Color to Black with an Alpha of 255.
The background color for the PlayButton now appears as a solid black.
The following settings involve alpha values. It's OK if your values differ slightly. The alpha ranges from 0 to 255.

**<Step 44>** In the Button section in the Inspector, change the normal color to white with 0 alpha.

**<Step 45>** For the Highlighted Color, select white with an alpha of 75.

**<Step 46>** For the Pressed Color, a light gray with alpha of 75.

**<Step 47>** For the Selected Color, white with alpha of about 128.
Finally, you can now test this out!

**<Step 48>** Press the Play icon and test the button. You should be able to highlight it with a light gray color, and select it with a darker gray color. You can also unselect it by clicking outside of the PLAY DOTGAME box.

So far all you did was to create the button, but it doesn't actually play the game yet. You'll do that later. Next, you'll use this button as a starting point for the other two buttons on this screen.

**<Step 49>** Duplicate the PlayButton by typing ctrl-d with the PlayButton selected.

The Hierarchy now shows two play buttons, one with a trailing (1) in the name. That's the new one and it's automatically selected.

**<Step 50>** Using the Move tool, move the new PlayButton to the center of the screen.

In order to keep the alignment, you use the green vertical arrow.

**<Step 51>** Rename the new button to "SettingsButton" and change the text for it to "SETTINGS".

**<Step 52>** Resize the button to better fit the new text. Be sure to select the button, not the text when you do this.

**<Step 53>** Make a QuitButton in a similar way.

**<Step 54>** Test your new buttons.

You do this by pressing the Play button and clicking on the buttons. Notice that you can use the arrow keys on your keyboard to move the selection up and down.

The menu should look like Figure 14.9.

**<Step 55>** Save the project.

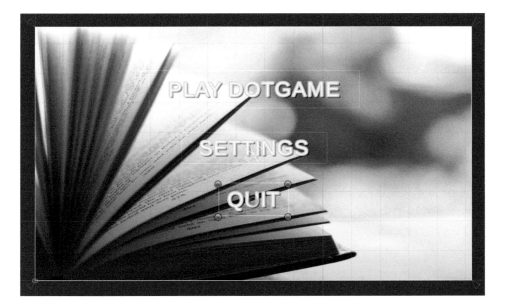

FIGURE 14.9   MainMenu.

You are now in the habit of saving your work often. You'll check your work into source control less frequently. When the two menus are operational, that will be a good time to do that.

You just finished creating the look and feel of the MainMenu. Next, you'll do the same for the Settings menu.

## SETTINGS MENU LAYOUT

The Settings menu is also laid out in three sections. The top has a title, the middle has a resolution dropdown and a FULLSCREEN checkbox side by side, and at the bottom, you have a back button that will take the player back to the main menu. In this section, you will create the UI elements of this menu without actually making them work. You might think that you now need to create a new scene for this menu, but it turns out to be a little easier to stay within the same scene and simply enable and disable the menus as needed.

<Step 1> In the Hierarchy, select the Canvas and do + – Create Empty Child.

<Step 2> Use the Rect tool to resize it with the Alt key to encompass the three buttons.
The Alt key is used to keep everything centered. Remember to click the left mouse button first before pressing the Alt key.

<Step 3> Rename the GameObject to MainMenu.
Your Scene panel should look like Figure 14.10.

<Step 4> Select the three buttons and move them under the MainMenu object.
You do this by selecting the three buttons while holding down Ctrl, then dragging the three selected buttons on top of the MainMenu in the Hierarchy. Your Hierarchy should now look like Figure 14.11.

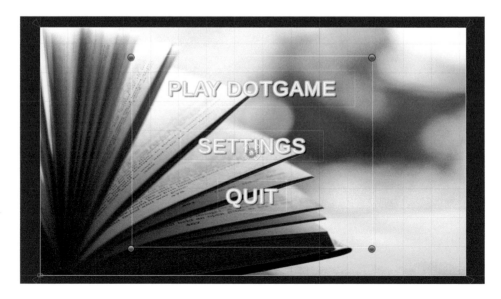

FIGURE 14.10 MainMenu layout.

FIGURE 14.11   Hierarchy for MainMenu.

**<Step 5>** Duplicate the MainMenu object and rename the duplicate object to SettingsMenu.

You're now going to start changing the SettingsMenu to gradually transform it to match the description at the beginning of this section. First, you'll temporarily disable the MainMenu.

**<Step 6>** Select the MainMenu object and disable it in the Inspector.

You do this, of course, but unchecking the checkmark next to the MainMenu title near the top of the Inspector. Notice that the Hierarchy still has the MainMenu, but it is displayed with a gray font, rather than a black one.

**<Step 7>** Select the SettingsMenu.

Your first task is to move the Settings button to the top and turn it into just text rather than a button.

**<Step 8>** Select the SettingsButton, expand the view in the Hierarchy, and then drag the Text (TMP) object to just below the SettingsMenu object.

The Hierarchy should now look like Figure 14.12.

**<Step 9>** Rename the Text (TMP) object to SettingsTitle.

**<Step 10>** Delete the PlayButton and the SettingsButton.

**<Step 11>** Move the SettingsTitle straight up to the top of the SettingsMenu.

You've been doing this with the Move tool, but since you have the Rect tool active right now, you can do this more efficiently as follows: Left-click and hold the Text in the Scene panel, press and hold the Shift key on your keyboard, and then drag up. Remember that you can undo any accidental moves with Ctrl-Z.

**<Step 12>** Select the text for the QuitButton, change the text to BACK, Font Size to 48.

**<Step 13>** Rename the QuitButton to BackButton.

Next, you'll add the fullscreen checkbox. Checkboxes are called Toggles in the Unity UI system.

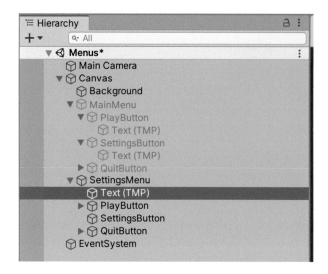

FIGURE 14.12    Working on the Hierarchy for the SettingsMenu.

**<Step 14>**  Select the Canvas, then + – UI – Toggle.

**<Step 15>**  Adjust the toggle to approximately match Figure 14.13.

This involves moving the toggle up and to the right, scaling the Background, increasing the Font Size, and changing the color of the Label Text. You also need to change the Label text to "FULLSCREEN".

You're getting a good workout in Unity. These skills will serve you well in the future as you deal with more advanced concepts later on.

FIGURE 14.13    Fullscreen toggle.

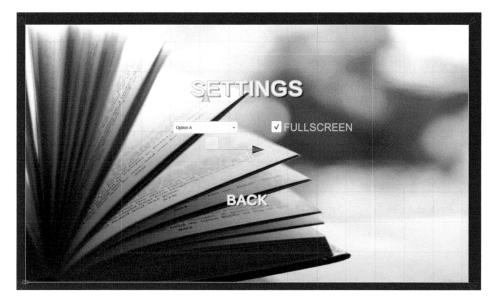

FIGURE 14.14    Resolution dropdown placed into the SettingsMenu.

<Step 16> Rename the Toggle object to "FullscreenToggle".

<Step 17> Move the FullscreenToggle to be a child of SettingsMenu.

<Step 18> Select the SettingsMenu.

<Step 19>  + – UI – Dropdown – TextMeshPro.

<Step 20> Rename the Dropdown to ResolutionDropdown.

<Step 21> Make the dropdown a little larger and move it up and to the left. Compare with Figure 14.14.

<Step 22> Make the ResolutionDropdown a child of SettingsMenu.

<Step 23> Test the menu.

If you click on the Play icon, you'll see that you can choose from among three options: A, B, C. These are placeholders for game resolutions. The Fullscreen toggle allows you to check and uncheck. The Settings Title isn't meant to do anything other than be a title, and the BACK button works just like the buttons on the MainMenu.

<Step 24> Save!

In the next two sections, you'll make the MainMenu and the SettingsMenu operate by writing code for them.

## MAINMENU FUNCTIONALITY

In this section, you'll add some code to make the three buttons in the MainMenu do the right thing. You might think that you'll need to make separate scripts for each button,

but you can easily achieve the needed functionality by creating a single script for the MainMenu.

**\<Step 1\>** Select the SettingsMenu and disable it. Then select the MainMenu and enable it.

You do this in the Inspector. If you have both menus enabled at the same time it looks pretty ugly, so you want to avoid that.

**\<Step 2\>** With the MainMenu selected, click on Add Component in the Inspector. Type the name MainMenu for the name, New Script, and then Create and Add.

**\<Step 3\>** Find the new script in the Assets panel and move it to the scripts folder. Then double-click on it to open it in Visual Studio.

**\<Step 4\>** In Visual Studio, enter the following code:

```
using System.Collections;
using System.Collections.Generic;
using UnityEngine;
using UnityEngine.SceneManagement;

public class MainMenu : MonoBehaviour
{
    public void PlayGame()
    {
        SceneManager.LoadScene(1);
    }

    public void QuitGame()
    {
        Debug.Log("Quitting Game");
        Application.Quit();
    }
}
```

This code needs some explanation. You have removed the Start and Update methods as you won't be needing them in this file. In the Using section at the top, you added a line to enable SceneManagement. Then you created two simple methods. The first, PlayGame, simply switches to Scene number 1, which, in the next step, you will set up to be the first level of the game. The QuitGame method has a debug statement to help you test this button inside the Unity Editor, followed by a call to Application.Quit function which exits the game, but only for built games.

**\<Step 5\>** Save your edits in Visual Studio!

Unfortunately, saving your edits isn't automatic, so if you forget to save, you'll be using the previously saved version of your code in Unity. This can lead to puzzling bugs, when really all you did wrong was to forget to save.

**\<Step 6\>** Drag the MainMenu.cs script onto the MainMenu in the Hierarchy.

This step is probably unnecessary, but if it is, do it. You should see the MainMenu script as a component of the MainMenu object.

**<Step 7>** File – Build Settings… and Add Open Scenes. You should have two scenes, Scenes/Menus and Scenes/SampleScene. Arrange the scenes so that Scenes/Menus is scene 0 and Scenes/SampleScene is scene 1.

Next, you're going to associate the PlayButton GameObject with the PlayGame method in your script.

**<Step 8>** Select MainMenu in the Hierarchy and expand it.

**<Step 9>** Select the PlayButton.

**<Step 10>** Look for the On Click() section in the Inspector near the bottom. Click on the + icon to add an event.

You now are ready to enter the information into the On Click event.

**<Step 11>** Drag the MainMenu object from the Hierarchy to the object entry in the On Click event dialog.

**<Step 12>** In the On Click dialog, click on No Function – MainMenu – PlayGame().

**<Step 13>** Test the PlayButton.

That's right, the PLAY DOTGAME button should work now and take you right to your static maze.

Making the Quit button work is very similar.

**<Step 14>** Select the QuitButton, and then repeat Steps 10–13 for the QuitButton. You'll use QuitGame() instead of PlayGame() in Step 12.

Testing the game is a little different. You'll need to have the Console panel open to see the Debug message. Or, you can build the game and test quitting that way.

Making the Settings button work requires no programming at all! Just do the following:

**<Step 15>** Select the SettingsButton, add an On Click event, and choose the SettingsMenu as the object. For the function, select GameObject – SetActive(). Check the checkbox below the function.

This will turn on the SettingsMenu. You also need to turn off the MainMenu, so do this:

**<Step 16>** Select the SettingsButton, add another On Click event, choose the MainMenu as the object, and for the function select GameObject – SetActive(). Uncheck the checkbox below the function.

**<Step 17>** Test the Settings button.

This is pretty easy. Click on it and if it enables the SettingsMenu and disables the MainMenu you're done.

**<Step 18>** Save.

You're now ready to tackle getting the Settings menu to work.

## SETTINGS MENU FUNCTIONALITY

Just as you did for the main menu, you'll need to create a script for the Settings menu with methods that are then linked to the UI elements in the Settings menu.

<Step 1> Disable MainMenu and enable SettingsMenu.

<Step 2> Select SettingsMenu.

Before you create the script for SettingsMenu, you're going to make the BackButton work. This is very similar to the way you implemented the Settings button for the main menu, just in reverse.

<Step 3> Select the BackButton.

<Step 4> Add an On Click event, and choose the MainMenu as the object. For the function, select GameObject – SetActive(). Check the checkbox below the function.

This activates MainMenu when the back button is clicked.

<Step 5> Add another On Click event, and choose the SettingsMenu as the object. For the function, select GameObject – SetActive(). Uncheck the checkbox below the function.

This deactivates SettingsMenu.

<Step 6> Test BackButton.

You can now go back and forth between your two menus. Next, you'll implement the FullscreenToggle.

<Step 7> Create a SettingsMenu script for the SettingsMenu GameObject. Edit it in Visual Studio.

<Step 8> Enter the following code for SettingsMenu.cs:

```
using System.Collections;
using System.Collections.Generic;
using UnityEngine;

public class SettingsMenu : MonoBehaviour
{
    public void SetFullscreen(bool isFullscreen)
    {
        Screen.fullScreen = isFullscreen;
    }
}
```

This code is fairly simple. You added a method called SetFullscreen which sets fullscreen mode to true or false depending on the value of isFullscreen.

Next, you'll need to tell the FullscreenToggle about this code.

<Step 9> Select FullscreenToggle and click on the + icon for On Value Changed (Boolean) in the Inspector.

This looks like the On Click event that you worked with earlier. Again, you need to enter a function and an object for this event.

**&lt;Step 10&gt;** Drag the SettingsMenu object to the OnValueChanged object slot, and for the function use SettingsMenu – SetFullscreen in the Dynamic bool section. Do not use SetFullscreen (bool) from the Static Parameters section.

**&lt;Step 11&gt;** Test the fullscreen toggle by building your project and running it.

You can't have fullscreen mode when running your game with the Play button, so you need to build it.

**&lt;Step 12&gt;** Save.

Finally, you're ready to add the resolution dropdown functionality. This one is a bit harder. Enter the following code into SettingsMenu.cs:

```
using System.Collections;
using System.Collections.Generic;
using UnityEngine;
using UnityEngine.UI;
using TMPro;

public class SettingsMenu : MonoBehaviour
{

    public TMP_Dropdown resolutionDropdown;
    Resolution[] resolutions;
    private void Start()
    {
        resolutions = Screen.resolutions;

        resolutionDropdown.ClearOptions();

        List <string> options = new List<string>();

        int ci = 0;
        for (int i = 0; i < resolutions.Length; i++)
        {
            string option = resolutions[i].width +
                    " x " + resolutions[i].height;
            options.Add(option);

            if (resolutions[i].width == Screen.currentResolution.width &&
                resolutions[i].height == Screen.currentResolution.height)
            {
                ci = i;
            }
        }

        resolutionDropdown.AddOptions(options);
        resolutionDropdown.value = ci;
        resolutionDropdown.RefreshShownValue();
    }

    public void SetResolution(int ri)
    {
        Resolution res = resolutions[ri];
        Screen.SetResolution(res.width, res.height, Screen.fullScreen);
    }

    public void SetFullscreen(bool isFullscreen)
    {
        Screen.fullScreen = isFullscreen;
    }
}
```

Here is a quick review of this code. At the top, you added two new using statements: using UnityEngine.UI and using TMPro. The UI using statement is necessary for some of the UI functions, and the TMPro statement is needed because you're using TextMeshPro for your dropdown.

The Start method creates a list of resolution strings and stores these options in the resolution dropdown for runtime use. The Start method also looks at the currently used screen resolution and refreshes the dropdown to show it.

Finally, the SetResolution method takes the currently selected option and uses it to set the screen resolution by making a call to `Screen.SetResolution` with the proper arguments taken from the selected option.

**<Step 13>** Test by playing it in Unity.

Well, it doesn't work yet. What went wrong?

Aha, you forgot to set the Resolution Dropdown for the SettingsMenu script.

**<Step 14>** Select the SettingsMenu, then drag the ResolutionDropdown to the Resolution Dropdown slot in the Inspector.

**<Step 15>** Test it again.

OK, you now have the resolution dropdown looking how you want it. Compare it with figure 14.15.

Still, the resolution isn't changing. That's because you can't do that inside of Unity, but if you build this project now it still doesn't work because you didn't quite finish your work yet.

**<Step 16>** Select the ResolutionDropdown.

**<Step 17>** In "On Value Changed(Int32)" click on the+icon, drag SettingsMenu to the object slot, and use SettingsMenu – SetResolution from the Dynamic Int section at the very top.

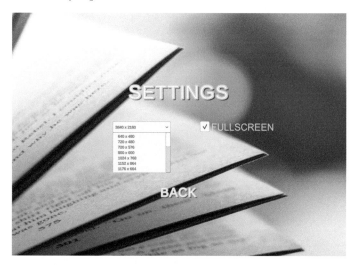

FIGURE 14.15   The Resolution dropdown.

**&lt;Step 18&gt;**   Save, Build, and Run.

Congratulations! You did it. You can try the different resolutions on your system, switch between fullscreen or windowed mode, and then play the game in your selected resolution and fullscreen mode. You still can't exit the game cleanly when you're in fullscreen mode, so be sure to find out how to close your application in that case. This depends somewhat on whether you have a PC or a Mac, and also on how many monitors you have set up.

The following steps are only necessary if you have set up for source control.

**&lt;Step 19&gt;**   Open SourceTree.

You should see a list of unstaged files. These are the files that you changed or added since the last commit.

**&lt;Step 20&gt;**   Stage all, add a commit message, commit and push.

This can go pretty quick. Your commit message can be as simple as "Added menus" or you can be more detailed. Because you're new at this, you may wish to clone this repository and test if it all worked.

Well, it's about time to get some kind of gameplay. Right now, playing the game consists of looking at a static screen.

# Animating the Player Character

I N THIS CHAPTER, you'll make Dottima, the player character, move about the playfield. You'll write some code to implement Dottima's motion using the four arrow keys. You'll also create some animations for Dottima and make the animations work inside the game. The animations will be very simple with just a few frames of animation, but that's a good way to get started with learning Unity's animation tools.

## SIMPLE PLAYER MOVEMENT

In this section, you'll put in simple player movement for Dottima. At first, you won't worry about collisions with the maze. You do the simple things first and gradually add more features, one by one, until you have a game! Well, that's a bit too simplistic, but you get the idea.

<Step 1>  Load the DotGame project.
You'll do some housekeeping first.

<Step 2>  Close the Tile Palette window.
While you were working on the Menus Scene, you had the Tile Palette window visible the whole time even though that wasn't necessary. You just closed it by clicking on the three-dot menu and selecting "Close Tab".
Next, you'll do something you should have done a long time ago.

<Step 3>  Rename the SampleScene to Game.

<Step 4>  Look at the Build Settings.
Yes, Unity updated the name there too. You now have two scenes with the names Scenes/Menus and Scenes/Game.

**\<Step 5\>** Switch to the Game Scene by double-clicking on it in the Scenes folder.

**\<Step 6\>** Select the Default Layout and the Scene panel.

**\<Step 7\>** Focus on the Maze1 Grid object with the f key. Scroll the mouse wheel to center the maze in the Scene panel.

**\<Step 8\>** Open the Assets/art folder in the Project panel.

Way back in Chapter 11 you created DottimaFace.png. Finally, you're going to bring her into Unity.

**\<Step 9\>** Drag DottimaFace into the Hierarchy.

Well, Dottima is a bit too large, as shown in Figure 15.1.

There are two ways to scale Dottima down. You could set the Scale factors, but instead you'll adjust the Pixels Per Unit in the Import Settings.

**\<Step 10\>** Click on DottimaFace in Assets/art.

**\<Step 11\>** Set Pixels Per Unit to 1024 and Apply.

**\<Step 12\>** Move Dottima to the lower left starting position of the Maze as in Figure 15.2.

The new Position for DottimaFace should be about (−7, −3, 0).

**\<Step 13\>** Select DottimaFace, create a script called DottimaController, and attach it to DottimaFace. Edit the script in Visual Studio and enter the following code:

```
using System.Collections;
using System.Collections.Generic;
using UnityEngine;

public class DottimaController : MonoBehaviour
{
    public float speed;
    private Rigidbody2D rb;
```

FIGURE 15.1  Large Dottima.

FIGURE 15.2    Dottima in the starting position.

```
void Start()
{
    rb = GetComponent<Rigidbody2D>();
}

private void FixedUpdate()
{
    Vector2 moveInput = new Vector2(
        Input.GetAxisRaw("Horizontal"),
        Input.GetAxisRaw("Vertical"));
    rb.velocity = moveInput.normalized * speed;
}
}
```

This code sets up a Rigidbody2D component in the Start method. It's done there because it can be time-consuming, so you don't want to do this every frame when you can do it just once at the start. In the FixedUpdate method, keyboard input from the four arrow keys is used to compute a 2D vector. That vector is then used to set the velocity of Dottima. The FixedUpdate method is used as opposed to the Update method to get a smoother and more controlled motion.

Next, you need to make this code work inside Unity.

<Step 14> Save the code in Visual Studio.

<Step 15> Enter a Speed of 7 for DottimaFace in the Inspector.

<Step 16> Click on Add Component. Type "rigid" in the search box, and select Rigidbody2D.

**<Step 17>** Change the Body Type in the Rigidbody 2D section of the Inspector to Kinematic from Dynamic.

> The Kinematic setting keeps Dottima from being affected by Gravity.

**<Step 18>** Press Play and move DottimaFace around the maze with the four arrow keys.

> Well, it's a start. You can move Dottima around, but she's going right through those books. Your next goal is to avoid that. The movement is probably jerky on your system. The next step will make the jerkiness much better.

**<Step 19>** Edit – Project Settings – Time. Set Fixed Timestep to 0.00833333.

> This setting assumes that your monitor refreshes at 60 or 120 Hz. The default Fixed Timestep in Unity is 0.02, which is 1/50 of a second. What you want is to match the refresh rate of your computer monitor. These days computer monitors usually refresh at 60 Hz, with some higher-end models refreshing at 120 Hz. Ideally you should do this in code rather than setting it to a fixed number, but for now, this is good enough for development, as long as your monitor is actually refreshing at 60 or 120 Hz.

## WALL COLLISIONS

In order to have collisions between objects, they need to be turned into physical objects. In Unity, you do that by adding rigidbody components as well as appropriate colliders. You'll start with Dottima.

**<Step 1>** Select DottimaFace.

**<Step 2>** In the Inspector, change the Body Type to Dynamic.

> This is necessary for the built-in collision detect to work.

**<Step 3>** Change the Gravity Scale to 0.

> If this were a platformer, you'd leave the gravity scale alone. In this top-down maze game, there's no gravity, at least not on this level.

**<Step 4>** Add a Circle Collider 2D component.

**<Step 5>** In the Scene panel, focus on DottimaFace with the f key.

> You can see that the Circle Collider is a bit too large.

**<Step 6>** Click on Edit Collider.

**<Step 7>** Reduce the Radius in the Inspector to have the circle collider fit Dottima.

> In general, you want colliders to be slightly smaller than the graphics. That way you will have a little bit of overlap when objects collide. This is better than having objects collide with a gap in between. You may wish to revisit these collider edits during the late stages of your project when the game is close to complete.

**<Step 8>** Run the game, move Dottima around, and then stop running the game.

> This isn't really necessary because there should be no visible difference. It's more of a sanity check to make sure you didn't break anything.

Next, you'll turn the books into rigid bodies with box colliders. This will be easier than you expect. No, you won't have to manually add a bunch of box colliders. Instead, you can use a Tilemap collider.

<Step 9> Select Maze1 Grid, expand it, and then select Tilemap.

<Step 10> Add a Rigidbody 2D.

<Step 11> Change the Body Type to Kinematic.

This makes the Tilemap stationary rather than subject to physical movement. The word Kinematic is a bit of a misnomer in this case as that word implies motion.

<Step 12> Add a Tilemap Collider 2D component.

This collider adds perfectly aligned box colliders to each of the tiles in Tilemap. You may keep the default settings.

<Step 13> Test it.

Wow, Dottima is moving around the maze, finally! As a bonus, Dottima is spinning when moving along a wall. This was not something you expected, but you like it, so you're making a mental note of this for future use. Then you're going to use the Constraints feature of Rigidbody 2D and stop the rotation of Dottima.

<Step 14> With DottimaFace selected, click on Constraints in Rigidbody 2D and check Freeze Rotation Z.

Now, when you run the game, Dottima no longer rotates. It was more fun when she rotated, but for now you're freezing the rotation.

<Step 15> Save and exit Unity.

<Step 16> Optional: Open Sourcetree, stage, commit, and push with the commit message: Dottima Collisions.

In the next few sections, you'll create sprite sheet animations for Dottima.

## IDLE ANIMATION

While not strictly necessary, idle animations have become standard for most video game characters. The idea is that characters should move just a little bit, even when they are idle, i.e. standing at a fixed location. You'll make Dottima stretch and squash up and down for her idle animation. This is simple to do both in Unity and in GIMP. You'll choose to do this animation in GIMP for the sake of consistency. Three sprites should be sufficient for this animation. You'll store the three sprites in separate .png files.

<Step 1> Load DottimaFace.xcf into GIMP.

<Step 2> Select – All.

<Step 3> Click on the Scale tool or type <Shift>-S.

FIGURE 15.3    Scaling Dottima in GIMP.

**<Step 4>**  Hold the Shift key, click and hold the mouse at the top of Dottima and drag down a little bit. Compare with Figure 15.3.

You can see that there is a double-curved outline near the top. This shows both the old and the new Dottima face, overlapping. You also see a Scale pop-up dialog.

**<Step 5>**  Click on the Scale button in the Scale pop-up dialog.

The original Dottima has disappeared, and you see the squashed image.

**<Step 6>**  Export at DottimaIdle1.png.

**<Step 7>**  Save as DottimaIdle1.xcf.

You're going to do this again and squash Dottima some more.

**<Step 8>**  Repeat Step 4, click on Scale, export to DottimaIdle2.png, and save as DottimaIdle2.xcf.

Now you'll of course want to see this animation in action in Unity. This is pretty easy to do if you know how.

**<Step 9>**  Open the DotGame project in Unity.

**<Step 10>**  Click on DottimaFace.

**<Step 11>**  Window – Animation – Animation.

You get a new window where you will be making animations. You can dock this into your layout as follows.

FIGURE 15.4   Unity layout with a docked Animation panel.

<Step 12> Drag the Animation tab at the top of the Animation window a bit below the Console tab. If you see just the tab, you're ready to release the mouse button. Your Unity layout should now look like Figure 15.4. If not, try again.

It is useful to have the Animation panel much wider than it is tall, as you will soon appreciate. You can lay out your screen some other way. It's up to you. You may want to experiment with various layouts from time to time and find a layout that works well for your monitor setup and monitor resolutions.

<Step 13a> If necessary, select DottimaFace in the Hierarchy.

Notice that the Animation panel has a message asking you to create an Animator and an Animation Clip. You'll do that next.

<Step 13b> In the Animation panel, click on Create.

<Step 14> In the resulting pop-up window, navigate to Assets/animations and name your animation Dottima_Idle.anim.

You'll be using the underscore to separate the name of the character from the names of the animations.

<Step 15a> Drag the three idle animation sprites from the art folder into the Animation timeline.

You will need to undock the Animation window to do this.

<Step 15b> As you did for DottimaFace, change the Pixels Per Unit to 1024 for the Idle sprites.

<Step 15c> Redock (is that a word?) the Animation window.

<Step 16> Click on the Play icon in the Animation window.

You now see a very rapid animation in the Scene panel. Be sure to focus on DottimaFace if you don't see Dottima in the Scene Panel. The next step is to slow down that animation.

**<Step 17>** Click on the Play icon again to stop the animation.

**<Step 18>** In the Samples text box, change 60 to 12.

This changes the time for each frame from 1/60 of a second to 1/12 of a second.

**<Step 19>** Run the animation again.

This time it looks better, but it's still not exactly what you want. It's looping this sequence 0, 1, 2, 0, 1, 2, etc. but what you really want is 0, 1, 2, 1, 0, 0, 1, 2, 1, 0,…

**<Step 20>** Drag DottimaIdle1 to the end of the sequence, and then drag DottimaFace to the end after that.

You now have five keyframes in the Animation Timeline.

**<Step 21>** Run the animation yet again.

This time you're going to accept it and move one. You will probably revisit this when the game is playable and adjust it.

**<Step 22>** Run the game.

You now have the idle animation running all the time, even when Dottima is moving. The next section will add movement animations.

**<Step 23>** Save!

## MOVEMENT ANIMATIONS

With a human or animal character, you'd now be doing a walk cycle. Dottima has no limbs, so you can't have a walk cycle for Dottima. Instead, you'll make the eyes bounce a little.

**<Step 1>** Load DottimaFace.xcf into GIMP.

You are once again starting with the base image of Dottima and making simple adjustments to create additional animation frames.

**<Step 2>** Click on the Ellipse Select tool.

**<Step 3>** Select the black pupil of Dottima's left eye. It's the eye on the right from your perspective. This should look like Figure 15.5.

**<Step 4>** Edit – Copy.

**<Step 5>** Edit – Paste As – New Brush. Use the name LeftEye.

**<Step 6>** Select – All.

**<Step 7>** Select the Color Picker tool (Shortcut O key).

**<Step 8>** Click on the Foreground color square.

FIGURE 15.5    Selecting the pupil of the right eye of Dottima.

**<Step 9>**  Click on the yellow eye color of Dottima.
The foreground color should now be that same shade of yellow.

**<Step 10>**  Click on the Pencil tool (Shortcut N key).

**<Step 11>**  Select the Pixel Brush, Size about 25.
This is the brush that looks like a single pixel.

**<Step 12>**  Draw over the Pupils for Dottima.
This should now look like Figure 15.6.

FIGURE 15.6    Dottima without pupils.

<Step 13> Save as Dottima_NoPupils.xcf.
You're saving this as a base sprite for possible future use. Dottima looks evil without pupils!

<Step 14> With the Pencil tool still selected, choose the LeftEye Brush.

<Step 15> Draw the pupils higher up in the eyes, as shown in Figure 15.7.
You can use Ctrl-Z to undo your attempts at placing the pupils.

<Step 16a> Save as Dottima_MoveU1.xcf.

<Step 16b> Export as Dottima_MoveU1.png.
Next, you'll move the pupils up again, but slightly to the left.

<Step 17> Load the no pupils sprite.
An easy way to do that is to do File – Open Recent – Dottima_NoPupils.xcf.

<Step 18> Draw the pupils near the top left of the eyes.
This image should look similar to Figure 15.8.

<Step 19> Save as Dottima_MoveU2.xcf.

<Step 20> Export as Dottima_MoveU2.png.
You could do additional sprites for this animation, but to keep things simple, you'll stop right here and move over to Unity.

<Step 21> Load DotGame into Unity as usual.

<Step 22> Select DottimaFace in the Hierarchy.

FIGURE 15.7   Dottima looking up.

FIGURE 15.8    Dottima looking up and to the left.

**<Step 23>** Look at the Animation panel and click on the small triangle next to Dottima_Idle.
This should look like Figure 15.9.

**<Step 24>** Click on Create New Clip …

**<Step 25>** Go to the Assets/animations folder.
You're probably there already from your previous work.

**<Step 26>** Type in the file name Dottima_Run in the File name field, and leave the Save As Type as anim. Click on Save.

**<Step 27a>** Change the Pixels Per Unit form the U1 and U2 sprites to 1024, just as you did earlier for the Idle animation sprites.

**<Step 27b>** From the Assets/art folder, drag Dottima_MoveU1 to 0 in the timeline.

FIGURE 15.9    Creating the Dottima_Run animation.

**<Step 28>** Drag Dottima_MoveU2 to 20 in the timeline.

**<Step 29>** Drag Dottima_MoveU1 to 40 in the timeline.

**<Step 30>** Click on the DottimaFace:Sprite expansion triangle and compare your window with Figure 15.10.

**<Step 31>** Click on the "Play the animation clip" icon in the Animation panel to preview the animation.

Dottima's eyes are bouncing left and right. You're now going to make the run animation the starting animation just to see what it looks like to move Dottima around with this animation.

**<Step 32a>** Select DottimaFace in the Hierarchy.

**<Step 32b>** Window – Animations – Animator.

**<Step 32c>** Compare your Animator window with Figure 15.11.

FIGURE 15.10   The Dottima_Run animation in the Animation timeline.

FIGURE 15.11   Initial view of the Animator window with an Idle and a Run animation for Dottima.

FIGURE 15.12    Rearranged Animator window.

**<Step 32d>** Rearrange the boxes to make them look like Figure 5.12.

As usual, you can use the scroll wheel on your mouse to center your view. You can see the green Entry box and an arrow connecting it to Dottima_Idle. Your goal is to have that arrow point at Dottima_Run. This is harder than it looks. No, you can't just drag it over there. Instead, do this:

**<Step 33>** Right-click on Dottima_Run and select "Set as Layer Default State".

**<Step 34>** Test the Game.

If everything went according to plan, you can now move Dottima around while her eyes are moving left-right. Of course, what you want is to have Dottima be in the Idle state when she's not moving. You'll implement that in the next section.

**<Step 35>** Save the project.

## MAKING THE ANIMATIONS WORK IN THE GAME

You have two animations, so next you'll make them run in the game depending on the player movements. First, you're going to explore a neat feature in the Animator window. You're still inside of Unity, so you're ready to go.

**<Step 1>** Select the Game panel and disable "Maximize on Play".

It's strongly recommended to usually have "Maximize on Play" enabled to avoid accidentally making changes to your game, not realizing that the game is still playing. If you do that, your changes will be lost when you eventually stop playing the game, which can be disastrous. Unity is truly wonderful, but it

isn't foolproof, and it can bite you if you're not careful. For these next few steps, you'll have "Maximize on Play" disabled.

**<Step 2>** Play the game.

**<Step 3>** Select DottimaFace.

**<Step 4>** Look at the Animator window.

> You'll see the Run animation displaying a rapidly moving progress bar below the Dottima_Run box. This feature can be useful when you want to see which of your animation is active.

**<Step 5>** Stop playing the game.

**<Step 6>** Enable "Maximize on Play".

**<Step 7>** In the Animator window, make Dottima_Idle the Layer Default State.

> If you play the game now, Dottima will be displaying Idle state animation. Next, you're going to put in a transition from the Idle state to the Run state.

**<Step 8>** Right-click on Dottima_Idle and select "Make Transition". Move the mouse to the Dottima_Run box and left-click to actually make the connection.

> If you run the game now, Dottima immediately does the transition to the Run state and stays there. What you want instead, is to only make that transition when Dottima moves. The basic idea of this is to check if the speed of Dottima is non-zero. If it is, you trigger the transition.

**<Step 9>** Select the newly created Transition in the Animator window.

> In the Inspector, you should see the properties of this transition. You will adjust those soon, but first you'll create the Speed parameter.

**<Step 10>** Click on Parameters, to the right of Layers at the top left of the Animator window.

**<Step 11>** Create a new Parameter by clicking on the Plus sign to the right of the search area in the Parameters panel.

**<Step 12>** Select Float.

**<Step 13>** Name the Parameter "Speed" rather than the default "New Float".

> The "New Float" is highlighted in blue, so that means you can just type "Speed" without having to select the text entry box. Type Enter to finish the text entry.

**<Step 14>** Select the Transition again, and then in the Inspector, click on the Plus icon in the Conditions area.

**<Step 15>** Change the zero next to the "Greater" to 0.001.

> The condition for this transition is that the Speed parameter is greater than 0.001. The 0.001 is just a small number. You could easily use some other small number as long as it is between 0 and the speed of your character after it starts moving.

**\<Step 16\>** Disable "Has Exit Time".

This setting would delay the transition once the conditions are met. In your case, you don't want to delay and to just start the run animation immediately.

**\<Step 17\>** Click on Settings below the "Has Exit Time" setting.

**\<Step 18\>** Set the Transition Duration to 0.

The transition itself should not take any time, so making the Transition Duration 0 accomplishes that. You can now test this transition by running the game and manually adjusting the Speed parameter.

**\<Step 19\>** Disable Maximize on Play.

**\<Step 20\>** Select DottimaFace.

**\<Step 21\>** Play the game.

**\<Step 22a\>**Look at the Animator window. You can see the Idle animation active.

**\<Step 22b\>**Change the Speed to 1.

Because the Speed parameter changed from 0 to something above 0.001, the Conditions were met which triggered the Transition to the Run animation. You can now see the Run animation as active.

**\<Step 23\>** Change the Speed to 0.

You want the Idle animation to become active now, but you didn't put in the transition for that yet, therefore you see no change and the Run animation continues.

**\<Step 24\>** Stop playing the game.

**\<Step 25\>** Make a transition from Dottima_Run to Dottima_Idle.

**\<Step 26\>** Disable "Has Exit Time" and change the Transition Duration to 0.

**\<Step 27\>** Add a condition that Speed is less than 0.001.

**\<Step 28\>** Repeat Steps 20–24.

This time the transition from Run to Idle gets triggered when the Speed gets set to 0.

All that's left to do now is to set the Speed parameter automatically depending on the movement of Dottima. You can do this with just a few lines of code.

**\<Step 29\>** Open DottimaController in Visual Studio.

**\<Step 30\>** Add the line:

```
public Animator animator;
```

after the Rigidbody 2D declaration near the beginning of the DottimaController class.

**\<Step 31\>** Save the script.

**\<Step 32\>** Back in Unity, select DottimaFace, and look at the Inspector. Drag the Animator component into the Animator slot for Dottima Controller (Script).

**\<Step 33\>** In the FixedUpdate function, insert the following line after rb.velocity = …;

```
animator.SetFloat("Speed", rb.velocity.magnitude);
```

**\<Step 34\>** Save and Test.

You're getting better at dealing with Unity. As Dottima moves around the maze she alternates between her idle animation and the run animation. It's starting to look like a game, step by step.

In this chapter, you created a fairly simple, usable player character for your game. In the next chapter, you'll create enemies to make the game more interesting.

# Enemies

## *Using Blender to Make Robot Sprites*

I N THIS RATHER LARGE CHAPTER, you'll start the development of enemies in DotGame. First, you'll tackle enemy robots. Then, you'll create spikers, blockades, and question marks. You'll be using Blender to make them, and then you'll export them as 2D sprites, ready for use in Unity. Finally, you'll code the basic movement of the enemies and put in collision detection.

You're going to spend only a moderate amount of time working on the graphics for this game at this early stage. Your goal is to make the game fun with simple graphics, and then, time permitting, you'll replace the graphics with better, more elaborate versions.

You've decided to use Blender to make what's called prerendered 3D graphics. Prerendering was pioneered by Rare in the Donkey Kong Country games for the SNES, way back in 1994. While it's true that Xevious from 1982 and Myst from 1993 also used this technique, Donkey Kong Country was first in its extensive use of the prerendering of animated characters. It's instructive to go online and look at videos of Donkey Kong Country on the SNES. Be aware that in those days, there was no HD video, so be sure to watch videos that use a 4:3 aspect ratio used by TVs in 1994. The 16:9 HD videos of Donkey Kong Country are stretched horizontally, which can be quite a distraction.

Prerendered 3D graphics is a way to display 3D graphics when the target hardware doesn't have 3D support. The SNES, for instance, could only display 2D sprites, so to get 3D animations the graphics were modeled, animated, and prerendered using very expensive 3D workstations, frame by frame, compressed and then stored in the very limited SNES memory. This technique introduced millions of game players to the wonders of animated 3D graphics in games. Today, prerendered 3D graphical elements are used to reduce battery consumption on mobile devices, even when 3D display hardware is available.

You already used prerendering in Part I when you used Blender to make the donut box sprite. You will be using this same technique to create some of the enemies in DotGame. Let's get started.

## BOX MODELING IN BLENDER

In this section, you'll use box modeling in Blender to create a robot for DotGame. You'll be making a simple character out of boxes. These instructions assume that you used Blender back in Chapter 4, but because that's been a while there's some review of Blender basics thrown in.

<Step 1> Open Blender 2.81a or later.

These instructions have been tested for 2.81a and should work for later versions. 2.81a was released in early 2020. If you're using a much later version from several years after you may need to make some adjustments to the steps.

You will start with the default cube, so don't delete it!

<Step 2a> File – Defaults – Load Factory Settings.

In this way, you will be able to follow the instructions in this book even if you set up your own preferences.

<Step 2b> Zoom in on the default cube somewhat so that it fills about half of the screen.

You can use the mouse scroll wheel to do that.

<Step 2c> If you don't have a numpad, set up Numpad Emulation as described in Chapter 4. You will be using the ordinary numbers at the top of the keyboard instead of the numpad numbers.

<Step 3> Press 1 on the numpad to get the Front Orthographic view.

You can see the view description in the top left corner where you will find the text "Front Orthographic". The 1 key got you to the Front View. It's possible that you're in Perspective mode right now, depending on the version of Blender you're using.

<Step 4> Press 5 on the numpad several times and look at the effect. Stop when you have "Front Orthographic" view.

This key toggles you between Perspective and Orthographic view. You'll be doing this a lot, so memorize this key.

<Step 5> Shift-Tab to enable "Snap during Transform" mode.

This mode makes various editing operations snap to the grid, which is often what you want. You can alternatively click on the magnet icon at the top middle of your window. This is a toggle as well, so when you click on the magnet (or type Shift-Tab) twice it toggles snap mode on and then off.

<Step 6a> Type g, then z and use the mouse to move the cube up so it lines up with the red horizontal line.

Your screen should look like Figure 16.1

The z key restricted your movement to the z axis, thus leaving your cube centered. You can see on the right side of the screen that the location of the Cube has changed from (0, 0, 0) to (0, 0, 1).

FIGURE 16.1    Starting Cube lined up with the X–Y plane.

Notice that there is a small orange dot in the middle of the cube. This is the origin for the cube. The location of Blender objects is actually the location of that object's origin.

Next, you'll move the origin to the bottom of the cube. You'll do that by moving it to the 3D Cursor, which happens to be at the bottom of the cube.

<Step 6b>  Right-click to bring up the Object Context Menu.

<Step 6c>  Set Origin – Origin to 3D Cursor.

This puts the origin of the cube to the 3D Cursor location, exactly at (0, 0, 0). Looking at the Transform section on the right side of the screen you see that the Location is now (0m, 0m, 0m).

You're now ready to do some *Box Modeling* using extrusions and loop-cuts among other operations. Box Modeling is a common technique used in 3D work. You typically start with a primitive shape such as a cube or sphere and add geometry to it step by step resulting in a rough shape for the desired model. A good example of this would be a chair where you start with a cube, squash it to make the seat, and then extrude four legs from the bottom and the back from the top. You would then add more details and adjust the locations of the faces to make the chair look more realistic.

For the robot you think of the cube as the body and then extrude the neck, head, arms, and legs. Along the way you adjust the geometry to get a robot look.

<Step 7>  Click on Modeling in the top menu.

This changes the layout to be especially suitable for modeling. It also changes the Object Interaction mode from Object Mode to Edit Mode. You also get new

icons on the left. In Edit Mode, you are able to select geometry of the currently selected object and edit it.

**<Step 8>** Try out Vertex Select, Edge Select, and Face Select.

To the right of the Object Interaction dropdown (where it now says Edit Mode, top left), there are three select mode buttons. The third one from the left is the Face Select mode button. You can choose Vertex Select, Edge Select, or Face Select mode. In Vertex Select mode, your left mouse button selects the nearest vertex, similarly for Edges and Faces. Try out all three select modes to get a feel for this.

**<Step 9>** Use Face Select mode.

**<Step 10>** Select the top face.

Compare with Figure 16.2.

As you can see, the selected face is a tan color whereas the other faces are gray. Before you go any further it's a good idea to save your work. You will do that in a newly created Assets folder called models for the DotGame project.

**<Step 11>** File – Save As … and save the file with the name DotRobot.blend in a newly created folder called DotGame/Assets/models.

The file interaction interface for Blender got a very nice facelift in 2.81. You can create the new folder directly in Blender and then save the file there. When you're done, check that the filename is displayed correctly at the top of the window.

**<Step 12>** Rename the default cube to DotRobot.

FIGURE 16.2    Selecting the top face of the default starting cube.

You do this by *double-clicking* on "Cube" in the Scene Collection panel at the top right of the Blender window. That's right, renaming is different in Blender vs. Unity where you single-click and wait instead. You should have done this rename earlier, but better late than never.

Now you're going to start adjusting the geometry of the cube.

**<Step 13>** Numpad 53.

This gets you into Right Orthographic view.

**<Step 14>** Select – All (or type a).

**<Step 15>** Type s y and scale the box to be about half the size.

**<Step 16>** Numpad 54488.

**<Step 17>** With the top face selected, type e s and move the mouse to create to base of the neck. Left-click when you're finished adjusting the neck.

Compare with Figure 16.3.

**<Step 18>** Type s x and move the mouse to make the base of the neck squarer.

**<Step 19>** Turn off Snap mode (Shift Tab).

**<Step 20>** Type e, move the mouse up, and left-click to make the neck, approximately the shape of a cube.

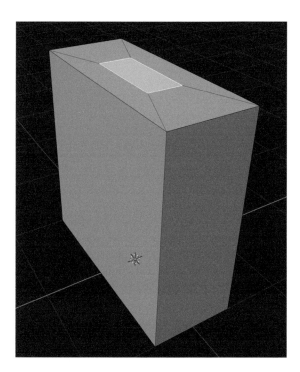

FIGURE 16.3   Creating the base of the neck of DotRobot.

**<Step 21>** Type e s and make the base of the head. Type e to extrude up and make the head.

> Compare with Figure 16.4
>
> The following step is optional. You will switch to the Blender Light Theme. This way your screen will more closely match the figures printed in this book. If you prefer the current Dark Theme you may skip this step.

**<Step 22>** Click on the Editor Type button in the upper left corner of the 3D Viewport. Select Preferences. Select Themes. Click on the Presets dropdown near the top and click on Blender Light. Change the Editor Type back to 3D Viewport.

> Your screen should now look like Figure 16.5. If you kept the dark theme, your screen would use darker colors, but it would otherwise be the same.
>
> Next, you'll add legs to your robot.

**<Step 23>** Numpad 5 1.

> You are back to using the Front Orthographic view.

**<Step 24>** Type the "a" key to select all.

> This is a very useful shortcut key and is well worth remembering. If you forget it, you can always click on Select and then All. You will also see a reminder for the shortcut key, a capital letter A. Blender is not case-sensitive, so a lower case a is fine.

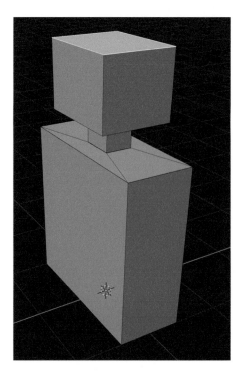

FIGURE 16.4   Body, neck, and head of DotRobot.

FIGURE 16.5    Using the Blender Light theme.

It's worth noting that because you are in Edit Mode the "All" refers to all of the geometry in the currently selected object and doesn't select the other objects in the scene such as the light or the camera.

**<Step 25>** Turn on Snap if it's not on already. Use Shift-Tab to do that.

Telling whether you're in snap mode can be confusing. Look at the magnet icon at the top middle of the 3D Viewport. If it has a light-blue background, it is active. If it has a white background, it is inactive, even though that white background makes it look active. Remember, blue is the color for active and this applies to any other toggle buttons in Blender. If you're still using the dark theme, a dark gray background indicates that it's inactive.

**<Step 26>** Type g z and use the mouse to move the robot up by 1.5 meters.

You can see how much you are moving the robot by looking at the numeric display at the top. Also, at the end of the move you see at small Move pop-up at the bottom left of the screen. You can expand that pop-up if necessary. Check that the Move Z box shows 1.5 m. If not, you can edit that box and change it to 1.5 m.

Next, you'll add a bunch of loop-cuts to prepare for adding the legs and arms.

**<Step 27>** Type t and t again.

This turns the toolbar off and on. The toolbar is on the left side of the screen.

**<Step 28a>** Hover the mouse near the right edge of the tool bar until you see horizontal arrows as the mouse icon. Drag the tool bar to the right until you see text for each toolbar icon.

This is a useful layout when you're learning about these tool icons.

**\<Step 28b\>** If the robot's head is cut off, zoom in and out with the mouse scroll wheel so you can see the entire robot as shown in Figure 16.6.

**\<Step 29\>** Select all.

**\<Step 30\>** Click on the Loop Cut icon in the tool bar. Then move the mouse over the robot.
    You will see yellow lines appearing as you move the mouse. These are potential loop-cuts.

**\<Step 31\>** Hover the mouse near the top of the head of the robot, then left-click.
    You should see an orange vertical line cutting through the robot. This is your currently selected loop-cut. You also get a "Loop Cut and Slide" pop-up at the bottom.

**\<Step 32\>** In the pop-up, change the Number of Cuts to 6.

**\<Step 33\>** Numpad 3.

**\<Step 34a\>** Hover the mouse again near the top center of the robot, then left-click.

**\<Step 34b\>** Change the Number of Cuts to 4.

**\<Step 35\>** Exit loop-cut and slide by clicking on Select Box in the tool bar, then click somewhere in the background of the 3D Viewport.

**\<Step 36\>** Numpad 5.

FIGURE 16.6   Expanded Toolbar and centered DotRobot.

**<Step 37>** Click and drag the red X button in the upper right of the 3D Viewport. This will give you a rotating view of the robot showing the loop-cuts that you just made. Compare with Figure 16.7. Adjust your view with the scroll wheel if necessary.

**<Step 38>** Numpad 15222.

**<Step 39>** Click on Face Select, above the User Orthographic text, upper left of screen.

**<Step 40>** Hold Shift, then click on six faces for each leg as shown in Figure 16.8.

**<Step 41>** Numpad 1.

**<Step 42>** Turn on Snap, if necessary.

**<Step 43>** Extrude down 1.5 meters.

**<Step 44>** Numpad 5, drag the mouse wheel to get a 3D view.

**<Step 45>** Loop-cut five cuts on each leg, and five cuts on the body. Exit the Loop Cut pop-up as before by clicking on Select Box, and then clicking in the background of the 3D View. Compare with Figure 16.9.

You added all those loop-cuts to give you starting faces for the feet and the arms.

FIGURE 16.7    Loop-cuts on the head and body of the robot.

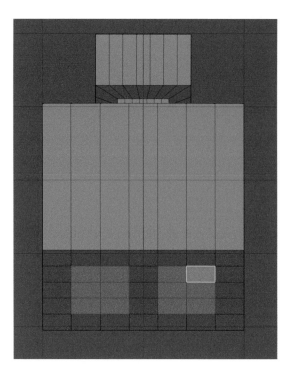

FIGURE 16.8    Selecting faces for the top of the legs.

FIGURE 16.9    Loop-cuts on the full-size robot.

**\<Step 46\>** Numpad 51.

        You should have a Front Orthographic view.

**\<Step 47\>** Select the bottom four faces, two for each leg.

        Hold down Shift while you make those face selections, as usual when selecting multiple items.

**\<Step 48\>** Numpad 3, extrude the feet to the left, 0.2 meters.

**\<Step 49\>** Select six faces on the body just below the top and in the center.

**\<Step 50a\>** Numpad 1.

**\<Step 50b\>** Extrude 0.5 meters.

**\<Step 51a\>** Numpad Ctrl-3.

**\<Step 51b\>** Select those same six faces on the other side.

**\<Step 52\>** Numpad 1. Extrude 0.5 meters.

**\<Step 53\>** Use loop-cuts and extrusions to make arms for the robot. Compare with Figure 16.10

        You added just one loop cut to each arm, and then extruded the outer three faces down by 1m.

        Now you'll add some simple eyes.

FIGURE 16.10    DotRobot with arms.

<Step 54> Add four horizontal loop-cuts to the head.

<Step 55> Select four faces for each eye as in Figure 16.11.

<Step 56> Disable Snap and extrude eye sockets into the head by about −0.25 meters. Compare with Figure 16.12.

  You now have the basic shape of the robot. Next, you'll set up the camera and lighting.

<Step 57> Select the Camera.

  The easiest way to do that is to click on Camera in the Outliner panel on the top right as in Figure 16.13.

FIGURE 16.11   Adding the eyes to the robot.

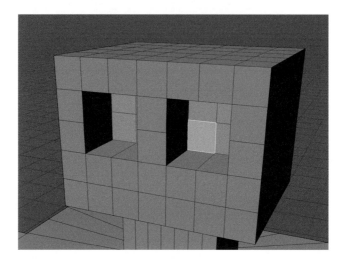

FIGURE 16.12   Negative extrusion to make eye sockets.

FIGURE 16.13    Selecting the Camera in the Blender Outliner panel.

**\<Step 58\>** Type n, then Numpad 0.

You'll see the camera pointing at the feet of the robot. The 3D View is showing what the camera sees. The n key brought up the settings for the camera. You can now adjust the camera, so it gets a good view of DotRobot.

**\<Step 59\>** Click on Layout.

You can't access the camera while you're still in Edit Mode for DotRobot.

**\<Step 60\>** Select the Camera again.

**\<Step 61\>** Set the Camera Location to (0, −10, 7), Rotation to (70, 0, 0). Compare your screen with Figure 16.14.

FIGURE 16.14    Viewing DotRobot through the camera.

FIGURE 16.15    Robot centered in the Camera view.

**<Step 62>** Hover the mouse over the Y coordinate of the Location. Drag it left-right until the robot is centered in the view as shown in Figure 16.15.

You're not finished yet with DotRobot, but you've done a whole lot of steps, so it's time to save your work and take a break. You'll wrap it up in the next section.

**<Step 63>** File – Save, and Exit Blender.

Exiting Blender isn't really necessary, but it's a good habit to exit your applications occasionally to make sure your save is working.

## LIGHTING IN BLENDER

In this section, you'll improve the lighting for DotRobot. You've been using the default light, and you haven't moved it or changed it. You'll quickly find out the dramatic effect that lighting can have on your renders.

**<Step 1>** Start Blender.

**<Step 2>** File – Open Recent – DotRobot.blend.

A quicker way to do this last step is <Ctrl><Shift>O. It's <command><shift>O on a Mac. The first item should be DotRobot.blend. If it is, just hit return to load DotRobot.blend.

Blender is free and competes with very expensive 3D programs such as 3D Studio Max and Maya. You might think that this makes Blender somehow worse than its competition, but that's not really the case. In many ways, Blender is better! One advantage of Blender over its competition is its very extensive keyboard shortcut support. Experienced Blender users can be incredibly fast

because of this. Search the web for "Blender Speed Modeling 2.8" for some examples of this. Those videos are typically sped up to give you a quick overview of what the artist did. As a novice Blender user, it may be beneficial for you to view some of these videos to get a feel for how the pros do it and to see the amazing advanced features of Blender in action.

After this detour, it's time to improve the render of DotRobot.

**<Step 3>** Select the "Rendering" Workspace.

You will see an empty Render Result because you haven't rendered anything yet in this project.

**<Step 4>** Render – Render Image (or type F12).

There is a pop-up entitled Blender Render as shown in Figure 16.16.

There are some obvious problems with this render. You'll fix these one at a time.

**<Step 5>** Close the Render pop-up window.

You now see the Render Result in the Rendering Workspace.

**<Step 6>** Use the mouse scroll wheel to adjust the size of the Render Result view.

This gets you a better view of the Render Result. The mouse wheel can seem jerky sometimes, so instead you can drag the magnify icon with the left mouse button. The magnify icon is at the top right corner of the view.

The next problem is that the background is a dark gray instead of transparent. This is easy to fix as follows.

FIGURE 16.16    Blender Render of DotRobot.

FIGURE 16.17    Render Properties for DotRobot.

**<Step 7>** Click on the Render Properties icon in the Properties Panel on the right. This should look like Figure 16.17.

**<Step 8>** Expand the Film section and check Transparent.

**<Step 9>** Render again.

The robot is now surrounded by a checkerboard pattern as shown in Figure 16.18.

Now, all that's left to fix is the lighting.

**<Step 10>** Select the Layout Workspace.

**<Step 11>** Type z8 to get Rendered Viewport Shading.

You just used the pie menu for the z shortcut key. Alternatively, you can also click on the Viewport Shading icons at the top right of the viewport to select different viewport shadings.

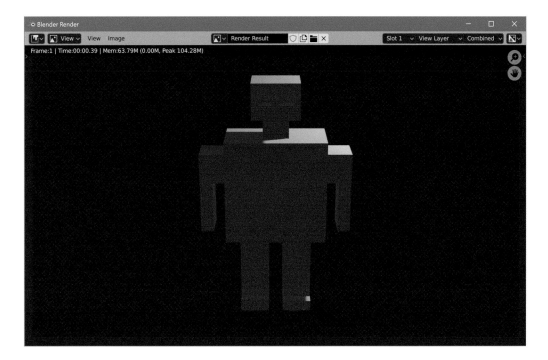

FIGURE 16.18    Robot Rendered on a Transparent Background.

## THE 3D VIEWPORT

Your 3D Viewport now looks very much like your last render. As you can see the lighting is coming from behind, but you'd rather have the light from the front. It's time to explore lighting in Blender. So far, you're using the default light. You'll continue to use it, but first you'll experiment with lighting.

**<Step 12>** Select the Light in the Outliner.

> Yes, you can have multiple lights in your scene, but for now, just one light is OK.

**<Step 13>** In the Properties Editor, click on the Light icon. Compare with Figure 16.9.

> There are four Types of Light in Blender: Point, Sun, Spot, and Area.

**<Step 14>** Click on all four of the Types of Light in turn and watch the effect in the Camera Perspective. Then select Point.

> The Point light is located at a specific 3D location and illuminates equally in all directions.

**<Step 15>** Disable the Light.

> You do that by clicking on the eyeball icon in the Outliner on the line for the Light. Disabling the light is the same as deleting it, except that you can bring it back easily.

FIGURE 16.19   Light Properties in Blender.

The surprising thing is this: Why can you still see anything at all in the 3D Viewport? The answer is this: There is something called ambient light in the scene. If you turn that off, you should then get an entirely black view. It's not obvious how to do that.

**<Step 16>** In the Properties Editor, select the World Properties icon and set the Surface Strength to 0.

You now have a totally black robot. This was just a test.

**<Step 17>** Enable the Light and compare with Figure 16.20.

This is a very stark view of the robot. Again, this was just a test. You'll go back to regular ambient lighting.

**<Step 18>** Set the Surface Strength back to 1.0.

Next, you'll look at the effect of moving the Light around in 3D space. To see what's going on you'll set up a second 3D Viewport.

**<Step 19>** Slowly move the mouse from the very top of the Blender window down until you see a vertical double arrow as shown in Figure 16.21.

**<Step 20>** Right-click and select Vertical Split.

**<Step 21>** Adjust the Vertical Split and left-click to choose where to split the 3D Viewport.

You now have two 3D Viewports as shown in Figure 16.22.

You can see that the left viewport is using Solid Viewport shading, whereas the right one is continuing to use Rendered shading.

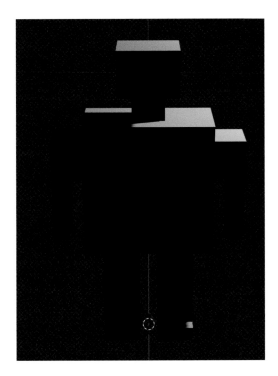

FIGURE 16.20    DotRobot with Dark Lighting.

FIGURE 16.21    Setting up for split screens in Blender.

<Step 22> Hover the mouse over the right viewport. Then type tn.

This toggles off the toolbar and the sidebar for that viewport. You now have a less cluttered view of the rendered robot.

<Step 23> Move the mouse slowly to the border between the viewports and drag to the right when you see the horizontal double-arrow.

You're doing this to make the left viewport larger. Compare with Figure 16.23.

<Step 24> Hover the mouse over the left viewport, then type Numpad 3. Adjust the view to see the robot, the light, and the camera as shown in Figure 16.24. Type Numpad 5 if necessary, to get an orthographic view.

FIGURE 16.22 Vertical Split in Blender.

FIGURE 16.23 Adjusted 3D Viewports in Blender.

**<Step 25>** Click on the light, type g and move the light around the left viewport while looking at the result in the right viewport.

**<Step 26>** Enter the following coordinates for the Location of the Light in the sidebar: X = 4m, Y = −2m, Z = 6m.

Compare your rendered viewport with Figure 16.25.

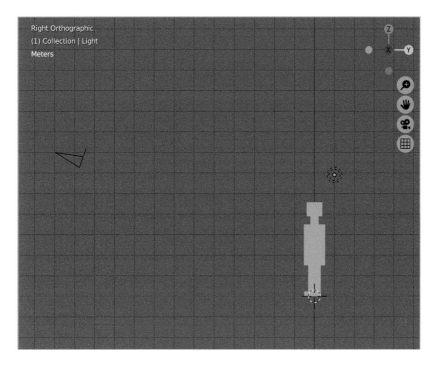

FIGURE 16.24    Right Orthographic view of the robot, light and camera.

FIGURE 16.25    Better lighting for the robot.

You could spend a lot more time adjusting the lighting. As you just saw, lighting has a dramatic effect on the quality of your renders. You have merely scratched the surface of this topic.

Here is one more easy adjustment.

**<Step 27>** Change the Color of the light to pale blue.

**<Step 28>** Save.

**<Step 29>** Render.

**<Step 30>** In the Blender Render pop-up, Image – Save As… and choose the filename DotRobot.png in assets/art.

**<Step 31>** Save the .blend file.

**<Step 32>** Exit Blender.

**<Step 33>** Open the DotGame Unity Project.

**<Step 34>** In Assets/art, select DotRobot.

**<Step 35>** In the Inspector, set the Pixels Per Unit to 1024 and Apply.

**<Step 36>** Drag DotRobot into the Scene panel as shown in Figure 16.26.

**<Step 37>** Test the game.

**<Step 38>** Save and exit Unity.

FIGURE 16.26   First appearance of DotRobot in DotGame.

This gives you a view of what the robot looks like in the game. The color is somewhat too close to the color of Dottima, but color adjustments can wait for now.

You just created a robot from scratch using Blender and took a peek at it in Unity. In the next section, you'll learn the basics of Blender animation before going on to animating the robot.

## BLENDER BASIC ANIMATION TUTORIAL

Before diving in and animating your robot, you'll do a side quest and learn the very basics of Blender Animation. You're going to create a Blender Animation of the default cube moving and spinning, and then you'll export that animation as a sequence of .png files, ready to be used by Unity.

Blender Animation is similar to animating game objects in Unity, so this will seem somewhat familiar to you. But of course, the details differ. You'll start by exploring the Animation Workspace built into Blender.

<Step 1> Open Blender and select the Animation Workspace. Compare your screen with Figure 16.27.

In this workspace, you see two 3D viewports, a Dope Sheet, a Timeline, and, on the right, the usual Outliner and Properties Editor. The left 3D viewport shows the default cube as seen from the default camera. The right 3D Viewport shows the camera, cube, and default light from the User Perspective. The Dope Sheet shows keyframes and other information about your animation. Immediately below the Dope Sheet, there is a very thin Timeline. The Timeline is there mainly for the animation controls.

FIGURE 16.27    The Blender Animation Workspace.

You're going to make that default cube bounce, so first you'll move it up above the X–Y plane.

**\<Step 2\>** Select the Cube, Turn on Snap, Hover the mouse over right 3D Viewport, type n, then type g z and move the cube up 3m.

The viewports should now look like Figure 16.28.

Next, you'll insert a keyframe into the Timeline.

**\<Step 3\>** Hover the mouse over one of the 3D Viewports and type i. Select Location.

You now see four yellow dots in the Dope Sheet at Frame 1.

**\<Step 4\>** Select Frame 10 in the Timeline as shown in Figure 16.29.

**\<Step 5\>** Move the cube down to location (0m, 0m, 1m).

**\<Step 6\>** Type i and select Location to create another keyframe at Frame 10.

**\<Step 7\>** Select Frame 20 and move the cube to location (0m, 0m, 2.5m).

To set the location, type the location in the sidebar because snap is still on.

FIGURE 16.28   Default cube moved up by 3m.

FIGURE 16.29   Selecting Frame 10 in the Dope Sheet.

**\<Step 8\>** Play the animation by clicking on the play button at the middle of the Timeline. Oops, the animation starts at Frame 20 when you do that.

**\<Step 9a\>** Pause the animation by pressing the pause icon (two vertical bars).

**\<Step 9b\>** Select Frame 1, then play the animation again.
You can now see the cube falling, bouncing up, and then getting stuck there. This is not a realistic animation at all, but that's not really your goal. You're simply trying to understand the basic controls. When the frame count reaches 250 the animation repeats.

**\<Step 10\>** Set the end of the animation to 30.
The text box for this is at the right edge of the Timeline. 250 frames are too many for this simple example.

**\<Step 11\>** Play the animation, then pause it.

**\<Step 12\>** Experiment with the other animation controls, but leave the Auto Keying off for now.
Your animation now consists of 30 frames. With the controls you can go to the beginning, end, skip forward and backward to the next keyframe, play the animation forward, backward, and pause it. There's also a record button, which is actually an Auto Keying feature that will allow you to avoid having to enter keyframes manually.

**\<Step 13\>** Turn on Auto Keying as shown in Figure 16.30.
Auto Keying will automatically insert the proper keyframes whenever you alter an object at a new frame.

**\<Step 14\>** Select Frame 25.

**\<Step 15\>** Select the cube, type g, and move to the side.
As soon as you do that a keyframe is inserted at Frame 25 because you have Auto Keying on.

**\<Step 16\>** Turn off Auto Keying.
You can leave Auto Keying on while you're doing an animation, but you need to remember to turn it off when you're done so that you don't unintentionally create keyframes later on.

**\<Step 17\>** Play the animation again, then stop it.

FIGURE 16.30   Auto Keying enabled in Blender.

Now that you're created your first animation in Blender, it's time to look at it. This animation is nothing to be proud of. It's more of a "Hello World" test to try out the interface.

You want to try out one more thing, rendering.

**<Step 18>** Use the Rendering Workspace.

**<Step 19>** Render – Render Animation.

You should see a pop-up window showing the 30 frames getting rendered, one after another. But, where did they go and how do you look at this rendered animation?

**<Step 20>** Click on the Output Properties icon in the Properties Editor. Look at the Output section.

There you will find the name of the folder where the 30 files got created, probably in PNG format. The Dimensions section allows you to adjust which frames to render, the pixel resolution, and the frame rate. Feel free to experiment with these settings. It's best to try these things out with a very simple animation so that you don't have to wait so long for the rendering process. One experiment worth doing is to set the File Format to one of the Movie Formats

**<Step 21>** Set the File Format to FFmpeg Video and render again. Then find the output file and play it using your operating system.

You should also notice that the size of the FFmpeg file is much smaller compared to the 30 png files. The choice of format for your renders really depends on the purpose of your work. As a game developer, you would render the .png files to be imported by Unity or possibly another game engine. Another possibility is a rendering of a cutscene as a movie file which your game engine would play as is.

**<Step 22>** Exit Blender and don't bother saving.

Of course, you can save, if you want, but this project won't be used again in this book. This Blender Animation tutorial has prepared you to tackle something a little more difficult: animating DotRobot.

## ROBOT SWINGING ARM ANIMATION

In this section, you're going to start the walk animation for DotRobot. Before you dive into that, you'll think about what this robot will do in the game. A good start is to look at the robots in Robotron 2084, the famous arcade game by Williams, released in 1982. In that game, there's a similar looking robot that simply walks around slowly and if it touches the player character it kills the player. In Robotron that robot is indestructible, and you sometimes have many of them on screen, which makes the game very difficult. Check out videos of Robotron online for a closer look.

Regardless of how you'll program the gameplay for DotRobot, a walk animation is going to be needed, so you're going to start with that. Once you have gameplay, you'll think about

what other animations you may wish to create. For example, if DotRobot has a special attack then you'll also create a new animation for that.

The plan for this first robot animation is to move the arms and legs without moving the robot. You'll look at the animation in 3D inside of Blender, but then place the camera in four positions in order to render the left, right, up, and down animations. This section shows how to animate the arms. In the next section, you'll complete the walk animation.

**<Step 1>** In Blender, File – Open Recent – DotRobot.blend.

**<Step 2>** Select the Animation Workspace.

**<Step 3>** Select DotRobot in the Outliner.

You might think that you can simply go into Edit Mode and start animating that robot by moving vertices and faces around and inserting keyframes just as you did in the previous section. Unfortunately, Blender doesn't work that way. Fortunately, Blender has a built-in addon called AnimAll that does allow you to animate vertices.

**<Step 4>** Change the Editor type of the right 3D Viewport to Preferences.

**<Step 5>** Click on Add-ons.

**<Step 6>** Scroll down, if necessary, until you see Animation: AnimAll, and check it. Compare your Preferences screen with Figure 16.31.

FIGURE 16.31    Selecting the AnimAll Add-on in Blender.

**<Step 7>** Bring back the 3D Viewport.

     By exiting the Preferences Editor, Blender autosaves the changes you made. There is a setting for autosaving preferences, so if you turned off that feature, you'll need to save preference changes explicitly.

**<Step 8>** With DotRobot still selected, go into Edit Mode in the right 3D Viewport.

**<Step 9>** Type n to show the Sidebar, or click on View – Sidebar.

**<Step 10>** Click on the Animate tab on the right side of the side panel.

**<Step 11>** Expand AnimAll by clicking on the small triangle next to it.

     The Sidebar should now look like Figure 16.32.

**<Step 12>** Click on Points.

     This setting lets the AnimAll add-on create keyframes for Points (also called vertices).

     You're now ready to animate the left arm of DotRobot.

**<Step 13>** In the User Perspective 3D Viewport, type Numpad 1 Numpad 5 and zoom in on the robot.

**<Step 14>** Select – None.

     You still had the eye sockets selected, so this unselects them.

**<Step 15>** Choose Vertex select (the box next to the Edit Mode) and use Rendered Shading with X-ray on. Compare your settings with Figure 16.33.

     The three settings you just made are circled in yellow.

FIGURE 16.32  The Sidebar interface for AnimAll.

FIGURE 16.33   Rendered Shading with X-ray, Vertex select.

**<Step 16>**  Select the two vertices at the end of DotRobot's left arm. It's the arm on the right from your view. You're actually selecting eight vertices because you have X-ray on.

**<Step 17>**  Type Numpad 3.

**<Step 18>**  Click on Insert in the AnimAll panel.
You just got three yellow dots in the Dope Sheet. Compare with Figure 16.34. You can see four highlighted vertices at the end of the arm.

**<Step 19>**  Go to Frame 10 in the Dope Sheet.

**<Step 20>**  Move the selected vertices to the left and up as in Figure 16.35 using the g key and the mouse.

**<Step 21>**  Click on Insert again.

**<Step 22>**  Test the animation so far in Object Mode.

FIGURE 16.34   Using AnimAll to insert Keyframes.

FIGURE 16.35    Animating the left arm of DotRobot.

You'll need to go into Object Mode, select Frame 1, then play the animation, stop it, and go back to Frame 10 and back to Edit Mode.

Next, in your animation, you want to move the arm back to its starting position at Frame 20. An easy way to do that is to copy and paste the keyframes from Frame 1.

**<Step 23>** Box-select the three dots at Frame 1 as shown in Figure 16.36.

This can be tricky. Be sure to select the upper left corner inside of the orange bar, or you'll just be selecting a new frame. Then drag the mouse down and to the right.

**<Step 24>** Right-click to look at the Context Menu as shown in Figure 16.37.

**<Step 25>** Select Copy.

FIGURE 16.36    Box-selecting Keyframes at Frame 1.

FIGURE 16.37    Dope Sheet Context Menu.

You could also, of course, have just typed <Ctrl> C, <command> C on a Mac.

**<Step 26>** Select Frame 20 and type <Ctrl> V, <command> V on a Mac.

**<Step 27>** Test the animation again as you did earlier.

You're halfway there. Next, you'll swing the arm backward. You lost the selection in the 3D Viewport, so you'll need to select the arm vertices again.

**<Step 28>** Hover the mouse in the right 3D Viewport, type Numpad 1, and box-select the end vertices of the left arm again.

**<Step 29>** Numpad 3.

**<Step 30>** Go to Frame 30.

**<Step 31>** Move the arm backwards and up a little.

**<Step 32>** Insert the keyframe by clicking on Insert in AnimAll.

**<Step 33>** Select Frame 40 and type  <Ctrl> V. It's <command> V on a Mac.

The copy-paste buffer should still have the keyframe from Frame 1, so you can just paste it again at Frame 40.

**<Step 34>** Set the end of the animation to 40.

**<Step 35>** Go to Object Mode.

You can only see animations created by AnimAll in Object Mode.

**<Step 36>** Play the animation.

The animation works, but it's a bit jerky at the start and end. To fix that, do the following steps.

**<Step 37>** Right-click on the top-left keyframe, and change the handle-type to vector.

**<Step 38>** Repeat for the top-right keyframe.

**<Step 39>** Play the animation again.

It's smoother now because the animation doesn't slow down and speed up anymore when it loops.

**<Step 40>** Save your work and exit Blender.

It's a good habit to save and exit at a good stopping point.

Next, as you would expect, it's time to animate the other arm.

**<Step 41>** Start Blender and File – Open Recent – DotRobot.blend.

You are surprised that you're back in Object Mode in the right 3D Viewport. Also, you're using Solid Viewport Shading with X-ray enabled. Just for fun, do this:

**<Step 42>** Play the animation.

The animation still works, but it looks quite a bit different in Object Mode with solid shading.

**<Step 43>** Switch to Edit Mode and Rendered Shading.

**<Step 44>** Numpad 1.

You did that so you can select the end vertices of the other arm.

**<Step 45>** Box-select the end vertices of the left arm as shown in Figure 16.38.

**<Step 46>** Go to Object Mode.

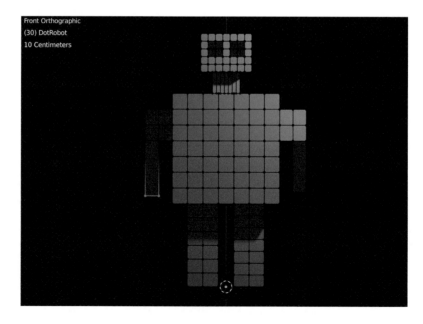

FIGURE 16.38 Selecting the end vertices of DotRobot's right arm.

This is important because the subsequent step only moves DotRobot when in Object Mode.

**<Step 47>** Drag the current frame marker left and right in the Dope Sheet and watch the effect on DotRobot.

**<Step 48>** Drag the current frame marker to Frame 1 in the Dope Sheet as shown in Figure 16.39.
Both arms of DotRobot should be hanging straight down.

**<Step 49>** Hover the mouse over the right 3D Viewport and type <Ctrl> Numpad 3.
You're now seeing the Left Orthographic view because you used the Control key when typing Numpad 3. DotRobot is dark because the light is on the other side.

**<Step 50>** Go to Edit Mode.

**<Step 51>** In AnimAll, check Points.

**<Step 52>** Click on Insert in AnimAll.

**<Step 53>** Switch to Object Mode, drag the current frame marker to Frame 10, then go back to Edit Mode. Compare your 3D Viewport with Figure 16.40.
You can see the left arm in a forward position. You'll move the right arm back.

**<Step 54>** Type g, move the selected arm back, and left-click to finalize the new position. Compare with Figure 16.41.

**<Step 55>** Click on Insert in AnimAll.

**<Step 56>** Object Mode, scrub to Frame 20.

**<Step 57>** Edit Mode, move the selected arm to hang down, click on Insert.

**<Step 58>** Object Mode, scrub to Frame 30.

**<Step 59>** Edit Mode, move the selected arm forward, click on Insert.

**<Step 60>** Object Mode, scrub to Frame 40.

**<Step 61>** Edit Mode, move the selected arm to hang down, click on Insert.

FIGURE 16.39    Dragging the current frame market in the Dope Sheet.

FIGURE 16.40    Setting up to animate the right arm of DotRobot.

FIGURE 16.41    Robot right arm moved back.

**<Step 62>** Object Mode and play the animation.

Congratulations, the robot arms are swinging just the way you wanted. The whole process was tedious, to say the least, but sometimes, in game development, you just have to deal with tedious work. It's worth thinking about how to automate tedious processes, but in this case you just did it. It was a good exercise, and maybe next time you'll think of a quicker way to do something like this.

**<Step 63>** Save your work.

Take a break, then go on to the next section where you'll animate the legs.

## ROBOT WALK ANIMATION

In this section, you're going to build on the work from the previous section and animate the legs of DotRobot. Go ahead, walk somewhere and pay attention to the timing of your swinging arms in relation to your legs. Chances are that when your left leg goes forward, so does your right arm, and when your right leg goes forward, your left arm moves forward, about at the same time. The actual physics of a human walk is very complex, but here you're animating a cartoonish robot, so you don't really need to be very realistic.

Moving the legs in Blender can't be done in quite the same way as moving the arms, because of all those vertices and faces that make up the legs. Rather than moving the feet, you'll select each leg entirely and rotate the vertices around a pivot point near the top of the legs.

**<Step 1>** Select Rendered Viewport Shading for the right 3D Viewport, X-Ray on.

**<Step 2>** Numpad 1. Go into Edit Mode.

You can quickly switch from Object Mode to Edit Mode and back by typing <Tab>.

**<Step 3>** In Vertex select mode, box-select the top of the robot, everything but the legs and the bottom of the chest, as shown in Figure 16.42.

That's right, you're going to hide the everything from the chest up to more easily work on the leg animation.

**<Step 4>** Type h (lower case).

This hides the top of DotRobot temporarily.

**<Step 5>** Type <Alt> h to bring DotRobot back, then type h again.

This is just to test that the geometry can be easily brought back.

Next, you're going to move the 3D Cursor to the top of the legs so you can put the pivot point there.

**<Step 6>** Box-select the bottom of the chest, type <Shift> S, Cursor to Selected.

This brings up a pie-menu and moves the 3D Cursor as shown in Figure 16.43.

FIGURE 16.42    Selecting the top of DotRobot in order to hide it.

FIGURE 16.43    3D Cursor moved to desired pivot point location.

<Step 7>  Numpad 7, Numpad 1.
            This shows you to top view of where the 3D Cursor went.

<Step 8>  Select the "Transform Pivot Point" icon and choose "3D Cursor" as shown in
            Figure 16.44.

FIGURE 16.44    Moving the Pivot Point to the 3D Cursor in Blender.

**<Step 9>**   Box-select the right leg of DotRobot (the one on the left from your view). Omit the vertices at the very top of the leg.

**<Step 10>**   <Ctrl> Numpad 3.

**<Step 11>**   Type r and move the mouse to rotate the selected leg, then right-click to cancel.

**<Step 12>**   Go to Object Mode.

**<Step 13>**   Drag the Frame marker to Frame 10 in the Dope Sheet.
        Make sure that in the camera view the right arm is back, the left arm forward.

**<Step 14>**   Go back to Edit Mode.

**<Step 15>**   Type r and swing the leg forward as shown in Figure 16.45. Left-click to finalize.

**<Step 16>**   In AnimAll, click on Points, then Insert.

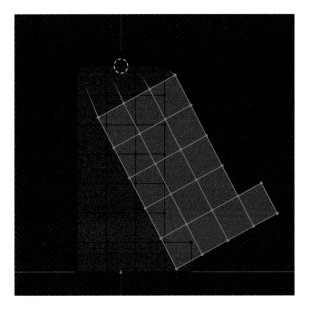

FIGURE 16.45    Swinging the right leg forward at Frame 10.

This created a keyframe for the leg rotated forward. You just realized that you need keyframes for Frames 1, 20, and 40, which are all the same, so you'll do that next.

**<Step 17a>** Type r and rotate the leg back to its original standing position.

**<Step 17b>** Drag the frame marker to Frame 1.

**<Step 18>** Click on Insert.

**<Step 19>** Frame 20 and Insert.

**<Step 20>** Frame 40 and Insert.

**<Step 21>** Rotate the leg back, go to Frame 30, and insert.

**<Step 22>** Object Mode, then play the animation.

You can see the right leg swinging back and forth.

**<Step 23>** Save.

**<Step 24>** Numpad 1, Edit Mode, and then Redo Steps 9–23 for the other leg.

You'll have to make some changes along the way. You might be able to do this without referring to the written steps, so give it a try. If something goes wrong, just start over from the save file and try again.

**<Step 25>** Save!

This is a major milestone. You have a very nice looking animated robot that you built from scratch in Blender.

You're still not quite finished. First of all, that hiccup in the animation is back. To diagnose it, do the following:

**<Step 26>** Find the border between the Dope Sheet and one of the 3D Viewports above. Then drag the border up to make the Dope Sheet fill most of your window.

**<Step 27>** Expand the Cube and compare with Figure 16.46.

Look carefully at the Keyframe for Vertex 188 and below. The handle types are circles, not squares. You need all of the Handle Types for Frame 1 and 40 to be of type Vector.

**<Step 28>** In the Summary row, click on the keyframe at Frame 1, <Shift> click on Frame 40.

You should have the entire left column and right column selected.

**<Step 29>** Right-click somewhere in the Keyframe area, Handle Type, Vector.

The selected handles should all be squares now, indicating that they are of type vector.

**<Step 30>** Collapse the Cube Keyframes and shrink the Dope Sheet to its original size.

**<Step 31>** Play the animation.

FIGURE 16.46   Massive Keyframes in the Dope Sheet for DotRobot.

That's much better. You no longer have hiccupping in the middle of the walk. All you have left to do now is to generate the walking animation png files.

**<Step 32>**  Save again.

**<Step 33>**  Select the Rendering Workspace.

**<Step 34>**  Select the Output Properties tab in the Properties Editor.

**<Step 35>** Change the Step to 2.

**<Step 36>** Change the File Format to FFmpeg video.

**<Step 37>** Render – Render Animation.

**<Step 38>** Go to the Output folder (the default is C:/tmp) and double-click on the mpeg animation to see it.

>    You should see a very short animation clip. In your video player, turn on repeat to see the walk cycle the way it will be displayed in the game. This was just a test. Next, you'll generate the .png files.

**<Step 39>** In Blender, change the File Format to .png.

**<Step 40>** Render – Render Animation.

**<Step 41>** Look at the first .png file in GIMP.

>    Notice that you don't have transparency. You should be seeing a checker-board pattern for the background, but it's black instead. What went wrong?

**<Step 42>** Back in Blender, look at the Output section of the Output Properties.

>    Below the File Format you see three choices for Color: BW, RGB, and RGBA. You have RGB selected, but you'll need the alpha channel for transparency.

**<Step 43>** Select RGBA for Color.

**<Step 44>** Render again and check out the first .png file in GIMP again.

>    You now see the checkerboard pattern in the background.

**<Step 45>** In Blender, go back to the Animation Workspace, save and exit.

>    You have one of the four directions for the walk cycle. You'll do the other directions later, after you've taken a look at your work so far in Unity.

>    You have 20 files to deal with here, with the names 0001.png, 0003.png, …, 0039.png. Create the folder Assets/art/DotRobotWalkDown and copy the 20 files there. They look like Figure 16.47 with Extra Large Icons selected, sorted by name in Windows 10.

>    You're now ready to get this animation working in Unity.

**<Step 46>** Start up Unity with the DotGame project.

>    It takes a few seconds to load the new .png files into Unity.

**<Step 47>** Select all the new .png files as a group and change the Pixels Per Unit to 1024.

>    To do the group selection, go to the DotRobotWalkDown folder, click the first .png file, then shift-click the last one. All 20 file names should be high-lighted in blue. You can then make the change in the Inspector for all 20 files simultaneously.

**<Step 48>** Select DotRobot in the Hierarchy.

**<Step 49>** Open the Animation window.

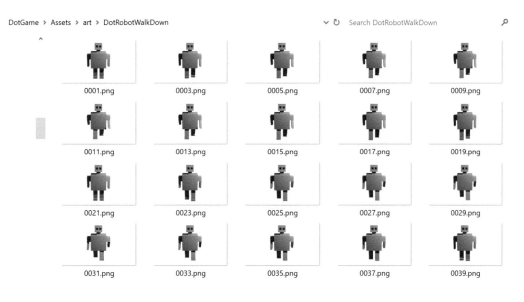

DotGame > Assets > art > DotRobotWalkDown          ✓ ↻   Search DotRobotWalkDown          ρ

| | | | | |
|---|---|---|---|---|
| 0001.png | 0003.png | 0005.png | 0007.png | 0009.png |
| 0011.png | 0013.png | 0015.png | 0017.png | 0019.png |
| 0021.png | 0023.png | 0025.png | 0027.png | 0029.png |
| 0031.png | 0033.png | 0035.png | 0037.png | 0039.png |

FIGURE 16.47    DotRobot walk cycle animation files, down direction.

**<Step 50>** Click on Create in the Animation window.

**<Step 51>** Name the new animation DotRobot_Walk_Down.anim and save it in Assets/animations.

**<Step 52>** Move the Animation Tab, and make it a separate pop-up window so that you can see the Project window and the Animation window at the same time.

**<Step 53>** In the Project window, select the 20 robot sprites and drag them to the Animation window at Frame 0. The result should look like Figure 16.48.
   There are now 20 frames, ranging from 0 to 19, in the Animation pop-up window.

**<Step 54>** Change the Samples setting in the Animation window from 60 to 12.

**<Step 55>** Preview the animation by pressing the play button in the Animation pop-up.
   You should see DotRobot going through the walk animation in the Scene panel.

**<Step 56>** Move the Animation window back to the bottom panel area next to Console.

**<Step 57>** In the Game panel, select Maximize on Play if necessary, then Play the game, then stop playing it.
   The robot looks pretty good. It might be better to make it larger, but you'll make that adjustment later. Next, you'll create the other three animations. All you have to do is rotate DotRobot, render and export to Unity, then do all that two more times. That's right, it's easier to rotate the robot rather than to move and reorient the camera and light.

**<Step 58>** File – Save. Leave Unity running, but minimize the window.

FIGURE 16.48    DotRobot Walk Down animation in Unity.

**\<Step 59\>**  Start Blender, reload the saved DotRobot.blend file.

**\<Step 60\>**  Hover the mouse in the right 3D Viewport, then Numpad 7.

**\<Step 61\>**  Type r 90  \<Enter\>.

**\<Step 62\>**  In the Timesheet at the very bottom, play the animation.
In the Camera View on the left you see DotRobot walking to the left.

**\<Step 63\>**  Select the Rendering Workspace.

**\<Step 64\>**  In the Output section, change the folder to Assets\art\DotRobotWalkLeft\

**\<Step 65\>**  Render – Render Animation.

**\<Step 66\>**  In Unity, change the Pixels per Unit of the new animation sprites to 1024 as you did before.

**\<Step 67\>**  In the Animation window, expand the DotRobot_Walk_Down text box, and click on Create New Clip… Use the name DotRobot_Walk_Left.anim in the animations folder.

**\<Step 68a\>**Drag the 20 sprites from the DotRobotWalkLeft folder to Frame 0, and change the Samples to 12 as before.

**\<Step 68b\>** Save.

**\<Step 69\>**  Repeat the steps you used to make the Walk_Left animation to make the Walk_Up and Walk_Right animations.

**\<Step 70\>**  The Animation window now has four animation clips set up for DotRobot as shown in Figure 16.49.
Wow, this is a long chapter, and you're not even done with DotRobot. Still, you've had enough of this for a while, so it's time to save your work and move on to making some different enemies for the game.
Traditionally, a small indie development team might consist of a programmer, an artist, a sound person, maybe a level designer or two and some testers.

FIGURE 16.49    The four walk directions for DotRobot in the Unity Animation window.

In this chapter, you took the role of the artist to make a single character, DotRobot. In the next chapter, you'll continue your artistic role and make the graphics for some more enemies.

Often, programmers can't draw, and artists can't program, but somehow, they can work together and make a game. It's a great benefit for the team when most everyone walks in the other people's shoes for a while. Still, this isn't a hard requirement. In this day and age of large teams, it's OK to specialize and just concentrate on your own little corner of the project.

# Making Textured Enemies with Blender

You're going to make three additional enemies for DotGame: spikers, blockades, and question marks. Spikers are simple rotating spikey things that attack whenever they see you. Blockades are square blocks that can be moved by pushing them. Question marks look like the usual English question mark. They do unknown things to you when you collide with them, anything from giving you points to moving you to another place on the level. Just as in the previous chapter, you'll use Blender to model and animate these enemies.

Along the way, you'll learn about textures and materials in Blender. Textures are typically square images that are applied to the surface of a 3D model. Materials combine possibly multiple textures and other surface properties which allow for the simulation of different types of materials in real life. An example of a material might be the shiny metallic surface of a hammer head, or the wooden surface of the handle of that hammer.

## SPIKERS

<Step 1> Open Blender and delete the default cube.
For this one, you'll start with the Ico Sphere.

<Step 2> Use the Modeling Workspace.

<Step 3> Add – Mesh – Ico Sphere.

<Step 4a> In the bottom left corner of the 3D viewport, expand the "Add Ico Sphere" menu and set Subdivisions to 1. Type Numpad 3 5.

<Step 4b> View – Frame Selected.
Your Screen should look similar to Figure 17.1.
This is an icosahedron, a polyhedron consisting of 20 equilateral triangles, one of the five platonic solids.

FIGURE 17.1   Creating an Ico Sphere in Blender.

**\<Step 4c\>** Save as Spiker.blend in Assets/models.

You're nowhere near done with this blend file, but you saved it now just to store it in the correct folder. This way, if you need to shut down your system quickly, you can just Save and power it down without having to think about it.

When you added the Ico Sphere, Blender went back to Object Mode even though you're in the Modeling Workspace.

**\<Step 5\>** Hit the \<Tab\> key to switch back to Edit Mode.

**\<Step 6\>** Rename the Icosphere to Spiker in the Outliner.

In Blender you double-click on the name to go to the rename entry mode, unlike Unity, where you do a single-click and wait instead.

**\<Step 7\>** Go to Edge Select Mode, then Edge – Bevel Edges. Type V to only bevel the vertices. Then move the mouse to get something like Figure 17.2.

**\<Step 8\>** Face – Extrude Faces Along Normals. Type 1 \<Enter\>. Zoom out a bit with the scroll wheel. Compare with Figure 17.3.

**\<Step 9\>** Change the Pivot Point to Individual Origins as shown in Figure 17.4.

**\<Step 10\>** Type s and move the mouse to turn the pentagon columns into spikes as shown in Figure 17.5.

You're going to animate the spiker, and it looks fairly good already, but before you do the animation, you'll start to learn the basics of textures and materials in Blender by creating a simple material for the spiker model. Alternatively, you could add a material after export to Unity using a Unity material, but you'll achieve better realism by working on the material in Blender.

FIGURE 17.2    Turning Vertices to Pentagons.

FIGURE 17.3    Extruding the Pentagons.

First, you'll go into the Animation Workspace and set up the camera and lighting. In order to be consistent with the other prerendered objects, you'll set up the light and camera the same way as in the DotRobot blend file.

<Step 11>  Select the Animation Workspace.

<Step 12>  Set the camera to location (0m, −13m, 7m), Rotation (70, 0 ,0).

The camera view has the spiker too low, so move up the spiker to be completely visible as follows:

FIGURE 17.4    Setting Pivot Point to Individual Origins.

FIGURE 17.5    Final Spiker Model.

**<Step 13>**  Select the Spiker, type g z 2.

**<Step 14>**  In the right 3D viewport, type Numpad 35.
    You now have a good view of the spiker in the camera view. You'll now turn the spiker red.

**<Step 15>**  Select the Shading Workspace. Zoom in on the spiker and compare with Figure 17.6.

**<Step 16>**  Select the Material Properties in the Properties Editor, and click on New. The Properties Editor now looks like Figure 17.7.
    You are likely seeing only the top of the Material section as it is too tall to show in its entirety. You can use the mouse scroll wheel to see all of it. Creating this material caused two nodes to appear in the bottom panel of the Shading Workspace.

FIGURE 17.6    The Shading Workspace featuring the spiker.

FIGURE 17.7    A new material in the Properties Editor.

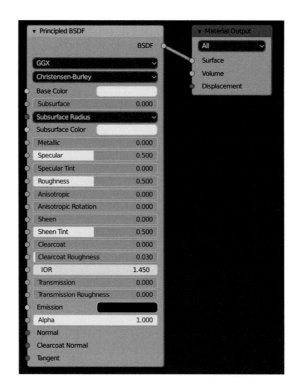

FIGURE 17.8   Nodes for a new material in Blender.

**<Step 17>** Use the mouse wheel to display the Principled BDSF and the Material Output nodes in the Shading Editor at the bottom. Compare with Figure 17.8.

**<Step 18>** Select the Base Color, currently white, in the Principled BDSF node and make it red by changing the Base Color to a red shade of your choice.

   The spiker should now be red. You can also access the Base Color in the Properties Editor, if you wish. You can see that it turned red there as well.

**<Step 19>** Go back to the Animation Workspace.

   OK, that's not good. The redness has disappeared. That's because you're using Solid Viewport shading.

**<Step 20>** Change to Rendered Viewport shading in both 3D viewports.

   Wow, that's much better. You just added a nice red material for the spiker. This is a simple as it gets. You didn't add a texture, just a solid color. You'll explore texturing later on. For this object, a plastic red material is just fine.

**<Step 21>** Save and exit Blender.

   This is a good time to save and exit, take a break, and come back to animate the spiker.

**<Step 22>** Start up Blender, File – Open Recent Spiker.blend.

   The Rendered Viewport shading got lost, so set it up again like this:

**<Step 23>** Select Rendered Viewport shading for both 3D viewports.

**<Step 24>** Numpad 7 while hovering the mouse over the right 3D viewport.
As you can see, the spiker has one spike pointing up, two rows of five spikes below, and another spike point straight down. You plan to do a rotation animation about the z-axis.

**<Step 25>** With the spiker selected, type r and move the mouse to watch the rotation. Right-click to cancel.
You'll notice that you don't need to rotate the spiker 360 degrees to generate a loop. 1/5 of 360 degrees works because of symmetry.

**<Step 26>** At the bottom right, set the End of the animation to 40.

**<Step 27>** In the right viewport, type I and select Rotation.

**<Step 28>** In the Dope Sheet, select frame 41.

**<Step 29>** In the right viewport, type r and rotate the spiker 72 degrees clockwise.
You do that by simply typing 72 and Enter.

**<Step 30>** Type i Rotation.
You now have keyframes at frame 1 and 41.

**<Step 31>** Play the animation.
Looking pretty good, but it slows down and speeds up. To fix that, change the handle as you did for DotRobot.

**<Step 32>** Right-click on the Summary Keyframes and change the handle-types to Vector.

**<Step 33>** Play the animation again.
This time the animation is smooth as silk. All that's left to do is to render.

**<Step 34>** Go to the Rendering Workspace.

**<Step 35>** In the output section, set the Step to 10.
This step setting is a bit of an educated guess. You'll get four sprites for each 72 degrees of rotation, which should be smooth enough. You can always rerender with a smaller step if the animation turns out to look too jerky in the game.

**<Step 36>** In DotGame/Assets/art create a subfolder called SpikerRotation.

**<Step 37>** Back in Blender, change the Output folder to the newly created SpikerRotation folder.

**<Step 38>** Make sure that you're still using PNG for the File Format with RGBA Color.

**<Step 39>** In Render Properties, check Transparent in the Film section.

**<Step 40>** Render – Render Animation.

<Step 41> Save and exit Blender.

> This object was much easier to create and animate than DotRobot. Next, you want to create the blockade, but first you'll learn how to make textures and use them in Blender.

## TEXTURES FOR BLENDER

In this short section, you'll explore how to create textures and use them in Blender. You'll texture the default cube with a rock texture that you're going to create in GIMP. The source material comes from pixabay.com.

<Step 1> Go to pixabay.com and search for stone wall rock. Likely the first image in your search will look like Figure 17.9. Log in and download the 1920 × 1280 jpeg of that image.

> You should still have an active account at pixabay from your previous usage earlier in this project. This texture is somewhat atypical. It's not square, and it's not seamless. This is OK for your purposes.

<Step 2a> Create the folder Assets/art/Blockade in the DotGame Unity project.

<Step 2b> Copy the texture file stone-3630911_1920.jpg.to this Blockade folder.

> When making your own textures, you would now typically edit the file in GIMP and make some adjustments. This won't be necessary here.

<Step 3> Open Blender and select the Shading Workspace.

> You are now looking at the default cube using the Material Preview Viewport Shading. This shading displays any textures that you may have set up, but no lighting effects. This will give you a clear view of the materials in use while you're working on them.

<Step 4> Select the default cube, if necessary, and select the Material Properties in the Properties Editor.

FIGURE 17.9    Image of Rocks by PeterH from pixabay.

**\<Step 5\>** Click on the small circle to the right of the Base Color (currently white). Then select Image Texture.

The bottom panel shows three nodes as in Figure 17.10.

**\<Step 6\>** Click on Open in the Base Color Section. Navigate to the stone texture from Step 2 and click on Open Image.

You immediately see a texture shown on the default cube. It's not quite what you expected.

**\<Step 7\>** Go to the UV Editing Workspace.

The UV letters refer to the coordinate system used for textures. UV coordinates are just like XY coordinates, just using different letters because you're already using XYZ coordinates for your 3D model.

**\<Step 8\>** In the right 3D viewport, select Material Preview Shading. Zoom in on the default cube. Then compare your Blender window with Figure 17.11.

**\<Step 9\>** In the UV Editor on the left, type a to select all, then s to scale, and move the mouse.

You can see that the texture is changing for the cube as you move the mouse to scale the unwrapped geometry on the texture. That cross-shaped arrangement of rectangles represents the faces and edges of the cube. You can imagine that cross getting wrapped around the cube.

You have control over the unwrapping as demonstrated in the following step.

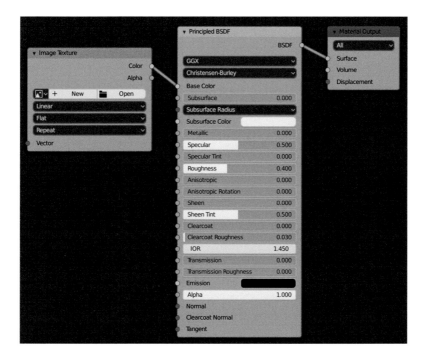

FIGURE 17.10   Using an Image Texture in Blender.

FIGURE 17.11    The UV editing Workspace in Blender.

**<Step 10>**  Go to Face Select mode in the right 3D viewport, type a to select all, then right-click and choose UV Unwrap Faces – Smart UV Project.

In the UV Editor, you now have six squares arranged differently.

**<Step 11>**  In the UV Editor, choose Face Select mode above, then select the top left face, type g and move the mouse.

This shows you how each face is mapped onto the texture. You can arrange the faces one-by-one, or by using one of the built-in UV Unwrap methods to let Blender do this for you.

This section is a demo to show the basic concepts of how textures work in Blender. You're now ready to move on and create a textured model in the next section. There's no need to save this project, so you can just exit Blender without saving.

## BLOCKADE

The plan for this game object is to have a heavy looking, cube-like object that can be slowly pushed or possibly pulled around the maze. You'll start with the default cube, alter the shape to make it more interesting, apply the rock texture from the previous section, and export it to Unity as a single image. There's no need to animate this object. You already set up the folder for this project so you can go ahead and create the .blend file.

**<Step 1>**  Start up Blender and save to Blockade.blend in Assets/models.

**<Step 2>**  Select the Modeling Workspace.

**<Step 3>**  Use the Front Orthographic view by typing Numpad 5 1.

**<Step 4>** Turn on Snap by clicking on the magnet icon at the top middle of the 3D viewport.

**<Step 5>** Type g z and move the cube up one meter.

**<Step 6>** Type a to make sure all vertices are selected.

**<Step 7>** Hover the mouse above and to the left of the cube. Then type <Ctrl> B to start the Bevel interaction. You'll see a dotted line from the center of the cube to the mouse cursor. Move the mouse away from the cube a little as shown in Figure 17.12 and click the left mouse button.

**<Step 8>** Expand the Bevel dialog at the bottom left of the viewport and change the Width to 0.2m.

**<Step 9>** Scroll the mouse wheel to zoom in on the default cube.

**<Step 10>** Change the name of the default cube to Blockade in the Outliner.

**<Step 11>** Hover the mouse near the blockade, type <Ctrl> R.
You have just entered into loop-cut mode.

**<Step 12>** Move the mouse near the left edge of the blockade until you see a single yellow horizontal line.
As you move the mouse in loop-cut mode, different possible loop-cuts appear. You want the horizontal one.

FIGURE 17.12 Beveling in Blender.

**<Step 13>** Scroll the mouse wheel to increase the number of loop-cuts to 6.

**<Step 14>** Left-click to go into position mode. In this mode, you can adjust the position of the loop-cuts. Try moving the mouse up and down to try this out.

**<Step 15>** Right-click to cancel the new position and choose the original centered position for the loop-cuts by left-clicking.

Once you become more experienced with this, you'll be able to do this loop-cut sequence in under a second. Try this now, if you wish, by undoing the loop-cut with <Ctrl> Z (<command> Z on Mac) and redoing it manually by repeating Steps 12–15.

**<Step 16>** <Alt> S (<option> S on a Mac) to Shrink/Fatten. Move the mouse toward the center of the Blockade a little and left-click.

**<Step 17>** Expand the Shrink/Fatten dialog at the bottom left, and make the Offset 0.2m. Compare your Blockade with Figure 17.13.

**<Step 18>** In the Properties Editor, click on the Modifier Properties icon.

**<Step 19>** Add Modifier Subdivision Surface.

**<Step 20>** Change the Subdivisions for the Viewport from 1 to 2.

**<Step 21>** Go to the Layout Workspace and zoom in on the Blockade. Compare with Figure 17.14.

Even without a texture, the blockade looks heavy. That's just what you want. Next, you'll add the texture, just as you did in the previous section.

FIGURE 17.13   The Shrink/Fatten command in Blender.

FIGURE 17.14   Blockade model.

<**Step 22**>  Go to the Shading Workspace.

<**Step 23**>  View – Frame Selected (or Numpad.).

<**Step 24**>  Go to Material Properties.

<**Step 25**>  Click on the small circle next to the Base Color. Select Image Texture.

<**Step 26**>  Open Assets/art/Blockade/stone3630911_1920.jpg.

<**Step 27**>  Modifier Properties.

<**Step 28**>  In the Properties Editor, click on Apply.
This makes the Subdivision Modifier permanent.

<**Step 29**>  Modeling Workspace.

<**Step 30**>  Face Select Mode.

<**Step 31**>  Use Solid Viewport shading.

<**Step 32**>  Hold the middle mouse button and move the mouse until your view looks like Figure 17.15.
You can now see the many faces generated by the Subdivision Surface Modifier. That modifier is very popular as it can quickly generate detailed geometry when starting out with a simple low-poly model.

<**Step 33**>  Use Rendered Viewport shading.
That's not quite what you had in mind, so you'll go and look at the UVs.

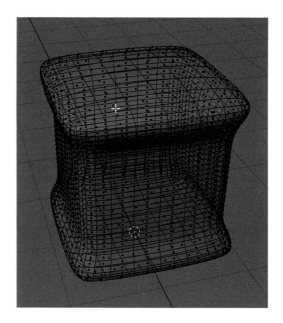

FIGURE 17.15    Blockade in Face Select Mode.

**<Step 34>** UV Editing Workspace.

**<Step 35a>** Hover the mouse over the right viewport, then type a to select all the faces. You need to still be in Face Select mode.

**<Step 35b>** Hover the mouse over the left viewport and type a there as well.

**<Step 36>** With the mouse still in the UV Editor, type s and scale up the mesh as in Figure 17.16.

FIGURE 17.16    Using the UV editor to adjust UV coordinates for the blockade.

<Step 37> Layout Workspace.

That's much better, although it's a bit jumbled and not realistic. You're going to live with that for now, maybe forever.

Your next goal is to set up the camera and lighting to match the other game objects, more or less. Rather than copying the camera and light coordinates you'll just adjust them manually.

<Step 38> Animation Workspace.

Yes, you're not going to do animation for this object, but this workspace is convenient for adjusting the camera and lighting.

<Step 39> Use Rendered Viewport shading in both 3D Viewports.

<Step 40> Top Orthographic View in the right viewport (Numpad 7). Zoom out to see the camera widget, the light widget, and the blockade.

<Step 41> Turn off Snap. Select the Camera. Type g and move it up to the red line (the x axis).

<Step 42> Type r and rotate the camera so you can see the blockade again in the camera viewport.

<Step 43> Move the light somewhat closer to the blockade. Compare with Figure 17.17.

All that's left to do is rendering.

<Step 44> Save.

It's a good idea to save your work before any render.

<Step 45> Render Workspace, Render – Render Image.

This was just a test to get a closer look. You can look at the details by scrolling the mouse wheel. You're seeing a horizontal band near the top of the blockade. How would you fix that? Simple, use smooth shading.

FIGURE 17.17   Blockade, textured and lit.

**<Step 46>** Shading Workspace. Select Blockade. Right-click to get the Object Context Menu.

**<Step 47>** Select Shade Smooth.

**<Step 48>** Render Workspace, Render – Render Image.

> The horizontal band is still there, but it's much softer and smoother. Now it's time to set up the render settings. This will be similar to the Spiker render settings, but it's different because you're rendering a single image, not an animation.

**<Step 49>** In Render Properties, Film, check Transparency.

**<Step 50>** Render – Render Image.

> You should see the checkerboard pattern in the background.

**<Step 51>** In the pop-up window, do Image – Save.

**<Step 52>** Make sure that you have png File Format, RGBA color.

**<Step 53>** Navigate to Assets/art/Blockade, and set the image name to Blockade.png.

**<Step 54>** Close the render pop-up, save and exit Blender.

> You're getting lots of practice with Blender and everything is starting to feel more familiar due to the repetitions. So far, you've been simply following along with the steps in this book, but you're getting much closer to having the skills to break out on your own to create entirely on your own.
>
> In the next section, you'll model one more enemy, if you can call it that.

## QUESTION MARKS

The question mark should be pretty easy to create. You merely model something that looks like a question mark, give it some kind of an animation, and you're done. You don't really need to make an animation nor a texture, but you'll do that anyway to continue your learning journey. Now that you think about it, animating the question mark is a good idea to draw the player's attention to it because it's probably just going to sit there otherwise. It's basically going to have a perpetual idle animation. You'll do a subtle squash up and down, and maybe mix in a left-right rotation.

Rather than modeling that question mark yourself you can use Blender's text features to create a very authentic looking question mark model automatically in just a few steps.

**<Step 1>** Create the folder Assets/art/QuestionMark in the DotGame project.

**<Step 2>** Start up Blender.

**<Step 3>** Delete that default cube.

**<Step 4>** Save the project in Assets/models/QuestionMark.blend.

**<Step 5>**  Shift-A and select Text.

> This creates a text object at the 3D cursor, which is currently at the origin.

**<Step 6>**  <Numpad> 7 to get a Top Perspective view.

**<Step 7>**  View - Frame Selected (<Numpad><dot>).

**<Step 8>**  Type <Tab> to get into Edit Mode. Check that you are in Edit Mode near the top left corner of the viewport. Your screen should look like Figure 17.18.

> You can see a very fat cursor on the right. You are looking at a giant text entry box. Try it out, if you like.

**<Step 9>**  Type a question mark.

> The built-in font for Blender has a strange looking question mark. That's not quite what you want, so you're going to use a different font to get a more standard looking question mark.

**<Step 10>**  In the Properties panel, select the Object Data Properties icon near the bottom of the icon column. The icon looks like the letter a.

> You see that there are quite a few options there. First things first: get a different font!

**<Step 11>**  Expand Font and click on the folder icon for the Regular font.

**<Step 12>**  Navigate to Assets\TextMesh Pro\Fonts and select LiberationSans. ttf.

> You could use any True Type Font with a.ttf extension, but the LiberationSans font is a good one to use because it is built into Unity and thus free to use in any Unity project.

FIGURE 17.18   Editing Text in Blender.

**<Step 13>** Click on Open font.

That's more like it. That question mark is skinny, but that can be easily fixed.

**<Step 14>** Delete everything but the question mark in your text.

You do that by typing a left arrow on your keyboard, then the backspace key four times to delete the four default letters.

**<Step 15>** <Tab> to go into Object Mode. Do a Frame Selected again i.e. <Numpad><dot>.

**<Step 16>** In the Object Data Properties, expand the Geometry section.

**<Step 17>** Offset 0.01m, Extrude 0.01m, Bevel Depth 0.01m.

Wow, what a difference. It's good to remember that beveling can make 3D object look a lot better. Next, you'll make the question mark yellow.

**<Step 18>** Select the Material Properties, add a new material, set the Base Color to yellow.

**<Step 19>** Select Rendered Viewport shading to see the new yellow color. Compare with Figure 17.19.

**<Step 20>** File – Save.

Next, you'll do the animation. In order to animate the question mark, you'll need to convert the text object to a mesh.

**<Step 21>** Object – Convert to – Mesh from Curve/Meta/Surf/Text.

**<Step 22>** Edit Mode.

The fat cursor is gone, and you can see the rather detailed mesh. You're now ready to do the animation for this mesh.

FIGURE 17.19   A very large yellow question mark in Blender.

<Step 23> Animation Workspace.

You're going to have to adjust the camera and lighting, just as with the previous enemies. In hindsight, it might have been better to start with one of those other projects and delete the mesh. Then you'd have the correct camera and light already set up. There is another way though. You can use the append feature in Blender to import specific objects from other blend files.

<Step 24> Select the light and type x to delete it. Hit the Enter key to confirm.

<Step 25> Delete the camera as well.

<Step 26> File – Append, select Spiker.blend and click on Append.

This next step isn't at all obvious. You do not click on the Light nor the Camera folders.

<Step 27> Double-click on the Object folder.

<Step 28> Click on Camera, Shift-click on Light, Click on Append.

As you can see in the Outliner, you once again have a Light and a Camera. You still need to update the view in the left viewport.

<Step 29> Hover the mouse over the left viewport, then type Numpad 0.

The camera shows a small question mark near the bottom. You'll need to make some adjustments to the question mark, leaving the camera and light as is.

<Step 30> In the right viewport, hover the mouse there and type Numpad 3 5.

<Step 31> Select the Text object in the Outliner, hover the mouse in the viewport, and do Frame Selected.

You now have a good view of the question mark from the side as shown in Figure 17.20.

<Step 32> Type r and move the mouse until the question mark is upright, then left-click to confirm.

FIGURE 17.20  Setting up the animation for the question mark.

FIGURE 17.21  Scaled up question mark.

**<Step 33>** Type s and scale the question mark so that it fills about half of the camera view as shown in Figure 17.21.

**<Step 34>** In the right viewport, type Numpad 1 Numpad dot.

**<Step 35>** Change both Viewport Shadings to Rendered.
You can see that you have a problem. The lighting is coming from the back. That works for the Spiker but not for the question mark.

**<Step 36>** In the right viewport, type Numpad 7 to get a top view, and then zoom out to see both the camera and the light.

**<Step 37>** Move the light toward the camera until the question mark is bright yellow.
While you're at it, you'll adjust the position of the question mark. But first, you'll do something you should have done earlier: renaming the Text object to QuestionMark.

**<Step 38>** In the outliner, rename Text to QuestionMark.

**<Step 39>** With the QuestionMark still selected, in the right viewport zoom in, type g and center it.

**<Step 40>** Adjust the light to be positioned in front and somewhat to the right of the question mark.
You now have a good view of the question mark in the camera viewport. You can finally do the animation.

**<Step 41>** Select the QuestionMark object.

**<Step 42>** Numpad 1 in the right viewport.

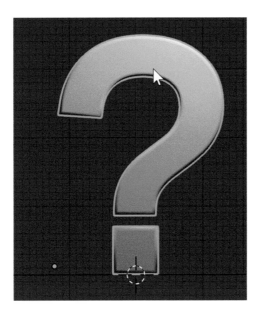

FIGURE 17.22    Adjusting the QuestionMark object position to line up with the 3D cursor.

**<Step 43>** Adjust the QuestionMark position so that the 3D cursor is at the center of the bottom, as shown in Figure 17.22.

You can see that the object origin is off to the side. The pivot point used for scaling is also there. Try a temporary scale if you like to see this. You'd like to have the pivot line up with the 3D cursor instead.

**<Step 44>** Click on the Transform Pivot Point icon at the top of the right viewport and select 3D cursor.

It's not really necessary right now, but you might as well put the object origin (that orange dot on the bottom left) at the 3D cursor position as well.

**<Step 45>** Object – Set Origin – Origin to 3D Cursor.

For future reference, it's good to know that you can manipulate the object origin and the pivot point using these menus. Now let's get back to animating.

**<Step 46>** Set the End of the animation to 40 at the bottom right of the Dope Sheet.

You're actually not in the Dope Sheet panel when you do that, but rather in the Timeline immediately below the Dope Sheet.

**<Step 47>** In the right viewport, type i and select LocRotScale.

**<Step 48>** Drag the frame counter to frame 20.

**<Step 49>** Type s z and scale down by about 0.9.

**<Step 50>** Type s x and scale up by about 1.1.

**<Step 51>** Type i and select LocRotScale.

**<Step 52>** Copy the keyframes from frame 1 to frame 41.

**<Step 53>** Play the animation.

Wow, that's eerie and spooky. Maybe you'll run this animation a bit faster in Unity.

**<Step 54>** Save.

This is getting to be familiar territory. Once again, all you need to do is to set up the Render.

**<Step 55>** Rendering Workspace.

**<Step 56>** In the Render Properties, check the Transparent checkbox in the Film section.

**<Step 57>** In the Output Properties, set Step to 4, and check that you have PNG and RGBA selected for File Format and Color.

**<Step 58>** Select the Assets/art/QuestionMark folder as the Output folder.

**<Step 59>** Render – Render Animation.

**<Step 60>** Animation Workspace.

**<Step 61>** Save and exit Blender.

In this section, you created yet another enemy and a simple animation for it. You're getting more familiar with the Blender interface and probably faster by using familiar keyboard shortcuts. Blender is famous for having keyboard shortcuts for just about everything, thus allowing you to be very productive as you learn the shortcuts for common commands. It's usually much faster to use the keyboard rather than the mouse, especially if you're a touch typist. In this age of technology, it's a huge advantage to be a fast typist.

In this chapter, you created three additional enemies. You learned quite a bit more about Blender. Switching between Blender and Unity can be challenging because of the different interfaces, so you resisted the temptation to look at the animations in Unity right away and concentrated on learning Blender for a while. In the next chapter, you'll work on getting all these new graphics into Unity. If you're lucky, you won't have to go back to Blender and redo anything, but that can happen, so don't feel bad if you need to do that.

# Enemy Movement and Collisions

I N THIS CHAPTER, you'll import the animations from the previous two chapters into Unity and make them work. You'll do them in order, starting with DotRobot, followed by the Spiker, Blockade, and Question Mark enemies. Your goal is to place them into the one and only level you have so far and make the game feel playable. This process is similar to the steps you took when you did Dottima several chapters ago.

## DOTROBOT MOVEMENT AND COLLISIONS

<Step 1> Load DotGame into Unity.

Unity will take some extra time to import the new animations in the Assets folder, but otherwise, nothing has changed since the end of the DotRobot chapter. You have one DotRobot in the level and he's just doing the down animation and not moving. Your goal for DotRobot is to have a single DotRobot walking in a circle at the right side of the level. Dottima simply has to avoid running into him to survive.

DotRobot will go clockwise around the brown book at the right, and use the following game logic: When DotRobot hits a wall he stops, turns 90 degrees to the right, and keeps going. If you implement this well, DotRobot will be in an infinite loop and continue to do that as long as the game is running on this level. After you have this working, you'll worry about how to make DotRobot do something more interesting.

<Step 2> Move DotRobot to a starting position at the right side of the level as shown in Figure 18.1.

You used the Move tool to do that, not the g command, which only works in Blender.

You're now going to put in some test code to move DotRobot and use the correct animation depending on the direction of the movement.

FIGURE 18.1    Starting position of DotRobot.

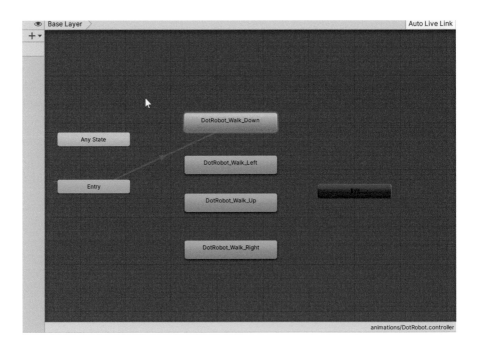

FIGURE 18.2    The DotRobot Animator window.

<Step 3> Window – Animation – Animator and rearrange the boxes to look like
Figure 18.2.
As you can see from this initial setup, DotRobot starts with the Down
animation and continues to run that animation indefinitely.

**<Step 4>** Create a DotRobot script in the scripts folder and assign it to the DotRobot object in the Hierarchy.

You'll start with a simple-minded attempt at moving DotRobot down upon starting the game.

**<Step 5>** Copy the code from DottimaController to replace the code in DotRobot and edit it to make it look like this:

```
public class DotRobot : MonoBehaviour
{
    public float speed;
    private Rigidbody2D rb;
    public Animator animator;

    void Start()
    {
        rb = GetComponent<Rigidbody2D>();
    }

    private void FixedUpdate()
    {
        Vector2 moveInput = new Vector2(0.0f, -1.0f);
        rb.velocity = moveInput.normalized * speed;
        animator.SetFloat("Speed", rb.velocity.magnitude);
    }

}
```

You simply replaced the contents of the Vector2 in the moveInput assignment to a 2D vector that points straight down. If you try to run this, it won't crash, but it will give you an error because you don't have a rigid body yet for DotRobot.

**<Step 6>** Add a Rigidbody 2D component to DotRobot. Run the game.

Well, the robot is moving down, but very slowly. It really should be stationary because the speed is set to zero right now. The slow downward movement is caused by the slight Gravity that you forgot to turn off.

**<Step 7>** Set the Gravity Scale to 0 and run the game again.

The robot is stationary, just as you would expect.

**<Step 8>** In the Inspector, set the Speed to 1 and run the game again.

Ok, now the robot is moving down, but too fast.

**<Step 9>** Set the Speed to 0.3 and try that.

The robot looks like he's skating, but this is probably as good as this is going to get without creating a more realistic walk animation. You'll keep this and fix the next pressing issue: DotRobot is running through the wall at the bottom.

**<Step 10>** Go back to the Scene panel, then in the Inspector add a Box Collider 2D to DotRobot, and edit the Collider to look like Figure 18.3. Zoom in on DotRobot with the mouse wheel to get a more detailed look while you're adjusting the collider.

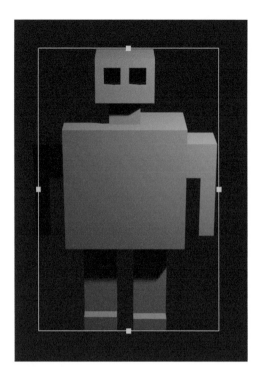

FIGURE 18.3   Box Collider in Unity for DotRobot.

**<Step 11>** Run the game and watch DotRobot get stuck at the bottom.

**<Step 12>** Run the game and collide Dottima with DotRobot.

Surprise! That actually works, sort of. DotRobot gets spun around when Dottima runs into him. That looks like fun, but of course this type of collision is not what you wanted. For now, all you'll do is freeze the rotation just as you did for Dottima.

**<Step 13>** In the Inspector, find the Constraints section for Rigidbody 2D of DotRobot. Then check Z.

The Z axis is perpendicular to the screen. Checking the Z Constraint prevents the kind of rotations you saw in the previous step.

**<Step 14>** Test that the Z Freeze Rotation works.

Your next goal is to have DotRobot show the four different animations under script control. The first baby step is to have DotRobot run the walk left animation in response to code in the DotRobot script.

**<Step 15>** In the Inspector, click on the small circle for Animator in the Dot Robot (Animator) section and select the DotRobot animator in the pop-up window.

**<Step 16>** Insert the following line in the Start method of DotRobot.cs:

```
animator.Play("DotRobot_Walk_Left");
```

**\<Step 17\>** Play the game.

DotRobot continues to act the same way, but plays the left walking animation instead of the down walk.

**\<Step 18\>** Add the following code to to the DotRobot class:

```
private void OnCollisionEnter2D(Collision2D collision)
{
    animator.Play("DotRobot_Walk_Left");
}
```

**\<Step 19\>** Change the initial animation to DotRobot_Walk_Down in the Start method.

**\<Step 20\>** Play the game.

DotRobot now changes to the left walk animation when it hits the bottom book. It's still stuck there though.

Next, you're going to introduce the concept of four directions in the code. Each direction gets a numeric code stored in the variable called "direction".

**\<Step 21\>** Enter the following code carefully into Visual Studio to replace DotRobot.cs:

```
using System.Collections;
using System.Collections.Generic;
using UnityEngine;

public class DotRobot : MonoBehaviour
{
    public float speed;
    private Rigidbody2D rb;
    public Animator animator;
    private int direction; // four directions 0,1,2,3
                           // down, left, up, right

    void Start()
    {
        rb = GetComponent<Rigidbody2D>();
        animator.Play("DotRobot_Walk_Down");
        direction = 0;
    }

    private Vector2 dirVector;

    private void FixedUpdate()
    {
        if (direction == 0) dirVector = new Vector2(0.0f, -1.0f);
        if (direction == 1) dirVector = new Vector2(-1.0f, 0.0f);
        if (direction == 2) dirVector = new Vector2(0.0f, 1.0f);
        if (direction == 3) dirVector = new Vector2(1.0f, 0.0f);

        rb.velocity = dirVector.normalized * speed;
        animator.SetFloat("Speed", rb.velocity.magnitude);

    }

    private void OnCollisionEnter2D(Collision2D collision)
    {
        direction = (direction + 1) % 4;
        if (direction == 0) animator.Play("DotRobot_Walk_Down");
        if (direction == 1) animator.Play("DotRobot_Walk_Left");
        if (direction == 2) animator.Play("DotRobot_Walk_Up");
```

```
        if (direction == 3) animator.Play("DotRobot_Walk_Right");

    }
}
```

Needless to say, a few words of explanation are in order. You added a variable called direction, and it is initialized to 0 in the Start method. In FixedUpdate, the current direction determines which of four 2D vectors are used to calculate the velocity vector of DotRobot. In the CollisionEnter2D method, you increase the direction code, causing DotRobot to turn to his right. There's a strange expression with a percent sign:

```
direction = (direction + 1) % 4;
```

This percent sign is a remainder integer function built into C#. It converts the number on the left to the remainder after division by the number on the right. When the direction is 3, the above expression changes the direction to 0, otherwise the direction is incremented. This has the effect of having DotRobot turn to the right. This method of increasing integers is commonly used when dealing with integers within a limited range.

**\<Step 22\>** Run the game.

Well, it works at the first turn, but after that DotRobot gets stuck. That's because he went too low and now is hitting the next book sprite. The following code fixes this problem.

**\<Step 23a\>** Insert this code at the beginning of the OnCollisionEnter2D function:

```
Vector2 newPosition = new Vector2(
    transform.position.x - dirVector.x * 0.1f,
    transform.position.y - dirVector.y * 0.1f);

rb.MovePosition(newPosition);
```

This isn't at all obvious. You're basically taking DotRobot and pushing him back from the direction he came by 0.1 units. DotRobot now happily runs around on a rectangular path. The 0.1 is one of those numbers found by experimentation. To better see how this code works you can temporarily change it to 0.3 and run it. Be sure to set it back to 0.1 when you're done.

You finally noticed that you're getting a warning error regarding the Parameter "Speed". This doesn't seem to cause any problems, but you'd still like to investigate.

**\<Step 23b\>** Run the game and then stop.

**\<Step 24\>** Look at the Console panel at the bottom.

You'll see multiple instances of the following error:

```
Parameter 'Speed" does not exist.
UnityEngine.Animator:SetFloat(String,Single)
```

**\<Step 25\>** Click on one of those error messages.

Voila! You get the following hint as to what's happening:

```
DotRobot:FixedUpdate() (at Assets/scripts/DotRobot.cs:31)
```

The 31 at the end is a line number. Your line number may be slightly different. You'll see in Visual Studio that line 31 has a left-over line of code from the Dottima animation. You don't need this anymore, but just in case, comment it out.

**\<Step 26\>** In DotRobot, change the `SetFloat` statement to:

```
//      animator.SetFloat("Speed", rb.velocity.magnitude);
```

The two slashes at the start of the line turn the code into a comment, which has the same effect as deleting it. You're doing this just in case you wish to resurrect this line later during development. The commented out code has also turned all green to show you that it's no longer being used. It's just a comment now.

**\<Step 27a\>** In the Console panel, click on "Clear on Play".

This will remove the old error messages when you run the game again.

**\<Step 27b\>** Test and Save.

Let's hope that you no longer see any errors or warnings in the Console panel. For future reference, it's good development practice to fix all compiler errors and warnings as soon as possible. By doing this, you will be aware of any new errors or warnings even if the game still runs.

In the next section, you'll work on the Spiker.

## SPIKER MOVEMENT AND COLLISIONS

The Spiker has just one animation, a simple rotation. First, you'll take a look in Unity to see what it looks like there.

**\<Step 1\>** In Assets/art/SpikerRotation, select the four sprites entitled 0001, 0011, 0021, and 0031.

As usual, you click on the first sprite, then shift-click on the others to select all four of them.

**\<Step 2\>** Set Pixels Per Unit to 1024.

**\<Step 3\>** Drag the 0001 Sprite into the Scene panel as shown in Figure 18.4.

**\<Step 4\>** Rename the 0001 Game Object to Spiker in the Inspector.

The Spiker is looking good as is, so you'll move on and put in the animation.

**\<Step 5\>** Window – Animation – Animation and click on Create.

**\<Step 6\>** In the folder Assets/animation, create the animation with the name Spiker_Rotation.anim.

FIGURE 18.4    Initial position of Spiker.

**<Step 7>** Select all four sprites in the SpikerRotation folder and drag them into the Animation.

**<Step 8>** In the Scene panel, select the Spiker, and focus on it by typing f.

**<Step 9>** If necessary, move the Animation window out of the way so you can see the Spiker. This should look like Figure 18.5.

**<Step 10>** Play the animation by clicking on the Play icon in the Animation window.

The Spiker is rotating much too fast. As you know by now, you can slow down these animations by adjusting the Samples/sec, which is currently 60.

**<Step 11>** Change the Samples to 12 and play.

That's a more reasonable speed, but it does look somewhat jerky at only 12 frames per second. It is called a Spiker though, so a little jerkiness is just fine for this object.

Next, you'll put in some basic movement and collision. You'll borrow the code from DotRobot and remove the animation control code as you won't need that. Later during development you'll experiment with the Spiker movement code to have it do something more interesting.

**<Step 12>** Add a Rigidbody 2D component to Spiker.

**<Step 13>** Set the Gravity Scale to 0.

FIGURE 18.5   Testing the Spiker Animation.

**<Step 14>**  Freeze Rotation Z.

**<Step 15>**  Add a Box Collider 2D to Spiker.

**<Step 16>**  Edit the Collider to fit the Spiker snugly as in Figure 18.6.

There's some judgment involved in how to edit colliders. Because the Spiker will kill Dottima when she gets too close, it's better to have the collider be small, thus allowing Dottima to escape a glancing touch.

FIGURE 18.6   Box Collider for Spiker.

**<Step 17>** Test the game.

As you expect, the Spiker just sits there, but Dottima can push the Spiker around.

Next, you'll add movement code.

**<Step 18>** In the scripts folder, right-click Create – C# script with the name Spiker.

**<Step 19>** Drag the Spiker script onto the Spiker Game Object in the Hierarchy.

**<Step 20>** Double-click on the Spiker script to open it in Visual Studio.

**<Step 21>** In Visual Studio, open DotRobot.cs.

You should still have a tab for this script, so you can just click on the tab.

**<Step 22>** With the mouse, select the contents of the DotRobot class, then type <Ctrl> C.

Note for Mac users: If you have selected the Windows key bindings, you are doing cut, paste, and undo with the <control> key rather than <command>. If you selected the Mac key bindings, you need to use <command>. This book assumes the Windows key bindings.

**<Step 23>** In Spiker.cs, select the contents of the Spiker class and type <Ctrl> V.

**<Step 24>** Remove all lines that call animator.Play. Compare with this code listing:

```csharp
public class Spiker : MonoBehaviour
{
    public float speed;
    private Rigidbody2D rb;
    public Animator animator;
    private int direction; // four directions 0,1,2,3
                           // down, left, up, right

    void Start()
    {
        rb = GetComponent<Rigidbody2D>();
        direction = 0;
    }

    private Vector2 dirVector;

    private void FixedUpdate()
    {
        if (direction == 0) dirVector = new Vector2(0.0f, -1.0f);
        if (direction == 1) dirVector = new Vector2(-1.0f, 0.0f);
        if (direction == 2) dirVector = new Vector2(0.0f, 1.0f);
        if (direction == 3) dirVector = new Vector2(1.0f, 0.0f);

        rb.velocity = dirVector.normalized * speed;
        //        animator.SetFloat("Speed", rb.velocity.magnitude);

    }

    private void OnCollisionEnter2D(Collision2D collision)
    {
        Vector2 newPosition = new Vector2(
            transform.position.x - dirVector.x * 0.1f,
            transform.position.y - dirVector.y * 0.1f);
```

```
        rb.MovePosition(newPosition);
        direction = (direction + 1) % 4;
    }
}
```

This code has a flaw at the beginning. Can you guess what? This one is tricky. You have a declaration for animator, but the animator variable isn't used, except in the commented out line. You can safely ignore this problem. Unity doesn't warn about this, so Unity thinks this is OK. Thinking ahead, you will probably want to access this animator in the future, so you'll leave it there.

If you test the game now, you'll see no difference, and the Spiker still just sits there. Can you guess why? That's right, the speed is set to zero.

<Step 25> Set Speed to 1.0 in the Inspector.

You might have noticed this before, but for some reason Unity capitalizes variables when displaying them in the Inspector. In C#, variables are case sensitive, so speed and Speed are different variables. This capitalization only happens within the Inspector for display purposes.

<Step 26> Test the game.

The Spiker works! Just for fun, try the following:

<Step 27> Test it again and collide Dottima with the Spiker to make it move over to the DotRobot. Watch what happens when they collide with each other.

Nothing special is happening, except that when the Spiker collides with DotRobot, both objects make a right turn and keep going.

<Step 28> Save.

You're almost done with this chapter. The Blockade and QuestionMark are easier because they don't move. In the next section, you'll import them into the scene and set up collisions for them.

## BLOCKADE AND QUESTIONMARK COLLISIONS

In this section, you'll continue to import the graphics for enemies in DotGame. Next on the agenda is the Blockade.

<Step 1> Go to the Blockade folder in Assets/art and select the Blockade sprite.

<Step 2> Once again, change the Pixels Per Unit to 1024, then click on Apply in the Inspector.

<Step 3> Drag the Blockade into the Scene at the exit gap near the top right corner of the level.

The Blockade is too small, so do this, to scale it up.

<Step 4> With the Blockade selected, change the Transform Scale to (2, 2, 1).

FIGURE 18.7    Placing the Blockade to block the exit.

**<Step 5>**  Adjust the position to center it, then compare with Figure 18.7.

This object needs no script, just the usual Rigidbody 2D and Box Collider Components.

**<Step 6>**  Add a Rigidbody 2D component to the Blockade.

**<Step 7>**  Set the Gravity Scale to 0.

**<Step 8>**  In the Constraints section, check Freeze Rotation Z.

**<Step 9>**  Add a Box Collider 2D and edit it to match the graphics.

**<Step 10>**  Test it.

This works well enough for now. You can push the Blockade object out of the way, allowing you to leave the level. You'll do more interesting things with this object later on. The exit probably ought to have a door instead of the blockade, but this is good enough.

**<Step 11>**  Save your work.

Next, you'll bring the question mark into the scene. This will be quite similar to the Spiker except it'll be easier because the question mark just sits there and is simply there to be collided with.

**<Step 12>**  Go to the QuestionMark folder in Assets/art.

**<Step 13>**  Change the Pixels Per Unit to 1024 in the Import Settings for all ten sprites.

This should be familiar territory for you. Select all the sprites first, then make the change in the Inspector.

**<Step 14>**  Drag the 0001 Sprite into the Hierarchy, rename to QuestionMark, focus on it with the f key, then move it to the middle bottom of the level. Compare with Figure 18.8.

FIGURE 18.8   QuestionMark placed into DotGame.

**<Step 15>** Open the Animation window.

**<Step 16>** With the QuestionMark object selected, click on Create in the Animation window.

**<Step 17>** In the animations folder, create QuestionMark_Idle.anim.

**<Step 18>** Drag the ten sprites from the QuestionMark folder into the Animation Window.

**<Step 19>** Play the animation and look at it in the Scene. Zoom in on the Question Mark to get a closer look.

**<Step 20>** Once again, this animation is too fast, so change the Samples entry to 12.

One slight annoyance is that when you enter the new number you need to remember to hit Enter before you hit the play icon. If you forget, the old Sample entry of 60 gets resurrected.

The animation is just like you want it now. You don't need a rigid-body for this object, just a Box Collider 2D.

**<Step 21>** Add a Box Collider 2D component to the QuestionMark object, and edit the collider to be smaller than the QuestionMark sprite as shown in Figure 18.9.

**<Step 22>** Test the game.

The QuestionMark is likely blocking your way. This is a temporary problem because you'll be adding code later on to make the QuestionMark disappear when you collide with it, rather than blocking you. For now, you'll simply move it out of the way.

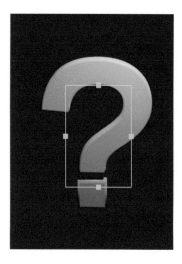

FIGURE 18.9    The Box Collider 2D for the QuestionMark Game Object.

**<Step 23>** In the Scene editor, move the question mark to a little to the right and down to allow Dottima to pass.

**<Step 24>** Test again.

The QuestionMark is doing enough for now. You have a working collider and the idle animation looks pretty good.

**<Step 25>** Save and exit.

You still don't have a game, but you'll get there soon enough. It's gradually getting to be fun to just move around the level and interact with the enemies. The graphics look fairly good even though they aren't really following a consistent art style. You're fine with having a strange mix of art styles in this game. You did everything from photographs of real-world object, 2D art drawn in a 2D art program, and of course using Blender, a very powerful 3D modeling and animation program.

In the next chapter, you'll add weapons and projectiles to bring some excitement and mild cartoon violence into this otherwise non-violent game. You'll stay away from blood and gore, of course, given the rather innocent nature of the story.

# Weapons and Projectiles

THIS CHAPTER COVERS the creation of the graphics and code for weapons and projectiles in DotGame. You'll start with arrows, which are lightweight weapons used by Dottima to damage her enemies. Then, you'll create bombs, which are much more powerful and can destroy most enemies in a single explosion. You'll also use Particle Systems in Unity to help animate the bomb animations.

## ARROWS

Before you even begin to design the arrow graphics you need to think about how they will be used in the game. You'll keep things simple graphically by having non-animated arrows going horizontally or vertically. They will be shot by Dottima and she'll magically shoot them without a bow. The arrows will simply be carried by her and point in the direction of the shot. You'll use the rotation available in Unity, so a single horizontal sprite is all you need to create. Arrows won't have gravity and will have unlimited range. Arrows will hit other objects and do damage, or not, depending on the object. Dottima will pick up arrows that are lying in the level. She can carry up to ten arrows, so if she tries to pick up too many arrows those arrows will just stay on the ground.

You could use GIMP, Blender, or an image from the web to make the arrow sprites. It seems that because they are associated with Dottima, it would be appropriate to use GIMP because that's how you made Dottima.

<Step 1> Create the folder Arrow in Assets/art.

<Step 2> Open GIMP and make the background color white.

<Step 3> File – New… and select 1024 pixels for the width and the height.
You should have a big white square on which to draw your arrow. It's easier to see what you're doing on a white background rather than the transparent checkerboard. You'll add transparency later.

**<Step 4>** Save the file as Arrow.xcf in the Arrow folder you just created.

As you've done before, you're saving the file right away with the proper name to make sure you can quickly do a save and shut down your system when necessary.

**<Step 5>** Make the foreground color black.

**<Step 6>** Select the Pencil tool (Shortcut key N) and set the Size to 36.

**<Step 7>** Select the Paths tool (Shortcut key B) and start to draw the outline of the arrow in Figure 19.1. You do this by clicking on the points in order, <Ctrl> click to close the loop. You can Undo actions with <Ctrl> Z if something goes wrong along the way. Use <command> instead of <Ctrl> if you're on a Mac.

**<Step 8>** Click on Stroke Path at the bottom of the Paths section, select the Pencil tool, and click on Stroke. Compare your result with Figure 19.2.

If you're not happy with this image, feel free to redo it, now that you know how this works. For example, you might want to make the arrow thicker, or change the shape slightly.

**<Step 9>** Fill the interior of the arrow with a red color.

Next, you'll make the background transparent. You can do this easily as follows:

**<Step 10>** Select – All.

FIGURE 19.1  Outline of the Arrow in GIMP.

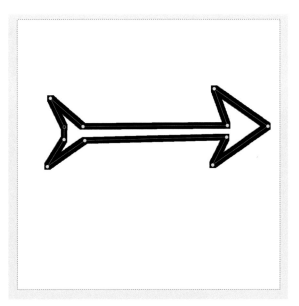

FIGURE 19.2   The Arrow Outline.

**<Step 11>**  Layer – Transparency – Add Alpha Channel.

There should be a channel display on the right. Instead of just seeing the Red, Green, and Blue channels, you now have the Alpha channel added, as shown in Figure 19.3.

Notice the tiny icons next the Channel names. They show a mini version of the contents of each channel. The Alpha channel is all white right now.

**<Step 12>**  Colors – Color to Alpha.

**<Step 13>**  Change the Opacity threshold to 0.0 as shown in Figure 19.4 and click OK.

The Opacity threshold needs to be set to 0 in order for the red color to be solid rather than partially transparent.

FIGURE 19.3   Alpha Channel added to Arrow.

FIGURE 19.4   Color to Alpha command in GIMP.

<Step 14> File – Export As… Arrow.png. Make sure you're still in the Arrow folder. The defaults are OK, so click Export.

<Step 15> File – Save and exit GIMP.
You now wish to see what the arrow looks like in in the game.

<Step 16> Open DotGame in Unity.

<Step 17> Go to Assets/art/Arrow and select the Arrow sprite.

<Step 18> Change the Pixels Per Unit from 100 to 1024 and click on Apply.
Yes, there is a way to automate this last step via Unity editor scripting. It's not exactly easy to do that, so you'll continue with the manual method for now. On larger projects, Editor Scripting is a useful way to improve the efficiency of workflow, but for smaller projects, especially for beginners, that's a topic best postponed for later. If you can't wait, go ahead and watch a tutorial video or two about Unity Editor Scripting, then search for Unity Pixels Per Unit Editor Scripting and try out the editor script for this at answers.unity.com.
We now return to looking at the arrow in Unity.

<Step 19> Drag the arrow into the Hierarchy. Then move it to be placed above Dottima as shown in Figure 19.5.
That looks reasonable, but the lack of symmetry for the arrow is bothersome. You may decide to redo the graphics later and make the arrow symmetric. For now, you'll forge ahead and make this arrow functional in the game.
The arrow is a little bit too large for you, so do the following:

FIGURE 19.5    Arrow above Dottima.

<Step 20>  Change the Transform Scale X and Y to 0.8 in the Inspector.
Now you'll set up the arrow pointing up and behind Dottima.

<Step 21a> Change the Z rotation to 90, Z position to 1, and move the arrow as shown in Figure 19.6.
The Z position at 1 puts the arrow behind Dottima. Try setting it to −1 to see the effect, if you wish, then set it back to 1. Imagine the Z axis running from

FIGURE 19.6    Arrow pointing up and behind Dottima.

your viewpoint pointing toward the screen. As the Z value increases the object moves away from you. The Z coordinate of Dottima is 0. When the Z coordinates are the same for two objects, it is not predicable which of the objects will be shown on top, so one way to ensure the display order is to give the two objects different Z coordinates. There are other methods available in Unity for this. You can read more about it in the Unity manual in the Sprite Renderer section, if you wish.

**<Step 21b>** Select the arrow, turn off Maximize on play, and play the game.

You see that the arrow just sits there, just as you would expect since the arrow has no script to control its movement. In the Inspector, the Position, Rotation, and Scale of the arrow are displayed, and they are not changing.

**<Step 22>** Select DottimaFace in the Hierarchy and continue to play the game.

As Dottima moves in the level in response to your controls, the Position X and Y are changing. When Dottima moves left-right, it's the X coordinate that changes, and when Dottima moves up-down, it's the Y coordinate that changes. The Z coordinate is constant at zero the whole time.

**<Step 23>** Stop playing the game, and then drag the arrow in the Hierarchy on top of DottimaFace. The Hierarchy should look like Figure 19.7.

You have just made the arrow a child of DottimaFace. DottimaFace now has an arrow icon next to it.

**<Step 24>** Collapse and Expand the children of DottimaFace.

You do this by clicking on the arrow next to it.

**<Step 25>** Play the game again.

You can now see the effect of making the arrow a child. It now follows its parent around. Notice that the position of the arrow doesn't change even though it's moving in the level. Those positions are relative to the parent, not absolute. The numbers are also very different from before. Both X and Y are less than 1 because the relative position of the arrow is not very far from the parent position.

As you're moving around you see that the arrow is behind the books, which seems a bit odd. The following step fixes that.

FIGURE 19.7  Hierarchy for DotGame with the arrow as a child of Dottima.

**<Step 26>** Change the Z position of DottimaFace to −2 and Play the game again.

In absolute terms, Dottima now has a Z of −2, the arrow −1, and the books are at 0. The arrow is still behind Dottima but in front to the books, just like you want.

Next, you'll make the arrow fly in response to a player button press. This requires a script. As always, when doing something complex such as this, you'll do this step by step. First, you'll write a script for the arrow movement.

**<Step 27>** Create a script named Arrow in the scripts folder and assign it to the Arrow.

**<Step 28>** Copy the contents of the Spiker class into the Arrow class, then edit to make it look like this:

```
public class Arrow : MonoBehaviour
{
    public float speed;
    private Rigidbody2D rb;
    private int direction; // four directions 0,1,2,3
                           // down, left, up, right

    void Start()
    {
        rb = GetComponent<Rigidbody2D>();
        direction = 2;
        rb.MoveRotation(90.0f);
    }

    private Vector2 dirVector;

    private void FixedUpdate()
    {
        if (direction == 0) dirVector = new Vector2(0.0f, -1.0f);
        if (direction == 1) dirVector = new Vector2(-1.0f, 0.0f);
        if (direction == 2) dirVector = new Vector2(0.0f, 1.0f);
        if (direction == 3) dirVector = new Vector2(1.0f, 0.0f);

        rb.velocity = dirVector.normalized * speed;
    }

    private void OnCollisionEnter2D(Collision2D collision)
    {
        Vector2 newPosition = new Vector2(
            transform.position.x - dirVector.x * 0.1f,
            transform.position.y - dirVector.y * 0.1f);

        rb.MovePosition(newPosition);
        speed = 0f;
    }
}
```

You only had to make a few changes. The arrow moves just like the spiker, except it doesn't make any turns upon collision. Rather, it just bounces back and sits still by setting the speed to 0.

Before testing this, you need to set up the scene. This arrow is independent of Dottima, so you'll need to unparent it as follows:

**<Step 29>** Drag the arrow in the Hierarchy away from DottimaFace up one level to the bottom below the QuestionMark.

**<Step 30>** Add a Rigidbody 2D component to the Arrow.

**<Step 31>** As usual, set the Gravity Scale to 0.0.

**<Step 32>** Drag the arrow up in the Scene so it no longer overlaps with Dottima.

**<Step 33>** Add a box collider 2D and edit it to fit the arrow.

**<Step 34a>** Set the speed for the Arrow to 6.

**<Step 34b>** Run the Game.

The arrow should fly up until it hits the book on top, then bounce back a little and stop. Just for fun, go ahead and collide Dottima with the stationary arrow. You can push the arrow around, and of course it doesn't do anything on its own because the speed got set to 0 when it collided on top.

It's time to be more discriminating with your collisions. What you want is for the arrow to not collide with Dottima at all.

**<Step 35>** Replace the OnCollisonEnter2D function with this:

```
private void OnCollisionEnter2D(Collision2D collision)
{
    if (collision.gameObject.tag == "Player")
    {
        Physics2D.IgnoreCollision(collision.collider,
            gameObject.GetComponent<Collider2D>());
        return;
    }
    Vector2 newPosition = new Vector2(
        transform.position.x - dirVector.x * 0.1f,
        transform.position.y - dirVector.y * 0.1f);

    rb.MovePosition(newPosition);
    speed = 0f;
}
```

You are checking to see if the collision is with the player, and if it is you ignore it. For this to work, you need to do this as well:

**<Step 36>** Select DottimaFace and in the Inspector select the Player Tag.

**<Step 37>** Test.

You test this by seeing if you can move Dottima on top of the arrow without collision.

**<Step 38>** Move the arrow back down to be on top of Dottima and test.

After some thought you've decided to make the arrows be independent objects, rather than children of Dottima. They will have three modes of existence. They can sit on the level, ready to be picked up by Dottima, they can be flying in a straight line until they hit a target, or thirdly they can be off-screen when Dottima is carrying them in an invisible quiver. Arrows should be destroyed when they cause damage.

You'll implement the shooting part in the next section.

## SHOOTING ARROWS

In this section, you'll continue to work on the arrows, including putting in code for shooting arrows. For now, you'll assume that Dottima has unlimited arrows.

You probably remember from the previous project that when you plan to have multiple copies of objects in a scene it's a good idea to use prefabs. In this way, you can easily modify all the copies at once by editing the prefab.

<Step 1> In the Project panel, select the prefabs folder.

You created this folder way back when you created the project. It's still empty, but not much longer.

<Step 2> Drag the Arrow object into the prefabs folder.

The Hierarchy panel now looks like Figure 19.8.

Unity allows you to edit the prefab assets directly. It's important to distinguish the prefab from instances of the prefab. You're going to try out two methods of looking at the Arrow prefab.

<Step 3> Click on the Arrow prefab in the prefabs folder in the Project panel.

This causes the Inspector to show the prefab, but without full editing support. To get full editing support do this:

<Step 4> Click on Open Prefab in the Inspector

Whoa. You're now editing the prefab. The Hierarchy is gone, replaced by just the Arrow prefab. You can now make changes to the prefab.

<Step 5> Change the Z Rotation from 90 to 0.

It seems that the default Z Rotation ought to be 0 for this prefab, so that's why you changed it.

<Step 6> Click on the < icon in the Hierarchy panel. It's in line with the Arrow heading on the left.

This takes you back to the regular Hierarchy and restores the Scene panel. Notice that the arrow is still pointing up. The Z Rotation is still 90 in the

FIGURE 19.8    Hierarchy panel with an Arrow prefab.

instance of the Arrow. The Inspector now has the entries for the Position and the Rotation in bold. This indicates that their values may be different from the default values of the prefab.

**\<Step 7\>** Click on the > icon to the right of the Arrow in the Hierarchy.

This once again takes you to the editing view of the parent prefab of the Arrow instance.

**\<Step 8\>** Go back to the Hierarchy as you did in Step 6.

None of this prefab manipulation changed the game in any way. At least, it shouldn't have. Just to make sure of this:

**\<Step 9\>** Test the game.

The game seems somewhat jerky on the author's system. It may be OK on your system, depending on your system. It's been a while since you built the game, so do that now.

**\<Step 10\>** File – Build and Run.

The game runs much smoother when run as a standalone app rather than inside of the Unity Editor. As your game becomes more complex, you will often see this kind of difference in animation smoothness.

It's a truly valuable feature of Unity to allow quick and easy testing of new features without having to wait for a build every time you want to test. Back in the early days of game development, it was common to have to wait five minutes or more for a build, so iterative development was much more difficult and time consuming.

**\<Step 11\>** Save.

The game is in good shape right now, and you even tested a build, so it was a good time to save. While you're thinking of it, you might as well create prefabs for the other enemies. Dottima herself doesn't need to be a prefab because you'll always have just the one Dottima object. Yes, in the far future, you might support multiplayer, but this is beyond the scope of things right now.

**\<Step 12\>** Make prefabs for DotRobot, Spiker, Blockade, and QuestionMark.

Your prefab folder should now look like Figure 19.9.

It's surprisingly easy now to have Dottima shoot arrows.

FIGURE 19.9  Prefabs for DotGame.

**<Step 13>** Add the following function to DottimaController.cs immediately after the FixedUpdate function:

```
private void Update()
{
    if (Input.GetKeyDown("space"))
    {
        Instantiate(
            shot,
            new Vector3(
                transform.position.x,
                transform.position.y, 1.0f),
                Quaternion.Euler(0, 0, 90.0f)
            );
    }
}
```

**<Step 14>** Add the following declaration line after the animator declaration at the top.

```
public GameObject shot;
```

**<Step 15>** Select DottimaFace in the Hierarchy, and in the Inspector, find the Shot entry in the Dottima Controller (Script) section. Click on the small circle on the right, and select the Arrow prefab.

Alternatively, you could drag the prefab from the prefabs folder into the Shot section. The Dottima Controller (Script) section now looks like Figure 19.10.

**<Step 16>** Test this.

You'll simply hit the space bar and watch arrows getting shot vertically starting at Dottima's position. It's worthwhile to review this new update code. First, you're using Update, not FixedUpdate, because that's what's required when checking for inputs. The GetKeyDown function is only true when the space bar is in transition to being pressed. The Quaternion.Euler function call sets the initial rotation of the arrow.

There are quite a few things to fix now. First, you'll stop the arrows from colliding with one another.

**<Step 17>** Change the if statement in OnCollisionEnter2D of Arrow.cs to this:

```
if (collision.gameObject.tag == "Player"
 || collision.gameObject.tag == "Arrow")
{
    Physics2D.IgnoreCollision(collision.collider,
        gameObject.GetComponent<Collider2D>());
    return;
}
```

FIGURE 19.10 Setting up the Dottima Controller.

The two vertical bars are the logical "or". This statement reads as follows: If the tag is "Player" or "Arrow" ignore the resulting collision.

Of course, you also need to add a tag to the Arrow prefab for this to work! There is no built-in "Arrow" tag, so you need to create it.

**\<Step 18\>** Edit the Arrow prefab.

**\<Step 19\>** In the Tag section at the top, expand the menu by clicking on the small downward triangle.

**\<Step 20\>** Click on Add Tag…

You are now looking at the Tags & Layers section.

**\<Step 21\>** Click on the plus icon in the Tags section and enter the name "Arrow" for the new tag.

**\<Step 22\>** Click on the Arrow object in the Hierarchy. It's the lower of the two Arrow lines.

**\<Step 23\>** In the Inspector, select the newly created "Arrow" tag instead of "Untagged".

Wow, it seems that should have taken fewer steps. This is the downside of Unity game development, but overall, it's well worth it when you consider all the benefits.

**\<Step 24\>** Test the game.

You can now shoot many arrows and it's now possible to create an arrow pile as in Figure 19.11.

Next, you're going to make the arrows go in the direction of movement of Dottima. This is easier said than done. You will have to make the direction variable public in the Arrow script. Then you'll set the proper direction when you Instantiate the Arrow. First, you'll edit the Arrow script.

**\<Step 25\>** Change the Arrow script to this:

```
using System.Collections;
using System.Collections.Generic;
using UnityEngine;

public class Arrow : MonoBehaviour
{
    public float speed;
    private Rigidbody2D rb;
    public Animator animator;
    public int direction; // four directions 0,1,2,3
                          // down, left, up, right

    void Start()
    {
        rb = GetComponent<Rigidbody2D>();
    }

    private Vector2 dirVector;

    private void FixedUpdate()
    {
```

FIGURE 19.11    Pile of Arrows.

```
    if (direction == 0) dirVector = new Vector2(0.0f, -1.0f);
    if (direction == 1) dirVector = new Vector2(-1.0f, 0.0f);
    if (direction == 2) dirVector = new Vector2(0.0f, 1.0f);
    if (direction == 3) dirVector = new Vector2(1.0f, 0.0f);

    rb.velocity = dirVector.normalized * speed;
}

private void OnCollisionEnter2D(Collision2D collision)
{
    if (collision.gameObject.tag == "Player"
     || collision.gameObject.tag == "Arrow")
    {
        Physics2D.IgnoreCollision(
            collision.collider,
            gameObject.GetComponent<Collider2D>()
            );
        return;
    }
    Vector2 newPosition = new Vector2(
        transform.position.x - dirVector.x * 0.1f,
        transform.position.y - dirVector.y * 0.1f);

    rb.MovePosition(newPosition);
    speed = 0f;
    }
}
```

You won't have to make a lot of changes, but this is a good time to make sure that your code matches the official code from this book. You'll take this opportunity to read this code and to try to understand it. The direction variable is now public, which means that other classes can see and change the direction of movement of the arrow. The Start function retrieves the Rigidbody2D component

and stores it in the rb variable for easier coding later on. The dirVector is a local variable used to calculate the velocity vector of the arrow. The collision code turns off collisions with the Player and other Arrows, otherwise it makes the arrow bounce back 0.1f units back from where the arrow came. The collision code also stops the movement of the arrow after a collision occurs by setting the speed to 0.

With the direction now public, you need to initialize it in the Arrow prefab.

**<Step 26>** Initialize the direction to 0 in the Arrow prefab.

And now you're going to take a big leap...

**<Step 27>** Replace DottimaController with this:

```
using System.Collections;
using System.Collections.Generic;
using UnityEngine;

public class DottimaController : MonoBehaviour
{
    public float speed;
    private Rigidbody2D rb;
    public Animator animator;
    public GameObject shot;
    private int direction;
    private float zrot;
    private Arrow arrow;

    void Start()
    {
        direction = 0;
        rb = GetComponent<Rigidbody2D>();
    }

    private void FixedUpdate()
    {
        Vector2 moveInput = new Vector2(
        Input.GetAxisRaw("Horizontal"),
        Input.GetAxisRaw("Vertical"));
        rb.velocity = moveInput.normalized * speed;
        animator.SetFloat("Speed", rb.velocity.magnitude);
    }

    private void Update()
    {
        float x, y;
        x = rb.velocity.x;
        y = rb.velocity.y;
        if (x != 0 || y != 0)
        {
            if (y < x) if (y < -x) direction = 0;
            if (y > x) if (y < -x) direction = 1;
            if (y > x) if (y > -x) direction = 2;
            if (y < x) if (y > -x) direction = 3;
        }

        if (Input.GetKeyDown("space"))
        {
            if (direction == 0) zrot = -90f;
            if (direction == 1) zrot = 180f;
            if (direction == 2) zrot = 90f;
            if (direction == 3) zrot = 0f;
```

```
GameObject ar = Instantiate(
    shot,
    new Vector3(
        transform.position.x,
        transform.position.y, 1.0f),
        Quaternion.Euler(0, 0, zrot)
    );

ar.GetComponent<Arrow>().direction = direction;
if (x!=0 || y!=0) ar.GetComponent<Arrow>().speed += speed;

        }

    }
}
```

That's quite a bit of new and gnarly code, but if you enter it carefully, it should work. Before you test it, you'll definitely want to review it. Near the beginning of the Update function, you're looking at the velocity vector and computing which of the four directions is closest. Imagine the x–y plane cut into four quadrants using the lines y=x and y=−x. The code determines in which quadrant the velocity vector is located and sets the direction accordingly. This is one of the few places in this book where you need a background in analytic geometry to understand the code. If you're lost here, don't worry about it, enter the code carefully, and move on.

One tricky part about this code is the condition that x and y may not both be zero when calculating a new direction. In other words, if Dottima is stationary the most recently computed direction is used to launch the arrow.

The section that instantiates the arrow also needs some explanation. First, you determine the rotation of the arrow depending on the direction. After you instantiate the arrow you set the direction of the arrow by copying the current direction of Dottima. And for a final touch, when Dottima isn't stationary you add the default speed of Dottima to the launch speed of the arrow. This makes the arrow go faster when Dottima is moving.

That was probably as much code as you'd ever want to type in all at once before testing. The ugly reality of how this code was originally developed is best left unwritten. Sometimes it's better to just copy someone else's code, try to understand it, and hope it works.

**<Step 28>** Test the game.

If you didn't have any typos, or other problems, you should now be able to shoot arrows in the direction of Dottima's movement. When she's stationary, the most recent direction of her movement determines the direction of the arrow.

You have a very nasty bug. When you shoot an arrow, Dottima bounces a bit to the side. Even though the arrow should never collide with Dottima, upon Instantiation there is one collision anyhow. This has to do with the way Unity handles collisions, and it's not easy to fix. There is, however, a very clever way to avoid the situation.

**\<Step 29>** Edit the Arrow prefab box collider to only surround the tip of the arrow.

Be sure, of course, to edit the prefab, not the Arrow object in the Hierarchy. Now that you have the arrow working, that Arrow game object is no longer needed.

**\<Step 30>** Remove the Arrow game object in the Hierarchy.

**\<Step 31>** Save and Exit.

There's more to do with arrows, but you'd like to take a break and do something else.

## BOMBS

In video games, bombs are often projectiles that are thrown or pushed for a fixed distance and then explode after a while causing big damage while displaying an explosion effect. In this section, you'll model the bomb in Blender and then import it into Unity to look at it there. You'll deal with throwing the bomb and ensuing explosion and damage in the following section.

It's fairly easy to model a bomb in Blender. You'll start by finding a reference image online. The use of a reference image is a popular technique for getting started with making a new 3D model of something. Often the goal is to replicate the geometry in the reference image precisely. You will be content with an approximate model.

**\<Step 1>** Go to Pixabay and search for "cartoon bomb".

You could, of course, just google that as well. You don't need to worry all that much about copyright and licensing of reference images because you won't be distributing the reference images directly. You'll simply use them to look at them for inspiration and maybe line up your geometry to them in Blender. Just to be legally safe you'll use the following free image from Pixabay as your reference.

**\<Step 2>** Pick the image depicted in Figure 19.12.

You don't even need to download this image, but you might as well, just for easier future reference. You *could* use the image directly in your game, but you decided against that. You would like to have better control over this graphic element by making a Blender model. Also, you don't want the explosion graphic on the fuse. Animating the fuse burning before the explosion would be, pardon the pun, overkill. You will, instead, put in a particle system that animates some sparks. You'll also put in a particle system for the bomb explosion.

**\<Step 3>** Open Blender and delete the default cube.

**\<Step 4>** \<Shift> A – Mesh – UV Sphere.

This is a good starting point for the bomb. Before you get into it, don't forget to save the file!

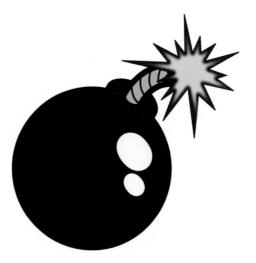

FIGURE 19.12    Free Cartoon Bomb found on pixabay.com.

**<Step 5>** File – Save As… bomb.blend in the assets/models folder, as usual.

**<Step 6>** Use the Modeling Workspace.

**<Step 7>** <Numpad> 1 5.

**<Step 8>** Edge Select, <Numpad> dot.

Just a reminder that the dot on the numpad is at the bottom next to zero. That focuses on the current selection.

**<Step 9>** Use Solid Viewport shading and turn on X-ray.

**<Step 10>** <Alt A> to deselect everything.

**<Step 11>** Type b and box select the top two rows of the sphere as shown in Figure 19.13.

**<Step 12>** Type x and select faces.

You just cut off the top of the sphere.

**<Step 13>** Box select the top edges, type e z, move the mouse up about 0.3 units, and click to stop the extrusion.

As usual, you can see the units at the top of the 3D viewport.

FIGURE 19.13    Selecting the top two rows of the sphere.

**<Step 14>** <Numpad> 7, dot, zoom out with the mouse. Compare with Figure 19.14.

**<Step 15>** Type e s and scale down by about 0.5 units.

**<Step 16>** <Numpad> 1, <Numpad> dot. Zoom out.

**<Step 17>** Type e z and move the mouse down about 1 unit.

**<Step 18>** Type f to close off the downward cylinder with a face.

**<Step 19>** Go to the Layout Workspace, <Numpad> dot. Compare with Figure 19.15.
This doesn't match the reference image exactly, but it's close enough. You ended up with a much larger fuse cylinder, which is what you want in order to see it better.
Next, you'll make the fuse.

**<Step 20>** <Shift> A – Mesh – Cylinder. Expand Add Cylinder (bottom left).

**<Step 21>** Depth 3m, adjust the Radius to fit snugly into the top opening of the bomb, about 0.18m. Compare with Figure 19.16.

**<Step 22>** Modeling Workspace.

**<Step 23>** In the Outliner, change the name of the Cylinder to Fuse, Sphere to BombBody.
In the next few steps, you'll adjust the fuse position, shorten it, and bend it.

**<Step 24>** <Numpad> 1, <Numpad> dot, zoom out.

**<Step 25>** Type g z and move the fuse up to be aligned with the top of the bomb body. Compare with Figure 19.17.

**<Step 26>** <Ctrl> R, scroll the mouse wheel to get 20 cuts, click twice to stop the loop-cut.
This loop-cut is done in anticipation of bending the fuse later on. The fuse is too long, so you'll scale it down.

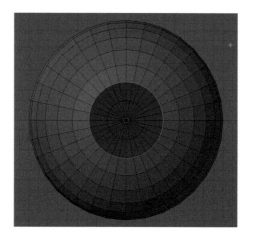

FIGURE 19.14 Top view of bomb modeling in progress.

FIGURE 19.15    The bomb casing completed.

FIGURE 19.16    Adding a Fuse to the Bomb.

**\<Step 27\>**  Type a to select all, s z and move the mouse to scale by a factor of 0.5 or so.
The fuse is floating above the bomb for now. That's OK. Next, you'll bend it.
You do that in the Layout Workspace.

**\<Step 28\>**  Go to the Layout Workspace. Type \<Numpad\> 5 1.

**\<Step 29a\>**  Select the Cursor icon on the left, or type the spacebar.

FIGURE 19.17    Moving the Fuse up.

**<Step 29b>** Click on the fuse, about 20% from the bottom.

        The 3D Cursor is now on the fuse, just where you want it.

**<Step 30>** Object – Set Origin – Origin to 3D Cursor.

**<Step 31>** In the Properties Editor, select Modifier Properties, then click on Add Modifier.

**<Step 32>** Select Simple Deform, click on Bend, Angle 90, Limits 0.20 and 1.00. Axis Y. Compare your screen with Figure 19.18.

**<Step 33>** Go back to the Modeling Workspace.

        You're seeing the effect of the modifier, but you're still seeing the fuse mesh before the modification as well. Blender does this when you haven't applied the modifier yet. Applying a modifier makes the modification permanent. If you click on Apply in Edit Mode, Blender will give you an error message. So…

**<Step 34>** Go back to the Layout Workspace, Apply the Modifier, then go back to the Modeling Workspace.

FIGURE 19.18   Bending the Fuse.

<Step 35> Move the fuse back into position. You may need to rotate it a little. Your goal is Figure 19.19.

You just completed the modeling of the bomb. Next, let's add some materials and lighting to make it look better.

<Step 36> Layout Workspace. Select the Camera. Type <Numpad> 0, g, and center the bomb.

<Step 37> Do a quick test render.

Notice that the lighting is bad, and the bomb isn't smooth.

<Step 38> Save and Exit Blender.

This is a good stopping point. Take a break! When developing games, it's all too easy to get on a roll and forget to take breaks now and then. Before you know it, it's 3am and you're going to be a wreck the next day. Don't do that!

<Step 39> Load bomb.blend into Blender.

<Step 40> Select the Select Box icon, upper left, if necessary.

<Step 41a> Go back to a User Perspective view by typing <Numpad> 5 and dragging the middle mouse button.

FIGURE 19.19    The bent fuse in the correct position.

<**Step 41b**> Select the BombBody object.

<**Step 42**> Object – Shade Smooth.

<**Step 43**> In Object Data Properties, select Normals and turn on Auto Smooth. The default 30 degrees for the Angle is fine.

<**Step 44**> Select the Fuse and repeat the last two steps.

<**Step 45**> Turn on Rendered Viewport Shading and zoom in on the bomb. Compare your screen with Figure 19.20.

You can see that smooth shading with Auto Smooth turned on can really improve the look of 3D rendered objects. This way of displaying 3D objects hides the creases between faces where the angle between the Normals is less than 30 degrees. If you look carefully, you can still see the corners along the outline of the bomb, but the interior looks convincingly round.

It's high time to add some materials to your bomb. Simply choosing some good colors goes a long way.

<**Step 46**> Go to the Shading Workspace.

FIGURE 19.20    Smooth Shading with Auto Smooth turned on.

**<Step 47>**  Select the BombBody, add a Material for it, and change the Base Color to a dark purple. Roughness 0.3, Metallic 0.5.

That's a good start. This thing is starting to look like a serious bomb.

**<Step 48>**  Select the Fuse, and make it red. Default settings are OK.

**<Step 49>**  Render – Render Image and compare with Figure 19.21.

There's no point in adding fancy textures to this bomb at this point. You can always do that later if you think it'll improve the look.

FIGURE 19.21    Dark purple and red materials for the bomb.

Now, what about the lighting? As before you'll import the light and camera from another blend file.

**<Step 50>** Delete the existing Camera and Light.

**<Step 51>** Append Spiker.blend and choose Object then choose the Camera and Light.

**<Step 52>** Select the Camera in the Outliner, then type <Numpad> 0.

**<Step 53>** Type g and center the bomb with the mouse.
This looks pretty good. The Fuse is in shadow, so you'll make one quick adjustment to the light.

**<Step 54>** <Numpad> 7. Zoom out with the mouse wheel. Select the Light and move it closer to the camera as shown in Figure 19.22.

**<Step 55>** <Numpad> 0.
That looks better. You're now ready to render. You've decided to delay animating the bomb for now and just go with a still image.

**<Step 56>** Use the Rendering Workspace.

FIGURE 19.22    Lighting and Camera setup for the Bomb render.

**<Step 57>** In Render Properties, click on Film and check Transparent.

**<Step 58>** In Output Properties, check that you're still using PNG File Format and RGBA Color.

**<Step 59>** Render – Render Image and compare with Figure 19.23.

**<Step 60>** In the Render pop-up, Image – Save As … and use the name bomb.png in Assets/art.

**<Step 61>** Close the Render pop-up, Save and Exit Blender.

**<Step 62>** Load DotGame into Unity and look at the Assets folder.

**<Step 63>** Select bomb in the art folder and, as usual, set the Pixel Per Unit to 1024, then Apply.

**<Step 64>** Drag the bomb into the Scene, then test the game.
   The bomb looks a little bit too small, but you're going to leave it as is for now.

**<Step 65>** Make the bomb into a prefab, test again, save and exit.
   These last few steps should feel very familiar to you if you went through this book step by step and paid attention. The productivity of game developers such as yourself can easily improve by factors of three, five, ten, or more by diligent practice and repetition. This is especially true for programming where productivity factors can go sky high. Super programmers can write code faster than you can read and understand it, have few bugs, and produce as much code with

FIGURE 19.23   Bomb render, ready to use in Unity.

better quality than teams of 50. The encouraging truth for us mere mortals is this: you don't need to be that talented to make great games. There's a lot more to game development than coding mastery and productivity, but it can definitely help to improve your skills with your chosen tool set.

## THROWING BOMBS

You'll start by thinking about how you want to interact with the bomb. The bomb will sit there on the level and when Dottima collides with it the bomb gets displayed on top of Dottima to indicate the Dottima has it. Then, when Dottima presses the spacebar, the bomb is dropped in place when Dottima is stationary, or else it gets thrown in one of four directions. The bomb will animate during the throw, get larger and smaller, and land someplace on the level. If the bomb lands on a book it will continue to slide until it reaches the level floor. At that time, the bomb delays for a fixed time, probably a second or two, and then it explodes, causing damage and a physical reaction in nearby objects.

Wow, that's quite a bit of work. You hope it'll be easy to do. You'll start with the bomb collider.

**<Step 1>** In the Scene panel, select the bomb and move it to be above Dottima.

You'll be testing this quite a bit, so you'll save time by having the bomb close to Dottima.

**<Step 2>** Edit the bomb prefab and change the Z Position to −3. Then go back to the instance in the Hierarchy and change it there to −3 as well.

You did this to have the bomb appear on top of Dottima, and everything else on the screen as well. You had to update both the prefab and the instance because the Transform position and rotation are no longer linked to the prefab. This is indicated by showing the coordinates in bold in the Inspector.

**<Step 3>** Temporarily move the bomb to overlap with Dottima and zoom in as in Figure 19.24.

As you can see, that's how you want the bomb to appear when Dottima is moving around the level with it. Be sure to move the bomb up again to where it was. This also tested that the rendering priority is working. Dottima has a Z value of −2, the bomb −3.

**<Step 4>** Add a circle collider 2D to the bomb prefab and edit it to fit the bomb body.

When you go back to the Scene, you'll see a green circle surrounding the bomb body. This shows the circle collider 2d. This green outline is only displayed when you have the Circle Collider 2D expanded in the Inspector.

**<Step 5>** Add a Rigidbody 2D to the bomb prefab, and set the Gravity Scale to 0.

**<Step 6>** Just for fun, play the game, collide with the bomb. Then push the bomb around the level for a while. Try shooting it with arrows.

FIGURE 19.24   Dottima holding the bomb.

This is not how the game is supposed to work! Nevertheless, it can be fun to play the game when it's incomplete. You never know what you might discover. For example, you might not have thought about what should happen when you shoot a bomb with an arrow. You could explode the bomb upon impact, delay the explosion, or have the arrow do nothing. For now, you'll make a mental note to test this again when the gameplay is further along.

You also noticed that the bomb is already doing a tumbling animation as a result of the physics engine handling the circle collider. So, all you'll need to do for that animation is start the bomb rotating when throwing it.

Next, you'll write some code for Dottima to deal with the bomb interaction.

<Step 7> Add the following code to the DottimaController class:

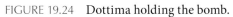

```
private void OnCollisionEnter2D(Collision2D collision)
{
    if (collision.gameObject.tag == "Bomb")
    {
        collision.gameObject.transform.SetParent(gameObject.transform);

        collision.gameObject.transform.localPosition =
            new Vector3(0.0f, 1.0f, -1.0f);

        Physics2D.IgnoreCollision(
            collision.collider,
            gameObject.GetComponent<Collider2D>()
            );
    }
}
```

This code only applies to collisions with bombs. First, it makes the bomb a child of Dottima by setting the bomb's parent. Then the local position is adjusted to make the bomb hover above Dottima as she moves. Those numbers for the offset are an educated guess. You plan to adjust them during testing. For this code to work, you need to make additional edits to the bomb prefab.

**\<Step 8\>** For the bomb prefab, create and add a "Bomb" tag.

**\<Step 9\>** Set the Body Type of the Rigidbody 2D to Kinematic.

This turns off the physics computations for the bomb as it is now linked to Dottima.

**\<Step 10\>** Test the game.

The code works, except that the bomb is displayed too high above Dottima.

**\<Step 11\>** Change the offset numbers to (0.0f, 0.6f, −1.0f) and test again.

That's much better.

**\<Step 12\>** Continue to adjust the horizontal and vertical offset and test until the bomb is centered horizontally and half of the bomb body overlaps with Dottima. Use Maximize on Play to get a closer look. You might try to use the Scale slider in the Game panel to zoom in even more.

Your offsets should be somewhere near (0.025f, 0.55f, −1.0f).

**\<Step 13\>** Test again and try to shoot arrows while carrying the bomb.

You might not have thought of this case before. Should Dottima shoot arrows while carrying a bomb? Right now, that's possible, but to make life easier for yourself you won't allow Dottima to shoot both projectiles simultaneously.

You will need to introduce a state variable to the DottimaController script.

**\<Step 14\>** In DottimaController.cs, do the following edits:

Add this line in the declaration section:

```
public int dottimaState = 0;  // 0 no bomb, 1 with bomb
```

Add this line immediately before the GetKeyDown line:

```
if (dottimaState == 0)
```

Add this line after the IgnoreCollision statement of the collision method:

```
dottimaState = 1;
```

**\<Step 15\>** Test these code changes.

You should be able to shoot arrows before but not after you pick up the bomb.

Next, rather than throwing the bomb, you'll just drop it when you press the space bar. After that you should be able to shoot arrows again.

**\<Step 16\>** In the declaration section of DottimaController, add the line:

```
private GameObject bomb;
```

**<Step 17>** After the GetKeyDown section, insert the following lines.

```
if (dottimaState == 1)
{
    if (Input.GetKeyDown("space"))
    {
        bomb.transform.SetParent(null);
        dottimaState = 0;
    }
}
```

**<Step 18>** In the collision code, add the line

```
bomb = collision.gameObject;
```

This code simply checks to see if Dottima has the bomb, and if so and the spacebar is pressed, then the parent of the bomb gets set to null, which makes the bomb just sit there. You also added a line to change the dottimaState back to 0, thus allowing Dottima to shoot arrows again.

**<Step 19>** Test it.

That works, except that you can't pick up the bomb anymore. That's OK because you'll be blowing up that bomb anyhow.

When looking at the collision code, you realize that you can improve its readability by using the bomb variable.

**<Step 20>** In OnCollisionEnter2D, replace "collision.gameObject" with "bomb" after the initial assignment for bomb. The resulting code should look like this:

```
private void OnCollisionEnter2D(Collision2D collision)
{
    if (collision.gameObject.tag == "Bomb")
    {
        bomb = collision.gameObject;
        bomb.transform.SetParent(gameObject.transform);

        bomb.transform.localPosition =
            new Vector3(0.025f, 0.55f, -1.0f);

        Physics2D.IgnoreCollision(
            collision.collider,
            gameObject.GetComponent<Collider2D>()
            );
        dottimaState = 1;
    }
}
```

This code change has no effect on your game other than readability of the code. It's often a good idea to improve readability of code so that weeks or even years later, the code is still maintainable by you or some future coder.

It's finally time for the bomb to get a script to handle the bomb's path when it's thrown, and the explosion, of course.

**<Step 21>** Create a script for the bomb prefab called Bomb.cs in the scripts folder.

**<Step 22>** Type in this code for Bomb.cs:

```
using System.Collections;
using System.Collections.Generic;
using UnityEngine;

public class Bomb : MonoBehaviour
{
    public int bombState = 0; // 0=idle, 1=fuse
    private float fuseTimer;
    public float fuseLength = 2.0f;
    // Start is called before the first frame update
    void Start()
    {
        bombState = 0;
        fuseTimer = fuseLength;
    }

    // Update is called once per frame
    void Update()
    {
        if (bombState == 1)
        {
            fuseTimer -= Time.deltaTime;
            if (fuseTimer <= 0.0f)
                Destroy(gameObject);
        }
    }
}
```

This code is familiar territory for you now. You have a countdown timer called fuseTimer which starts at two seconds and when it reaches zero or less, the bomb destroys itself. The bomb state variable is initially set to 0, so if you test this code right now there is no testable change in the game's behavior.

**<Step 23>** In DottimaController.cs, insert this line at the beginning of the GetKeyDown section:

```
bomb.GetComponent<Bomb>().bombState = 1;
```

This line changes the bomb state to a countdown toward the explosion. You don't have the explosion just yet.

**<Step 24>** Test.

Pick up the bomb, drop it, wait two seconds, and the bomb disappears. Perfect.

You like this interaction quite a bit, so maybe you won't throw the bomb at all. Maybe, just placing it and running away would work well as a weapon for Dottima. You've decided to code the explosion next to try this out.

All of this code will reside in Bomb.cs. Rather than just destroying the bomb when the fuseTimer reaches zero, you will find all nearby objects and damage them somehow. You'll check to see if the object is a robot or a spiker, and if it is, you'll just destroy it. The real damage system will be added later.

**<Step 25>** In the Bomb script, replace Update with this:

```
void Update()
{
    if (bombState == 1)
    {
        fuseTimer -= Time.deltaTime;
        if (fuseTimer <= 0.0f)
        {
            DamageNearbyObjects(gameObject.transform);
            Destroy(gameObject);
        }
    }
}

void DamageNearbyObjects(Transform tr)
{
    Collider2D[] colliders = Physics2D.OverlapCircleAll(tr.position, 3.0f);
    for(int i=0; i<colliders.Length; i++)
    {
        if(colliders[i].gameObject.tag == "Spiker")
        {
            Destroy(colliders[i].gameObject);
        }
        if (colliders[i].gameObject.tag == "Robot")
        {
            Destroy(colliders[i].gameObject);
        }
    }
}
```

Wow, that looks worse than it is. The Update function just has one new line that calls your new function DamageNearbyObjects. You have to tell that function the position of the center of a circle. All objects inside that circle get destroyed if they are a Robot or a Spiker. Of course, you also need to do this:

<Step 26> Add a "Spiker" tag to the Spiker prefab, and a "Robot" tag to the Robot prefab.

<Step 27> Place a second bomb in the level somewhere.

<Step 28> Test it by placing each bomb next to an enemy and try to destroy them.

Now that you see how this works you will review the code. The Unity built-in function Physics2D.OverlapCircleAll returns an array of colliders that intersect with the specified circle. You then loop through the array, pick the objects you want, and destroy them.

The game is now actually playable. Finally! You've decided to leave well enough alone and abandon the plan to throw the bombs. Placing them is fun too. If time permits you can always add the throwing mechanics later.

The arrows don't work yet, so the next section will fix that.

## ARROWS REVISITED

Now that you have the bombs playable, it's time to revisit the arrows. Just as with the bombs, you're wondering if you could just keep things simple and make the current arrow mechanic acceptable. You decide to give Dottima infinite arrows and just have the arrows disappear on impact. You'll have the arrows change the direction of the robots and destroy the spikers. That's about as simple as you can make it and still have a game.

**<Step 1>** Replace the collision method in Arrow.cs with this:

```
private void OnCollisionEnter2D(Collision2D collision)
{
    if (collision.gameObject.tag == "Player"
     || collision.gameObject.tag == "Arrow")
    {
        Physics2D.IgnoreCollision(
            collision.collider,
            gameObject.GetComponent<Collider2D>()
        );
        return;
    }

    if (collision.gameObject.tag == "Spiker")
    {
        Destroy(collision.gameObject);
    }

    Destroy(gameObject);
/*
    Vector2 newPosition = new Vector2(
        transform.position.x - dirVector.x * 0.1f,
        transform.position.y - dirVector.y * 0.1f);

    rb.MovePosition(newPosition);
    speed = 0f;
*/

    }
}
```

You simply added some code to destroy any spikers that collide with the arrow. You also put in a line to destroy the arrow after any collision. The code at the end which does a 0.1 unit rebound is no longer needed because the arrow is destroyed. Still, you'd like to keep the code there in case you change your mind later about what happens to arrows after a collision, so you merely commented out those five lines.

**<Step 2>** Test the game by shooting the spiker and bombing the robot.

You can now use both of your weapons using just a single button and you can clear the level of all enemies. You are rapidly turning all of your hard work into a fun game. There's still much to do, however. Next, you'll add particle systems to make the game look better.

**<Step 3>** Save!!

## PARTICLE SYSTEMS IN UNITY

Your next task in DotGame is to add particle systems to the bombs. One system simulates sparks for the fuse and the other an explosion effect when the bomb destroys nearby objects. These visual effects are purely cosmetic, but they will make the game look much better.

In this section, you'll learn about particle systems in Unity and experiment with them a little before adding them to the bomb in the next section. A particle system in Unity simulates and renders many small images to produce a visual effect.

**\<Step 1\>** Read the "Particle systems" introduction in the Unity manual.

You can just search the web for "Unity Particle Systems" to get there quickly. Feel free to watch a couple of videos too. There's nothing like seeing particle systems in action to quickly grasp this concept.

**\<Step 2\>** Open the DotGame project in Unity.

**\<Step 3\>** GameObject – Effects – Particle System.

Your scene now has the default particle system operating in the middle. As you can see, there are a lot of settings in the Inspector, plus a Particle Effect panel in the Scene view as shown in Figure 19.25.

**\<Step 4\>** To get an appreciation of what Unity is doing here, check the Show Bounds checkbox, and zoom out as shown in Figure 19.26.

You can see a large yellow box which contains all of the particles in the particle system.

**\<Step 5\>** Try out the Pause, Restart, and Stop buttons on the Particle Effect panel.

**\<Step 6\>** Use the mouse wheel to zoom back in and center the level.

**\<Step 7\>** Uncheck Looping and Restart.

The particle system stops after five seconds. The 5 is set in the Duration slot in the Inspector. The Duration is ignored when Looping is checked.

**\<Step 8\>** Check Looping and Restart.

**\<Step 9\>** Hover the mouse over Start Lifetime and drag until the value is about 1.

**\<Step 10\>** Hover the mouse over Start Speed and drag until the value is about 2.

Compare your particle system with Figure 19.27.

FIGURE 19.25   Particle Effect Panel.

FIGURE 19.26    Default Particle System.

FIGURE 19.27    Reducing the size of a particle system.

**<Step 11>** Experiment with the other setting of the Particle System in the Inspector.

You don't need to understand all of these settings, but it's useful to get an idea about what's there.

**<Step 12>** Delete the Particle System in the Hierarchy.

You're not going to save this particle system. Rather, you're just trying out some things, and now you're ready to build a system of sparks and an explosion effect.

## FUSE SPARKS AND EXPLOSIONS

The first particle system you'll build is intended to sit at the end of the fuse of the bomb prefab. It'll get turned on by the bomb script when the bomb is dropped, and the countdown timer is started. You want tiny bright sparks with trails emanating in a spherical pattern.

**<Step 1>** GameObject – Effects – Particle System.

You immediately see the default particle system located somewhere on the screen.

**<Step 2>** Change the Transform Position to (0, 0, −3) in the Inspector.

The particles have orange boxes around them. You would prefer to not have those boxes, so do the following:

**<Step 3>** Expand the Gizmos menu and uncheck Selection Outline.

The Gizmos menu is at the top middle of the Scene panel. You can also turn off all Gizmos there if you wish by clicking on the Gizmos button. You currently have two Gizmos in the scene, a Camera icon and a thin large rectangle indicating the camera view. You might wish to make that camera gizmo smaller by sliding the 3D icons slider to the left a little bit.

**<Step 4>** Play the game and take a look at the Particle System in the game.

It's basically the same, except that it looks different against the tan background.

**<Step 5>** Rename the Particle System to Sparks.

**<Step 6>** Change the Start Lifetime to 0.07.

This makes the Sparks much smaller because the particles only live for 0.07 seconds.

**<Step 7>** Start Size 0.25

The particles are much smaller now.

**<Step 8>** In the Emission section, Rate over Time 200.

You now have a horizontal strip of particles. You want the particles to emanate from a point.

**<Step 9>** In the Shape section, Change the Shape to a Sphere, Radius 0.

That's more like it. It's starting to look like sparks from a fuse.

**<Step 10>** Select Sparks in the Hierarchy and type f to focus on the sparks.

**<Step 11>** Change the Start Color to a Random Color with a gradient as in Figure 19.28.

First, you expand the drop-down menu at the far right of the Start Color dialog. Select Random Color. Then click on the color bar to open the Gradient Editor. There, you enter three colors, red, yellow, and orange, by typing 0%, 50%, and 100% for the Location and then enter the color for each location by clicking on the Color. That's easier done than said!

The sparks have a fun, colorful look to them. It's time to move them to a bomb.

**<Step 12>** Move Sparks to the end of the fuse of one of the bombs. Zoom in to precisely place it.

**<Step 13>** Test the game.

The bomb with the sparks looks like Figure 19.29.

A few adjustments might make this look even better, but this is good for a very simple Particle System. You can definitely tell that this bomb is about to blow up!

Next, you will make this particle effect a child of the bomb prefab so that the sparks don't get left behind when Dottima picks up the bomb.

**<Step 14>** Delete the other bomb, the one without sparks.

**<Step 15>** Drag Sparks on top of the bomb in the Hierarchy.

Take a look at the Position of Sparks. X and Y should be close to 0, and Z should be exactly 0.

**<Step 16>** Delete the bomb prefab. Then recreate it by dragging the bomb into the prefabs folder.

FIGURE 19.28  Gradient Editor showing gradient with three colors.

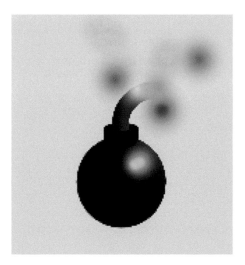

FIGURE 19.29    Bomb with Sparks.

**<Step 17>**   Drag the newly created bomb prefab back into the scene someplace near the robot so that you again have two bombs in this scene.

**<Step 18>**   Test the game.

The game pretty much works the same way except that now both bombs have Sparks all the time. You have one more thing to do: only have the sparks active during the bomb countdown.

**<Step 19>**   In Bomb.cs, insert the following lines in the declarations section:

```
private ParticleSystem sparks;
```

**<Step 20>**   Insert the following lines in the Start function:

```
sparks = GetComponentInChildren<ParticleSystem>();
sparks.Stop();
```

This code assumes that there is a particle system in some child of the bomb. Only then can GetComponentInChildren find it. You're taking a risk here. Best practice would be to put in code to check if sparks in valid before using it in your code.

**<Step 21>**   Insert this code in the Update function, inside of the bombState == 1 section:

```
if (sparks.isStopped)
{
    sparks.Play();
}
```

That's it. Try to understand this new code before proceeding to the next step.

**<Step 22>**   Test it.

You might wonder why there's a test for sparks being inactive when calling sparks.Play(). The reason is that every time you call the Play() function, the

particle system gets reset. Resetting the particle system in the Update function would reset it every frame, which would result in a very boring display of nothing. Try it out, if you're curious, by commenting out the if statement.

**\<Step 23\>**   Save.

All that's left for this section is to put in a bomb explosion. You'll start this by getting some fire.

**\<Step 24\>**   Log into your pixabay account and search for "fire flame".

**\<Step 25\>**   Pick the image that looks like Figure 19.30 and download the 1280 × 852 version.

**\<Step 26\>**   Create the folder Assets/art/Explosion and store this jpg there.

**\<Step 27\>**   In GIMP, create a new 1280×852 image, fill background with transparency.

**\<Step 28\>**   Drag the new jpg image into GIMP.

**\<Step 29a\>** Layer – Transparency – Add Alpha Channel.

**\<Step 29b\>** Color – Color to Alpha and choose a black color. Make sure the color is perfectly black.

**\<Step 30\>**   Compare with Figure 19.31.

**\<Step 31\>**   Save this image as explosion.png in the Explosion folder.

**\<Step 32\>**   Back in Unity, look for the explosion.png file in Assets and drag it into the Hierarchy just to look at it, then delete it in the Hierarchy.

You're ready to create the explosion effect.

FIGURE 19.30   Fire Image by Rudy and Peter Skitterians from Pixabay.

FIGURE 19.31   Adding transparency to the fire.

**\<Step 33\>** In the Project panel, select the art/Explosion folder and click on the + icon.

**\<Step 34\>** Select Material from the very large pop-up menu.

**\<Step 35\>** Enter "ExplosionMat" for the name of the new Material.

**\<Step 36\>** Drag the explosion asset from the Explosion folder to the Albedo in the Main Maps in the Inspector.

**\<Step 37\>** Change the Rendering Mode to Transparent.

**\<Step 38\>** Change the Shader to Sprites/Default.
You now have a Material to use in your explosion Particle System.

**\<Step 39\>** GameObject – Effects – Particle System.

**\<Step 40\>** Change the Transform Position to (0, 0, −3).

**\<Step 41\>** Change the name of the Particle System to "Explosion".

**\<Step 42\>** In the Renderer section, change the Material to ExplosionMat.
You can drag the material there, or you can click on the small dotted circle in select the material in the pop-up menu. Compare your Renderer section with Figure 19.32.
You should see some fireballs in the Scene panel.

**\<Step 43\>** In the Shape section, change the Shape to Sphere, Radius to 0.

**\<Step 44\>** In the Emission section, change the Rate over Time to 0.
The particle system is doing nothing right now because no particles are getting emitted.

FIGURE 19.32    Renderer section of Explosion Particle System.

**<Step 45>**  Click on the+icon in the Bursts section and watch the effect on the particle system.

The default settings for Bursts emit 30 particles all at once at the beginning. That's what you want for an explosion.

**<Step 46>**  Change the Duration to 1 at the very top of the Explosion section.

You now see a burst of 30 particles every second.

**<Step 47>**  Change the Start Lifetime to 1 also.

That's starting to look like an explosion every second. When you're done developing this particle system, you'll turn off looping because the explosion will happen just once for each bomb.

**<Step 48>**  Change the Start Size to 2, Start Speed to 2.

Now you have something that actually looks like an explosion! If you were lazy, you'd stop right here, but there's more to do. You want the explosion to last longer and settle a bit at the end.

**<Step 49>**  Change the Duration to 2, Start Lifetime 2.

**<Step 50>**  Turn on the Velocity over Lifetime by checking the checkbox next to it.

**<Step 51>**  In Velocity over Lifetime, change the Speed Modifier to Curve.

You open the Curve dialog by clicking on the triangle on the right.

**<Step 52>**  Select the fifth curve preset at the bottom, as shown in Figure 19.33.

The explosion slows down its expansion over time and settles down at the end of its two second duration. The size of the explosion may have to be adjusted to look right in the game. You'll do just one more thing to this explosion. You'll make those particles spin.

**<Step 53>**  Change the Start Rotation to Random Between Two Constants, and then set the constants to −180 and 180.

**<Step 54>**  Enable Rotation over Lifetime.

The default settings for this are OK.

FIGURE 19.33    A Particle System Curve for the Speed Modifier.

This explosion ends too abruptly, so you'll fade it out toward the end using Color over Lifetime.

**\<Step 55\>** Enable Color over Lifetime.

**\<Step 56\>** Click on the color bar to enter the gradient editor. Click on the top right flag and make the alpha 0. Drag the top left flag to the middle to the alpha 1 in the middle. Your gradient should look like Figure 19.34.

This has the desired effect of fading out the explosion near the end of the animation. You can't resist and you'll make just one more adjustment.

**\<Step 57\>** Change the burst setting from 30 to 50 in the Emission section.

This fills in some gaps in the explosion.

Next, you'll put this into the game, much as you did with the sparks.

**\<Step 58\>** Uncheck Looping.

You won't be looping this, so all you have to do is play the explosion effect and you'll be done.

FIGURE 19.34    An alpha gradient to fade out the explosion.

Your plan is to have two variables for the two particle effects for the bomb. You'll set those variables up in the Start function. The following code does that:

**<Step 59>** In Bomb.cs, add the following variables to the declaration section:

```
private ParticleSystem explosion;
private Component[] comparray;
```

**<Step 60>** Replace the Start() function with this:

```
void Start()
    {
        comparray = GetComponentsInChildren<ParticleSystem>();
        foreach (ParticleSystem p in comparray)
        {
            if (p.gameObject.name == "Explosion") explosion = p;
            if (p.gameObject.name == "Sparks") sparks = p;
        }
        bombState = 0;
        fuseTimer = fuseLength;
        sparks.Stop();
    }
```

In this code, you're looping through all particle systems of the children of the bomb and checking their names. When the name matches, you set the explosion and the sparks variable. One more thing:

**<Step 61>** Insert this line in the Update function immediately before the DamageNearbyObjects call.

```
explosion.Play();
```

That's where the explosion actually happens! For this to work, you need to make the explosion a child of the bomb prefab. One easy way to do this is as follows:

**<Step 62>** Delete one of the two bombs in the Hierarchy. Remember where it was.

**<Step 63>** Drag the Explosion on top of the other bomb in the Hierarchy. That bomb now has two children. Check that the Transform Position of the Explosion is (0, 0, 0).

**<Step 64>** Delete the bomb prefab in the prefabs folder and then drag the bomb from the Hierarchy into the prefab folder.

**<Step 65>** Drag the bomb prefab into the Scene and put it where the old second bomb was.

**<Step 66>** Test it!

Well, that wasn't a success. Both Explosions played as soon as the game started. Then, when you placed the bomb and used it, there was no Explosion animation. What went wrong?

The immediate Explosions are caused by the default "Play on Awake" setting for Particle Systems. You forgot to uncheck that.

**<Step 67>** In the bomb prefab, find the Explosion prefab, and uncheck "Play on Awake".

**<Step 68>** Test it again.

The Explosions no longer play at the start. However, they still don't play even though you put in that line into the Update function. The answer is in that code, just a few lines later. You're destroying the bomb! Guess what, that means that all the children get destroyed as well, so no explosion. The simple fix is to unparent the Explosion before destroying the parent.

**<Step 69>** Insert the following line before the explosion.Play line in Bomb.cs:

```
explosion.transform.SetParent(null);
```

**<Step 70>** Test it one more time.

You now have an explosion when the fuse Timer reaches zero. There is only one slight problem. The Explosion animation is too small considering the 3 unit radius of the bomb explosion. Rather than making that Explosion larger, you've decided to reduce the radius to match the animation.

**<Step 71>** In the Physics2D.OverlapCircleAll call in DamageNearbyObjects, change the 3.0f to 1.5f.

Success! It's fun to run through the explosion. Yes, Dottima is fireproof.

Congratulations. You have gameplay, and it's looking good. For most game projects, reaching first gameplay is a truly satisfying experience. Depending on the scope of the final release, you might still be weeks, months, or even years away from completion. This project still has some work to do, but it definitely helps to see the progress so far.

**<Step 72>** Save and exit Unity.

In the next chapter, you'll create a few additional levels, put in scoring, and make life more difficult for Dottima.

# Lives, Level Design, and Old School Scoring

This CHAPTER COVERS lives for Dottima, the creation of additional levels, and a scoring system. You'll use the Unity GUI system to display the lives, scores, and any needed text. Also, you'll put in a game state system to handle messages like "level complete" and "game over."

So far Dottima is invincible in the game, but that is about to change. You'll keep it simple, and kill Dottima when she touches a Spiker or a DotRobot. Dottima gets a fixed number of lives, and when she runs out of lives it's game over.

You'll create additional levels with the current tile-set. You'll design the difficulty ramping to make the game easy at first and more difficult for subsequent levels. You'll also add an old school scoring system: You get points for killing enemies and for completing levels. To make the scoring more interesting, you'll add a timer for each level, and you'll award extra points for any remaining time.

## THE UNITY GUI

You've had some experience with UI work in previous chapters. It's time to get an overview of what's available.

<Step 1> Go to the Unity manual version 2019.3 and search for User Interfaces and read the introduction.

There you can see the three User Interface toolkits available in the 2019.3 version of Unity: UIElements, Unity UI (Package), and IMGUI. In the future, UIElements will be the recommended way to make User Interfaces, but it is still under development. UIElements is a great improvement, but it is complex and not for beginners just yet. It's probably safer and easier to stick with the old system, the Unity UI (Package).

<Step 2> Click on Unity UI in the tree view on the left.

There you can see the somewhat overwhelming documentation for Unity UI. No, you don't need to read all that, but it's good to know where this is in case you need it in the future.

The Unity manual is written for experienced Unity users, so don't feel bad if you don't understand everything in the manual. Feel free to explore the manual on your own, mainly to get an overview. Then it's time to get back to making your game.

## LIVES

You did something like this before in the Bouncing Donuts game. In that game, you had levels and a score, but just one life. So, rather than reinventing the wheel you're going to copy over some code from that project. You'll bring it in piece by piece and edit it to make it work where necessary. Then you'll add the lives.

<Step 1> Use your operating system to copy GameState.cs and Scoring.cs from the Bouncing Donuts project scripts folder into the DotGame scripts folder.

<Step 2> Open DotGame in Unity and test it.

As you start up Unity, you might see a message that Unity is importing the "new" scripts. You're not using those scripts yet, so the game should still work without any visible difference. In the operating system display of the scripts folder, you would see that the new script files now have .meta versions, just as all the other scripts. These .meta files are important auxiliary files used by Unity to keep track of its files. Just to make sure you're on the same page as this book, compare your display of the scripts folder with Figure 20.1.

The names for DottimaController and SettingsMenu are truncated. There's a slider at the bottom right corner of the Assets panel where you can adjust the view and see the complete names when necessary.

Before using these newly imported scripts, it's a good idea to read the code and make any necessary changes.

<Step 3a> Double click on the Scoring script and look at it in Visual Studio.

There are no errors in the Error list section. That's a good sign. There's only one public variable, gamescore, and it gets initialized to 0. That is definitely OK. The OnGUI function displays the score and the level, and the game over and level complete messages. You want to keep all that, so you won't make any

FIGURE 20.1    The scripts for DotGame so far.

changes to this file for now. You also have the Awake function. You're not sure if you still need this, so you'll comment it out.

**\<Step 3b\>** Comment out the Awake function in the Scoring script, then save it.

**\<Step 4a\>** Double click on the GameState script and look at it.

**\<Step 4b\>** Also comment out the Awake function, then save.

Again, there are no other changes necessary. In this file, you initialize the state to GamePlay, and the level to 1. These two files should just work, but you'll need to bring them into the game.

**\<Step 5a\>** Create a new empty GameObject and name it GameState. Then add the GameState script component.

**\<Step 5b\>** Create a new empty GameObject and name it `Scoring`. Then add the Scoring script component.

**\<Step 6\>** Test this.

You have a score of 0 and level 1 displayed in the upper left and right corners. So far so good. You'll make those work later on. For now, it's time to add a lives display.

**\<Step 7\>** In OnGUI in Scoring.cs, insert this after the two GUI.Box statements:

```
GUI.Box(new Rect(Screen.width / 2 - 100, 20, 200, 50), "Lives " + lives);
```

**\<Step 8\>** Also, after the gamescore=0 declaration insert this:

```
public static int lives = 5;
```

You just put in the lives counter. Now you just need to deal with death, which is easier said than done. First, you'll do this the simple way:

**\<Step 9\>** In DottimaController.cs, insert the following code near the end of OnCollisionEnter2D:

```
if (collision.gameObject.name == "DotRobot")
{
    Scoring.lives--;
    gameObject.transform.position = new Vector3(-7.0f, -3.0f, -2.0f);
}
```

**\<Step 10\>** Test it.

Pretty bad, but this is a great example of iterative development. Each step in development is as small as you can stand it, even if the step results in an obviously flawed result. This code simply reduces the lives by one and warps Dottima back to the beginning of the level. Your next steps will move you closer to something resembling a death sequence. You need to replace the name test with a tag test, which is more robust when you have multiple robots.

**\<Step 11\>** Check that the Spiker prefab has a Spiker tag, DotRobot a Robot tag.

**<Step 12>** Replace the .name test for DotRobot in the collision code with this:

```
if (collision.gameObject.tag == "Robot" ||
    collision.gameObject.tag == "Spiker")
```

Notice the logical "or" operator consisting of two vertical bars ||. You read this as follows: If the tag equals DotRobot or the tag equals Spiker then reduce the lives and warp Dottima to the beginning. This is a situation where typing accurately is crucial. A typo in the string constants won't be caught by the compiler. Instead, your code simply won't work. In other words, make doubly sure that you don't have a typo in the string constants and that they match the tag names precisely.

**<Step 13>** Test it.

Dottima now dies if she touches a spiker or a robot. During testing, you just discovered a fairly serious bug. When Dottima is carrying a bomb, she can pick up a second bomb! Then when she places it, the bomb works, but she's still carrying a bomb. That second bomb can't be dropped, and Dottima is forever carrying that bomb.

There's, of course, a simple way to fix this: Dottima shouldn't be able to pick up a second bomb. True to your principles, you're dropping everything (no pun intended) and fixing this immediately.

**<Step 14>** Insert this line as the first line in OnCollisionEnter2D in DottimaController.cs:

```
if (dottimaState == 0)
```

This makes sure that Dottima isn't carrying another bomb when she's picking one up.

**<Step 15>** Test this.

That's right, even this simple and obviously correct line needs testing. Why? Well, when Dottima tries to pick up the second bomb she now collides with it. This actually is OK, but you probably didn't know that the code would do that. It might be better to have Dottima run through that second bomb, but you'll just leave things as is.

Next, you'll think about what should happen when Dottima dies. Surely you don't want an instant warp to the starting point. What you really want is a death animation, followed by a reset of the level. You'll use the existing state variable for Dottima and add a death sequence state.

**<Step 16>** Edit DottimaController.cs and change the dottimaState declaration to this:

```
public int dottimaState = 0;  // 0 no bomb, 1 with bomb, 2 dying
```

This is, strictly speaking, unnecessary, but you're going to attempt to maintain the very few comments in the code. You really ought to create constant variables for those states, just as you did for the game states, but you're in a hurry, so you'll put that off, possibly forever.

**\<Step 17\>** Insert this code at the end of `Update`.

```
if (dottimaState == 2)
{
    float shrink = 0.9f;
    float rotspeed = 1.0f;
    rb.rotation += rotspeed;
    transform.localScale = (
        new Vector3(
            transform.localScale.x * shrink,
            transform.localScale.y * shrink,
            transform.localScale.z));
}
```

This code rotates and shrinks Dottima when she's in the dying state. In Unity, you need to build a new Vector3 when adjusting transform.localScale. All you need now is a way to get Dottima into this state.

**\<Step 18\>** In the collision function, replace the death section with this:

```
   if (collision.gameObject.tag == "Robot" ||
       collision.gameObject.tag == "Spiker")
   {
       dottimaState = 2;
       Scoring.lives--;
//     gameObject.transform.position = new Vector3(-7.0f, -3.0f, -2.0f);
   }
```

You're switching to the "dying" state and you commented out the warp code so you can see the animation.

**\<Step 19\>** Test this by killing Dottima in the game.

Well, that works, but Dottima shrinks much too quickly. Time to adjust the shrink factor;

**\<Step 20\>** Move the spiker close to Dottima, change shrink to 0.99f and test again.

You moved the spiker to make testing faster. In fact, Dottima will probably die in less than a second without you doing anything. That's not how you want to release the game! The animation looks better, but you'd like the rotation to be faster and to go clockwise instead.

**\<Step 21\>** Change rotspeed to −2.0f.

That's much better. You just realized though that you need to use Time.deltatime in order to have the same animation speed regardless of the performance of the target computer. Here is the improved code:

**\<Step 22\>** Replace the shrink and rotspeed declarations with this:

```
    float shrink = 1.0f - 2.0f * Time.deltaTime;
    float rotspeed = -400.0f * Time.deltaTime;
```

`Time.deltaTime` is the time, in seconds, between updates. You were estimating 200 updates per second, so you inserted a fudge factor of `Time.deltaTime * 200`, and then rearranged the constants. The `0.99f` had to be replaced with `(1.0f - 0.01f)` because it's the `0.01f` that determines the amount of shrinking.

**<Step 23>** Test.

The animation is approximately the same as before. Feel free to adjust the constants `2.0f` and `400.0f` in your code.

Next, you're going to fix an obvious bug. The lives display goes to −1 instead of to 4 during the death sequence. Why is that? That's right, the dying Dottima is still on the level and is continuing to collide with the spiker. Here's an easy fix:

**<Step 24>** Insert this line at the very beginning of OnCollisionEnter2D:

```
if (dottimaState == 2) return;
```

The return skips all of the subsequent code. Collisions are still happening, but the associated code is not running in the dying state.

**<Step 25>** Test this.

You should see that the lives counter at the top of the game decrements from 5 to 4. It probably would make more sense to wait with that decrement until after the death sequence is complete. You'll implement that while putting in a countdown timer.

**<Step 26>** In DottimaController.cs, put the following into the declarations section:

```
private float deathTimer = 1.0f;
```

**<Step 27>** Insert this code after the localScale statement:

```
deathTimer -= Time.deltaTime;
if (deathTimer < 0.0f)
{
    Scoring.lives--;
    dottimaState = 0;
    rb.rotation = 0.0f;
    gameObject.transform.localScale = new Vector3(1.0f, 1.0f, 1.0f);
    gameObject.transform.position = new Vector3(-7.0f, -3.0f, -2.0f);
}
```

See explanation below.

**<Step 28>** Change the robot and spiker collision code to this:

```
if (collision.gameObject.tag == "Robot" ||
    collision.gameObject.tag == "Spiker")
{
    // drop the bomb first
    if (dottimaState == 1)
    {
        bomb.GetComponent<Bomb>().bombState = 1;
        bomb.transform.SetParent(null);
    }
    dottimaState = 2;
}
```

You have some very interesting code here. The `deathTimer` is the usual countdown timer, initialized to `1.0f`, that is one second. When `dottimaState` is 2, it counts down, and when it reaches zero, the lives counter gets decremented, and then there's a bunch of code to restore Dottima to a playable state, and then

she gets warped to the beginning position. You had to restore the rotation, the scale, and the state, and then Dottima is ready to continue to play. The collision code has to handle the case of Dottima carrying the bomb when dying. The simplest and the most fun way is to drop the bomb and explode it when that happens.

**<Step 29>** Test this.

Things work fairly well, but you might discover a nasty bug. After playing for a while Dottima doesn't do the death sequence anymore. Why? This is a typical bug during development when there's no obvious hint as to why the death sequence breaks. After testing some more, you discover that the death sequence works upon the first death, but not after. Aha! It looks like an initialization problem. You're not reinitializing the `deathTimer` when you restore Dottima. So…

**<Step 30>** Insert this line before the `Scoring.lives` decrement.

```
deathTimer = 1.0f;
```

**<Step 31>** Test multiple deaths for Dottima. The death sequence should run every time.

You've decided that you like the way the game operates right now, so you're giving up on doing a complete level reset upon death. This could have some gameplay ramifications. For example, if you need a certain number of bombs to get through a level, and you lose them, then you'll be stuck. That may seem unfair, but you'll deal with this problem later.

**<Step 32>** Save.

Yes, you aren't handling the case where the lives reach zero. This is a problem for another day. In the next section, you'll create some additional levels. Finally!

## LEVELS

All this time, you've worked with just a single level. You're now going to create additional levels by making new scenes in Unity, just as you did in Bouncing Donuts.

**<Step 1>** In Unity in the Scenes folder, select the Game scene.

You have two scenes right now, Game and Menus.

**<Step 2>** Rename the Game scene to Level 1.

**<Step 3>** Select the Menus scene and test it. Try to play the game.

This should still work even though you renamed the Game scene. That's because of the way that scene is loaded. Your code doesn't use the name but rather the scene number. Take a look at MainMenu.cs for this code.

**<Step 4>** With Level 1 selected in the Scenes folder, do Edit – Duplicate.

Unity named the duplicate level "Level 2", just what you want.

<**Step 5**> Create Level 3 by doing another Edit – Duplicate.

Even though you just created those new scenes, your Scene panel is still looking at Level 1.

<**Step 6**> Make some small changes to Levels 2 and 3 so you can tell them apart.

An easy way would be to delete a bomb or the question mark. You're not designing these levels yet. Rather, they are place holders for later.

Your next goal is to put in logic for what happens at the end of a level. This is very similar to Bouncing Donuts. In that game, you reached the end of the level when the main character (the bouncing donut) collided with the donut box. In this game, you'll put in an invisible collider at the end near that Blockade.

<**Step 7**> Double click on Level 1 in the Scenes folder.

<**Step 8**> Create an empty GameObject and rename it ExitLocation.

<**Step 9**> Move it to the exit, superimposed on top of the Blockade.

<**Step 10**> Change the Z position to 0, if necessary.

This doesn't really matter, but 0 just looks better.

<**Step 11a**> Delete the Blockade.

You no longer need the Blockade there.

<**Step 11b**> Add a Box Collider 2D Component to ExitLocation and adjust it to look like Figure 20.2.

<**Step 12**> Insert this code at the end of OnCollisionEnter2D in DottimaController.cs:

```
if (collision.gameObject.name == "ExitLocation")
{
    GameState.state = GameState.levelComplete;
}
```

FIGURE 20.2   The Exit Location Box Collider.

**\<Step 13\>** Test colliding with the ExitLocation.

> The collision works, and you get the Level Complete message, but you can still play the level!

**\<Step 14\>** In DottimaController.cs, insert this line in the declarations section:

```
public float levelCompleteTimer = 2.0f;
```

> This doesn't really need to be public, but having it public allows you to see it in the Inspector while playing the game.

**\<Step 15\>** Insert this code at the beginning of Update:

```
if (GameState.state == GameState.levelComplete)
{
    rb.velocity = Vector2.zero;
    levelCompleteTimer -= Time.deltaTime;
    if (levelCompleteTimer < 0.0f)
    {
        SceneManager.LoadScene(2);
    }
}
```

> This code counts down the levelCompleteTimer and goes to the second level after it reaches 0. This is pretty much the same code as in Bouncing Donuts.
>
> The SceneManager line needs the appropriate "using" statement.

**\<Step 16a\>** Insert this line at the top of the file as the last "using" statement:

```
using UnityEngine.SceneManagement;
```

**\<Step 16b\>** Test by starting at Level 1. Try to get to Level 2.

> It doesn't work. Look at the error message at the bottom of the Unity window.

**\<Step 16c\>** Add Level 2 and Level 3 to the build settings.

> Be sure to have the build numbers match the Level numbers.

**\<Step 17\>** Test and Save.

> You should now be able to get to Level 2.
>
> The level display is incorrect at the top right of the game screen.

**\<Step 18\>** Replace the LoadScene code with this:

```
if (levelCompleteTimer < 0.0f)
{
    GameState.level++;
    SceneManager.LoadScene(GameState.level);
}
```

> You're eventually going to get to the end of the game, currently that's Level 3. At that point the LoadScene line is going to break. You'll deal with that later. Next, you're going to put the ExitLocation into Level 2.

**\<Step 19\>** At Level 1, drag the ExitLocation object into the prefabs folder.

**\<Step 20\>** Edit Levels 2 and 3, remove the Blockades there as well and put in the ExitLocation object.

**\<Step 21\>** Test it, starting at Level 1.

The level display is fine until you get to the non-existent Level 4. At that point, you get error messages in the Console and at the bottom of the Unity screen, just as you might expect.

In order to handle this, you will add another GameState: theEnd.

**\<Step 22\>** In Scoring.cs, insert this code at the end of OnGUI:

```
if (GameState.state == GameState.theEnd)
{
    GUI.skin.box.fontSize = 60;
    GUI.Box(new Rect(
        Screen.width / 2 - 250,
        Screen.height / 2 - 50,
        500,
        100),
        "T H E     E N D");
}
```

**\<Step 23\>** Insert this in GameState.cs:

```
public const int theEnd = 4;
```

**\<Step 24\>** At the end of DottimaController, replace the ExitLocation code with this:

```
if (collision.gameObject.name == "ExitLocation")
{
    if (GameState.level < 3)
        GameState.state = GameState.levelComplete;
    else
        GameState.state = GameState.theEnd;
}
```

**\<Step 25\>** In the Update function of DottimaController, insert this near the beginning, after the levelComplete section:

```
if (GameState.state == GameState.theEnd)
{
    rb.velocity = Vector2.zero;
    levelCompleteTimer -= Time.deltaTime;
    if (levelCompleteTimer < 0.0f)
    {
        GameState.level = 1;
        SceneManager.LoadScene(GameState.level);
    }
}
```

**\<Step 26\>** Test it, starting at Level 1.

You can now get to the end after Level 3, and then, because you don't have a real ending yet, the game simply restarts at Level 1. This is very old-school. Many of the arcade games of the eighties did this. They didn't have an ending but just started over from Level 1, sometimes with increased difficulty.

Next, you're going to add three more levels, so you'll have six levels set up. This can be done with one click and three keystrokes!

**\<Step 27\>** In the Scenes panel, click on Level 3, then type \<Ctrl\> D three times.

You now need to fix DottimaController because that code still assumes that you have three levels. To make that code more maintainable, you'll add a constant for the number of levels.

**<Step 28>** In the declarations section for DottimaController.cs, insert

```
public const int lastLevel = 6;
```

**<Step 29>** Replace the ExitLocation section with this:

```
if (collision.gameObject.name == "ExitLocation")
{
    if (GameState.level < lastLevel)
        GameState.state = GameState.levelComplete;
    else
        GameState.state = GameState.theEnd;
}
```

You're pretty sure that this will work, and it would take a while to test this, so you'll delay testing until you add another feature or two. This goes against the principle of testing every testable change immediately, but sometimes it's OK to test multiple changes in order to save time. You just hope that you won't regret this.

You still have that bug, in that the lives counter doesn't handle the case of running out of lives. You're going to try this one-liner:

**<Step 30>** Insert the following at the end of the `deathTimer < 0.0f` section:

```
if (Scoring.lives == 0) SceneManager.LoadScene(0);
```

**<Step 31>** Test, starting from the Menus scene.

Sure enough, when you get to level 4 your get an error message. You forgot to add the new Scenes to the build settings. Before you fix that you'll test the lives handling. It turns out that doesn't work either. The game ends when you run out of lives, but the next game starts with 0 lives.

**<Step 32>** Replace the LoadScene(0) line with this:

```
if (Scoring.lives == 0)
{
    Scoring.lives = 5;
    SceneManager.LoadScene(0);
}
```

**<Step 33>** Add Levels 4, 5, and 6 to the Build Settings. Make sure that the index for each scene matches the Level number.

**<Step 34>** Test it again.

Looks like it's working. The game is getting to be more complex, so you'll keep an eye out for unknown bugs during future testing. You really should be displaying the game over message when you run out of lives, but for now you'll abruptly go back to the menu.

**<Step 35>** Save it and exit Unity.

It's healthy for your project to save and exit periodically, so you're doing that here. In the next section, you'll add some old-school scoring.

## SCORING

Just as you did in Bouncing Donuts, you'll only have one type of score: points. Points can easily become meaningless if you're not careful. There are plenty of examples of hugely successful published games with mostly meaningless scoring due to unlimited points exploits, or on the other extreme, an easily obtainable optimal score. In the arcade, scoring was sometimes very meaningful, with world record attempts still happening on thirty-year old games.

As you put in the scoring for this game, you'll choose a simple mechanism for scoring and plan to revisit the topic of having a meaningful score once you're closer to completion.

Clearly, you'll want to award points for killing robots and spikers. You should also award big points every time you complete a level.

<Step 1> In Bomb.cs, replace the Spiker and Robot sections at the bottom with this:

```
if(colliders[i].gameObject.tag == "Spiker")
{
    Scoring.gamescore += 50;
    Destroy(colliders[i].gameObject);
}
if (colliders[i].gameObject.tag == "Robot")
{
    Scoring.gamescore += 100;
    Destroy(colliders[i].gameObject);
}
```

This is pretty easy. You simply inserted the scoring lines before the Destroy calls. You need to do the same sort of thing in Arrow.cs:

<Step 2> In Arrow.cs in the collision code, insert a 50-point gamescore line before the Destroy call for the Spiker, just like you did for the Spiker in Bomb.cs.

<Step 3> Test.
This should just work.

<Step 4> In DottimaController.cs, add scoring lines of 500 points for levelComplete and 1000 points for theEnd.

<Step 5> Test.
So far so good. Next, you'll put in a level timer that counts down from 100 points down to 0. When Dottima reaches the end of a level, she gets the remaining points in the count down timer. This feature is put in to make scoring more meaningful. The faster you complete a level, the more points you get. It's up to the player to decide if it's worth to kill all the enemies, given that it'll take more time to do that. You, as the game designer and developer, need to think about how to lay out the levels and adjust the scoring so that this player decision isn't obvious, at least on some of the levels.

**\<Step 6a\>** In Scoring.cs, insert this in the declarations:

```
public static float levelTimer = 100.0f;
```

You created a float that keeps track of the time spent on a level.

**\<Step 6b\>** Replace the Update function with this:

```
void Update()
{
    if (GameState.state == GameState.gamePlay)
    {
        levelTimer -= Time.deltaTime;
        if (levelTimer <= 0.0) levelTimer = 0.0f;
    }
}
```

This `levelTimer` variable decreases at a rate of 1 unit per second during gameplay, and then gets stuck at 0.

**\<Step 7\>** In OnGUI, replace the first GUI.Box call with this:

```
GUI.Box(new Rect(20, 20, 400, 50), "Score: " + gamescore +
                " Timer: " + (int)levelTimer);
```

Make sure to add spaces inside of the quotes as indicated. If you don't, the display elements won't be separated properly.

You added the Timer display to the right of the Score display. You had to change the box width from 200 to 400. Way back at the beginning of this book you learned about casting. Here, you are casting the float variable levelTimer to an int in order to display just the seconds.

**\<Step 8\>** In Update for DottimaController.cs, insert these two lines before the level++ statement and the level=1 statement:

```
Scoring.gamescore += (int)Scoring.levelTimer;
Scoring.levelTimer = 100.0f;
```

These lines award the points to the player at the end of the level and reset the levelTimer.

**\<Step 9\>** Test.

So far so good, but you found two new (or are they old?) bugs. When you lose all your lives, the score doesn't get displayed, and when you start a new game your score isn't reset, nor is the levelTimer. Also, Dottima can still move after reaching the end of a level. You'll fix the Dottima issue first.

**\<Step 10\>** In DottimaController.cs, insert these lines at the beginning of FixedUpdate:

```
// At the end of a level, stop updating Dottima
if (GameState.state == GameState.theEnd) return;
if (GameState.state == GameState.levelComplete) return;
```

**\<Step 11\>** Insert those same two lines in Update immediately after the levelComplete and theEnd sections.

**\<Step 12>** In MainMenu.cs, replace PlayGame with this:

```
public void PlayGame()
{
    Scoring.gamescore = 0;
    Scoring.levelTimer = 100.0f;
    SceneManager.LoadScene(1);
}
```

This isn't exactly clean code, but it works. Or does it?

**\<Step 13>** Test by playing several games.

You're almost there. You now need to handle game over properly.

**\<Step 14>** In DottimaController, insert the following after the levelComplete section in Update:

```
if (GameState.state == GameState.gameOver)
{
    rb.velocity = Vector2.zero;
    levelCompleteTimer -= Time.deltaTime;
    if (levelCompleteTimer < 0.0f)
    {
        Scoring.lives = 5;
        GameState.level = 1;
        GameState.state = GameState.gamePlay;
        SceneManager.LoadScene(0);
    }
}
```

**\<Step 15>** Insert this in the "stop updating Dottima" sections:

```
if (GameState.state == GameState.gameOver) return;
```

You'll insert this twice, once in `Update` and once in `FixedUpdate`.

**\<Step 16>** At the end of `Update`, replace the `Scoring.lives == 0` section with:

```
if (Scoring.lives == 0)
{
    GameState.state = GameState.gameOver;
}
```

**\<Step 17>** Test it.

Well, this should work, except that the Game Over display is quite short, only two seconds. This is OK for now as you will likely replace the Game Over display with its own scene later on.

Upon further reflection, you've decided to have "The End" actually end the game.

**\<Step 18>** Replace the "The End" section in Update with this and test it.

```
if (GameState.state == GameState.theEnd)
{
    rb.velocity = Vector2.zero;
    levelCompleteTimer -= Time.deltaTime;
    if (levelCompleteTimer < 0.0f)
    {
        Scoring.lives = 5;
```

```
        Scoring.gamescore += 1000;
        GameState.level = 1;
        GameState.state = GameState.gamePlay;
        SceneManager.LoadScene(0);
    }
}
```

You're now basically doing the same thing as in the Game Over section, except you're adding the points.

**<Step 19>** Save.

Your code has slowly but surely gotten ugly, at least in some parts. Whenever you see repetitious code, or functions that have gotten over a page long, you're ripe for refactoring the code. No, you're not going to do that now, but you feel bad about it and hope to find the time for that soon.

It's time to move on and build a bunch of levels.

## LEVEL DESIGN

In this section, you'll make the first few levels of DotGame. Games such as this can easily grow to have hundreds or even thousands of levels. There won't be room in this book to do that, but you're going to make enough levels to make the game interesting.

It's a tradition in game design to have the first few levels very easy so that the players get a chance to learn the game before getting to the real challenge of the later levels. Alternatively, some games put in tutorials to teach the game. You can't go wrong with Bushnell's Law, attributed to Nolan Bushnell:

> All the best games are easy to learn and difficult to master. They should reward the first quarter and the hundredth.

This law emerged from the days when it cost a quarter to play an arcade game, with an average game time of three minutes.

You're decided to make the first few levels very easy and gradually increase the difficulty all the while introducing new game elements. You'll start with a blank level:

**<Step 1>** On Level 1, remove all enemies. Compare with Figure 20.3.

Even this level has a challenge. How fast can Dottima get to the exit? Your score depends on that. This level teaches the players how to get to the exit. They can't really get this wrong as long as they know to use the arrow keys to move Dottima around. You'll make a mental note to put in instructions about the controls.

**<Step 2>** On Level 2, remove all enemies, then put in four spikers, as shown in Figure 20.4, then test.

This level teaches the player to shoot arrows. You will need to tell the players about the space key, otherwise they will have a hard time with this level.

**<Step 3>** Make Level 3 look like Figure 20.5 and test.

Now the game is getting slightly more difficult. You will have to select the Maze1 Grid Tilemap and open the Tilemap Editor so you can remove that one

FIGURE 20.3    Level 1 of DotGame.

FIGURE 20.4    Level 2 of DotGame.

square. Why did you remove that square? Try playing the game without that change and wait a while to see what those spikers will do to the Blockade.

<Step 4>    Make Level 4 look like Figure 20.6 and test.

You're introducing the bomb and the robot. You should say something about the bomb controls. This level is also fairly easy. In the next level, you'll introduce multiple robots and bombs. You'll also change the layout of the level.

FIGURE 20.5    Level 3 of DotGame.

FIGURE 20.6    Level 4 of DotGame.

<Step 5> Make Level 5 look like Figure 20.7 and test.

This level is actually quite easy if you don't care about killing the robots. Just wait a little and walk out of the exit. This level would be more interesting if you had to kill all the robots in order to get through it. Maybe you could put in logic

FIGURE 20.7   Level 5 of DotGame.

for the Blockade that makes it disappear when all the robots are gone. Maybe you'll implement this in the future.

You haven't done anything with the question mark, so Level 6 puts it in there.

<Step 6> Make Level 6 look like Figure 20.8 and test it.

There's not much to testing this. You're stuck because those question marks don't do anything yet other than block you.

<Step 7> Add the following script to the QuestionMark prefab with the name QuestionMark.

```
using System.Collections;
using System.Collections.Generic;
using UnityEngine;

public class QuestionMark : MonoBehaviour
{
    private void OnCollisionEnter2D(Collision2D collision)
    {
        if (collision.gameObject.name == "DottimaFace")
        {
            int randomscore = Random.Range(10,101);
            Scoring.gamescore += randomscore;
            Destroy(gameObject);
        }
    }
}
```

This script should fix your problem. You get a random score between 10 and 100 when you collide with a question mark, and it destroys itself. Of course,

FIGURE 20.8   Level 6 of DotGame.

there are many other possible random actions for those question marks, but a random score is good enough for now.

**<Step 8>**   Test Level 6.

This is a puzzle! How are you going to get past those two robots? Try to figure this out before reading on. Here's a hint: Use the bomb to blow up one of them, then steer the other robot by hitting it with arrows.

Congratulations, you have a game. It's short, and fun, and probably way too easy, but it's a great start. Who knows where this will lead? Time and space are limited, so this will be all the gameplay development before your initial release. You're not done yet, though. You don't even have audio, and there's no title screen, no credits, etc.

**<Step 9>**   Test the game from the Menu. Then save it.

You're making sure that the game is playable and that there are no obvious flaws.

# Sound and Music for DotGame

This chapter covers sound and music for your 2D maze game. You'll use several different audio creation techniques, starting with speech, some sound effects for the actions in DotGame, and you'll use Scott Joplin's Peacherine Rag as background music.

## RECORDING SPEECH

These days it's really easy to add speech to a video game. Just record someone speaking, and put it into the game. It wasn't always that easy.

In 1980, the arcade game Berzerk by Stern was one of the first games to use speech synthesis. Using a vocabulary of 32 works including "intruder," "chicken," and "robot," a few taunting phrases added excitement and humor to a fun shooting maze game. The gameplay of Berzerk is somewhat similar to DotGame in that the robot starts at the left and tries to find an exit to get to the next level.

<Step 1> Watch a video or two of Berzerk by Stern from 1980.

Notably missing is the background music. They spent all of their audio budget on the speech. For 1980, it was quite a technical achievement. It is one or two decades before speech became commonplace and inexpensive for video games.

You've decided to put in a few phrases into the game, just for fun. "Game Over", "Find the Exit, Dottima", "Yikes", and "Level Complete" is a good starting point.

<Step 2> Create an "Audio" subfolder in the DotGame Assets folder. Create a Reference subfolder in Audio.

<Step 3> Record the four phrases and store them in separate .wav files stored in Audio/Reference.

You can do this by recording yourself saying those phrases, one after another, and storing them in a single .wav file. Store the original recording in Reference. Then use Audacity to cut out the four phrases and store them as .wav files, also

in Reference. Don't forget to normalize. These phrases will be inserted into the game together with the other sound effects.

## MORE FREE SOUND EFFECTS ONLINE

In Bouncing Donuts, you used freesound.org to find a boing sound. For DotGame, you'll start by making a list of desired sound effects and then you'll see what you can find at freesound.org to match that list.

    **<Step 1>**  Make a list of possible sound effects.

            Each action by each character can result in a sound effect. Starting with Dottima, she shoots arrows, picks up bombs, and collides with walls. Arrows can bounce off walls or destroy something. Bombs do a fuse countdown, plus an explosion afterward. The question mark gets picked up, and the blockade gets pushed. That's quite a few sound effects. Let's see what you can find.

    **<Step 2>**  In the following steps, store the downloaded files in Assets/Audio/Reference.

    **<Step 3>**  Get an explosion sound from freesound.org.

            That's the most important sound. Freesound has a lot of explosions, so search for "explosion" and pick one of the many free explosion sound effects.

    **<Step 4>**  Get a "bounce" sound from freesound.org.

            Again, there are many "bounce" sounds to choose from.

    **<Step 5>**  Get a "Whoosh" sound from freesound.org

            You can use the "Whoosh" sound by qubodup. That one is in the public domain, and it's in the .flac sound format. Fortunately, Audacity can import that, so you'll be able to work with this.

    **<Step 6>**  Search for "ding" at freesound.org and choose one of those sounds.

            This one is for picking up something good like a bomb or the question mark. That's enough for now. You can always add more sound effects later.

## MORE SOUND EFFECTS IN AUDACITY

Next, you'll explore Audacity some more for getting synthetic sound effects. You're just going to play around with the settings and try get some random sounds that you like. You'll figure out later where to use them. While you're in Audacity, you'll also process the other effects that you collected so far.

    **<Step 1>**  Open Audacity.

    **<Step 2>**  Generate – Risset Drum. Use the default settings and click on OK.

            The Windows version of Audacity 2.3.0 has three versions of the Risset Drum effect. You can pick any of them.

            It's time you took a look at the Audacity Manual.

**\<Step 3\>** Help – Manual.

> This will open the manual in your default browser.

**\<Step 4\>** Click on Audacity GUI – Effects. Then click on Risset Drum.

> There, you can see a complete description of the Risset Drum, a sound based on the work of composer Jean Claude Risset.

**\<Step 5\>** Select – All, Effect – Change Pitch… Percent Change 100 – OK.

**\<Step 6\>** Effect – Change Tempo… Percent Change 300 – OK.

> For lack of a better word, you'll call this one a thud. It's ready to be exported, no need to normalize this one.

**\<Step 7\>** Save the project in Reference. Also export in Reference as thud.wav.

**\<Step 8\>** Review all the audio files in Audacity, trim any silences before or after the sound, and save them as .wav files and the corresponding .aup files in Reference.

**\<Step 9\>** Copy the sounds from Assets/Audio/Reference to Assets/Audio.

> You now have nine sound effects and speech files ready to import into Unity. Here's a list in alphabetical order:

- Bounce.wav

- Ding.wav

- Explosion.mp3

- FindTheExit.wav

- GameOver.wav

- LevelComplete.wav

- Thud.wav

- Whoosh.wav

- Yikes.wav.

> You did all those sounds yourself this time, with extensive help from the generous artists who supply free sound effects online. In a fully realized commercial game, you would probably hire a professional to make original sounds for you. Typically, you would supply a list of the desired sound effects to the sound effects artist and when the job is done, you'll squeeze the sounds into the game. It helps to decide ahead of time about file formats (.wav vs. .mp3 or other) and the memory budget. The nine sound effects are mostly using .wav format and all the sounds together are using up less than two Megabytes, so you're OK as far as memory usage goes.

## SOUND EFFECTS CODING FOR DOTGAME

This is going to be easy. The process is very much the same as for Bouncing Donuts.

<Step 1> Load DotGame into Unity.

<Step 2> Look at the Audio folder and play all the sounds. The nine sounds should match the sound list from the previous section, also in alphabetical order.

<Step 3> Review how you did sound effects for Bouncing Donuts in the file donut.cs
You declared AudioSource variables, accessed the components of donut to get the sounds, and then called Play at the appropriate spot in the code. You'll be doing the same thing here.

<Step 4> In Arrow.cs, insert this in the declarations section:

```
AudioSource whoosh;
```

<Step 5> In the Start function, insert:

```
whoosh = GetComponent<AudioSource>();
whoosh.Play();
```

<Step 6> In the arrow prefab, add an AudioSource component with the whoosh sound as the clip and the Play on Awake unchecked.

<Step 7> Test it.
It works, except that the sound cuts off as soon as the arrow is destroyed. The best solution is to not destroy the arrow, but rather to have it bounce away from its collision and only get destroyed a bit later. You'll do this next because you need to put in the Bounce sound anyhow. You just realized that the Arrow will actually have two audio sources, so you'll need to revamp the arrow sound code.

<Step 8> In Arrow.cs, insert this in the declarations section:

```
AudioSource bounce;
```

<Step 9> Replace the Start function with this:

```
void Start()
 {

     rb = GetComponent<Rigidbody2D>();
     AudioSource[] audios = GetComponents<AudioSource>();
     whoosh = audios[0];
     bounce = audios[1];
     whoosh.Play();
 }
```

<Step 10> In the collision function, insert this after the IgnoreCollision section:

```
bounce.Play();
```

<Step 11> Comment out the Destroy(gameObject) statement after the Spiker section.

**<Step 12>** In the arrow prefab, add another AudioSource component with the Bounce audio clip and the Play on Awake unchecked.

**<Step 13>** Test.

You took out the `Destroy(gameObject)` statement so that you can hear the Bounce sound. The arrows no longer disappear when colliding. The arrows are more powerful now and can take out multiple Spikers. That's kind of fun, but this just doesn't feel right. You're going to put in a deathTimer and dying state for the Arrow similar to the way you did that for Dottima.

**<Step 14>** In the declarations section, insert:

```
private float deathTimer;
private int state;  // 0 = alive, 1 = dying
```

**<Step 15>** In `Start`, insert:

```
deathTimer = 1.0f;
state = 0;
```

**<Step 16>** In `FixedUpdate`, insert this at the beginning:

```
if (state == 1)
{
    rb.velocity = Vector2.zero;
    return;
}
```

**<Step 17>** Create this `Update` function:

```
private void Update()
{
    if (state == 1)
    {
        deathTimer -= Time.deltaTime;
    }
    if (deathTimer < 0.0f) Destroy(gameObject);
}
```

**<Step 18>** Edit `OnCollisionEnter2D` to look like this:

```
private void OnCollisionEnter2D(Collision2D collision)
{
    if (state == 1) return;

    if (collision.gameObject.tag == "Player"
     || collision.gameObject.tag == "Arrow")
    {
        Physics2D.IgnoreCollision(
            collision.collider,
            gameObject.GetComponent<Collider2D>()
            );
        return;
    }

    bounce.Play();

    if (collision.gameObject.tag == "Spiker")
    {
        Scoring.gamescore += 50;
        Destroy(collision.gameObject);
    }
```

```
        state = 1;
    }
```

Ok, that was quite a bit of editing, but it was fairly easy. You're shutting down that arrow when it's dying. You just want it to sit there for one second and then destroy itself.

**<Step 19>** Test.

The game almost plays as before. The arrows look like they might be interfering with the Robots when you shoot at them, but this is likely just an illusion. You've only put in two sound effects so far. Let's hope the rest are easier.

**<Step 20>** In the Question Mark prefab, add a Ding AudioSource. Uncheck the Play on Awake.

**<Step 21>** Replace the QuestionMark class in QuestionMark.cs with this:

```
public class QuestionMark : MonoBehaviour
{
    private AudioSource ding;
    private float deathTimer = 1.0f;

    void Start()
    {
        ding = GetComponent<AudioSource>();
    }

    private void Update()
    {
        if (deathTimer < 1.0f)
        {
            deathTimer -= Time.deltaTime;
            float shrink = 1.0f - 1.0f * Time.deltaTime;
            transform.localScale = (
                new Vector3(
                    transform.localScale.x * shrink,
                    transform.localScale.y * shrink,
                    transform.localScale.z));
        }
        if (deathTimer < 0.0f) Destroy(gameObject);
    }

    private void OnCollisionEnter2D(Collision2D collision)
    {
        if (deathTimer < 1.0f)
        {
            Physics2D.IgnoreCollision(
            collision.collider,
            gameObject.GetComponent<Collider2D>());
            return;
        }

        if (collision.gameObject.name == "DottimaFace")
        {
            int randomscore = Random.Range(10,101);
            Scoring.gamescore += randomscore;
            ding.Play();
            deathTimer -= 0.01f;
        }
    }
}
```

OK, that wasn't a whole lot easier, but the result is worth it. You added just a deathTimer and rather than having a state variable you made the deathTimer do double duty as a state variable. You once again decided to keep that question mark alive so you can hear the ding sound. You're shrinking the Question Mark during that second using a technique similar to the Dottima shrink code. The IgnoreCollision section is necessary to shut down collisions during the death sequence.

**<Step 22>** Test.

This should just work. Start your testing at level 5 by selecting the Level 5 scene first.

You've waited long enough to hear that explosion in the game. Here you go:

**<Step 23>** In Bomb.cs, insert this in the declarations:

```
public AudioClip clip;
```

**<Step 24>** In the Update function, insert this in the fuseTimer section before the SetParent.

```
AudioSource.PlayClipAtPoint(clip, Camera.main.transform.position);
```

**<Step 25>** In the bomb prefab, set clip to point at the Explosion sound.

**<Step 26>** Test this on Level 4.

The camera reference needs an explanation. You're using `PlayClipAtPoint` to play the entire explosion sound even after the bomb gets destroyed. This means you need to tell the code where the sound is located. The sound system then computes the distance to that location from the camera in order to compute the volume. To make that explosion loud you're putting that explosion sound on top of the camera.

You still don't have a fuse sound, so that'll have to wait for later. Next, you'll put in the Thud whenever a robot collides with something.

**<Step 27>** Put the thud sound into DotRobot, with the Play call at the beginning of the collision function.

You do this similarly to Steps 4 and 5, but with the Play call in a different spot. All you need to do now is put in the speech clips. You'll put them in all at once.

You have some bad news. Dottima needs to be a prefab. You'll see why soon enough.

**<Step 28>** Go to Level 1.

**<Step 29>** Make DottimaFace into a prefab by dragging it into the prefabs folder.

**<Step 30>** Go to Level 2. Delete DottimaFace in the Hierarchy. Drag the DottimaFace prefab into the Hierarchy.

**<Step 31>** Repeat Step 30 for Levels 3–6.

In the future, you'll turn all of your GameObjects into prefabs if you think those objects might get reused, whether in the same or a different scene.

**<Step 32>** Insert the following lines into the declarations of DottimaController.cs.

```
public AudioClip yikes;
public AudioClip gameOver;
public AudioClip levelComplete;
public AudioClip findExit;
```

**<Step 33>** Insert this in Start.

```
AudioSource.PlayClipAtPoint(findExit, Camera.main.transform.position);
```

**<Step 34>** Insert this at the end of Update immediately after the gameOver assignment.

```
AudioSource.PlayClipAtPoint(gameOver, Camera.main.transform.position);
```

**<Step 35>** Insert this near the end of the file, immediately after the dottimaState=2 statement.

```
AudioSource.PlayClipAtPoint(yikes, Camera.main.transform.position);
```

**<Step 36>** Insert at the beginning of the "ExitLocation" section at the end of the file.

```
AudioSource.PlayClipAtPoint(levelComplete, Camera.main.transform.position);
```

**<Step 37>** In the DottimaFace prefab, Select the Audio Clips for Yikes, Game Over, Level Complete, and Find Exit in the Dottima Controller (Script) section in the Inspector.

As usual, you can do that by dragging the clips from the Audio folder or by selecting the clips from a menu in the Inspector. The Dottima Controller (Script) section now looks like Figure 21.1.

FIGURE 21.1   Dottima Controller (Script) section in the Inspector.

**<Step 38>** Test and Save.

All the sound effects are in the game now, except for the missing fuse sound. You'll visit Freesound again to look for something.

**<Step 39>** At freesound.org, download fuse_burning_48khz.wav.

This is an eight-second sound. You'll trim it to be just 2.5 seconds. Unity has the fuse, go two seconds, so a little bit longer is good.

**<Step 40>** Create a 2.5 second fuse sound in Audacity and store in the Reference and Audio folders as usual.

**<Step 41>** Put the sound into Bomb.cs with a PlayClipAtPoint after sparks. Play.

**<Step 42>** Test it.

Wow, that sounds great. You're finished with sound effects. Time for some music.

## BACKGROUND MUSIC IN DOTGAME

**<Step 1>** Find some free music, or create some original music.

**<Step 2>** Put it into the game. But wait…

Before you go and do all this work by yourself, how about a simple way to put great music into the game with very little work. You can always add other music later on, if you wish.

**<Step 3>** Go to MuseScore.com, log in, and download the Peacherine Rag by Scott Joplin, entered into MuseScore by James Brigham.

The score for this piano piece is in the public domain, so you can use it without fear of lawsuits. James Brigham entered it into MuseScore and assures us that it's faithful to the original public domain score.

**<Step 4>** In MuseScore, load the Peacherine Rag and export it as an mp3 file. Create a new folder in Assets/Audio called Music and store the MuseScore file as well as the mp3 file there.

**<Step 5>** Back in Unity, check to make sure you can play the Peacherine Rag mp3 file.

**<Step 6>** In the Menus scene, create an empty game object, rename it to MusicLoop.

**<Step 7>** Add an Audio Source to MusicLoop, check Play on Away and loop. Use the Peacherine Rag clip.

**<Step 8>** Attach the following script to MusicLoop:

```
using System.Collections;
using System.Collections.Generic;
using UnityEngine;

public class MusicLoop : MonoBehaviour
{
```

```
    // Start is called before the first frame update
    void Start()
    {
        DontDestroyOnLoad(gameObject);
    }

    // Update is called once per frame
    void Update()
    {
        if (GameState.state == GameState.gameOver)
        {
            Destroy(gameObject);
        }
    }
}
```

This script ensures that the MusicLoop game object stays active even after a new scene is loaded. You can check this by playing the game and looking at the Hierarchy. There is an exception though. In the Update function, you destroy this music object as soon as the GameOver state is reached. This is necessary because the game soon goes back to the Menus scene and creates the MusicLoop again, thus restarting the music.

<Step 9> Test it. Save.

This works pretty well. It's not perfect, but it sounds like a real game now. It's kind of annoying that the voice keeps saying "Find the Exit, Dottima". You'll live with that for now. Later on, you plan on writing and recording a different phrase for each of the levels.

# Cutscenes

THIS SHORT CHAPTER COVERS the creation of cutscenes and other similar scenes such as a title screen or the ending for DotGame. The word "cutscene" is usually reserved for short, animated interludes where the player simply watches. Typically, cutscenes tell the story of the game, chopped up into short interludes interspersed throughout the game.

This chapter is not about how to make cutscenes. That would take us too far afield from the purpose of this book, which is learning how to develop games. Technology has come so far that now there is little difference between movie making and cutscene making.

A good place to learn about cutscenes is the YouTube video "A complete history of cutscenes in games" by Logitech G. Watch it in your spare time, it's fun and inspirational. You'll learn about the most famous cutscene of them all, with the text "All your base are belong to us!", an example of what can happen when your translator doesn't know English.

No, you won't be making elaborate cutscenes for DotGame. You have a concept for a story, but the game just isn't large enough to warrant cutscenes at this time. Instead, you'll do the absolute minimum for the first release. This means putting in a Title Scene. Even the animation isn't really necessary, but it's easy enough and gets you a framework for making other cutscenes in the future.

## AN ANIMATED TITLE SCENE

The title scene for DotGame needs to show the title with a short animation and then go on to the menu scene. You're going to put in a short animation of a very large Dottima scrolling onto the screen. That's it, short and sweet.

Yes, you've decided to keep the title DotGame, at least for now. The domain dotgame. com is not being used by anyone, so that's a good sign that no major publisher owns this name.

First, you're going to fix a problem with the Menus Scene.

<Step 1> Select the Menus Scene.

<Step 2> In the Hierarchy, select the Settings Menu, and then uncheck it in the Inspector.

**\<Step 3\>** In the Hierarchy, select the Main Menu, and check it in the Inspector.

**\<Step 4\>** Test.

This simply has you starting on the Main Menu rather than on the Settings Menu.

You're going to use Level 6 as the starting point for making a Title scene.

**\<Step 5\>** Duplicate Level 6. This generates Level 7. Rename Level 7 to TitleScene.

**\<Step 6\>** In the TitleScene, delete everything except for the Main Camera and DottimaFace.

**\<Step 7\>** For DottimaFace, change the Transform Position to (0, 0, −2), Scale to (5, 5, 1). The Game panel should look like Figure 22.1.

**\<Step 8\>** Select DottimaFace. In the Inspector, remove the Dottima Controller (script) and the Rigidbody 2D components.

**\<Step 9\>** Add a new script component, call it DottimaTitle, and use this code:

```
using System.Collections;
using System.Collections.Generic;
using UnityEngine;
using UnityEngine.SceneManagement;

public class DottimaTitle : MonoBehaviour
{
    float timer = 7.0f;
    // Start is called before the first frame update
    void Start()
    {

    }

    // Update is called once per frame
    void Update()
```

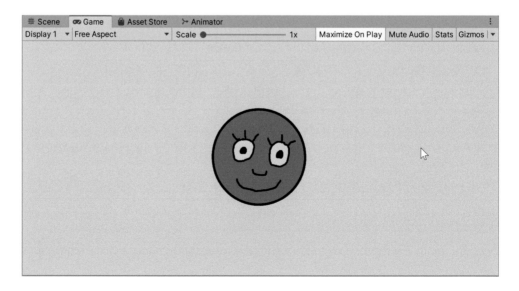

FIGURE 22.1  Dottima in the Title Scene.

```
    {
        float delta;
        delta = Time.deltaTime;
        gameObject.transform.Translate(new Vector3(delta * 4.0f, 0.0f, 0.0f));
        timer -= delta;
        if (timer < 0)
        {
            SceneManager.LoadScene(0);
        }
    }
}
```

This code moves Dottima to the right for seven seconds, then loads the Menus Scene.

**<Step 10>** Test it.

Dottima moves to the right, leaves the screen, then the Menus Scene starts together with the music.

**<Step 11>** In the Scene panel, move Dottima to the left until she's barely off-screen and a little lower. Then test this again.

All that's missing now is the text for the game name.

**<Step 12>** Insert the following function into DottimaTitle:

```
private void OnGUI()
{
    GUI.backgroundColor = Color.clear;
    GUI.color = Color.yellow;
    GUI.skin.box.fontSize = (int)(Screen.width / 9.0f);
    GUI.Box(new Rect(
        0.0f,
        Screen.height * 0.1f,
        Screen.width,
        Screen.height * 0.3f),
        "DotGame");
}
```

This code displays the name "DotGame" in big yellow letters as shown in Figure 22.2.

**<Step 13>** Test and Save.

## MORE CUTSCENES

What other cutscenes should you create? It's up to you. You now know enough to make a wide variety of cutscenes using the techniques you learned throughout this book. Here is a partial list:

**Instructions for the Controls:** Display the text: Use arrow keys to move Dottima toward the exit.

**Game Over Scene:** A scene that shows an animated text "Game Over", displaying the score and the level attained.

**Ending Scene:** A scene showing Dottima getting back to her original book.

FIGURE 22.2   DotGame Title Animation.

**Credits:** A scene showing credits for the game developers.

**Story Scenes**: Periodically showing text telling the story of Dottima.

Congratulations. You have finished all the development steps for this book. You're not quite finished yet. There's still testing and releasing, which will be covered in the following chapters.

# Testing

THIS CHAPTER COVERS testing. You'll start by reviewing the history of software testing, in general, and video game testing, in particular. You'll then review the testing for DotGame during development, and finish by testing just one more time before release.

## A BRIEF HISTORY OF VIDEO GAME TESTING

It's going to be *really* brief. In the beginning, the customers were the testers. And guess what, today, the customers are the testers too. In the intervening years, professional video game testers did the testing. We've come full circle, amazingly. Well, it's not quite that simple.

Games hit the big time in the eighties arcade era. At that time, testing was done in the field. The games were put out into arcades, and if they made enough money, they were manufactured. Of course, crash-bugs were a very bad thing, because then the game would stop earning money. Eventually, the arcade manufacturers put in special hardware that detected when the game crashed and then triggered a reboot. This was called a watchdog. It was crude, but it was better than having a frozen screen. The arcade companies of that time had no professional testing. It was the customers who tested the games.

A decade later cartridge-based home consoles took over the game industry. This absolutely required extensive testing because the games were manufactured as ROM cartridges. There was no ability to patch or fix bugs after release, so the games had better be free of bugs. Sometimes bugs would slip through with disastrous economic consequences. A common rule from that time was the 200-hour rule: Games had to withstand 200 hours of brutal testing without problems, no crashes, no serious bugs. Game companies hired professional testers to play the games for 200 hours, often multiple times, before they were willing to take the chance and release the games to manufacturing. You might have had a team of five testers playing your game for forty hours each. They weren't just looking for bugs but also gave valuable feedback on whether the game was good and fun to play.

Fast forward to the internet era. Games could now be released to customers for essentially no cost, thus allowing, once again, the customers to take on the role of testing. The large companies would still hire professional testers, but a more prevalent testing technique

would be a limited release to a smaller country such as Turkey or New Zealand to get the needed testing time before committing to a worldwide release.

For a small independent game developer, the bulk of the testing is actually done after release. If your game is a success, you will get feedback from your customers. You will then use that feedback to make a better version, release that, and the cycle starts all over again.

As you have seen during your development of DotGame, it's advantageous to begin testing during development. Good software development practices are the secret to avoiding bugs or to catch them early on before they become difficult to find and fix. In the next section, you'll review your testing for DotGame during development.

## TESTING DURING DEVELOPMENT

Of the hundreds of steps taken to build DotGame, a large number simply say "Test." The old way of writing all of your code first and then to test is very risky and should be avoided. Even so, as you look back on how things went, so had some bugs along the way, and there's a good chance that there are still some undiscovered bugs lurking in the code.

Currently, the most serious known bug isn't even a bug but rather a feature omission. Nowhere do you tell the player to use the arrow keys to control Dottima. You will definitely need to fix that before release.

You had a sequence of bugs during the development of the game states, for example, "Game Over" and "Level Complete." In retrospect, now that you're more experienced, you might be able to avoid those bugs. A tough, but useful exercise is to rebuild the whole game from scratch. You may want to go through that exercise twice: Once without changing anything (on purpose) and another time where you make changes along the way and hope nothing falls apart as a result.

To sum things up, you had only a few bugs along the way, and you didn't have to redo very much. The worst thing was the decision to not bother creating a DottimaFace prefab early on. You probably had typos along the way. This book has to assume that you don't have typos because there are really too many possible typos to discuss in a book. You probably learned the hard way that you need to save and back up your work early and often. The only way to really learn this is the hard way.

## TESTING BEFORE RELEASE

Traditionally, software developers test their products before release and hope they don't find anything really awful. Here are some tips for how to test games before releasing them.

- **Do a feature freeze, then test.**

  It's tempting to keep adding features, even the day before release. Especially on the day before. Don't do it! You need to have the discipline to stop adding new features. It's hard enough to find the bugs. Occasionally, you'll need to add a feature in order to fix a bug. Avoid that if possible.

- **Test all bug-fix changes, even tiny ones.**

    Did you change the code in some way that can't possibly cause a new bug? Guess what, it can, so test it.

- **Give yourself a good night's sleep before release.**

    If you think you're done testing, stop. Go to sleep. Wait a day or two if you can. Then release. You'll be amazed what some time spent reflecting on the release can produce. You might think of a bug that you didn't bother to fix.

- **Don't release if there's a mysterious, rare, crash bug.**

    Give yourself the time to find it. Ask for help, talk it through with yourself, your dog, or a trusted coworker.

    The phase of testing before release is the best, but also the worst part of game development. You're so close and yet, you might be weeks away from release if things go horribly wrong. This is where experienced developers shine. They've been there before, so they know what to expect, and they build their code in a way that avoids the really terrible bugs. Still, software development is difficult and no one, however experienced or talented, is immune from writing buggy code sometimes.

- **Play the game.**

    Pretend you just bought this game for $5. Play it for a while. Give it a chance. Forget everything you know about the game before you start.

- **Watch people play the game.**

    This is often a true wakeup call. You'll be shocked at what people will do with your creation. Of course, this should be done all through development, but it's never too late to do this and learn.

    In the next, also very short chapter, you'll get some advice on how to release your game.

# Release

Y OUR GAME IS READY FOR RELEASE. Or is it? The nitty-gritty details of this are beyond the scope of this book, mainly because they have changed so radically over the years. This brief chapter includes some general advice that was valid forty years ago and should be valid forty years from now.

First and foremost, your game should be an experience worthy of your audience's time. Whether it's mindless fun, a tough challenge, or a way to tell your story, make it good, whatever that means. You are the ultimate arbiter of goodness. By the time you reach your release date, check to make sure that you're still mostly pleased with your creation. Don't release something that you know to be a bad game! On the other hand, if you like it and believe in it, then release the thing and ignore the critics. Even the very best games don't appeal to everybody, so as long as you have some fans who love it then you've succeeded.

Of course, the decision to release or not to release may not be yours to make. Regardless, let's assume that, right or wrong, you're releasing your game to an unsuspecting public. You then need a way to transmit the game and maybe even sell it to your customer. There are dozens of main-stream ways to release video games. Pick one or more of those and get ready! Your next step is to finalize the code and other assets.

Once that's done you need to back up your source code, all reference assets, including videos, paper sketches, even the email trails: anything else you or your heirs may wish to look at in ten or twenty years when all is forgotten and obsolete. Save it all, especially if you were smart enough and lucky enough to keep the long-term intellectual property rights for your game. When you actually release, keep a good log. You'll likely be doing this infrequently, so you'll want those notes as a reference for the next release.

In the next section you'll use Unity to build a releasable version of DotGame.

## RELEASING A UNITY GAME

Unity makes it fairly easy to get your game ready for release. Simply build it, and you're done. Well, not quite. In this section, you'll explore Unity's build settings, specifically for DotGame. No, you're not actually releasing DotGame in this chapter, but you are going to get it ready for release.

You are dismayed to see that the TitleScene is missing in the build settings. Furthermore, you just found out that Unity builds always start with Scene 0, so you'll need to shuffle the scenes a bit and change your code! Yikes.

**\<Step 1\>**  Load DotGame into Unity.

**\<Step 2\>**  Select TitleScene.

**\<Step 3\>**  File – Build Settings … Add Open Scenes.
          TitleScene in Scene number 7.

**\<Step 4\>**  Move TitleScene to position 0.
          This will break your code very badly. How can you deal with this?

**\<Step 5\>**  In GameState.cs, insert the following lines in the declarations section:

```
public const int MenuScene = 1;
public const int FirstLevelScene = 2;
public const int SceneOffset = FirstLevelScene - 1;
```

This setup makes it easier to maintain your scenes if you decide to change the layout of the scenes in the future.

**\<Step 6\>**  In MainMenu.cs, replace the LoadScene line with this:

```
SceneManager.LoadScene(GameState.FirstLevelScene);
```

**\<Step 7\>**  In Update for DottimaController.cs, replace the LoadScene calls with these:

```
SceneManager.LoadScene(GameState.level + GameState.SceneOffset);
SceneManager.LoadScene(GameState.MenuScene);
```

That first line goes into the LevelComplete section, the second into the GameOver and the theEnd sections.

**\<Step 8\>**  In DottimaTitle.cs, replace the LoadScene call with this:

```
SceneManager.LoadScene(GameState.MenuScene);
```

**\<Step 9\>**  Test the game!
          Unfortunately, you had to do quite a bit of coding to get this to work. And wouldn't you know it, you found a bug! The music doesn't stop when you reach the end, and you get two versions of the music playing, which is not good!

**\<Step 10\>**  In MusicLoop.cs, insert this into Update:

```
if (GameState.state == GameState.theEnd)
{
    Destroy(gameObject);
}
```

<Step 10> Test again, and Save.

Yes, this is typical. You continue to find bugs when all you're doing is trying to release the game and you've already frozen the code!

<Step 11> Build DotGame, and test the build.

Before you release to the world you will, once again, need to do a complete save and backup.

## LOCALIZATION

Localization used to be called translation. Either way, it's a process that makes your game more accessible to customers in other countries. This can be fairly easy if the other country uses English as its main language, or if the population tends to know English. For example, Norway teaches English starting in first grade, with over 80% of the population fluent in English. So, should you localize your games? Yes, if you have a hit on your hands, otherwise, English is OK for your first release. This is a two-way conundrum, though. If you localize, you will increase your chances of your game becoming a global hit.

A really great way to deal with localization is to avoid text as much as possible. In Dottima, that didn't happen. The good news is that the text is limited, and the spoken words are short, so it wouldn't cost much to translate Dottima into another language.

How much does it cost to translate your game text? A rough estimate is $0.10 US per word. So, for Dottima you've got a few words on the Menu and the GUI, plus the speech. You can probably put in subtitles for the speech, so all in all you've probably got less than $10 US translation cost per language. If you're going to bother to translate, you'll also need to translate your marketing materials: App Store descriptions, etc.

If you don't have a budget for localization and you'd like a free option, there's two basic methods. You can search online for a translation sheet. In DotGame, words such as "Level" and "Play" can be found in such translation sheets, so maybe that'll work. The other method is to have your fans do the translations for you. You'll need to publish the words and phrases that you wish to have translated, and rely on the kindness of your players to help you out.

## GAMES AS A SERVICE

Want to read something funny? Go and read the game design document (GDD) from Chapter 11. That document has some very nice ideas in it, but guess what, some of them got lost along the way. Oh well, that's what future releases are for.

Somewhere along the way you need to make a major decision. How are you going to support your creation next week, next month, and next year? Are you going to make more levels or add those features from the GDD that you conveniently forgot about for the first release? Will you follow in the footsteps of countless mobile games that release new levels and game elements every month or even more often? This approach is called Games as a Service (GaaS).

Would DotGame work with the GaaS model? Definitely yes! The game lends itself to the creation of more levels, more characters, and more cutscenes. Rather than lumping

all that new content into a sequel, it can be easier to simply release the new content in smaller chunks.

## THE END?

No, this is not the end of your game development journey. Rather, it's a beginning. You still have much to learn, but you're ready to make more games. Young or old, there's a good chance you'll enjoy playing and making games for the rest of your life. The game industry will change. Simply look back ten or twenty years. In 2005, flip phones were common and most people had landlines. Mobile gaming was in its infancy, and phrases such as "free to play" or "monetization" would result in blank stares. There was no consumer VR, no facetime, no app stores, no Steam, no Twitter, and Unity just got released as version 1.0 for Macs only. But, Super Mario, Zelda, Pac-man, and Halo were hit gaming franchises then, and they still are! Coding was an important skill then, as it is today.

The game industry has grown at an astounding pace over the past fifty years. Not bad for what was once called "only a fad, like the pet rock." It's impossible to predict what things will look like twenty years from now. Some of your game development skills will become obsolete. Your toolset will be different. That's the nature of the business. Still, much of what you learned in this book will continue to be relevant. Good games have a way of sticking around, so make good games and keep playing.

# Appendix I

## *Game Development Glossary*

THIS IS AN ALPHABETICAL LIST of words, acronyms, and phrases commonly used by game developers. This glossary will allow you to quickly look up words and acronyms that may be unfamiliar to you. If you're new to this, go ahead and read this glossary and find out what you don't know.

### A

**Algorithm:** a process or set of rules typically used by a computer to perform a calculation or solve a problem.

**Alpha:** the first letter of the Greek alphabet. In the context of computer graphics, a floating point number from 0 to 1 which determines the opacity of a graphic element. Zero alpha means transparent, 1 opaque. For 8-bit integer values, alpha ranges from 0 to 255.

**Ambient Sounds:** sounds in the background usually unaffected but the game action.

**Animation:** a series of frames which, when played in sequence, are interpreted by the brain as motion.

**App:** an application, typically on a mobile device.

**Application:** a computer program together with its necessary data files.

**Array:** a table of numbers or other objects used by a computer program. Arrays may be single- or multi-dimensional.

**Asset:** a graphic element, sound, code, or other object used to build an application.

### B

**Background Music (BGM):** music that loops in the background of a level.

**Beta:** a version of an application that is close to final and is released to potential customers for testing purposes.

**Bit:** 0 or 1. An abbreviation for binary digit.

**Bitmap:** a representation of an image using an array of bits.

**Bot:** a computer program that is designed to behave like a human player.

**Box Modeling:** a technique used to create 3D models where you start with a cube and add details.

**Bug:** a programming error in a game. Severe bugs may make a game unplayable. See glitch.

## C

**camelCasing:** a naming convention where each word in a multi word name starts with a capital letter, except the first one, for example, eBay or myVariableList.

**Camera:** a device that displays a portion of the game world to the player.

**Casting:** type conversion by placing the type you are casting to in parentheses. For example, (int)x where x is a float. This cast converts the float to an int resulting in possible data loss.

**Cheat Code:** a usually secret sequence of characters or button presses which exposes a hidden game feature.

**Checkpoint:** a location in a game where, if reached by the player, the player may subsequently restart his game.

**Code:** expressions of one or more computer languages, stored in a text file.

**Coding:** the creation of code.

**Coding Standard:** rules for writing code in a particular programming language. These rules aim to make code readable and maintainable.

**Colliding:** what happens when two objects touch in a game world.

**Collision:** this happens when two objects touch or overlap.

**Comment:** part of computer code that can be read by programmers but has no effect on the execution of the code.

**Comment Out:** converting computer code into a comment. In C#, single lines are quickly commented out by putting two forward slashes at the beginning of the line.

**Compatibility:** the ability of two or more systems to work with one another.

**Coordinate System:** a two or three axis system that can determine the location of objects by specifying two or three numbers. The individual coordinates are usually called X and Y, or X, Y, and Z.

**Cutscene:** a non-interactive portion of a game to show some of the story. Cutscenes may be short prerendered videos, or they may be implemented in game using the game assets.

## D

**Design Document:** document used by designers to describe the design of a game.

**DirectX:** game development software by Microsoft

## E

**EULA:** end user license agreement

## F

**Face:** flat surface on a 3D model, usually three or four sided.

**Float:** a floating point number, a number with a decimal point. There are digits before and possibly after the decimal point, hence the name floating point. In C# and similar computer languages floats are represented by 32 bits.

**First Person Perspective:** view of a game where the player sees the world through the eyes of the player character. See Third Person Perspective.

**FPS:** First Person Shooter

**Frame:** a single image displayed on a monitor or other display device.

**Frame Rate:** the number of frames displayed in one second, often expressed as frames per second, FPS. Good frame rates for video games are 60 and above, though 30 FPS is considered acceptable.

## G

**Game Design Document:** a formal, living document describing the software for a video game as it is being developed. It is often used to help organize how development teams create the game.

**Game Engine:** a set of tools and computer programs to help create video games.

**Gameplay:** the actions of game characters and rules of a game affecting the outcome. If it's cosmetic, such as the graphic look of a character, then it's not gameplay. See reskinning.

**GDD:** see game design document.

**Genre:** a major category of games with similar gameplay.

**Geometry:** mathematics of shapes. Also, the set of shapes in a game or game object.

**Glitch:** a minor bug in a game, typically not affecting the ability of players to play the game.

**Graphics:** the visual elements of a game seen on one or more screens.

**Graphical User Interface (GUI):** a form of user interface using graphical icons rather than text. Also, an interface using a mouse to point and click rather than keyboard entry.

## H

**Hierarchy:** an arrangement of items where the items are above, below, or at the same level as other items.

## I

**Indie:** independent creator of a movie or game.

**Integer:** a whole number without a fractional or decimal part. See Float.

**IP:** Intellectual Property.

**IP:** Internet Protocol.

**Intellectual Property:** a work or invention that is the result of creativity.

**Internet Protocol:** a set of rules governing the format of data sent over the internet or other network.

**Iterative Development:** a method of development where many versions are created, one after another, each version attempting to improve upon the previous versions.

## J

**Joystick:** input device typically providing a two-dimensional direction. Gaming joysticks usually include one or more buttons as well.

## K

**Kill Screen:** a level in a game which cannot be completed due to a severe bug. Famous classic arcade games with kill screens include Donkey Kong and Pac-Man.

## L

**Lossless:** a method of compression that doesn't change the content of the original version.
**Lossy:** a method of compression for images that sacrifices clarity for compression efficiency.

## M

**Magic Number:** a number inserted into source code without explanation. Code becomes more maintainable and understandable when magic numbers are replaced by named constants.
**Massively Multiplayer Online Game (MMO):** online game with large numbers of players on the same server.

## N

**Natural Number:** numbers used in mathematics, starting with 1, 2, 3, etc. There is no such thing as a largest natural number. 0 is usually not considered a natural number.
**NES:** Nintendo Entertainment System, an 8-bit game console released in 1985.
**Non Player Character (NPC):** any character in a game that's not controlled by the players.
**Noob:** a new player, usually someone who knows very little about a game.

## O

**Obsolete:** outdated and no longer useful.
**Overhead View:** a view looking down from a high perspective.

## P

**PascalCasing:** a naming convention where each word in a single or multiword name starts with a capital letter, and the words are concatenated together.
**Physics:** in gaming, the use of physical laws to make games more realistic.
**Physics Engine:** specialized software used by a game engine to simulate the physics of game objects.
**Pixel:** an abbreviation of picture element, typically a very small rectangle or square displaying a single color.
**Platform:** in game development, a computer game system, PC, or mobile device used to host games.
**Player:** a human who is playing a game.
**PlayStation:** one of a series or game consoles by Sony.

**Polygon:** a geometric shape bordered by straight line segments.

**Porting:** converting a game from one platform to another.

**Postmortem:** a review of the game development process by the developers. Usually postmortems are created after some time has passed after release.

**Probability:** a mathematical concept dealing with randomness. Probability is often represented by a single floating point number from 0 to 1, ranging from impossible to certainty.

**Prototype:** a very early version of a game used for testing a game concept or development method.

**Public Domain:** creative material not protected by intellectual property laws such as copyrights, trademarks, or patents. Anyone can use a public domain work, and no one can ever own it.

**Puzzle:** a game where the goal is to find a solution.

**Puzzle Game:** a game that feels like a series of puzzles.

## Q

**Quality Assurance (QA):** a methodology for testing games in a systematic manner. The goal of QA is to find and categorize bugs.

## R

**Random Number Generator:** software that generates numbers that appear to be randomly distributed. Sometimes called pseudo-random number generator.

**Rational Number:** numbers of the form a/b with a and b integers and b non-zero.

**Real Number:** numbers with possibly infinitely many decimal digits, such as pi or the square root of 2. Real numbers are often approximated in computers by floating point numbers, for example pi as 3.14159.

**Refactor:** process of restructuring existing computer code without changing its external behavior.

**Render:** producing a 2D image of a 2D or 3D model with lighting and shadow effects.

**Reskinning:** changing the graphic look of a game without affecting gameplay.

**Reverse Engineer:** to reconstruct a game, software, or device without access to the original source code or designs.

**RGB:** red, green, blue. A common graphics format for displaying color images.

**RGBA:** red, green, blue, alpha. A common graphics format for images with transparency (alpha).

**Role-Playing Game (RPG):** game which allows the player to assume the role of a character, often immersed in a complex game world.

**Rules:** for games, directives to be followed by the players in order to play the game according to its design.

## S

**Scale:** the size of objects, or to alter the size of an object in one or more dimensions.

**Scene:** in Unity, a particular level or menu screen with its own scripts, game objects, and properties.

**Scrolling:** moving the camera view laterally, usually in order to keep the player character visible as the character explores a scene.

**SNES:** Super Nintendo Entertainment System, a 16-bit game console system, released in 1990.

**Source Code:** a collection of commands used to build a game or other software.

**Spam:** unwanted textual message such as email, text, or fax.

**Sprite:** two-dimensional graphic element, usually stored as a rectangular array of solid and transparent pixels.

**String:** an ordered sequence of letters or other symbols such as special characters or digits.

**Switch:** a game console by Nintendo, first released in 2017.

**Syntax:** in computer science, the rules that govern the arrangement of symbols to form valid computer code. Invalid syntax will generate a syntax error message with information about the cause of the error.

## T

**Testing:** in game development, the process of discovering and documenting bugs in game software.

**Third Person Perspective:** gameplay view of a spectator, as in a soccer game, rather than the view of the player character. See First person perspective.

**Three D Game:** a game developed using a 3D engine, usually with a first-person perspective for the camera.

**Two and One-Half D Game:** a game developed using a 3D engine but with 2D gameplay.

**Two D Game:** game developed using a 2D game engine with 2D gameplay.

## U

**User Interface:** software used to connect the player with the game, menus, and player settings.

## V

**Variable:** in programming, a value that may change, as opposed to a constant.

**Vector:** a quantity that contains direction and magnitude. In game programming, vectors usually consist of sequences of two or three floating point numbers.

**Vertex:** a point in two- or three-dimensional space, usually represented by two or three floating point numbers. A vertex designates a single location, whereas a vector designates a direction from one location to another.

**Vertices:** more than one vertex. Often misspelled as "vertexes," but "vertices" is the proper usage.

**Video Game:** a game played on a television, computer monitor, or mobile device, often using specialized controllers.

**Virtual Reality (VR):** user interface that can detect the player's body motion and adjusts the display accordingly in real time, giving the illusion of being a part of a 3D environment.

## W

**Walkthrough:** a video of someone playing a game from beginning to end. Also, a document which describes how to do that. Usually a walkthrough shows a particularly easy way to play the game.

**Waterfall:** a game production methodology that precedes from design documents, to developing a budget and schedule, and finally development that strictly follows the design documents and budgets. This method may ensure that you won't run over budget and that you ship on time, but it surely won't guarantee a fun and successful game.

**Will Not Fix (WNF):** a bug that is minor and too expensive to fix in relation to the benefit of fixing it.

**Wireframe:** a view of a 3D or 2D object with only the edges visible.

**Workflow:** a repeatable pattern for the way work gets done. Often, a workflow can be described as a sequence of steps, or as a flow diagram.

## X

**x-Axis:** one in a system of coordinates, typically horizontal.

**Xbox:** a family of game consoles made by Microsoft.

## Y

**y-Axis:** one in a system of coordinates, vertical in 2D.

## Z

**z-Axis:** one in a system of 3D coordinates, vertical or away from the viewer.

# Appendix II

## *Rules for Game Developers*

H ERE ARE SOME RULES for game developers in no particular order. It can be helpful to read these when you're looking for inspiration. If you break these rules, you'll probably regret it…

- **Test everything early and often**.

- Avoid writing untestable code, or code that won't get used until later during development.

- Fix all major bugs before continuing with development. This is the most important rule!

- Fix most minor bugs before continuing with development. Minor bugs are a sign that something is going wrong. It's best to fix it to make sure your minor bug isn't a wolf in sheep's clothing.

- Maintain a bug list.

- Keep your bug list small.

- Don't try to design the entire game all at once. Instead, prototype, then iterate.

- Make the game really easy early on, but not without challenge.

- Use a working title, preferably a bad one that you'll change later. This has the advantage of preparing you for the day when you have to change the title.

- Search the web for your game idea and/or title to find out if it's been done.

- When testing, try to break the game.

- Jiggle it. All objects should bounce, throb, wobble, or something.

- Check for "borrowed" assets and remove them ASAP.

- Every player action should have a fun reward, even dying.

- Under commit and over deliver.

- Make a game you yourself would love to play and pay money to own.

- Get to gameplay as quickly as possible after launching the game.

- Don't waste the player's time explaining things they don't yet need to know.

# Appendix III

## *Game Development Checklist*

W HEN DEVELOPING A GAME, it pays to go through a checklist to make sure you didn't forget something along the way. Here is one possible checklist. As you gain experience as a game developer, add to this list, or change it to suit your needs and goals.

- **Before You Start Development**

  - Are you excited about the game? If not, toss it and do something else.

  - Are you doing this for the money? If so, do something else if you can afford to.

  - Do you have an excellent, original concept?

  - Does it all make sense?

  - What are some competing games? Did you play them? Did you at least look at videos of them?

- **During Development**

  - Is it fun?

  - Do you enjoy playing it yourself?

  - If it's not fun, what's your excuse? Don't be afraid to kill the project if it's not fun.

  - Are the controls responsive? If not, make them responsive ASAP. The controls should feel good all by themselves even when you're just moving a character around or driving a vehicle for no reason, for example.

  - Is the learning curve OK? This needs to be tested.

  - What rewards are you giving the player?

  - Good UI. Make the UI experience fast and easy to understand.

- Does gameplay start ASAP?
- If you have cut scenes, make them skippable. Not everyone cares about the story, especially if they're playing the game a third time.
- Do you have a schedule?
- What are your platforms? For example: PC first, then Mac, then mobile.
- What is the audio plan for the game? Do you have speech, music, and sound effects?

- **Marketing**
  - How are you promoting this project?
  - When and how are you making GIFs?
  - Do you have a domain and a website for the game?
  - Do you have a twitter account?
  - Facebook account?
  - Trailer?
  - Playable demo?
  - Do you have cheat-codes? If so, what are they and what do they do?
  - Who are the testers during development? Before release?

- **Before Release**
  - Does the game use the new title everywhere, or do you have the working title in there someplace?
  - Do you have a copyright notice?
  - Trademarks?
  - Did you put in a credits screen?
  - Do you have accurate names in the credits?
  - Did you check all licenses and observe all associated terms?
  - Are the credits easily accessible, even for players who didn't finish the game?
  - Is the website operational?

# Appendix IV
## Legal

THIS APPENDIX IS A SHORT and somewhat personal introduction to legal issues for game developers. Your goal as a game developer is to make good games, which is easier said than done. Along the way, you'll need to deal with copyrights, trademarks, patents, etc. First things first: I am not a lawyer and everything in this section is for educational purposes and not legal advice.

If you can afford it and are planning to release your game commercially, it might be beneficial for you to hire a lawyer to help you, preferably a specialist in game development law or intellectual property (IP). If you work for a company of any size your employer should let you know about your legal obligations when developing games for them. If you are an independent developer with a very small budget, you can always search the internet for legal information. A good starting point is to search the web for videos about "law for game development." You will find several excellent video presentations from the Game Developer's Conference. Watch them and learn!

The best one for starters is by Chris Reid: Practical Law 101 For Indie Developers: Not Scary Edition. This video is aimed at indie game developers, but you will benefit greatly from this video whether you're an indie, a student, a hobbyist, an employee at a large game company, or a veteran such as myself.

Why bother? If you are making games just for your own personal entertainment, never to release them to the public, then by all means, skip the legal stuff. As soon as you try to sell or even give away your creations to anyone else such as friends, family, or the public, then yes, you need to know about game development law. Even if you work as a professional game developer for a large company, and especially then, you need to know the basics of game development law.

We'll conclude this very short appendix with a list of do's and don'ts:

- **Dos**

  - DO watch one or two good video game law videos to learn about the basics.

  - DO protect your intellectual property.

  - DO find a good video game attorney to help you, if you can afford one.

  - DO make good original games.

- **Don't**

  - DON'T blatantly copy someone else's game.

  - DON'T make fan games based on Mario, Zelda, Sonic, or anything owned by someone else.

  - DON'T make spiritual successor games. At least, know what you're getting into with this.

  - DON'T infringe on copyrights, trademarks, and/or patents.

  - DON'T sign contracts without reading them.

And to wrap things up, my personal most important DON'T. People always ask me if I still get royalties from Crystal Castles. The short answer is no, nor do I get credit. Yes, it's been thirty seven years, and the game is still being sold. Yes, I wrote and created the code, the design, and much of the graphics for that game, pretty much solo with significant contributions from the Atari coin-op department. Not only don't I get royalties, I don't get credit, nor do I get notified when a new product gets released with Crystal Castles in it. How did I let this happen? Well, I worked for Atari as an employee from 1982 to 1984 and signed away all my rights on day one of my employment.

DON'T sign away your long-term rights.

In recent years, I vowed to never let such a thing happen to me again. When I create a game, I keep the long-term rights for myself, if at all possible. Sometimes, if you wish to work for a game company, you have no choice but to sign away your rights, especially when you're new to the industry. At the very least, be aware of what you're signing, and ask for credit and notification of sequels or derivative products in the future. Maybe you can get your rights back if the company goes out of business or is acquired. It can't hurt to ask.

IP can have a very long commercial life, possibly centuries. Whatever you do, avoid creating a game or any other IP on your own and then selling the copyright to someone else. Instead, license it for a limited time period so that you and your heirs can control and benefit from your creation in the future.

# Appendix V

## *The C# Coding Standard for this Book*

THIS APPENDIX LISTS the coding standard for C# and Unity as used in this book. This is a fairly simple and short coding standard. More extensive and detailed coding standards can be found on the internet.

- **Tabs:** Never use tabs. Instead, indent using spaces, either two or four spaces.

- **Line Width:** Limit line width to 72 characters. This is to help with readability and with formatting the code for this book.

- **Bracing:** Open and closed braces are at the beginning of lines and are the only thing on the line. Never omit braces for blocks of just one statement. Single line blocks may have the braces on the same line.

For example:

Bad
```
if ( x > 9 ) y = 3;
```

Good
```
if (x > 9)
{
  y = 3;
}
```

Also OK
```
if (x > 9){ y = 3;}
```

The bad example is shorter, but harder to maintain and just asking for someone to change the code to something like this:

Really Bad
```
if (x > 9) y = 3; z = 4;
```

- Why is this really bad? Well, the programmer probably wanted the z assignment statement to only be executed when x > 9. The code will, however, always do the z assignment regardless of the value of x.

- **Comments:** Use comments only when necessary. Use the // style of comments rather than the /* */ style. Put comments above the code rather than after or on the side of it.

- **Spacing:** Add spaces to improve readability where appropriate. In particular, separate arguments in function calls with spaces.

Good

```
DisplayScore(score, 20, 30);
```

Bad

```
DisplayScore(score, 20,30);
```

- There are many such situations where adding a space can make your code look clearer. C# doesn't care about these extra spaces. Just don't put spaces inside of identifiers.

- **Vertical Spacing:** Add single blank lines generously to separate methods and blocks of functionality. If you have too many of these, consider refactoring them into multiple methods.

- **Large Methods:** Avoid them. Break them into smaller methods to improve clarity and readability.

- **Naming:** Use camelCasing or PascalCasing. Avoid underscores.

Good

```
public void MyFunction();
```

Bad

```
public void my_function();
```

- PascalCasing is used for functions and class names.

- GameObjects names should use PascalCasing because the associated script uses the name as the class name.

# Index